LAVI

LAVI

THE UNITED STATES, ISRAEL, AND
A CONTROVERSIAL FIGHTER JET

JOHN W. GOLAN

Potomac Books
An imprint of the University of Nebraska Press

All rights reserved. Potomac Books is an imprint of
the University of Nebraska Press.
Manufactured in the United States of America.

♾

Library of Congress Cataloging-in-Publication Data
Golan, John W.
Lavi: the United States, Israel, and a controversial
fighter jet / John W. Golan.
pages   cm
Includes bibliographical references and index.
ISBN 978-1-61234-722-6 (cloth: alk. paper)
ISBN 978-1-61234-783-7 (epub)
ISBN 978-1-61234-784-4 (mobi)
ISBN 978-1-61234-785-1 (pdf)
1. Lavi (Jet fighter plane) 2. United States—Foreign
relations—Israel. 3. Israel—Foreign relations—
United States. 4. United States—Foreign relations—
1981–1989. I. Title.
UG1242.F5G624 2016
358.4'183—dc23
2015021063

Set in Scala by M. Scheer.

CONTENTS

ILLUSTRATIONS

PHOTOGRAPHS

TABLES

PREFACE

This is the story of an airplane, its mission, and its time. It is a tale of trust and betrayal, of two allies with much in common, and of the events, and the people, that endeavored to divide them. The Lavi was conceived out of the uncertainty of the 1970s and evolved amid the optimism of the 1980s. It began as a project to provide Israel with an attack jet for the twenty-first century, and evolved to become a binational program, deeply involving both American and Israeli industry and American and Israeli politics. Ultimately it would perish amid the harsh fiscal realities of the latter 1980s. In its wake, however, are lessons that live on for both nations. The hope behind this book is that those lessons might yet be absorbed.

This book was written, in part, to dispel some of the misconceptions that have arisen around the Lavi in the years since it first flew. The most common have been attempts to arbitrarily equate the Lavi with such very different American fighters as the F-16 or F-20, all of which fail to grasp the fundamental distinctions in role and philosophy that separated the Israeli design from these and other American warplanes. They were different airplanes, intended for different missions. More importantly, such misconceptions reflect a more basic failure to grasp the unique political and military environment in which the Lavi was forged.

No nation in modern history has faced the kind of military and political questions that Israel has had to deal with on a daily, ongoing basis. No other nation lives with neighbors who have pledged to wipe it off the map, and no other nation in history has stood so few against so many for so long. The threat that Israel faces is not merely of a different order than what Americans have known, but of a different kind.

It is easy to forget that prior to June 1967 there was no special U.S.-Israeli relationship. There was no memorandum of understanding, no exchange of intelligence and military know-how, no security assistance. It was not until Israel demonstrated its permanence as a feature of the Middle East, and its potential value as a military ally, that the United States began to sell arms to Israel on a regular basis and to enter into cooperative agreements.

The story of the Lavi unfolded under one of the most intensely pro-Israel presidents in the history of U.S.-Israeli relations. It was not merely that President Ronald Reagan had a tender place in his heart for Israel. Under previous administrations, American-Israeli ties had remained largely unwritten, with no formal basis for regular communication or exchanges between the two armed forces. The Reagan administration would change all of that. Moreover, under the Reagan White House, the scale of bilateral U.S.-Israeli weapons development, testing, and production was expanded manyfold. For the first time, the United States not only took advantage of Israel's battlefield experiences as an example to learn from but also took advantage of Israeli technology and weapons know-how to help flesh out the American military arsenal.

All of which makes the chain of events leading from the decision to launch the Lavi to the decision to cancel the program several years and billions of dollars later only more disturbing. What emerges is a picture of an American foreign and defense policy apparatus that first failed to define clear policy objectives and then subsequently failed to follow through on those objectives once they had been set. Instead policy was made, and then redirected, at the whim of competing factions, fighting their own private wars deep inside the government. Moreover, this chain of policy direction, misdirection, and then redirection was not an isolated event. Rather, it constituted a pattern that was to haunt the administration throughout the Reagan presidency. Indeed, the problem goes deeper than that. It is a pattern of fragmented foreign policy and decision making by bureaucracy that has plagued virtually every American presidency of the past century and has become endemic to the American foreign policy apparatus.

In many respects, the story of the Lavi forms a microcosm of U.S.-Israeli relations and of the inner workings of both the American and Israeli political systems. It also, however, offers a glimpse into the Israeli defense establishment: a reflection of the fears and traumas that have shaped Israeli military and political thinking for the past half century and that continue to shape Israeli society to this day.

I have had the good fortune to have known friends in Israel from across the political spectrum. No people, no nation, have fought as long or as hard for their freedom as have they. Israelis have seen the face of battle, up close, for far too long to romanticize it. There is no great honor in losing your friends, your family members, or your children in battle. In all my travels I have never encountered a nation that has produced so many popular songs about peace as has this small nation. No people yearn for an end to bloodshed more than the Israelis do. But make no mistake about it: no one is more prepared to fight for their freedom when need be than they.

LAVI

1. The First Lion

There is a shadow that hangs across Israeli society, a pervasive presence that lurks in the background of consciousness, intruding, unbidden, into everyday life. It is the ever-present specter of war. Both in its tactical, military aspects and in its broader implications—political, economic, personal—it is the one common reality that every Israeli has shared and struggled to come to grips with. To understand what the Lavi was, and the airplane that it was intended to be, requires an understanding of the underlying pressures behind it and the crucible out of which it was forged. It is therefore rightful that this story begins with the outbreak of one such war, in June 1967.

As the month of June dawned that year, Israel again found itself surrounded by a hostile alliance, its sea lanes cut off, and a world community indifferent to the prospect of its imminent annihilation. During the month of May Egyptian president Gamal Abdel Nasser had ordered the evacuation of the United Nations peacekeeping observers from Sinai. Eliminating the buffer zone created after the previous Arab-Israeli war, Nasser began to mass troops and tanks along Israel's border. The whole process was accompanied by great fanfare, together with promises that this time Nasser would fulfill his threats: this time the Arab armies would succeed in driving the Jews into the sea. The announcement sent the Arab Middle East into euphoria, and pro-Nasser street demonstrations swept through the region. It was a rallying cry for genocide, amplified by the voice of Cairo Radio and promises that "the Arab people is firmly resolved to wipe Israel off the map."[1] There could be no mistaking the blood-soaked aims of Israel's neighbors. As Nasser himself had promised only two years before, "We shall not enter Palestine with its soil covered in sand, we shall enter it with its soil saturated in blood."[2]

Leaders from across the Arab League soon climbed on the Egyptian bandwagon, propelled by popular demand and fears of retribution should they stand in the way of the glorious victory. By mid-May military treaties had been signed between Egypt, Syria, and Jordan, placing the military assets of all three nations, as well as a considerable contingent of Iraqi troops, at Egypt's disposal. The Egyptian army again cut off Israeli shipping through the Gulf of Aqaba, halting Israeli trade to Africa and the Pacific for the second time since Israel's modern-day rebirth.

The promises of previous administrations in both the United States and Europe "guaranteeing" Israel's right of free passage through the Straits of Tiran in return for an Israeli withdrawal from Sinai had been long forgotten by the time that Nasser's army closed its noose. Neither France, nor Britain, nor the United States, which had worked so hard to convince Israel to withdraw, was prepared to maintain the commitments of previous administrations or of prior convenience. Not only were none of them willing to protect Israel's right of free passage through international waterways, none of them were prepared to aid Israel in fending off the impending invasion.

The all-encompassing, gripping tension of those days is often difficult to convey to succeeding generations. In 1967 the standing Israeli army, in its entirety, numbered fewer than 100,000 soldiers. Even with all of its civilian reservists called up, Israel's total armed force would number a meager 264,000. Arrayed against them was a standing Egyptian army of 240,000 soldiers, another 50,000 Syrian troops, 50,000 Jordanians, and a 70,000-man Iraqi army—not to mention contingents sent from Arab states as far away as Morocco or the Arab League's own military reserves. In terms of both combat aircraft and main battle tanks, Israel's air force and armored corps were outnumbered by nearly three to one. And to add to its dilemma, Israel was facing the prospect of an imminent invasion on three fronts, from borders where Arab guns were already within artillery range of Israel's major population centers.[3] Israeli schools rehearsed air raid drills. Blood plasma was stockpiled. Over fourteen thousand hospital beds were readied for the wounded, and ten thousand graves were dug in anticipation of the worst.[4] In the words of Israeli foreign minister Abba Eban, "The chilling wind of vulnerability penetrated to every corner of the Israeli consciousness. When we looked out at the world we saw it divided between those who wanted to see us destroyed, and those who would not raise a finger to prevent it from happening."[5] Israel again tasted the bitter truth. When crisis came, it could depend on no one but itself.

The way Israel responded next, however, was to forever reshape the Middle East. This small strip of sun-bleached sand, this nation of farmers, peddlers, and refugees, would again do the one thing that so many had never expected Jews to ever do: they fought back. On the dawn of June 5, 1967, the Israeli air force, the Heyl Ha'Avir, staged a preemptive strike on the Egyptian airfields and laid waste to 204 Egyptian warplanes—destroying most of them while they were still on the ground. Within six days Israeli armor and paratroopers had smashed through the Egyptian lines and seized the whole of the Sinai, a territory some 120 mi (190 km) across; had conquered the Jordanian-held territories of Judea and Samaria, including Jerusalem and its holy sites; and had captured the Syrian-held Golan Heights. For the first time in Israel's nineteen years of existence there were no terror bases operating on its borders, no snipers within rifle range of its cities, and no Jordanian or Syrian artillery to open fire on its farmlands from their commanding heights above. Against all odds, outnumbered and outgunned, Israel had won.

The Six-Day War was a turning point in many ways. It marked the first time that the United States began to see Israel as a potential partner, with a significant role to play in the balance of power in the Middle East. The war taught both the Middle East and the world the rising importance of airpower in modern warfare. But it was also the point at which Israel relearned valuable lessons about dependency and about the hazards of relying on foreign powers for its supply of weapons.

Until the Six-Day War, France had been Israel's principal supplier of modern combat aircraft, with the French-built Mirage IIIcj forming the backbone of the Heyl Ha'Avir. In practice, the Mirage III was less agile than the Soviet-built MiG-21s, which then filled out the front lines of the Arab air arms. Further, although it had been designed primarily with the interceptor role in mind, in 1967 the Mirage had been called upon to play a pivotal role in the air-to-ground operations that had devastated the Egyptian air bases in the opening hours of the war. In spite all of its shortcomings, however, the Mirage III was the most potent all-around fighter in Israel's arsenal and had been the centerpiece of Israel's air force modernization plans.

Israel had ordered a follow-on batch of fifty specially reconfigured Mirage fighters, known as the Mirage 5, which were to be built to Israeli specifications and optimized for the attack role. The sale had already been finalized, and the aircraft paid for, prior to the outbreak of war. The Mirage 5 increased the number of weapons pylons available on the airplane from the three seen under the Mirage III to seven. These and other modifications increased the airplane's bomb load from a maximum of 2,000 lb (910 kg), to 9,260 lb (4,200 kg). The new airplane also eliminated much of the original French electronics suite, including the Cyrano radar that had proven so troublesome. Simplifying the electronics package had also provided the Mirage 5 with additional space for an extra 110 gal (420 L) of fuel.[6] While the Mirage IIIcj might have been the star performer in Israel's air-to-air success of 1967, in the view of Israel's tactical planners, what they needed to win the next war was a fighter with more range and more bomb load. The Mirage 5 was intended to provide them with that airplane.

All of this came to an end in June 1967 when the French government of Charles de Gaulle reversed its arms sales policies and imposed an embargo on sales to Israel. The embargo included the fifty Mirage 5 fighters as well as a deal for a dozen missile patrol boats. For over a decade, the unwritten Israeli-French alliance had played a pivotal role in Israeli defense planning. Israel's naval commandos had received some of their very first training from their counterparts in France.[7] Israeli officers attended French military academies. French and Israeli intelligence agencies regularly exchanged reports on developments throughout the region. There had even been a pilot-exchange program, providing Israeli fighter pilots with all-weather flight training in Europe—which they would otherwise seldom have exposure to in the skies of the Middle East.[8] The French-Israeli alliance that had been forged during the Algerian civil war in the early 1950s began to unravel as the French withdrew from Algeria and sought to ingratiate themselves with the oil-rich Arab Middle East. The French would go on to sell the Mirage 5 fighter, with all of the refinements that the Israelis had requested, to both Egypt and Libya, but not to Israel.

The loss of the French warplanes and missile boats came as a severe blow to the Israeli armed forces. Although the United States would eventually step in as Israel's principal arms supplier, the Heyl Ha'Avir was left with no immediate replacements for lost or damaged fighters and without a source of spare parts for the ones that they already had. The memory of this betrayal would be etched deep into the minds of those Israeli officers who, decades later, would champion, and ultimately oversee, the development of the Lavi fighter. Moreover, France was not the only European power to renege on its arms deals with Israel following the Six-Day War. Within a short time Britain too would succumb to visions of cheap oil and would likewise back out of an agreement to supply weapons to Israel.

Under a covert agreement made in the early 1960s, the British had agreed to supply Israel with a number of 1950s-era Centurion tanks, as part of a larger deal that was to have included supplies of the British Chieftain main battle tank, then under development. The British wanted Israeli assistance in adapting the Chieftain for desert conditions, and two prototypes were sent to Israel for testing in 1966. The aging Centurions, which the British badly wanted to unload, did arrive. The promised supplies of Chieftains did not. Britain joined France in publicly declaring an arms embargo against Israel in 1967, and in 1972 it terminated the secret Chieftain-Centurion arms agreement, with no Chieftains having ever been delivered for Israeli use.[9] For decades to come those same battle-worn and many times updated Centurion main battle tanks would form a central component of Israel's armored corps. The Chieftain, meanwhile, went on to arm Israel's neighbors in the Jordanian Arab Legion. Both the French and the British were short-lived arms partners. Betrayal was an experience that Israel's logistical planners had grown accustomed to.

But 1967 was a turning point for this also. For the first time Israel's leadership determined that they would not accept the prospect of being forced to find a new source of arms with every shift in the political winds, nor would they accept making due with upgrading hand-me-downs already several years out-of-date by the time that they arrived. The Israeli government determined that it would have the fighters that the French had promised, as well as the missile boats. And U.S. arms supplies or no U.S. arms supplies, the Israel Defense Forces (IDF) would never again be held hostage to the politics of a foreign power.

When the Israeli government moved next, it was with all the stealth and cunning that its intelligence agencies could muster. The embargoed missile boats were quietly sold off to a Brazilian "fishing" company. A few days later they showed up in Haifa harbor, flying the Israeli flag. As for the fighter planes, while the French government might have been unwilling to supply weapons to Israel, the leadership of Dassault Aviation—which produced the Mirage—was equally unwilling to return payments already made. Dassault continued to supply aircraft components, assembly jigs, and even blueprints in secret, all in accordance with the previously signed arrangement. This left only the jet engine, which was produced by the French manufacturer Snecma, for which the Israelis still needed fresh deliveries and spare parts. As it turned out, Switzerland had also entered into a contract to license-produce the Mirage. Through the good offices of a few Swiss agents, the Israeli intelligence institute, or Mossad as it is more commonly known, borrowed the blueprints for the Snecma design. With the blueprints in the hands of Bet Shemesh Engines, and with a steady supply of parts and production tooling from Dassault, Israel Aircraft Industries (IAI)—a company that only a decade earlier had been known for maintenance of propeller-driven transports—had entered the jet fighter age.[10] This was the beginning of an IAI fighter legacy that would one day lead to the Lavi.

When Israel had declared its independence in May 1948, Lod Airport—the future site of Israel Aircraft Industries' factory and headquarters—had been on the front lines of a contested battleground. The Israeli air force had comprised a few light monoplanes and transports. Under British rule, the Jews of Palestine had been forbidden from bearing arms and the new state's arms industries had been confined to those few that could be carried out in secret—with a handful of underground factories producing homemade hand grenades and Sten guns. The future site of Israel Aircraft Industries was on the edge of a dusty airstrip that was barely distinguishable from any other far-flung corner of the British Empire. Herds of sheep and goats could routinely be seen scrambling among the rocks and nearby hills. At the time, the site looked more likely to produce a donkey cart than a jet fighter in the next twenty years.

Israel Aircraft Industries would begin its existence in 1953 as Bedek Aviation, providing repair and maintenance services for the newly formed Israeli air force as well as for El Al, the Israeli national airline. The first real opportunity for Israel Aircraft Industries to become a manufacturer of airplanes, and not merely a repair house, came when they were awarded a license to deliver the French-designed Magister trainer for the Israeli air force. The Fouga Magister was a two-seat, subsonic jet trainer, which was to provide Israeli Flying School cadets with their first introduction to jet-powered flight. Only the most imaginative of minds could conceive of the Magister as being the forerunner to a modern jet fighter. But while the Magister may have been a far cry from the sleek Mirage, it did provide valuable experience, introducing IAI to basic techniques for component manufacture, airframe assembly, and quality control.

The initial fighter aircraft produced by IAI were manufactured directly from the French design. The Israelis called the aircraft the Nesher (eagle). It was a carbon copy of the Mirage 5, with only minor changes from the French prototype, mostly to the avionics suite. Some forty of these aircraft were produced in time to see service in the 1973 Yom Kippur War.

But the Israeli air force was not completely satisfied with the airplane, and in the following years IAI's engineers set about developing a new, evolved aircraft. The result was the Kfir (lion cub), the first prototype of which flew in 1973. While clearly paying homage to their earlier Nesher production experience, the Kfir afforded the IAI development team with their first experience in integrating a complex weapons system, balancing between the competing demands of aerodynamics, structures, avionics, and weapons. Among its many differences from its predecessors, the Kfir utilized an American-built J79 jet engine. Far more powerful than the Atar engine that the Mirage had relied upon, the J79 boasted up to 17,900 lb (79.6 kN) of thrust, compared to the 13,230 lb (58.8 kN) that the Atar 9B had produced. The Kfir was slightly more compact than the earlier Mirage, and the new American engine also operated at higher temperatures, requiring the addition of an air scoop at the base of the vertical tail to cool the aluminum structure that housed the engine. In virtually every performance category that mattered for an attack jet, however, the Kfir was superior.

The Kfir could handle more payload and carry it farther, and the fact that it was also faster than the Mirage was icing on the cake. When twenty-five of these early model Kfir fighters were later leased to the U.S. Navy and Marine Corps, the American pilots would speak highly of the Kfir's excellent acceleration qualities, acknowledging that it was one of the few airplanes that could out-accelerate the U.S. Navy's F-14 Tomcat.[11] In the words of one Israeli Kfir pilot, "On this engine . . . it's like lightning."[12] Equally important from the standpoint of operational effectiveness, the Kfir had a newer, more capable avionics suite, vastly enhancing its lethality in the attack role.

But the Israeli engineers were not yet finished tinkering with their design. The one area where the early Kfir had suffered in comparison to its Mirage III predecessor was in its air-to-air agility. The added structural weight needed to accommodate a more powerful engine and to carry a heavier bomb load had increased its wing loading, making it slightly "lazier" in a turning engagement than its lighter-weight Mirage predecessor. The solution that the Israeli development team arrived at was the addition of canard foreplanes.

Adding canards to the Mirage design was not a foregone conclusion. The development team at Dassault had experimented with the addition of canards on the Mirage Milan flying test bed—built from a converted Mirage 5 airframe. They had advised the Israeli development team against this approach. Fly-by-wire technology was not an option for either French or Israeli developers during the 1970s, and the incorporation of a canard complicated the aerodynamic behavior of the airplane, shifting the aerodynamic center forward and reducing static margin. While not ideal for the Mirage III or Mirage 5 airframe, however, the canard proved to be a perfect fit for the Kfir—whose static margin had been increased inadvertently by virtue of its shortened length and added weight. The canard not only reduced the static margin of the Kfir back to the levels experienced under the earlier Mirage III but also provided the airplane with the ability to reach higher angles of attack than either the Mirage or Nesher had been able to achieve. In 1976, only a year after it was first introduced, Israel began to deploy the new, canard-equipped Kfir—labeled as the Kfir C2. In addition to the canard foreplanes, the new version featured an extended wing leading edge, or "dog-tooth," which simultaneously increased the effective wing area and reduced buffeting at high angles of attack. Taken together, these refinements increased the sustained turn rate of the Kfir C2 from 7.8 deg/sec to 8.7 deg/sec and increased the maximum instantaneous turn rate from 16.5 deg/sec to 18.7 deg/sec.[13] The Kfir C2 would later be followed in production by the Kfir C7 in 1983, boasting updated electronics and a "combat plus" modification to the J79 engine that provided an additional 1,300 lb (5.8 kN) of thrust. The maximum bomb load was also increased, from the 9,430 lb (4,280 kg) available under the Kfir C2 to some 13,390 lb (6,070 kg) for the Kfir C7. Israel's Kfir C2s would subsequently be upgraded to the Kfir C7 standard.

The Kfir was but one example of Israel's drive for arms independence, a pattern that was repeated throughout Israel's armed forces in the aftermath of the 1967 war. Others included the Merkava main battle tank, the Saar 4 missile boat, the Gabriel antishipping missile, and the Shafrir 2 and Python 3 air-to-air missiles. This did not mean that Israel ceased to buy foreign arms. Israel's defense requirements were too diverse for Israel to develop and manufacture everything that it might need. But it did mean that Israeli alternatives would exist in the event that one arms supplier or another later reneged on an agreement. It was with this legacy of foreign arms-supplier inconsistencies and a dual-track procurement policy that the Lavi would be ushered in.

The Six-Day War was the first Arab-Israeli war that was to profoundly shape the character of the Lavi. Many lessons came out of this conflict, events that shaped the Israeli psyche for decades to come. The Six-Day War had underscored the vital role of Israel's air force as the nation's first line of defense. It had taught the Israeli government, and the Israeli people, that when the bullets started flying, Israel could depend on no one but itself. It sent a message that foreign arms suppliers could, and often would, terminate arms contracts for their own political reasons, often suspending deliveries at the worst possible time. And it taught the Israeli people that when they did depend upon themselves, whether on the battlefield or to supply arms for their own defense, there was very little that they could not do.

2. Superpower Relations

I t is easy to forget that when Charles de Gaulle declared an embargo on arms shipments to Israel in 1967, there was no "special" U.S.-Israeli relationship for Israel to fall back on. America's reliability as an ally was largely untested, and in the coming years the actions of successive American presidential administrations would continue to cast doubt over the wisdom of relying exclusively on American arms.

The Israeli government had approached the United States on numerous occasions prior to the outbreak of the Six-Day War, seeking to diversify its selection of weapons. In the early 1960s the Kennedy administration had agreed to authorize limited shipments of U.S. arms to Israel, offering to sell Hawk antiaircraft missile batteries. Although no jet fighters were offered, the fact that the United States would sell arms to Israel at all was in itself a breakthrough.[1] Prior U.S. administrations had maintained a strict embargo on the supply of weapons to Israel since the establishment of the Jewish state in 1948.

In June 1964 Israeli prime minister Levi Eshkol attempted to expand further on the gains made under the Kennedy administration and approached President Lyndon B. Johnson with a request for additional arms deliveries. With the French having recently withdrawn from their colonies in North Africa, it was already apparent that alternative sources of weapons needed to be cultivated. The airplane that the Israelis wanted most from the Americans was the supersonic F-4 Phantom. With its combination of range and payload, it would have significantly improved Israel's ability to repulse any threatened invasion. But in 1964 the United States had already made it clear that the Phantom was not for sale. As an alternative, Prime Minister Eshkol therefore inquired into the possible purchase of A-4 Skyhawk or A-6 Intruder strike jets.

The A-4 was a subsonic attack jet that had first flown in June 1954. It had been developed to provide the U.S. Navy with a carrier-borne light attack capability and was a dedicated close air support and strike jet, not an air-to-air fighter. However, it could provide an able complement to the role of the Mirage. With a maximum 8,200 lb (3,720 kg) bomb load, it far surpassed the payload of the French aircraft, providing Israel with an alternative to the Mirage 5 fighters, then years away from development.[2]

As for the A-6, the Intruder represented an even greater leap in strike capabilities, offering expanded range and payload. Like the Skyhawk, it was a dedicated attack jet, but with far more reach. The Johnson administration, however, made it clear that the Intruder was, like the F-4 Phantom, not available for discussion.

President Johnson was willing to consider a sale of Skyhawks to Israel but insisted on tying the deal to plans for the supply of weapons to Israel's neighbor to the east, the Hashemite Kingdom of Jordan. This was the first time that an American president attempted to tie promises of arms sales to Israel to proposals for similar arms sales to an Arab government. Offering arms to Israel was a means of deflecting some of the opposition that the latter sale was sure to encounter in Congress. It would not, however, be the last time that such a linkage was made. The negotiations for the sale of the Skyhawks were protracted, with the Johnson administration attempting to tie additional conditions to their delivery, including stipulations limiting when and how the aircraft could be used. A final deal was not cemented until 1966, together with the requisite promise that the Israeli government would not lodge protests with the U.S. Congress opposing the sale of an arms package to Jordan. Under the agreement finally reached, the United States would sell forty-eight A-4 Skyhawks to Israel, with the first aircraft scheduled to be delivered in November 1967.[3]

Following the Six-Day War, however, the United States followed the example of its European allies and officially suspended all arms deliveries to Israel. Weeks passed, and it appeared for a time that the United States would turn out to be no more reliable than the Europeans had already proven to be. Eventually the embargo was lifted, and the first Skyhawks arrived in Israel in 1968. But the pattern that had been set by the Skyhawk experience was one that was to be repeated many times over. American arms sales to Israel were often tied to arms sales to Israel's Arab neighbors. And whenever Israel took military action, it ran the risk of a punitive arms embargo, precisely as had happened in June 1967.

The United States was nonetheless different, in many ways, from the European arms suppliers that Israel had relied upon in the past. To begin with, America was less dependent on Middle Eastern oil. More importantly, American foreign policy was governed by a different set of underlying precepts, which shaped the decision-making process. In spite of all of the social reforms of the previous century, European governments still retained many features of a class-based society. It was always understood that decisions would need to be made by the ruling elite that might be unpopular with the commoners. This political tradition was not supplanted by the advent of democracy. Rather, the parliamentary systems adopted by European governments guaranteed that prime ministers could expect their party or coalition to approve their foreign policies when they came before the legislatures.

The American political system, on the other hand, was rooted in a different tradition, with a distinct separation between the executive and legislative branches. No president could assume that his policies would automatically be approved and budgeted by the legislature. Rather, it was a process of negotiation between the two political offices. This division was further magnified by tying each representative or senator to a specific voting district, ensuring that he or she was directly accountable to his or her constituents, not a political party. American governmental policy, including American foreign policy, was at least partly dictated by the need to ensure that the American people believed that their government was doing the right thing.

In the aftermath of the Six-Day War, American public support for Israel was at an all-time high. The United States was then embroiled in a protracted battle in Vietnam, where it faced some of the same Soviet-made arms that Israel had defeated so handily. Israel's victory dawned upon the American consciousness like a new spring day. A tiny, modern-day David had defeated the Goliath of four Arab armies and the Soviet empire that stood behind them. It therefore came as no surprise when the Johnson administration lifted its arms embargo and allowed the Skyhawk deliveries to proceed. After all, 1968 was also a presidential election year.

The wheel of the American election season had not yet finished turning, however. Later that same year, Republican presidential candidate Richard Nixon would promise that, under his administration, the United States would sell Israel not only Skyhawks but the coveted F-4 Phantom as well. It was therefore only natural that the Johnson administration would preempt Nixon's campaign pledge and approve the sale of fifty F-4E Phantoms to Israel. Within a matter of months the United States had gone from embargoing arms shipments to Israel to selling Israel the most sophisticated fighter in the U.S. inventory. For Israel's policy and defense planners, America was a strange and bewildering place.[4]

It would be September 1969 before the first Phantoms actually arrived in Israel, but the fact that the United States would sell Israel its frontline fighter signaled a sea change in the Arab-Israeli conflict. For years, the Arab armies of Egypt, Syria and Iraq had received the majority of their arms from the Soviet Union. But with Israel now a direct recipient of American weaponry, the Arab-Israeli conflict shifted from the international back-burner, to become a frontline battleground in the Cold War.

From Israel's standpoint, the American weapons could not have arrived too soon. Hardly had the dust settled from the Six-Day War than a new Middle East war had begun. From September 1969 to August 1970 Egypt engaged Israel in what became known as the War of Attrition. Nasser's concept was to wear Israel down by taking advantage of Israel's sensitivity to casualties—military and civilian. Using a combination of terrorist attacks and artillery barrage, Egypt's president hoped to engage Israel in a protracted conflict that was sure to maximize casualties on both sides. He was convinced that in an exchange of bloodletting, Egypt could better absorb the casualties than tiny Israel. Israel responded to the Egyptian attacks by launching commando raids and air strikes deep into Egyptian territory. The strategy behind these raids was not merely to inflict more damage than Nasser had inflicted on Israel. Rather, the Israeli strategy was aimed at challenging Nasser's authority as the supreme ruler over the Nile. When Israeli jets streaked across the skies of Cairo, Egypt's president could hardly pretend to be the victorious general that he boasted of being. In so doing, Israel hoped to undermine Nasser's grip over Egypt.

Only now this was not merely an Arab-Israeli conflict. With the two sides receiving their respective arms from the Soviet Union and the United States, every new battle had the potential of spiraling into a superpower confrontation. The Soviets sent not only jet fighters to replace the Egyptian losses but also advisors to train the Egyptians, North Korean technicians to man the antiaircraft batteries, and even Red Army fighter pilots to patrol Egypt's skies.

By March 1970 the Soviets had deployed three squadrons of Red Army MiG-21s to Egypt. The Israelis knew only too well from the chatter across the airwaves precisely which language was being spoken at the air bases surrounding Cairo. The potential for a superpower confrontation had never been greater. On June 31 President Nixon personally sent a carefully worded message to the Soviets, warning that the Middle East was "a very dangerous region, like the Balkans before World War I. The two Great Powers would have to be very careful in their action to prevent a confrontation which neither wants."[5] With the threat of a third world war looming, the Israeli government halted its deep penetration raids into Egypt and limited its retaliatory raids to Egyptian encampments in the Suez Canal zone. Every effort was made to avoid a direct confrontation with the Soviet pilots. That is, until July 1970.

On July 25 a flight of Soviet MiG-21s jumped a pair of Israeli Skyhawks that were on a bombing run over the Suez Canal, badly damaging one of them before the Israeli pilots escaped into the

Sinai. The Skyhawks lacked the speed, acceleration, and air-to-air weaponry of the MiGs. From this point forward, the Israelis knew that they had no alternative but to respond. No further erosion in Israel's freedom to retaliate could be tolerated.

On July 30 the Heyl Ha'Avir sprang its trap, luring sixteen Soviet-piloted MiG-21s into an aerial ambush. The Soviet air controllers peering into their radar screens had expected to find four A-4 Skyhawks over the canal zone, with a single, harmless Mirage on a reconnaissance mission high above. They had been convinced that it was another routine day in the exchange of Israeli bombing raids and Egyptian artillery fire and had vectored the Russian fighter pilots for what they were sure would be easy prey. But in place of the Skyhawks, the Russians found four Israeli Phantoms, mimicking the call signs and flight patterns of A-4 strike jets. And in place of the lone Mirage reconnaissance jet circling overhead, they found four Mirage IIIs. From behind the mountain ridge to the east, another four Mirage fighters broke from their cover to join the fray, while an additional four Mirage IIIs were scrambled from a nearby airstrip. In that single afternoon five Russian-piloted MiG-21s would be shot down, without the loss of a single Israeli aircraft.

The aerial debacle helped bring an end to the War of Attrition. At long last, the Russians shared President Nixon's concern that the Arab-Israeli war might escalate into a superpower face-off. Within a week the Soviets had notified Egypt's President Nasser that they could no longer guarantee Russian fighter coverage for Egypt's airspace, and a cease-fire, which the United States had been struggling to achieve for months, finally went into effect on August 7, 1970.[6]

Yet, once again, Israel discovered that there was a price to pay for foreign dependency. As part of the cease-fire agreement, Egypt was required to refrain from deploying surface-to-air missiles within 19 mi (30 km) of the Suez Canal. The Egyptians would violate this clause within a month. Israel, however, was unable to take action to remove the missiles or to otherwise retaliate, due to U.S. pressure to maintain the cease-fire. These same missiles would later cost the lives of Israeli pilots and cripple the effectiveness of the Israeli air force during the next round of war.[7]

In October 1973 the Egyptian and Syrian armies launched a surprise attack during Yom Kippur, the most holy day of the Jewish calendar. Most of Israel's frontline troops were at home, on leave for the holiday. On the Sinai front, nearly 300,000 Egyptian troops and over 2,000 Egyptian tanks were arrayed against a mere 436 Israeli soldiers, who were all that manned the Bar Lev Line, Israel's series of fortifications on the eastern side of the Suez Canal. The majority of Israeli armored formations in the Sinai were held in reserve to the east and could count on no more than 280 tanks between them. On the Golan front with Syria the situation was no better, with some 1,200 Syrian tanks devoted to the invasion, opposed by a meager reserve of 170 tanks on the Israeli side. The joint Egyptian-Syrian assault had caught the Israeli armed forces completely by surprise, with only a razor-thin margin of troops on the front.[8]

During the first days of the Yom Kippur War, Israel relied on that handful of troops at the front line, together with the Israeli air force overhead, to hold off the invading armies long enough for Israel's reserves to be mobilized. But the battle was too unequal. Within a short time Israeli forces were teetering on the verge of collapse, while the bulk of the Israeli army was still many hours away, rushing to mobilization centers. The Israeli government had gravely misjudged the likelihood of another war and, once engaged, had similarly misjudged its ability to repulse the invasion. Precious hours were lost before the Israeli government would formally request resupply from the United States. The Israelis, however, were not the only ones who had misjudged the situation.

In the United States, the supply of additional arms and ammunition to Israel was delayed while the U.S. government wrangled over how to supply the weapons without offending the Arab powers. Plans were laid out for utilizing civilian air carriers to transport the weapons—plans that were then shelved when no civilian freight carriers proved willing to fly into a war zone. The magnitude of the threat that Israel faced was completely lost on the White House. Everyone was expecting a swift Israeli victory, a repeat of the Six-Day War. For eight crucial days the United States delayed the resupply of munitions to Israel.

There were a variety of opinions regarding the source of the delay in U.S. assistance. Secretary of State Kissinger described the delay as being the result of a combination of miscalculation and misplaced apprehensions on the part of various Defense Department officials. As Kissinger would later tell it, Defense Secretary James Schlesinger was nervous regarding the possible reaction in the Arab world: "Schlesinger saw no problem with sending auxiliary equipment not requiring American technicians. But his concern was that meeting Israel's requests and thus turning around a battle that the Arabs were winning might blight our relations with the Arabs."[9]

Not every U.S. official shared Kissinger's recollection of these events, however. At the time, Adm. Elmo R. Zumwalt Jr. was America's chief of naval operations. He reported a different interpretation of those same events, placing responsibility for the delay squarely on the shoulders of the secretary of state himself:

> There has been a great deal of public controversy over the causes of the delay in the American airlift. In various backstage, not-for-attribution colloquies Henry Kissinger, in his familiar role as a "senior official," has let it be known that his effort to resupply Israel fast was frustrated by Secretary [of Defense] Schlesinger who feared to antagonize the Arab oil producers. This tale is just a tale, and an extraordinarily disingenuous one at that. It was Henry himself who stalled the airlift. I do not mean to imply that he wanted Israel to lose the war. He simply did not want Israel to win decisively. . . . He wanted Israel to bleed just enough to soften it up for the post-war diplomacy he was planning.[10]

Regardless of the source of the delay, whether the secretary of state or the secretary of defense, the result was clear: only when it became obvious that neither the Arab leaders nor their Soviet patrons would agree to a cease-fire while the Arab armies were winning the war did the United States overcome its internal disagreements and finally airlift the munitions and spares that Israel so desperately needed. The U.S. arms did come. But they came late. Once again, the reliability of America as the primary source for Israeli arms had been called into question.

On balance, the United States not only supplied fresh arms to Israel but for the first time also supplied a portion of those arms in the form of outright grants. Out of $2.2 billion in arms that were approved by President Nixon, $1.5 billion came in the form of grants that did not have to be repaid.[11] Thus began another shift in the U.S.-Israeli relationship. In the past, in spite of the rising cost of arms, Israel had always been able to expand its defense spending at a rate credible enough to deter its neighbors from launching new invasions with every turn of the month. But in the 1970s, and particularly after the flexing of Arab oil power in 1973, Israel found itself facing neighbors who were able to so vastly outspend it as to make Israel's own monetary resources seem trivial. For the first time, Israel began to depend on a foreign power not only for arms shipments but for assistance in paying for those shipments.

The American response in the 1973 Yom Kippur War consequently carried a mixed message to Israel's leaders. On the one hand, the United States ultimately did supply arms to Israel. Moreover, for the first time the United States supplied Israel with the economic assistance necessary to pay for those arms. But the American response had also come late, delayed by political maneuvering and concerns about how the Arab world would react to U.S. assistance. This delay had proven costly. Caught off guard at the beginning of the war, Israel lost over 2,400 soldiers killed in the ensuing weeks of conflict, with another 500 listed as missing in action. And once Israel did overcome the initial shock of the invasion and launched a counteroffensive, the United States would press Israel to agree to a quick cease-fire, rather than face the possibility of Soviet intervention.

The Yom Kippur War was the second Arab-Israeli war that was to profoundly shape the Lavi fighter. From the standpoint of those in Israel who were proponents of Israeli arms independence, the Yom Kippur War was one more example of the hazards of dependency. The inherent dangers of depending on an unwritten foreign alliance had once again proven to be very costly. This would not be the last time that America's reliability, both as an ally and as a source of arms, would be called into question.

The timing of the public unveiling of the Kfir fighter was itself another case in point. As a nation at war Israel has always maintained a policy of maximum secrecy in connection with military research and development. The entire Kfir development effort was carried out as a "black" program. There were rumors in the press, some claiming that Israel was developing a jet fighter under the code name of Barak (lightning), but it was not until after the Kfir had actually reached production that the project was officially acknowledged, in 1975. The timing of the announcement, however, would be dictated by new strains in the U.S.-Israeli relationship.

At the time, the Ford administration was in the midst of coordinating a new disengagement treaty between Israel and Egypt. The Ford administration still carried with it a certain taint, left over from the Watergate scandal, and a new agreement between Egypt and Israel—however limited in its scope—just might be the boost that they needed going into the upcoming elections. Equally important, an agreement that was brokered by the United States would weaken the political standing of the Soviets and drive a wedge between Moscow and its Egyptian clients. But the Egyptian and Israeli positions remained far apart. In return for an Israeli withdrawal from the Sinai oil fields of Abu Rodeis, the Egyptians offered only a two-year, "nonuse of force" agreement, rather than a permanent cease-fire. The talks also continued to stumble over the subject of Israeli withdrawal from the Gidi and Mitla Passes, the strategic "gates" to the Sinai. The Egyptians insisted that all Israeli troops would have to be withdrawn from the passes, a condition that the Israeli government rejected. Lacking the ability to bring the two sides together by pressing the Egyptians to moderate their stance, the U.S. government instead played the only card that it had. In late March the Ford administration announced that U.S. policy in the Middle East would need to be "reassessed." For the next six months the White House declined to entertain new arms sales to Israel—including ongoing requests for the delivery of America's newest jet fighter, the F-15 Eagle.[12]

This was yet another first in U.S.-Israeli relations: the use of arms deliveries as a tool for pressuring Israel into making concessions at the bargaining table. The White House announcement also had the potential, however, of sending a dangerous message of vulnerability to Israel's adversaries. It was therefore no accident when in April the veil of secrecy was finally lifted and the Kfir was officially unveiled. The rollout was intended to send a clear message to the Arab world that, with or without an agreement on F-15 deliveries, Israel was still more than capable of defending itself.[13]

The negotiations with Egypt dragged on throughout the remainder of the year, and ultimately the Israeli government gave in to most of the Egyptian demands. The Egyptians received control of the Abu Rodeis oil fields, and Israeli troops withdrew from both the Mitla and Gidi Passes, although they continued to control the mountains that flanked the passes. The new Egyptian-Israeli Sinai accord was signed on September 1, 1975, and President Ford approved the sale of the first batch of F-15s to Israel soon afterward. The belated deal did little, however, to assuage the concerns of those in Israel who believed that an independent source of Israeli arms was a necessity.

In the first decade following the Six-Day War, America's record as a strategic ally therefore remained a mixed message of contradictions and policy reversals. On the one hand, Israel was seen as an important part of America's network of Cold War alliances and partnerships. The United States went from supplying virtually no arms to Israel to becoming almost the exclusive source for Israeli weapons. American military assistance went from providing loans to giving outright grants to pay for the flow of arms that Israel relied on. But dependence on American arms always carried a price. Sometimes the price was the acceptance of American policy goals, as was the case in 1970 when Egypt had violated the terms of a cease-fire. At other times the price was a suspension in arms deliveries at an awkward moment, as occurred in the opening days of the Yom Kippur War. Many times, arms shipments to Israel would be tied to arms deals to the Arab world.

Israel's reliance on the United States was therefore a mixed blessing for Israel's leadership. The United States had proven to be a better friend than the European powers. But the future was by no means certain. It was with this mixed legacy that Israel's policy makers entered into their next round of arms decision making, during the latter 1970s.

3. The Lion's Den

The emergence of the United States as Israel's new, principal arms supplier following the Six-Day War presented new challenges for Israel's arms procurement process. Compared to the narrow selection of weapons that Israel's leadership had been accustomed to, the United States provided a teeming arms bazaar. But Israel's purchasing power was still limited. The Israelis could not afford to haphazardly allocate their budget on every new weapons craze. To a degree that had not been true in the past, order was desperately needed: a thought-out process to evaluate both needs and resources. The development of this process and the men whose visions shaped it were to be at the heart of the chain of decisions that eventually led to the Lavi.

Throughout the first two decades of the Heyl Ha'Avir's existence, the selection process for evaluating new fighter aircraft had been a relatively informal procedure—depending more on which fighter aircraft were available than on the assessments of Israel's pilots and planners. Procurement recommendations would be submitted to General Headquarters by the commander of the air force, based on the impressions of one, or at best two, pilots. From there it became a matter of campaigning for budget allocations. Very few nations would contemplate the sale of warplanes to Israel, leaving few alternatives. There had therefore never been a need for a more systematic process to measure Israel's air force requirements against what the available aircraft had to offer.

At the end of the 1960s, however, all of this changed. The introduction of America as Israel's new, principal supplier of arms meant that the variety of aircraft that might potentially become available had multiplied manyfold. The Israelis had gone from working with a single French manufacturer to selecting between competing designs and contractors. This transformation, combined with the parallel drive to develop an indigenous Israeli manufacturing capability, led Israel's leadership to rethink the process by which Israeli aircraft had been selected in the past.

This change in the Israeli approach was led by the deputy air force chief, Brig. Gen. Benjamin Peled, the first air force officer assigned to form and lead a dedicated Hadish (modernization) team.[1] The purpose of this team was not only to better organize Israel's fighter evaluation process but also to determine what Israel's air force needs truly were. For such a task, no better candidate could have been chosen than Benny Peled.

For Benjamin Peled, a lifetime of service was, in his own words, a "high calling."[2] He had been only a young man with a fascination for aviation when he was first admitted to the mechanical engineering program at Israel's Technion in 1947. The thought that he might one day be placed in charge of overhauling Israel's fighter modernization efforts could hardly have been more remote. But war intervened, and the young would-be engineer found himself a mechanic in Israel's fledgling air force, repairing piston-powered fighters during Israel's War of Independence.[3]

When the war ended, Benny applied for admission to Israel's newly formed flying school, and in 1950 he graduated at the head of his class. From there he was assigned to fly Spitfires in the 105th Fighter Squadron. As was immediately evident, however, Benny Peled was among the most naturally gifted pilots to enter the young air force's ranks. Only months after having been assigned to the piston-powered Spitfires, he was reassigned to Israel's very first jet fighter squadron, flying the newly delivered Meteor.[4] Assignment to the squadron was an honor bestowed on only the very best of pilots.

Within a few short years Capt. Benny Peled would be handed command of his own jet fighter squadron, the 113th, in 1955—flying the French-made Ouragan. Although a strictly subsonic platform, the Ouragan was nonetheless an improvement over the Meteor and inaugurated the era of close cooperation between Israel and France. By the time that the 1956 Sinai War erupted, Major Peled would be promoted once again and given command over Israel's first squadron of newly delivered Mystere fighters. Time and again he was selected to lead Israel's newest and best. By the Six-Day War, Lt. Col. Peled had risen to command the air base of Hatzor.[5]

But it was not merely his skill as a pilot or commanding officer that made Benny Peled the ideal candidate to reinvent Israel's fighter selection process. Rather, Benny Peled combined his flying skills and command experience with broad technical knowledge. Benny took a leave of absence in 1958 to complete his work on the engineering degree that had been interrupted years before. This combination of flying skills, combat experience, and engineering expertise made Benny Peled uniquely qualified to one day redefine Israel's air force modernization process. Inside the Heyl Ha'Avir, Peled was known for three traits: his fierce temperament, his insistence on discipline, and the breadth of his technical knowledge. It was routine for him to come home after a long day at the air base and spend hours more pouring through the latest aviation journals, while his wife sat patiently waiting. As one Israeli fighter pilot recalled, "If you didn't have an engineering degree, he treated you as if you were an idiot, and a moron. It was up to you to prove that you were not."[6]

Moreover, his assignment to the Hadish team was not Benny Peled's first experience with Israel's fighter selection process. Benny had been Israel's chief test pilot in the early 1950s, when he was first sent to evaluate the French and Swedish fighters available at the time.[7] It had been in this context, in April 1954, that he had become the first Israeli pilot to break the sound barrier, while flying a prototype for the French Mystere II in a dive. But Benny Peled gained much more than firsthand experience as a test pilot that day. He also gained a firsthand look at the way Israel's early fighter selection process both worked, and potentially, failed them. Benny had immediately recognized that the Mystere II had severe shortcomings. The airplane had almost no useful bomb load and a highly limited range. Worse, the Mystere II was unstable at high speeds. It didn't take much inquiry to determine that the French themselves had no intention of purchasing the airplane until these design shortcomings were resolved. Convinced of his assessment, it would nonetheless require several exchanges between Benny Peled and Israel's air force leadership, including some heated arguments, before he was able to convince them to cancel their existing deal for the Mystere II, and wait instead for the redesigned Mystere IV.[8]

Long before taking the reins of Israel's Hadish team, Benny Peled had observed Israel's previous fighter selection and procurement process from the inside, with all of its flaws. In the past, aircraft had been selected largely on the basis of availability. Moreover, too much had rested on the opinion of a few senior officers—many of whom had never flown the airplane. As he had done with every challenge that he faced, Benny Peled approached his role as Hadish team leader with the single-minded focus of a pilot executing a bombing run. He was determined to correct the flaws in Israel's fighter selection process—flaws that he had witnessed firsthand in years past.

Assisting Benny Peled on the Hadish team would be two individuals who would also play pivotal roles in Israel's fighter procurement strategy. As young lieutenants, David Ivry and Amos Lapidot had begun their air force careers together, assigned as eager new pilots under Benny Peled's leadership in Israel's 113th Fighter Squadron in 1955. Like Benny, these two young men had been among the handful of fighter pilots selected to serve in Israel's first French-equipped jet squadron.[9] Each of this trio of pilots, both commanding officer and pupils, would leave his mark on Israel's weapons procurement process, across a period spanning more than two decades. Their common experiences, and vision, would ensure continuity in Israel's procurement efforts. Before joining the Hadish team, both David Ivry and Amos Lapidot had likewise gone on to command fighter squadrons of their own, and each, like Benny Peled, was known for his meticulous attention to detail. Each member of this trio would one day play a pivotal role in shaping the Lavi fighter program. Each one, in his turn, would also one day command the Heyl Ha'Avir.

Among the first tasks that were given to Brigadier General Peled's Hadish team was overseeing the production of the Nesher fighter from the French blueprints and the subsequent development of the Kfir. The first Nesher flew in September 1969, with the airplane entering production in 1972. The prototype for the Kfir fighter would follow soon afterward, with its first flight in June 1973. But the Nesher and Kfir programs were only part of the Hadish team's efforts.

Although the Kfir was certainly a step beyond the Mirage, it could not fulfill all of Israel's needs. The Israelis had pushed the basic Mirage-style airframe as far as it would go, and any new break-throughs would require a more radical departure. More importantly, the Arab air arms would soon be fielding a newer, more lethal gen-eration of Soviet-designed aircraft, not to mention the best West-ern fighters that oil money could buy. There was never any doubt that, in order to keep up, Israel would need the next generation in fighter technology.

In the early 1970s the U.S. military was also in the initial stages of developing a new generation of fighters for their own use. Del-egations of Israeli pilots were therefore sent to evaluate the Amer-ican aircraft, whether flying or still on paper, to determine their suitability for meeting Israel's needs. The Israeli planners came down in favor of purchasing the F-15 relatively early, years before it would be made available to them.[10]

The F-15, however, was not in itself a complete answer to Israel's fighter inventory needs. At the time, the Heyl Ha'Avir had a fleet of some 120 F-4E Phantoms, nearly 200 A-4 Skyhawks, and some 80 Mirage III and Nesher fighters, as well as a handful of the old Mystere jets, all of which would eventually need to be replaced. There was no way that they could afford enough of the big, expen-sive F-15s to fill their requirements. Moreover, while it was a superb high-speed interceptor, the F-15 did not necessarily fit all of Isra-el's objectives. For Israel, the strike role was every bit as important as the air-to-air mission, and in a bombing run an airplane with a smaller profile would have a distinct advantage. As one Israeli pilot commented with regard to the Eagle, "I don't want to be the biggest target in the sky."[11] Long before the first F-15s arrived, it had already become apparent that Israel would need to procure a high-low mix of fighter designs, much like the U.S. Air Force and Navy.

There were two aircraft on the horizon that could potentially fill Israel's need for a smaller, cheaper fighter to complement the F-15: the General Dynamics YF-16 and Northrop's YF-17. The U.S. Air Force would eventually choose the single-engine F-16 to complement the role of the F-15 in American inventory. The U.S. Navy, for its part, would choose to develop a slightly larger aircraft based around the twin-engined YF-17. Assigned to McDonnell Douglas, the navy fighter would be relabeled as the F/A-18. Although the first flight of each prototype was still years away, the Hadish team already had two likely candidates to fulfill their future lightweight fighter needs. The choice between them, however, was not unanimous. Many of the Israeli pilots were worried about the vulnerability of the YF-16 to ground fire, and the addition of a second engine made the YF-17 an attractive option. Even before the prototypes flew, however, Benny Peled would be convinced that the F-16 would provide the better match in capability and price.[12]

In May 1973 Maj. Gen. Benny Peled became Israel's new air force commander. Brig. Gen. David Ivry was promoted to become his deputy air force chief, and Col. Amos Lapidot became the new leader of the Hadish team. Continuity had been preserved for Israel's fighter modernization plans. The F-15 was still viewed as Israel's first choice for a new air superiority fighter, and there was still time to contemplate a buy of either the single-engined F-16 or the twin-engined F-17. None of them, however, could have foreseen the war that would break out in October of that same year—a war that was to forever reshape Israel's air force planning.

Within a matter of weeks the Israeli armed forces would lose more soldiers than at any time since the War of Independence. But the Yom Kippur War was not only a tremendous blow to the Israeli armed forces; it was also a particularly grave blow to the Israeli air force. With too few soldiers on the ground to stem the tide, the Heyl Ha'Avir had been called upon to perform close air support and attack missions, without having the opportunity to first suppress the enemy air defenses. The network of missile batteries that had been built up on the Egyptian side of the Suez Canal, in violation of the cease-fire agreement signed in 1970, took a heavy toll on Israeli aircraft. They faced a similar missile network arrayed against them on the Syrian front. A total of 102 Israeli aircraft would be shot down during the course of the war, 37 percent of them during the first seventy-two hours of fighting.[13] Nearly half of the Israeli fighter losses would be due to surface-to-air missile batteries, with a similar number lost to antiaircraft artillery.[14] The Egyptian and Syrian air defenses not only succeeded in downing Israeli aircraft in numbers that the Arab air forces could only dream of approaching, but they also forced many attack missions to be aborted while the Israeli pilots attempted to evade the missiles. In spite of heroic efforts, the Israeli air force was unable to supply anything approaching the degree of frontline support that they had been accustomed to. The loss in men, material, and morale was devastating. Losses were particularly high among Israel's fleet of A-4 Skyhawk strike jets, where fifty-three aircraft would be lost. By the end of the war twenty-six Skyhawk pilots would be either killed or missing in action, with another twelve becoming POWs.[15]

Many strategists, far removed from the battlefield, took the Yom Kippur War to be a sign that the preeminence of the fighter-bomber had ended and that surface-to-air missiles now held the upper hand. Within Israel's air force, however, it was understood all too well that the high casualty rate was as much a product of the tactics that were employed as it was the result of missile technology. Had the Israeli air force been given the opportunity to target the missile network before assigning aircraft to attack the advancing Egyptian and Syrian tanks and soldiers, the losses suffered could have been far less. It was a luxury that they simply had not had.

Following the Yom Kippur War, Maj. Gen. Benny Peled was given new impetus to rebuild the Heyl Ha'Avir and to absorb the lessons of the war. Intelligence gaps were filled, communication lines were cleared, and focus was given to developing the necessary combination of tactics and technology needed to counter the surface-to-air missiles. It would be another decade before the fruits of this labor would become visible. But to truly understand what kind of fighter the Lavi became, the impact of this war on Israeli military thinking must be understood. It has often been said that generals have a tendency to refight the last war. For Israel's air force, the Yom Kippur War was that last big war, and the losses that they experienced would weigh heavily on the minds of the developers behind the Lavi.

In 1974 Israel Aircraft Industries presented their own proposals for a next generation of Israeli-developed fighters. The concept studies referred to the proposed airplane as the Aryeh (lion) and spanned a variety of possible designs. These concept studies would be expanded upon and refined several times during the course of the next six years. Studies for both single- and twin-engined fighters were assembled, featuring a range of possible inlet geometries and designs with both single and twin vertical tails. Alternative missions and different weapons options were likewise examined. The one common element retained by all of these concepts, however, would be the canard-delta layout that had been pioneered by the Kfir.

A good sense for the various trade studies being weighed can be gathered by examining one such design concept: a configuration known as Layout 28. Layout 28 was the focus of extensive wind tunnel studies as well as weapons and avionics integration efforts. It featured a twin-engine design with two vertical tails, combined with the trademark canard and delta wing that was common to so many of IAI's conceptual studies. Layout 28 featured two-dimensional, variable geometry inlets mounted on the sides of the fuselage, similar to those found on the F-15, allowing the airplane to maximize its supersonic performance. Had it been built, it would have been only slightly smaller than the F-15.[16]

Many of Israel's leading military and political figures would likewise come down in favor of developing a new, twin-engined fighter, designed to meet Israel's unique air force needs. Seed funding continued to be approved in successive years by the Knesset Foreign and Defense Affairs Committee, helping to keep the concept studies alive. It was a budget decision that also had the support of Israel's Hadish team, whose members deemed it prudent to keep Israel's options open. But however widely this strategy was endorsed elsewhere it was not endorsed by Israel's air force commander, Maj. Gen. Benny Peled.

In an unusual move, Peled submitted a confidential letter addressed to a closed-door session of the Knesset's Committee for Foreign and Defense Affairs, notifying them that the Hadish team's recommendation to continue funding further design studies had been submitted without his own concurrence. To Peled's way of thinking, spending additional resources on exploring a domestic fighter program was a waste of precious resources.[17]

Benny Peled was still convinced that Israel's next fighter, beyond the F-15, should be a single-engined airplane. It was a question of weighing payload, as well as the airplane's size and agility, against the cost. As leader of the Hadish team only a few years before, Peled had closely followed the development of the Kfir and had concluded that while a homegrown fighter would offer the opportunity to precisely match a new airplane to Israel's operational needs, it would also prove a more costly alternative. Like others in the defense establishment, Peled was mindful of Israel's sensitivity to future suspensions in arms deliveries. But he believed that there were other, less costly means for ensuring Israel's vital flow of weapons.

Rather than develop an all-new fighter from the ground up, Benny was convinced that licensed production of an existing American fighter design would prove to be a less costly alternative. It would not have completely freed Israel's armed forces from reliance on American weapons deliveries. A variety of key aircraft and engine components still would have needed to be imported. But it would have cushioned the Israeli armed forces from short-term suspensions while the politicians sorted out their differences. Moreover, licensed production would have offered Israel the opportunity to uniquely customize an American design to meet Israeli needs, without the full development expense of an all-new fighter.

Israel Aircraft Industries was, understandably, less enthusiastic about the licensed production concept. IAI officials complained that they were "not a garage" and that their talents could better be applied to the development of an all-new airframe.[18] But there was no escaping the logic of Benny Peled's position.

The proposals from Israel Aircraft Industries were therefore placed on the back burner. They were not shelved completely and continued to curry favor among elements of Israel's political establishment. Wind tunnel studies continued, as did the evaluation of alternative engine and weapons integration options. However, the prime path for Israeli arms procurement remained focused on American weapons.[19]

The fly-off for America's Air Combat Fighter took place in 1974, beginning with the first flight of the YF-16 in January and the first flight of the YF-17 in June. Throughout the ensuing months, the U.S. Air Force put both aircraft through an intensive flight-test program before announcing the selection of the YF-16 as the winner on January 13, 1975. The U.S. Navy, meanwhile, announced in May of that year that it had selected the YF-17 as the basis for its own future development efforts.[20] In Israel the Hadish team, now led by Col. Amos Lapidot, had been closely following the results of the American competition. They likewise came down in favor of the F-16 as the preferred alternative for Israel's next jet fighter order.

By the mid-1970s, as Israel's leadership planned for the restructuring of Israel's air force in the shadow of the Yom Kippur War, long-term procurement plans had begun to take shape. With the F-15 slated to become Israel's next air superiority fighter, the Hadish team had come around to Benny Peled's previous assessment, concluding that the F-16 constituted the best complement to the F-15. Moreover, given Israel's past experiences with the fickle nature of foreign arms supplies, the Israeli leadership saw licensed production as an essential part of that procurement strategy. The Heyl Ha'Avir was also deep in the process of absorbing the lessons of the Yom Kippur War and developing strategies to deal with the surface-to-air missile threat. The stage was therefore set to make the procurement decisions that would profoundly shape Israel's air force for the next two decades, and beyond. By all appearances, those decisions were expected to center around licensed production of the U.S.-developed F-16. This was provided, of course, that other events did not intervene.

4. The Next Lion

In March 1977 the Israeli government submitted its proposals for licensed production of the F-16 to the newly elected Carter administration. Under the original proposal, Israel was expected to purchase the first 50 examples directly from the U.S. manufacturer, with assembly to thereafter shift to Israel for the next 200 aircraft. It was estimated that a further 150 to 200 aircraft would eventually be needed to flesh out Israel's fighter wings.[1] Such a proposal not only would have satisfied Israel's fighter inventory needs but would have allowed the Israelis to modify the F-16 on the assembly line to suit their own requirements.

The ability to modify the F-16 while it was still on the assembly line was a central part of Maj. Gen. Benny Peled's proposed procurement plans. For most air forces, the more glamorous role of the air-to-air dogfight tended to draw attention away from the seemingly mundane job of dropping bombs on the enemy. But for Israel's air force, ignoring the ground war was a strategic error that they could never afford. It was in the attack mission that the vast majority of Israeli fighters had been shot down during the Yom Kippur War. To a greater degree than in other Western air forces, the Heyl Ha'Avir had to tailor its procurement and mission planning to support the ground war. In the words of Maj. Gen. Mordechai Hod, the commanding officer of the Heyl Ha'Avir during the 1967 Six-Day War, "Air superiority in itself is not an aim. Its object is to enable airpower to be used correctly and wisely. . . . Air superiority is a necessary evil."[2] Just as Israeli air force planners had found it necessary years before to develop the Mirage III into the multirole Mirage 5, so too Israeli arms planners had something more in mind for an Israeli-produced F-16 than merely a carbon copy of the American fighter.

Table 1. Israeli air force, 1995: Early 1977 projection

Aircraft	Number
Kfir	80
F-15	60
F-16 (various models)	450
Total	590

Had the go-ahead been given for Israeli manufacture, at least two versions of the F-16 would have emerged from the Israeli assembly floors. One, following the lines of the standard F-16A/B and F-16C/D models, would have been biased toward air defense duties. The other, a very different sort of airplane, would have been tailored for the attack and close air support (CAS) missions. We can gain some idea of what this other airplane might have looked like by reviewing other F-16 derivative fighters that were developed years later in the United States and Japan.

The first such F-16 derivative to emerge was the F-16XL, which was also marketed to the U.S. Air Force (USAF) in the mid-1980s as an alternative to the F-15E Strike Eagle. The F-16XL, or F-16E as it was proposed, featured a stretched fuselage and a cranked arrow wing. The design more than doubled the wing area, from the 300 sq ft (27.9 m²) of the conventional F-16A to 646 sq ft (60.0 m²) on the F-16XL. It also increased the number of available hard-points from nine to seventeen, vastly increasing the weapons load that could be carried. The result was an aircraft capable of carrying twice the payload up to 44 percent farther than a conventional F-16.[3] The F-16E ultimately lost-out to the F-15E as the USAF's next long-range strike platform. Had Israel been permitted to license produce the F-16, however, it is entirely plausible that this version might have made its way into Israeli service.

The other derivative of the F-16 was the Japanese-developed Mitsubishi F-2. Developed in the 1990s under Japan's FS-X fighter program, the F-2 was a less radical design departure, featuring a stretched fuselage and a 25 percent increase in wing area. The Japanese aircraft did incorporate an all-composite wing, however, and also increased the number of available weapons stations from nine to eleven. The F-2 also retained the conventional F-16 wing and tail combination.

Licensed manufacture would have given the Israelis the opportunity to do much more than merely gain some degree of arms independence or install their own electronics. Licensed manufacture would have given them an opportunity to optimize the airframe for their own particular needs. It would have required a redesign of certain features, but it would still have been far less expensive than attempting to extend their Kfir experience to a new generation of aircraft.

Yet if Israel's leadership had learned the lessons of foreign dependency, so had the foreign governments. The Carter administration turned down Israel's request to license produce the F-16, indicating that the United States would need to consult with its four NATO allies who were also coproducing the airplane. The excuse was absurd. When the United States later extended local production rights for the F-16 to Turkey, South Korea, and Japan, it was without requests for comment, much less permission from Europe. However, the excuse served the ends of the Carter administration, which knew full well that its NATO partners were too dependent on Arab oil to publicly agree to an arms sale to Israel.[4]

The Carter administration was not the only element in the United States to express reservations about allowing the Israelis to set up their own F-16 assembly line. General Dynamics, the American developer of the F-16, also expressed concern with the prospect that Israel might eventually be offering an improved version of the F-16 for export. General Dynamics was well aware that Israel would not be leaving the design untouched. However, there was also an irrational side to General Dynamics' concerns. There was no reason that General Dynamics could not have incorporated Israeli innovations into their own production line. The mutual exchange of lessons learned and airframe features need only have been written into the contract. General Dynamics could have benefited from Israeli-developed refinements without having to pay for the development costs. Furthermore, by law the United States had to approve any Israeli arms exports incorporating American technology, as the Israelis had most recently discovered when they had sought an export license for the sale of Kfir fighters. The Israelis would have been no more free to reexport copies of the F-16 than were the European partner nations that were already producing the airplane.

We can only wonder at what opportunities were lost in 1977, for both the United States and Israel. By marrying an American fighter design to Israeli combat experience, both nations would have benefited. For Israel, such an arrangement would have conserved Israeli defense resources while still incorporating the features and capabilities that it needed and insulating Israel's arms supply from short-term policy disagreements. For the United States, such an arrangement could have paved the way for the transfer of Israeli-developed innovations into U.S. warplanes. Both nations could have gained from the exchange of technology and experience.

In October 1977 Maj. Gen. Benny Peled stepped down as air force chief, without having closed a deal for the licensed production of the F-16. Maj. Gen. David Ivry became the next head of Israel's air force. Ivry shared Peled's reputation for organizational skills and attention to detail. In 1975 Ivry had even followed in his predecessor's footsteps by taking time off from his duties to complete a degree in aeronautical engineering at Israel's Technion. A reserved war veteran who demanded the utmost from Israel's pilot corps, Ivry had authored Israel's *Air Gunnery* manual, which together with Yak Nevo's *Aerial Combat* formed the basis for Israel's pilot-training regimen throughout the 1950s and 1960s.[5] Israel's air force may have had a new commanding officer at the helm, but under the gaze of Ivry's steel-blue eyes, the course that had been laid out would remain unaltered. Negotiations would continue, seeking the licensed production of the F-16 in Israel.

After much delay, the Carter administration finally offered the Israeli government an alternative to the coproduction proposal: the direct sale of seventy-five American-produced F-16A/BS. The Israeli government, eager to maintain its qualitative edge, accepted the offer in August 1978, with the hope that it might still convince the administration to reconsider Israeli coproduction of the F-16. But even as the Israeli government agreed to accept the American offer, there were other voices in Israel's leadership suggesting other ideas. They advocated an Israeli alternative to Israeli needs.

This revived proposal for an indigenous Israeli fighter was to have two principal advocates within Israel's political leadership. But the two had very different visions of just what this proposal entailed. At the time, the preeminent one of the two was Israel's minister of defense, Ezer Weizman. A former commander of the Israeli air force, Weizman had earned his pilot's wings with the Royal Air Force (RAF) during the final days of World War II. Throughout his military career, the flashy image of the World War II RAF pilot, complete with goggles and scarf, remained part of the mystique that Weizman cultivated. As air force commander, Major General Weizman would insist on maintaining a lone black Spitfire as his personal mount, using it to shuttle between air bases and parking it alongside the sleek jet fighters on the flight line. Impetuous and flamboyant, the tall, lanky Ezer Weizman had been responsible for instilling a spirit of elitism among the fighter jocks of the Heyl Ha'Avir.

When Weizman left the air force in 1966 to take the role of chief of operations at Israel's General Headquarters, it was only a matter of time before he would enter the world of politics. No other post that he might have been offered in the military could have replaced his beloved air force. But while it was obvious to many that Ezer Weizman would eventually seek a role in politics, it was not altogether obvious where that political career might land the ambitious former pilot. It would not have been unreasonable to suspect that Weizman might join the elite of Israel's Labor Party, with which his uncle Chaim had been so closely associated. But as a nation at war, Israel was replete with war heroes and ex-generals. There was little room in Israel's ruling Labor Party for yet another former general to make it to the top. Weizman instead set his sights on joining the opposition Likud Party.

By the mid-1970s the heavy casualties from the Yom Kippur War, combined with the decades of sacrifice demanded from Israel's citizens, had taken their toll. Dissatisfaction was running high, and Ezer Weizman joined the leading opposition party as campaign manager just as it stood poised to overtake Labor at the polls. In 1977 voters handed the Labor Party its first defeat and propelled the Likud bloc into command of the Israeli government. Weizman was appointed as Israel's new minister of defense, and it was only natural that the former air force chief would take a special interest in modernization plans for Israel's air force.

In 1978 Weizman directed Israel Aircraft Industries to dust off its conceptual designs from the Aryeh studies and focus on options for a small, single-engined airplane to "succeed" Israel's Kfir. What Weizman had in mind was a lightweight attack jet focused around the narrow objective of replacing Israel's aging A-4 fleet. The airplane was meant to be the successor to the Kfir in production, not in operational service. Weizman described it as "small, cheap, and a bastard."[6] In other circles it was described less charitably as a "jet Spitfire."[7] For Ezer Weizman, it could hardly have been any different.

Weizman also wanted to keep the new airplane free from American involvement and interference. Israel had recently had a sale of twenty-four Kfir fighters to Ecuador put on indefinite hold by the Carter administration. As long as the Israelis depended on American components for their airplanes, even if only for the engine, Washington would still have veto power over export sales. As a consequence, Weizman directed IAI to investigate the prospects for purchasing an engine from Europe, where export policies were expected to be more lenient. As Weizman stated at the time, "We want the Aryeh to be as free as possible from political interference."[8]

But Ezer Weizman's vision of a completely homegrown fighter had long since died on the vine. None of the European jet engine manufacturers was prepared to sell to Israel. If they had once been willing to enter into discreet arms sales during the 1950s and 1960s, they were not willing to do so in the 1970s and 1980s. The power of the petrol majority had become too great. Nor could Israel develop and produce a new jet powerplant on its own. Jet engines had become far too complex for a nation with no experience and limited resources to consider such an endeavor. The conclusion drawn at Israel Aircraft Industries was that any new Israeli fighter, like the Kfir before it, would have to depend on the United States for its engine.

One other prominent political figure was also a vocal advocate for developing a new Israeli-produced fighter: the chairman of the Knesset Foreign Affairs and Defense Committee, Moshe Arens. Arens had been born in 1925 in Kovno, Lithuania. His family moved to Riga, Latvia, a short time later, in 1927, and it was there that Arens spent much of his childhood. Jews had always lived uneasily in those lands. The memory of the last round of pogroms was never more than a generation away. Even this history of persecution, however, could not have prepared the Jews of Latvia and Lithuania for the tragedy that would befall them.

Moshe Arens's father was a businessman with numerous contacts in America—contacts that eventually allowed him to escape with his family to the United States in 1939. Moshe was thirteen years old at the time. Within less than a year, Nazi Germany would overrun Latvia and Lithuania, and all of the friends and family members whom he had grown up with would perish in the Holocaust. It was a reality that the young Arens would never escape.

Moshe Arens would go on, seemingly, to integrate well into his new homeland, but the memories of his lost family members would continue to shadow his footsteps. Arens served in the U.S. Army Corps of Engineers from 1944 to 1946, and in 1947 he completed his bachelor's degree in mechanical engineering at MIT. Yet even in this measure of success, the young man could find no ground in which he could lay those painful memories to rest.

It would be no accident therefore that Arens would heed Israel's pleas for help and leave the United States to volunteer in Israel's War of Independence in 1948. There Arens would join the Irgun Tsvai Leumi (national military organization), one of several Jewish underground armies that had been founded in prestate Palestine, under the leadership of Menachem Begin. Arens was part of a wave of volunteers from the industrial, Western world who would to come to Israel in its hour of need. Jews as well as non-Jews came from America, Canada, and Britain, lending their skills, and often their military expertise, during the war. Although relatively few in number, they would make an important contribution to Israel's war effort, providing the first pilots for its new air force and experienced officers to lead and train its army. Most of the volunteers would return to their lands of origin shortly after the war was over.[9]

Like many other volunteers, Moshe Arens returned to the United States in 1951, after the fighting had settled down. Returning to his studies, he completed his master's degree in aeronautical engineering at the California Institute of Technology in 1954. From there he went on to work at Curtiss-Wright Corporation while he continued to work toward his PhD. Had he followed his own father's advice, Arens would have perhaps stayed in the United States, partaking in a postwar prosperity that could have promised him a comfortable future. But for Arens, the memories of his childhood friends, of the family members that he had left behind in Lithuania, were too vivid: "My father wasn't happy about me going to Israel, and he wanted me to stay in the United States and become a millionaire. But this was something that I had to do. When people of a certain age ask me why I went to Israel in 1948, I reply, 'Why didn't you?' I came out of Lithuania and Latvia where the Germans destroyed everything. Ninety-five percent of the Jews there didn't survive. In 1948 this was our last stand after the Holocaust; this was the chance that Jews had to show they would survive."[10] After completing his PhD, Arens returned to Israel in 1957 to become an associate professor at Israel's Technion. In 1962 he became vice president of engineering at Israel Aircraft Industries and later went on to oversee the development of the Kfir jet fighter. In 1971 he would be awarded the Israel Defense Prize for his contributions to Israel's defense industries.

In the 1970s Moshe Arens was convinced to join the Likud's list of candidates for the Knesset, under the leadership of Menachem Begin—the former Irgun leader under whom Arens had served during Israel's War of Independence. Arens was elected to the Knesset for the first time in 1974, and in 1977, when the Likud Party soundly defeated Israel's Labor Party in national elections, Arens returned to the Knesset as head of the Foreign Affairs and Defense Committee.

It was in this capacity, in 1978, that Arens was indeed warm to the idea of an Israeli-developed airplane, and his committee was quick to recommend an initial budget of $450 million to launch the program.[11] As Arens related during one interview, continuing to rely on the United States to meet Israel's jet fighter needs would be "a very bad mistake from every point of view. It would be a death blow to the design and development potential of IAI . . . . I hope and believe the new government will show greater independence and reliance on our own capability for developing and manufacturing our procurement needs."[12]

But the airplane that Moshe Arens wanted was very different from that envisioned by Ezer Weizman. Arens was not interested in a simple light-attack airplane but rather advocated the development of a state-of-the-art fighter, an aircraft that he saw as being equal or superior to either the F-15 or the F-16. But of course, Weizman was minister of defense, and Arens was not. Arens's ideas remained only brewing.

Two years later, in 1980, the first batch of twenty-five F-15s had been delivered to Israel, and the first deliveries of F-16s, out of the seventy-five that were then on order, were expected to follow shortly. The Israeli air force was easily the strongest in the region, with some 550 combat aircraft on hand, as compared to 450 in the Syrian inventory, 80 Jordanian fighters, and some 350 Iraqi combat aircraft. More importantly, the Egypt-Israel peace treaty signed in 1979 had removed the immediate threat of war with the largest of the Arab armies. But Israel's military planners knew that they could not sit content. The F-4E Phantom and A-4 Skyhawk were still Israel's principal fighter and attack aircraft. The F-4 had first flown in May 1958 and the A-4 in June 1954. They were old and tiring aircraft, and a modernization plan would have to be approved soon.

It was also at this time that the Israel Defense Forces completed a study on projected Arab military capabilities in the 1990s and on Israel's defensive requirements.[13] This report is still classified, but some of its contents and conclusions can nonetheless be guessed at. As part of the Middle East arms package approved by the Carter administration in 1978, a package that had included Israel's order for seventy-five F-16s, Saudi Arabia was to receive sixty-two F-15C/D aircraft, together with five E-3 airborne warning and control system (AWACS) command centers. The Hashemite Kingdom of Jordan, meanwhile, was eagerly bargaining for the purchase of F-16s, and several of the other oil states were also busily shopping in the Western arms bazaar. All of these nations could potentially be dragged into a future Middle East war.

Israel's most direct threat at the time of this particular IDF study, however, was most obviously Syria. Prior to the initiation of peace talks in the mid-1970s, Egypt had been the principal Soviet client state in the Middle East. With Egypt realigned to the Western camp, that distinction now belonged to Syria. The Israelis still outnumbered the Syrians at the time in terms of aircraft, tanks, and artillery. But it was already clear in 1980 that this situation was purely temporary. In 1967 the Syrian air force had numbered only 120 combat aircraft. In 1973, at a time when Egypt was still the principal recipient of Soviet arms in the region, this number had grown to 210. And by 1980, with the Syrians now firmly in position as the Soviets' principal client in the region, that number had grown to no less than 450 fighter and attack aircraft. At that rate of growth, the Syrian air force would approach 800 combat aircraft by 1990 and surpass 900 by 1995. The best that the Israelis could hope to sustain was a fleet of perhaps 600 aircraft.[14] In addition, rumors were already beginning to leak out regarding a new generation of Soviet fighters that, benefiting from a series of successful espionage operations, had worn thin the much-vaunted Western technological edge.[15] Worse, the Syrians were now at the top of the Soviet export list. Syria, Libya, Iraq, and India had been the only client states to have received the Soviets' most secret fighter of the 1970s: the MiG-25 Foxbat. And as of 1980, Syria was the only nation to field the new T-72 tank outside of the Red Army. These were weapons that even the Soviets' Warsaw Pact allies had not yet received, and there could be little doubt that when the next generation of Soviet fighters became available, Syria would be among the first to field them.

The Israeli government approached the Carter administration once more in 1980 to request that it be allowed to license produce the F-16 in Israel. It was once again turned down.[16] The Israeli government could not delay an air force modernization program forever, hoping that the United States would eventually change its mind. Nor was Israel willing to accept the prospect of continuing to be at the mercy of fickle foreign governments, left without aircraft or spares. One French disaster was enough.

So it was that in March 1980 the State of Israel publicly announced the go-ahead for the development of an all-new fighter called the Lavi, meaning "lion" in Hebrew. As would eventually be evident, a new breed of warbird was in the making.

5. The Power of Decision

Once the Lavi program was given the go-ahead, many key decisions regarding the shape of Israel's air force modernization plans could fall into place. In the air-to-air role, Israel's 1990s air force could be expected to consist of a combination of F-15s plus the initial batch of F-16s then on order. They would also need a new long-range strike fighter to replace the F-4, for which Defense Minister Ezer Weizman appears to have had either the F/A-18 or a version of the F-16 in mind. This left the Lavi squarely in the short-range attack role, with the Heyl Ha'Avir expecting to procure some four hundred of the aircraft.[1]

As originally envisioned by Weizman, the Lavi was to have been powered by a single General Electric F404 turbofan, the engine chosen personally by Weizman and the only powerplant then named in the U.S. authorization.[2] The F404 also powered the F/A-18 and was a favorite among nations looking to build their own lightweight fighters. At the time that Weizman announced his decision, the F404 was already the leading candidate to power Sweden's JAS-39 Gripen and was expected to power the first prototypes of India's Light Combat Aircraft. In its production version, the F404 could deliver up to 16,000 lb (71.2 kN) of thrust in afterburner and 10,600 lb (47.1 kN) of thrust at military power.[3]

Table 2. Israeli air force, 1995: Early 1980 projection

Aircraft	Number
F-15	55
F-16	75
U.S. fighter (type undetermined)	70+
Lavi (F404-powered)	400
Total	600

It appears likely that at least some of the performance figures later quoted for the Lavi were derived from initial estimates made for this smaller, F404-powered fighter. These included an estimated combat radius of 244 nm (450 km) when flying on internal fuel and carrying eight 1,000 lb (450 kg) Mk 82 bombs.[4] As fighter-bombers go, these values reflect a very short legged aircraft—the "jet-Spitfire" approach to the Lavi design.

As envisioned, the Lavi had a canard-delta planform featuring an all-moving canard. The fighter was expected to be a single-seat aircraft, with a two-seat version available as a trainer. The aircraft was to have had a fixed ventral inlet, in contrast to the variable, supersonic inlet featured on the Kfir. But if we are to believe the early artists' impressions released by IAI, the inlet was originally expected to have had a boxier, rectangular shape to it, unlike the rounded inlet seen on the F-16 or on later incarnations of the Lavi. This early vision of the Lavi fighter had evolved from an Aryeh concept study identified at IAI as "Layout 33." The Layout 33 design study had centered on an airplane with an empty weight of no more than 11,110 lb (5,040 kg), and a maximum takeoff weight of 28,500 lb (12,930 kg).[5] This airplane was significantly smaller than Israel's prior jet fighter, the Kfir, which had an empty weight of 16,060 lb (7,280 kg) and more closely resembled the 10,450 lb (4,740 kg) empty weight of the A-4 Skyhawk. Minimizing the cost of the new airplane was also a priority, mandating that the Lavi be fitted with an austere, minimalist avionics suite.

The program reflected Ezer Weizman's vision for what the Lavi should be, but it did not necessarily reflect the preferences of the air force commander at the time, Maj. Gen. David Ivry, nor those of the current leader of the Hadish team, Brig. Gen. Amos Lapidot—who would be expected to oversee the new airplane's initial development. It was only later that the views of Israel's senior air force staff would become evident.

All of this early planning changed just two months after the program got the official go-ahead. On May 28, 1980, Ezer Weizman resigned as Israel's minister of defense. The reason given was a budget disagreement with Finance Minister Yigael Hurwitz, who had recently ordered a temporary freeze on all new contracts, including those for the Defense Ministry. However, this was far from the first time that Weizman had run into conflict with another member of the Begin Cabinet, a situation that certainly had not been helped when he had offered to run as a candidate for the opposition Labor Party just a few months earlier. Weizman had joined the Likud Party as a political newcomer: one more former general, looking to launch a political career. But there could be only one prime minister, and in a Likud-led government that man was Menachem Begin. Weizman therefore sought more fertile ground elsewhere. Six months after his resignation, Weizman would vote against the government that he had once been a member of and in favor of a no-confidence measure in the Knesset. Had the vote passed, the road could have been cleared for new elections, offering an opportunity for Weizman to rise under the banner of a new political party. But the no-confidence vote failed, and the future of Israel's air force would no longer be directed by the former general.

This political shift, however, was the opportunity that Moshe Arens, and others who had been leaning in favor of a more capable aircraft, had been waiting for. Arens, who had earlier spearheaded support for the Lavi in Israel's parliament, was by then among the highest-ranking members in Israel's Likud Party. His personal friendship with the two leaders at the top of the Likud hierarchy,

Foreign Minister Yitzhak Shamir and Prime Minister Menachem Begin, dated back to his days as a volunteer in the Irgun movement during Israel's War of Independence. He could be assured of their attention on any matter of substance, particularly concerning a subject on which he was viewed as being something of an expert. It was consequently no surprise that in September Arens would be offered the newly vacated post of defense minister. It was also no surprise to anyone who knew Moshe Arens that he would decline that offer.

Politics is never a simple matter in Israel, and for Moshe Arens there was more at stake than just the future of the Lavi. Under the 1979 Egypt-Israel peace treaty, Israel had agreed to withdraw completely from the Sinai, a measure that Arens had argued was too great of a concession. It meant that Egypt, which had precipitated the Six-Day War, was to receive back the entire territory from which it had once launched cross-border terror raids and where it had massed troops for its threatened invasion of Israel in June 1967.

It was not merely the Sinai that was at stake, however. Arens was convinced that Israel's other neighbors would expect that the pattern set by these agreements would likewise be applied to Israel's other frontiers, including far more sensitive areas near the heart of Israel's population centers. Surrendering the Sinai, in its entirety, could make it more difficult to press Israel's case for territorial adjustments on other frontiers.

The agreed-upon surrender of the Sinai was scheduled to take place over the course of three years following the signing of the treaty. However much he may have wanted the post, Arens was not willing to go down in history as the defense minister who presided over Israel's withdrawal from the Sinai. Ever a man of his principles, Arens declined the offer to take over Israel's Defense Ministry.

There were other people, however, equally interested in developing the Lavi into a world-class fighter, willing to take up the role of defense minister. One such individual, Ariel Sharon, was eventually appointed to the post. What was more, with Weizman out of the picture, Arens now had the ear of the prime minister on this issue, and he began to put his vision for what the Lavi should be into motion.

"The original concept of an a-4 replacement was an unusual one and not very good," Arens later explained. "It would not have been a survivable aircraft."[6] In another interview he put it even more bluntly: "Ezer wanted to feed into the bottom of the pile, and I wanted to feed into the top."[7] The first step toward changing this bottom-of-the-pile fighter into a top-of-the-line warbird was to change the engine selection. Without a more powerful engine there was no way that the airplane's capabilities could be expanded.

The Lavi had long since outgrown the outlines of the Layout 33 concept study that had once formed its basis. The original design study had attempted to more evenly balance air-to-air and air-to-ground capabilities, with a thrust-to-weight ratio of 1.11 in an air combat configuration. The Israeli air force, however, would later allow this value to slip to 1.07, in return for better range and payload. The Israelis had already begun sizing up an airplane built around a more powerful version of the f404, which increased the available thrust to some 18,000 lb (80.1 kN). This still left them with a platform that fell short of their requirements. There happened to be two other power-plants, however, that had been proposed for the Lavi: Pratt & Whitney's f100 and their pw1120.

Capable of delivering up to 23,830 lb (106.0 kN) of thrust with afterburner, the f100 had powered the American f-15 and f-16 fighters. It was a proven, operational design. The pw1120, meanwhile, was a derivative of the f100, sharing some 60 percent of its components but incorporating a new fan design and a simplified afterburner. It could deliver up to 13,550 lb (60.3 kN) thrust at military power and 20,620 lb (91.7 kN) thrust in afterburner.[8] It had been specifically targeted for the fighter export market, featuring fewer parts and improved reliability.

Yet despite the pw1120's potentially attractive qualities, Pratt & Whitney had yet to find a customer for their derivative engine, and the corporate leadership was growing anxious. The company was therefore willing to offer an investment package in order to entice the Israeli government into changing its engine choice—a package that included an offer to purchase a 42 percent share in Bet

Shemesh Engines, the state-owned company expected to license produce whichever engine was chosen.[9]

The PW1120 turned out to offer precisely the balance of thrust and affordability that Moshe Arens, and those like him who wanted to see the Lavi evolve into a more capable platform, were looking for. It was this engine that Arens's Foreign Affairs and Defense Committee officially endorsed, with the full backing of several of Israel's senior air force officers. They, too, it would seem, were looking for a little more than merely a short-range A-4 replacement.[10]

It was this support among Israel's senior air force staff, and from the commanding officer, Maj. Gen. David Ivry, in particular, that ultimately tipped the balance in the debate. Weizman had come from a generation of stick-and-throttle flying, unencumbered by surface-to-air missile batteries or electronic countermeasures. His experiences as an RAF pilot in World War II, and when he later went on to select the Mirage to become the backbone of Israeli airpower in the 1960s, did not coincide with the electronic necessities of the modern battlefield. Ivry's experiences suggested a different story. As Maj. Gen. Benny Peled's deputy during the Yom Kippur War, Ivry knew only too well the difference that effective countermeasures, had they been available, might have made. During Cabinet briefings, Ivry strongly endorsed the PW1120, seeing in the Lavi an opportunity to deliver the kind of survivable strike fighter that the Heyl Ha'Avir desperately needed.[11] Ivry's support was the final, decisive factor. As Prime Minister Begin was heard to remark on the subject, "Count on the air force commander to know what is best for his troops."[12] In May 1981 Weizman's preliminary choice of the F404 was overturned, and the PW1120 became the new engine for the Lavi.

In hindsight, it is remarkable that the significance of this engine change was largely lost on the aviation community. The traditional rule for airplane design dictates that the smallest engine that still meets all of the design criteria should invariably be the one that is chosen. A smaller engine will weigh less, demand less fuel, and require a smaller airframe. When raw materials and manufacturing costs are totaled up, a slightly smaller engine can be the deciding factor in whether a fleet of four hundred aircraft is possible or whether only three hundred can be procured. What no one in the aviation journals or general news media caught on to was that for the Israelis to change the engine choice after the program had already been launched meant that they were changing the mission requirements for the airplane.

For Weizman's vision of an inexpensive A-4 replacement to have been realized, the Lavi design should have been frozen by the end of 1982, with production to begin as soon as 1986. But in 1982 "Arik" Sharon was minister of defense, and the Lavi design was not being frozen, but rather reinvented. Like Moshe Arens, Sharon had in mind a far more capable attack jet than Weizman's small A-4 replacement.

If the Six-Day War had taught the Israelis that they could depend on no foreign allies in times of war, the Yom Kippur War had taught them that sometimes even their own leadership could fail them. In the hours preceding the Egyptian and Syrian attack, the Israeli military had received last-minute intelligence that confirmed that an invasion was imminent. By that time it was already too late to call up the army's reserves in time to reach the front lines. But it was not too late to stage a preemptive air strike. The air force commander, Major General Peled, came out vocally in favor of staging a preemptive strike to destroy the Arab air forces and cripple their air defense networks before the impending invasion was underway. He wanted to ensure air superiority from the start, freeing the air force to provide close air support without impediment. His request, however, was rejected. It was the opinion of Prime Minister Golda Meir that Israel was too reliant on foreign goodwill in the United States and elsewhere to be seen as staging an attack that the Arab governments could then claim as the excuse for their planned invasion. The Israeli leadership let the Arab armies fire the first shots of the war, weighing the political costs against the lives of Israeli soldiers on the front line.

It was this wartime experience, more than any other, that indelibly shaped the reforging of the Lavi. All of the leading figures in Israel's military establishment at the time that the Lavi program was retooled and relaunched, from Defense Minister Ariel Sharon to army chief of staff Lt. Gen. Rafael "Raful" Eitan to air force commander Maj. Gen. David Ivry, had directly experienced the impact of this political decision on the battlefields of the Yom Kippur War.

In 1973 Maj. Gen. (Res.) Ariel Sharon had commanded the 143rd Armored Division on Israel's Sinai front, securing the beachhead for Israel's eventual counterattack across the Suez Canal.[13] Wounded on the battlefield, Sharon had refused to be evacuated from the front line. In true Israeli tradition, he had led his soldiers from the front, not from a headquarters hundreds of miles away. Sharon had watched from below as Israeli aircraft suffered painful losses in futile attempts to supply air support to troops on the ground. As Sharon later wrote in regard to the Lavi, "We knew for sure that we wanted to build an aircraft that was based on our experience in the Yom Kippur War, when we had faced the most complicated problems of antiaircraft weaponry. We believed that on the basis of this experience we could produce the best so-called second-line aircraft in the world, which would emphasize survivability. This was an especially significant issue for us because of our relatively small number of planes."[14] As Sharon knew all too well, it was the "second-line aircraft" that the ground troops would depend on to supply close air support. In spite of, or perhaps because of, his experience as an army general who had commanded troops on the ground, and not pilots in the air, Ariel Sharon understood the need for a survivable close air support and attack platform.

Maj. Gen. Raful Eitan, meanwhile, had been in command of the Golan front during that same war and had seen his own field headquarters overrun by Syrian tank divisions—while the Israeli air force had been effectively hamstrung by the Arab missile network. Eitan would subsequently become among the most vocal critics of the political decision to withhold Israel's first-strike option during that war. Like Sharon, he would go on record as a supporter of a more versatile attack platform.

And of course, it had been Brig. Gen. David Ivry who had been deputy air force chief during the Yom Kippur War and who had witnessed firsthand how Benny Peled's call for a preemptive air strike had fallen on deaf ears. He had seen for himself the devastating impact that this decision had inflicted on Israel's fighter pilot ranks. Thirty-one Israeli pilots had lost their lives flying in that war. Another fourteen had been captured, and more still were injured.[15] For the small community of Israel's fighter pilots, these were deep wounds. These were men that David Ivry had known by name, pilots and navigators he had flown with and commanded. Ivry, Eitan, and Sharon: each of these men had his own reasons for seeing the Lavi transformed from an austere A-4 replacement into a more capable, multirole fighter, one that would "emphasize survivability" above all else.

The Lavi therefore became the Israeli air force's newly domesticated pet project, fulfilling their own visions for what an attack jet should be and for an airplane that could do the one thing that no counterpart at that time, American or otherwise, was capable of doing: fly straight into the jaws of a fully functional air defense network, deliver its bomb load, and survive. Survivability thereafter became the central, driving concept behind the Lavi, the principle by which all aspects of the airplane were measured. The airplane was up-sized to fly farther and to carry a heavier payload. This meant that fewer sorties would need to be flown to ensure that its target had been destroyed. Improved airplane subsystems were added as rapidly as they became available, all with the aim of reducing vulnerability to enemy missiles and allowing the pilot to focus on his mission. The airplane's cost went up, but the Lavi had become truly a warbird without peer—an airplane built with a distinctively Israeli approach.

There have always been subtle differences between Israeli and American philosophies toward weapons design and procurement. The United States has far more resources to devote, and in America the realities of war can sometimes become lost somewhere between the bureaucrats and the glitz of the latest "high-tech" weapons craze. In Israel, a nation with no other natural resources to rely on, military doctrine has tended to emphasize the all-importance of the human element. To a nation vastly outnumbered by its enemies, every pilot lost represents an irreplaceable investment in time and resources. Israel has no vast manpower reserves. As a result, American and Israeli weapons efforts tend to differ in emphasis.

The differences in U.S. and Israeli military doctrine, and emphases, came to be exemplified during the latter 1950s and early 1960s when the conventional wisdom of the day dictated that the long-range, radar-guided missile had made dogfighting a thing of the past. Popular thinking suggested that all future air-to-air engagements would occur beyond visual range, with pilots combating opponents that they could see only on their radar screens. As the United States set out to develop its next fighter, the F-4A Phantom, emphasis was placed on speed and the ability to carry lots of missiles. Pilot training became focused on long-range interception rather than dogfighting skills.

In Vietnam it was fast discovered that those early long-range missiles were appallingly unreliable. American F-4s would ripple-fire radar-guided missiles in salvos and were still being shot down in close-quarter dogfights for which the F-4 was never designed, and for which the pilots had never been trained. The bureaucrats and technology experts had allowed all of the edge in air-to-air training and experience built up during World War II and the Korean War to waste away. Later F-4 variants, including Israel's F-4Es, would add a cannon. But the airplane would never be a natural dogfighter.

Yet at the same time that the United States and Europe had abandoned dogfight training as a leading component of their air force regimens, the Israeli air force had continued to emphasize close-range air-to-air combat as central to pilot training. At the same time that the venerable cannon was being omitted from the early versions of the F-4 Phantom, the Israelis were insisting that a cannon be added to the Mirage III fighters that were supplied by France. In 1967, in the skies over Egypt, Syria, Jordan, and Iraq, the Israeli air force demonstrated for all to see just how right they had been. It was the human element, the Israeli soldier, that had allowed a tiny nation, vastly outnumbered on the battlefield, to win a war that many had believed would spell the end of Jewish history. And it was the cannon, a weapon that had been abandoned by the American and European air forces, that had wreaked devastation on the Egyptian air force, both on the ground and in the air. The Israelis had chosen the weapons that would best build upon their own pilots' capabilities and training.

The reasons that Israeli arms procurement and development patterns have been so different from those of their counterparts in America and Europe should be readily evident. In Israel, virtually everyone involved in defense manufacture has served in the Israeli armed forces and has experienced war firsthand. For Israelis, war is not some distant phenomenon. Everyone has friends and family members who were lost in battle or during a terrorist attack. A number of the engineers involved with the Lavi were themselves reserve fighter pilots, veterans from the 1967 and 1973 wars. The Israeli government's director of development for the program, Menachem Eini, was himself a reserve brigadier general in the Israeli air force: a battle-tested soldier, not a bureaucrat. Eini had been a navigator during the 1969–70 War of Attrition, when his F-4E had been shot down by an Egyptian surface-to-air missile. It was an experience that had been forever etched into his psyche.

On July 18, 1970, Menachem Eini's Phantom had crossed the Suez Canal as part of a coordinated assault on Egyptian missile batteries. It was the first time that the Israelis had attempted to employ a new electronic warfare pod, recently provided by the Americans, that was supposed to jam the Egyptian radar and allow Israeli fighters to penetrate and attack the missile batteries themselves. Unfortunately, electronic warfare was still a new science at the time, and the American pods failed to provide protection. Even decades later, Eini's memories of that day would remain vivid:

> The missile, of course, was not impressed by our wonder weapon, coming in underneath us and exploding like they do in the movies. It felt as if someone had thrown a handful of gravel against the aircraft's skin. . . . We immediately released our bombs and banked eastwards towards home. We were already descending and building up speed to avoid any further missile hits. . . . Then, the moment when everything happens at once: just fifteen seconds away from the Canal I noticed the aircraft was slowly rolling left and downward. . . . Without think-

ing I pulled my ejection handle and flew from the cockpit. . . . When I left the aircraft, we were flying at 600 knots, a tremendous speed, and from the shock of hitting the air I lost consciousness. I remember, as if through a fog, the parachute opening and, afterwards, me crawling wounded on the ground, my left leg with a compound fracture, lying lifeless and askew. My right arm was broken in three places, and I couldn't move this either.[16]

After bailing out over enemy territory, Eini would remain a prisoner of war for the next forty months. The pilot of the Phantom and Eini's closest friend, squadron commander Lt. Col. Shmuel Hetz, would be less fortunate. Over the next three years Eini would mull over everything that had gone wrong that day. Three years, while he endured the pain of his injuries in an Egyptian prison camp:

> Hetz was the most outstanding individual of our age-group in the air force, head and shoulders above everyone else. He radiated a special kind of intensity; he was smart and always charming. He was an obvious choice as the first Phantom squadron leader, though it was the first time they had picked someone from the younger generation and not a veteran and more experienced pilot. We started basic training together, then pilot school. He went on to fighters, I to navigation. . . . I sat in an Egyptian prison for forty months, including a year in a military hospital at Maadi, and not a day went by without my thinking about the aircraft going down and Hetz's death.[17]

As director of development for the Lavi, Eini made one point exceedingly clear: no Lavi pilot should ever have to endure forty months as a POW for lack of an adequate electronic countermeasures suite. He expected the Lavi to survive, and to excel, in the same environment where his American mount had once failed both him and his closest friend decades before.[18]

The Lavi had become Israel's fighter pilots' own. Veteran aces were interviewed to determine every detail, from how the head-up display should appear to where the dials should go to how the control stick should be placed and how far back the seat should be inclined. They were asked what features they wanted to see and how best to present data on the displays. In Menachem Eini's own words, "Even foreign experts and pilots, when they see our plans and the aircraft itself, admit that it's every combat pilot's dream come true."[19]

The Lavi developers knew, better than most, just how important that edge in man-machine interface could be. It had been the superior experience of the American pilots, not the machines they flew, that had given them a kill-to-loss ratio of 10.6:1 in air combat over Korea and, despite the inferior handling qualities of the F-4, an overall ratio of 2.6 by the end of the Vietnam War. In the 1973 Yom Kippur War, the Israelis, despite all of the troubles that they faced from the surface-to-air missiles, brought home a kill-to-loss ratio of 21:1 in air-to-air combat. And in Lebanon in 1982, where for the first time they were flying truly superior fighters against the Syrian air force, the Israelis inflicted over eighty air-to-air kills, with no air-to-air losses of their own.[20]

As for survivability, this was the hallmark against which Israeli weapons engineers had historically measured their product. The Israeli-developed Merkava (chariot) main battle tank was a case in point. The Merkava had been among the very few tanks to be built with its engine located in front, ahead of the crew, so that if the tank were ever to be hit and its armor pierced, the projectile would destroy the engine and not the crew. The Merkava was built with a uniquely Israeli emphasis to its design. While its American and European counterparts would continue to emphasize speed, mobility, or firepower, the Merkava stood alone in emphasizing armored protection and crew survivability. Israel simply had too few soldiers to be able to afford being careless about losing them on the battlefield.

The Lavi very much followed in the footsteps of this same tradition, boasting the most advanced electronic warfare suite yet seen on a fighter of its kind. At every turn, the Lavi developers were haunted by the ghosts of the Yom Kippur War, by their friends and comrades who had never returned from the enemy missile nests. It was this kind of war that the Lavi was intended to fight, and win: a surprise attack in which Israel's air force would not have the luxury of suppressing the opposing air defense network. It was built to deliver ordnance, in spite of both guns and missiles, and to live to tell about it. No equivalent to this experience, or to this design emphasis, existed elsewhere.

It is sometimes difficult for those who have had no direct contact with Israel or with Israelis to fully comprehend the depth of responsibility that Israel's leaders, officers, and even weapons developers have toward the lives of individual soldiers on the battlefield. Israel and America have a great deal in common, from the noisy campaign pageants that are an intrinsic part of democracy to basketball games and pop music. But the two nations are also subtly different. In Israel, Independence Day, or Yom HaAtzmaut, is always preceded by Memorial Day, or Yom HaZikaron. The two are intrinsically connected, in ways that their counterparts are not in American culture. On the morning of Yom HaZikaron, from Tel Dan in the north to Beersheva and Eilat in the south, sirens wail across Israel, in unison, for two minutes. In that moment, every Israeli will stop what he or she is doing and stand at attention in memory of their war dead. Highways come to a standstill as cars halt where they are and drivers climb out to stand at attention. Every secretary, every clerk, stops his or her daily routine to pause in unison and remember those who fell on the battlefield to ensure Israel's freedom. They owe their country, their freedom, their lives to those who have fallen in the line of duty. It is something taken very seriously in a small nation with so many war dead. For Israelis, the connection is unmistakable: there can be no Yom HaAtzmaut, no Independence Day, without first having Yom HaZikaron.

War touches the lives of Israelis, in great and small ways, every day. A friend once described to me an experience that he had while riding on a bus, traveling to visit relatives for the weekend. The regular news broadcast came over the radio, as it does on every hour. On this day, the announcer told of an Israeli soldier who had died earlier that morning intercepting a band of would-be terrorists who were attempting to cross into Israel. The entire bus fell silent. Everyone awaited more details, waiting to see if they might know the soldier who had died, if they had lost a friend or a family member. In the seat across from my friend sat a middle-aged woman laden with heavy eyes. Only God could tell who she was remembering. Perhaps a brother or a father, a husband or a son. Combat losses are taken very personally in Israel. Today it might be your neighbor's son who dies for his country, tomorrow it might be your own, or it might be you. Israel is much less like a country as Americans conceive of a nation and much more like an extended family: a lone community trapped in the surreal landscape of the Middle East. One soldier, every soldier, is the most precious commodity that they have. It is not merely an expression of sentiment. To a nation so small, it is a strategic fact. This was why the Lavi, from the moment that its Israeli developers were free to reinvent it, became a uniquely Israeli war machine. The pilots who would one day fly it would be people that all of them knew.

In late 1981 Israel began to negotiate with a number of American aerospace firms for the development of a composite wing and tail structure for the Lavi. This effort marked yet another departure from the original Lavi concept approved by Weizman. Composite materials, with graphite epoxy being the example most widely in use, had also been applied in a more limited degree to earlier aircraft. They offered an opportunity to reduce the weight of aircraft structural components while providing greater tensile strength than comparable aluminum or titanium alloys. The Lavi, however, was expected to see much more widespread use of composites than had been found in any previous production fighter. By weight, some 22 percent of the Lavi structure was expected to be made up of composite materials.[21] Above and beyond the weight savings that this technology could afford, composites were also expected to reduce the airplane's drag. It was estimated that conventional aluminum or titanium construction would have increased drag on the Lavi by up to 10 percent and would have lowered its overall performance statistics by 5 percent on average.[22] However, the manufacture of composite components was by no means cheap, and it was highly doubtful that Weizman's earlier concept for an inexpensive A-4 replacement would have contemplated the same degree of composites usage.

Some of the airplane's composite components, such as the airbrakes, could easily be developed and manufactured in Israel. But for major structural items, such as the wing and vertical tail, Israel Aircraft Industries turned to the proven expertise of American aerospace firms. Designing a composite component was not as simple as substituting one material for another. To obtain the maximum benefit from the composite materials, the wing and vertical tail would require the application of aeroelastic tailoring. While the Israelis certainly had a fair deal of composites manufacturing experience of their own and could eventually have developed ply tailoring techniques given sufficient resources and time, doing so would have delayed the development effort and drained resources. The Israeli developers therefore held talks with a number of U.S. manufacturers, including McDonnell Douglas, General Dynamics, Grumman, Northrop, and LTV. Industry observers, mindful that Israel was rumored to be negotiating a purchase of the F/A-18, cited McDonnell Douglas as the front-runner in the competition.[23] But it was Grumman that would eventually be awarded a $100 million contract to develop and build the first twenty shipsets of wings and vertical tails for the Lavi, with production thereafter to shift to Israel. Grumman, of course, emphasized that they could also extend their production of Lavi wing and tail units indefinitely. Like the decision to change the Lavi engine selection in favor of a more capable but also more expensive alternative, the revelation that a significant portion of the airplane would be constructed from composite materials was yet another indication that fundamental changes had been made.

From 1980 to 1982, the Lavi fighter had evolved considerably—in only two short years. From the moment that Ezer Weizman had stepped down as defense minister, the race had been on to remold the Lavi. No longer an austere, short-range A-4 replacement, it had become a much longer range, multirole strike fighter, for which survivability was the overarching emphasis. Outwardly, the only change immediately visible to the public eye was a redirection in the airplane's engine selection and, later, the decision to employ composite materials on a large scale. Few outside observers, however, would recognize the underlying changes to the design intent that these decisions reflected. The Lavi program had made great strides during its first two years of development—but the skies ahead were far from clear.

6. Encountering Turbulence

At the same time that the Lavi program was launched, the United States welcomed a new administration into the White House. President Ronald Reagan formally took the oath of office in January 1981. A man of deep convictions with a strong sympathy for the State of Israel, Reagan and his administration would present both new opportunities and new challenges for the developers of the Lavi.

President Reagan's personal commitment to Israel's security was well established. For more than a decade, Reagan's stances on major foreign policy issues had been clearly and consistently stated, during his term as governor of California as well as in his numerous radio addresses, personal correspondence, and editorials and interviews. In a handwritten letter to a constituent, for example, dated a decade before he became president, Governor Reagan clearly explained his own convictions regarding Israel and the Middle East: "Let me sum up the Middle East situation as I believe it is and has been. Israel, outnumbered one hundred to one in the population of unfriendly surrounding nations, has held its own with the help of American military supplies. In addition, the U.S. presence in the area has kept the Soviet Union outside the Middle East, at least as an active participant. . . . I feel that the United States is morally bound to protect Israel's right to nationhood and I support that position without reservation."[1]

In yet another instance, during a radio address made in April 1977, the president-to-be would go even further, declaring his opposition to territorial compromises that endangered Israel's defensive posture: "The real issue in the Middle East has to do with the Arab refusal to recognize that Israel has a right to exist as a nation. To give up the buffer zones Israel took in the Six Day War would be to put a cannon on her front walk aimed at her front door by those who have said she must be destroyed."[2] For the newly elected president, his support for Israel was not some one-time campaign pledge that had materialized during the race for the Oval Office.

However, Reagan's affinity toward Israel was also tempered by the fact that the new president saw the principal focus of his foreign policy as being an unrelenting drive to win the Cold War. The new administration also had a number of senior staff members who had long-standing business interests in the Arab world, as well as others whose positions were less well known. Precisely how these competing elements would play themselves out was unclear.

The first test of the new administration's ability to formulate a coherent policy in the face of crises in the Middle East would not be long in coming. On June 7, 1981, eight Israeli F-16s, escorted by six F-15s, bombed Iraq's nearly complete Osirak nuclear reactor into oblivion. The Israeli government had pleaded for years for France to halt the reactor's construction, or at the very least to prevent Italy from providing the "hot cell" laboratories needed to separate plutonium from the spent reactor fuel. While Iraq was scouring the world market for uranium ore with which to feed its nuclear ambitions, the Europeans had been providing it with the means to convert that ore into plutonium and to extract that plutonium to produce atom bombs.

The Israeli government had agonized for months over how to deal with the nuclear menace on its doorstep. None more so than Prime Minister Menachem Begin. For Begin, the threats of annihilation aired regularly on Iraqi radio were all too familiar. Out of all of Israel's prime ministers, it was the Polish-born Begin who identified most closely with the victims of the Holocaust. Born in Brest-Litovsk, he had grown up in a community that, prior to the

Second World War, had included some thirty thousand Jews, 70 percent of the town's population. By the end of the war fewer than ten Jews remained.[3] Most of Begin's family members would perish in the Nazi death machine, including his parents and older brother. On his desk Prime Minister Begin would keep a photograph of a young boy, arms raised into the air, led away at gunpoint by German soldiers.[4] It was with these ghosts that Menachem Begin conferred when making fateful decisions.

For Begin, there could be only one response to Saddam Hussein, with or without the approval of the American or European governments. At a press briefing held shortly after the raid, Prime Minister Begin put his defiant resolve on stage, in the face of the international censure that he knew would follow:

> Israel has nothing to apologize for. Ours is a just cause. We stand by it and it will triumph. . . . During the Second World War a bomb of twenty kilotons caused at least two hundred thousand casualties in killed and afflicted. . . . With three such bombs . . . they could have destroyed completely, utterly, the Dan [Tel Aviv] district, the basis of our industrial, commercial, agricultural and cultural life. Six hundred thousand casualties we would suffer, which would mean, in terms of the United States, forty-six million casualties, in terms of Egypt over eight million casualties. Where is the country which would tolerate such a danger knocking at its door? . . . Another Holocaust would have happened in the history of the Jewish people. Never again, never again! Tell so your friends, tell anyone you will meet, we shall defend our people with all means at our disposal. We shall not allow any enemy to develop weapons of mass destruction turned against us.[5]

Having exhausted all diplomatic means available, and with only days remaining before the reactor's scheduled start-up, the Israeli government had responded with the only means left open—leaving Saddam Hussein's dreams of nuclear hegemony in craters and ashes.

A total of seventeen bombs had scored direct hits on the reactor core, fracturing its foundation beyond repair. The single bomb that had missed the dome would fall only feet away, striking the neutron guide hall that would have irradiated raw uranium ore to produce plutonium. The damage to the site would set back Saddam Hussein's nuclear ambitions by more than a decade, and Osirak would never be rebuilt.[6]

However, the Carter administration had failed to relay Israel's concerns surrounding the Iraqi nuclear weapons program to the incoming staff of President Reagan. Moreover, not all members of the new administration shared the president's favorable attitude toward Israel. The new defense secretary, Caspar Weinberger, happened to be among them.

Caspar Weinberger came to the Reagan administration with many years of public service under his belt. Weinberger had been appointed as deputy director of the Office of Management and Budget (OMB) under President Richard Nixon in June 1970. Two years later, in May 1972, he would be promoted to become the director of the OMB. Following his years in the Nixon administration, Weinberger would take a post as an executive at the Bechtel Corporation, a California firm known for its extensive construction contracts throughout the Arab Middle East.

By the time of Israel's raid on Iraq's Osirak nuclear facility, Weinberger had already earned a reputation in Washington for forging his own foreign policy priorities, often to the dismay of other members of the president's staff. On February 3, 1980, just days after the new administration had been sworn into office, Weinberger would hold a press conference in which he informed the public that the new administration intended to reconsider many of the policy decisions made by its predecessor, including the Carter administration's ban on the development of a neutron bomb. The neutron bomb was a controversial weapon that was intended to use the intense radiation from an atomic blast to kill all plant and animal life within its destructive radius, relying on the radiation rather than on the effects of the explosive blast to wreak its devastation. It was the ultimate antipersonnel weapon, theoretically allowing an invading army to capture their opponent's key industrial facilities intact while killing all inhabitants. The Carter administration had previously forsworn developing this concept into an operational weapon, a stance that the Reagan administration had no intention of reversing.

At the time that Caspar Weinberger was espousing his personal views on nuclear weapons, the Reagan administration was beginning the delicate process of convincing America's NATO allies to proceed with the deployment of American Pershing II nuclear missiles in Europe. Unlike the neutron bomb, which had no place in the administration's defensive doctrine, the Pershing II was at the heart of the Reagan administration's efforts to restore America's nuclear deterrent in Europe. Weinberger's press statements elaborating on his own personal sentiments could hardly have been more poorly timed. The U.S. State Department delivered a series of frantic cables to the various European capitals, retracting the defense secretary's pronouncements. Ronald Reagan's secretary of state, Alexander Haig, would recall this incident as but one of many occasions when Weinberger would overstep his authority: "His tendency to blurt out locker-room opinions in the guise of policy was one that I prayed he might overcome. If God heard, He did not answer in any way understandable to me. The arduous duty of construing the meaning of Cap Weinberger's public sayings was a steady drain on time and patience."[7]

Haig had followed a slightly different path on his way to the Reagan Cabinet. A graduate of West Point Military Academy, he was a veteran of both the Korean and Vietnam Wars. He had earned three medals for his actions during the Inchon landings in Korea and the Distinguished Service Cross for "extraordinary heroism" during Vietnam. Haig had served as deputy secretary of defense under President Johnson and in the Nixon White House had served both as an advisor to the National Security Council and subsequently as White House chief of staff. In addition, from 1974 to 1979 General Haig had been the supreme allied commander over NATO forces in Europe.

President Reagan's Cabinet was divided over how to react to Israel's raid, from Secretary of State Haig, who was appreciative of Israel's security concerns regarding Iraq's nuclear ambitions, to Vice President George Bush and White House Chief of Staff James Baker, who believed that Israel should be punished for bombing America's "ally," Saddam Hussein.[8] The strongest voice in favor of "punishing" Israel for the raid on Iraq's nuclear reactor, however, was Secretary of Defense Weinberger. After two days of debate, agreement was finally reached on a plan that would temporarily delay the delivery of four F-16 fighters that had been scheduled for shipment to Israel over the coming weeks. It was not the tacit nod of approval for the raid that Haig had argued in favor of, but it was also not the all-encompassing embargo that Weinberger and others had proposed.

It seems, however, that Secretary of Defense Weinberger could hardly contain his enthusiasm for the planned suspension and chose to announce the news to the world personally at a press briefing that same day. Once again, Weinberger's public grandstanding could hardly have been more poorly timed. Secretary of State Haig had previously assured the Israelis that he expected no such embargo to occur. Having lost the internal debate, Haig had hoped to at least notify the Israeli ambassador in advance of any public announcements. Instead, the Israeli ambassador learned of the arms suspension through the news media.[9] After the press briefing, an irate Secretary of State Haig immediately telephoned the secretary of defense to vent his frustration: "Cap, you have an obligation to tell us about your concerns, but not to go public. Please, let's have no more press briefings at the Pentagon on this subject."[10]

But there was still more to come on this score. In announcing the suspension of jet fighter deliveries, Weinberger went beyond merely delaying the shipment of the next four F-16s then being prepared for transfer to Israel and extended the suspension to include all U.S. fighter shipments over the succeeding months. As the weeks passed, F-15s and F-16s scheduled for delivery continued to accumulate in storage while the political process dragged on. The defense secretary's announcement also marked another new turn in the history of Israel's arms dependency on the United States. For the first time, Israel's dependency on the United States had made its arms deliveries vulnerable not merely to administration fears regarding Arab reactions but to the political leanings of individual policy makers inside the White House.

Weinberger's propensity to forge his own policy from the podium of the Washington press corps was duly noted by a number of White

House officials. President Reagan's press secretary, Larry Speakes, would likewise comment on this pattern: "I had my own problems with Cap, because he was the only one in the administration who consistently refused to follow our game plan for dealing with the press, which originated in my office. . . . Cap was always getting out of line. He was the worst. When he traveled, you'd wake up one morning and there would be Cap from London or Karachi or wherever on the 'Today' show. . . . Cap was just the loosest of the cannons, the baddest boy."[11] Once stated in public, either Weinberger's views had to be "clarified" by other members of the Reagan administration or, more often than not, they simply became official policy. In most instances, it was easier to give in to Weinberger's policy tantrums than it was to expose the dissension that existed within the administration's ranks. Caspar Weinberger's decision to extend the suspension in Israeli fighter aircraft deliveries to include as many aircraft as possible was but one more example of this process.

A U.S. congressional inquiry eventually confirmed Israel's justifiable concerns over Iraqi nuclear intentions, and the jet fighters were delivered, albeit many months behind schedule. But the episode contained painful echoes of the French betrayal of just fourteen years earlier. The administration's reaction to the Israeli raid on Iraq's nuclear weapons plant had been but the first exercise in a disjointed U.S. foreign policy.

Israel's next experience with an inconsistent and confused U.S. policy stance was to occur following its 1982 invasion of Lebanon. Ever since Yasser Arafat's Palestine Liberation Organization (PLO) had been expelled from Jordan in 1970, Lebanon had become the primary center for recruitment, training, and coordination for the many branches of the terrorist organization. Beset by its own internal ethnic divisions, which finally erupted into a civil war in 1975, Lebanon had disintegrated into a chaotic web of local warlords who were powerless to control the heavily armed PLO gunmen in their midst. The PLO training camps in Lebanon had become the springboard for terrorist attacks carried out throughout the world.

June 1982 did not mark the first Israeli foray against the PLO training camps. In March 1978, in a particularly brutal incident, a squad of PLO gunmen infiltrated Israel by sea from Lebanon and hijacked an Israeli bus carrying vacationing families. In what became known as the "Coastal Road massacre," thirty-five civilians were killed and another seventy-five wounded. Within days Israel had launched Operation Litani, sending troops into southern Lebanon in an attempt to dismantle the PLO terror bases on Israel's border. The operation, however, was only partially successful. The PLO's terror network merely retreated northward, and within a month Israel was pressured into withdrawing.

In July 1981 the PLO opened up a barrage of artillery fire on Israel's northernmost communities, sending the civilian population of Galilee into bomb shelters. For ten days PLO forces equipped with Soviet-made 130 mm guns and Katyusha rockets rained their deadly fire on Israeli towns and villages, while Israel retaliated with aircraft and artillery. The Reagan administration hastily arranged a cease-fire agreement, but the underlying problem remained.

The final straw would come on June 3, 1982, when Israel's ambassador to Britain was gunned down by assassins from a PLO splinter group. Israel retaliated by bombing PLO command centers in central Lebanon, an action that again brought PLO artillery fire on Israeli communities in Galilee. On June 6, in the largest Israeli military action since the end of the Yom Kippur War, Israel launched Operation Peace for Galilee, sending thousands of Israeli troops across the Lebanese border. This time, however, the goal of the Israeli army was not merely to root out the PLO bases closest to Israel's border but to drive the PLO out of Lebanon in its entirety.

The Reagan administration once again had difficulty reaching a consensus regarding how to react to the Israeli military action. Secretary of State Haig argued that Israel had a right to self-defense and that Washington's interests would best be served by taking advantage of the situation to promote new diplomatic initiatives. In the opposing camp, once again, was Secretary of Defense Weinberger, who again promoted the idea of suspending arms deliveries to Israel as "punishment" for its military actions. Drawing on support from National Security Advisor William Clark, Weinberger again won the debate, and in mid-June the administration suspended shipment of a follow-on batch of seventy-five F-16s that were slated for delivery to Israel over the coming months.

In September the Defense Department went even further, announcing that the suspension of the shipment of combat aircraft to Israel would be extended to approval of export licenses for the Lavi wing and vertical tail. At the time, the Israeli government was in the midst of negotiating a contract with Grumman, and the embargo brought these talks to a standstill. Once more, the driving force behind the decision to extend the scope of the arms suspensions had been Defense Secretary Weinberger.[12]

With the Lavi program stalled before it had even left the drawing board, it was once again up to the airplane's most ardent political supporter to come to its rescue. Moshe Arens had not been idle in the intervening years since he had passed up the opportunity to become minister of defense. In January 1982 Arens had given up his post as chairman of the Knesset Foreign Affairs and Defense Committee to become Israel's ambassador to the United States. This Washington assignment was to prove crucial to Arens's efforts on behalf of the Lavi, allowing him to forge personal contacts within the Reagan administration and with the new secretary of state, George Shultz.

In Israel, meanwhile, the aftermath of the Lebanon War found the Israelis embroiled in the internal chaos of Lebanon's civil war. The Israelis had succeeded in driving the PLO out, but they had yet to find an exit strategy that ensured that the PLO bases would not be restored. During this chaos, Defense Minister Sharon had been pressured to resign, following a massacre perpetrated by Lebanon's Christian Phalange militia, one of Lebanon's many private armies and one with which Israel had allied itself against the PLO. The position of Israel's defense minister was vacant once more. In February 1983 the Defense Ministry was again offered to Arens. This time, with the Sinai withdrawal already an accomplished fact, Arens accepted.

Moshe Arens's appointment to the Defense Ministry coincided with a number of changes in leadership inside of Israel's armed forces. Maj. Gen. David Ivry, who had been among the leading advocates for expanding the role of the Lavi, had retired from the Israeli air force in December 1982. In April 1983, however, in one of his first appointments, Defense Minister Arens would call Ivry back into active duty, to serve as deputy chief of staff for Israel's armed forces.[13] Arens thus ensured that an air force voice would be clearly audible among Israel's highest military ranks. Maj. Gen. Amos Lapidot, who had formerly led the Hadish team and the initial Lavi development effort, meanwhile became the new commander of the Heyl Ha'Avir, on December 31, 1982. Among his previous assignments, Lapidot had served as the commanding officer of Israel's 101st Fighter Squadron, flying Mirage fighters during the Six-Day War, and had also headed Israel's air force intelligence branch in the years immediately following the Yom Kippur War.[14] In this latter capacity he had been made responsible for absorbing the lessons of the war, as well as for assessing Arab military capabilities and the tools and tactics necessary to counter them. Lapidot understood in detail the threats that the Israeli air force would face on future battlefields and remained convinced of the need for the Lavi.[15] As Arens took over as Israel's new minister of defense, he knew that he could count on the new air force commander to continue to press for the development of the Lavi as one of his highest priorities.

With the domestic scene secure, Arens gave the task of removing the remaining obstacles to the Lavi's development his full attention. If he had possessed any doubts before about the necessity of securing an independent Israeli means for arms production, the Reagan administration announcement that came in April 1983, confirming that American aircraft shipments would continue to be withheld until Israel withdrew from Lebanon, would no doubt have cured him. As Arens remarked at the time,

> I'm afraid that there is no precedent to such a statement in relations between Israel and the United States during 35 years. It has never happened that an American President has said that the supply of aid to which the United States obligated itself is conditioned on concessions in policy. Today in Lebanon, tomorrow on another front. . . . This is a statement that is hard for us, and it will force us to make a re-evaluation

of the situation, of our arms-buying policies. I can say quite surely that such a re-evaluation will bring us to the conclusion that we have to reduce our dependence on arms supplies from outside.[16]

That Israel could not again afford to allow the sources of weapons and spare parts on which it depended to be cut off by the winds of foreign politics had been made painfully clear.

In his quest to free-up American export approval for the Lavi contracts, Arens had two major advantages that his predecessor in the Defense Ministry had lacked. The first was that he was at least on speaking terms with Caspar Weinberger. Ariel Sharon had little patience for Weinberger, whom he considered a novice in military affairs, and had not been averse to showing it. Even if they didn't happen to see eye to eye, at least Arens could still pick up the telephone and talk with his American counterpart. More importantly, Arens had already formed an excellent working relationship with the newly appointed secretary of state, George Shultz.[17]

Shultz was an economist by training and tended to view the Lavi program, and foreign relations in general, through the lens of that experience. An artillery officer in the U.S. Marine Corps during World War II, Shultz received a PhD in economics from MIT in 1955. He later served on the Council of Economic Advisors under President Eisenhower, and in 1970 he was appointed director of the newly formed Office of Management and Budget under President Richard Nixon. It was in the OMB that Shultz and Caspar Weinberger had first crossed paths—with Shultz serving as Weinberger's superior. In 1972 Shultz became Nixon's secretary of the treasury, and after leaving the Nixon White House he served as executive vice president at California's Bechtel Corporation. At the Bechtel Corporation Shultz and Weinberger would once again work side by side, and in a repeat of their roles at the OMB, Shultz would once again be the senior administrator.

As a fresh, incoming secretary of state, George Shultz had visions of launching a new round of negotiations in the Arab-Israeli conflict. The continued delay in the approval of the Lavi contracts was an impediment to that goal. Moreover, Shultz did not share Weinberger's automatic enthusiasm for suspending arms deliveries. Shultz also saw the Lavi as a way to provide a much-needed boost to Israel's ailing economy. For Shultz, improving Israel's economic footing went hand in hand with reviving the Middle East peace process. As he later wrote, "As part of this overall economic effort, I favored U.S. approval of the licenses required to enable Israel to design and build the next generation of Israel Aircraft Industries' fighter, the Lavi, which would replace the Kfir, an aircraft built on the model of a 1960s-era French Mirage. This project, of special interest to Defense Minister Arens and others in the Likud leadership, helped keep some high-tech jobs in Israel at a critical time."[18] Moreover, compared to his predecessor in the role of secretary of state, Shultz was also better equipped to navigate the internal landscape of the Reagan White House. Unlike Alexander Haig, Shultz had developed a personal friendship with the president that in turn gave him greater freedom to maneuver.

It was George Shultz whom Moshe Arens telephoned shortly after taking office as defense minister. Both men wanted to move beyond the painful series of policy blunders that had strained U.S.-Israeli relations in the preceding months, in order to find a mutually beneficial path out of the Lebanon tinderbox. Within two days of their telephone conversation, on April 17, 1983, Arens was able to announce the fruits of his labor: the American embargo on the Lavi contracts had been lifted. At the subsequent press conference, Arens would extend his thanks to those who had made this accomplishment possible, adding that "I'm grateful to the President of the United States, and particularly to the Secretary of State George Shultz, who I know has worked hard to bring about this release."[19] The Lavi program was once again underway.

During its first two years of development, the Lavi had already overcome the first of the many political hurdles that it was destined to face. Even more so than its predecessors, the Reagan administration had been wracked by internal political strife and subjected to the confused policy priorities of competing political factions. In spite of Ronald Reagan's own warm attachment to Israel, divisions among senior administration officials were already leading to confusion regarding American policy and goals. Sadly, it was a trend that was to continue.

7. Mysterious as a Ghost Ship

I f the American foreign policy apparatus has been confusing for Israeli leaders, it has been only marginally less confusing for most Americans. This would be the first battleground that the Lavi would have to face, navigating through the tangled maze of the halls of power in Washington. Under the U.S. Constitution foreign policy is the responsibility of the executive branch, led by the president. In theory, the president provides the outlines for a U.S. foreign policy agenda, while the State Department and other affected agencies are expected to faithfully carry out the president's directives. The reality, however, is somewhat more complicated.

In practice, the role of president has long been too complex for any one man to keep track of all of the details involved with executing policy. The amount of time that the president has to review and approve policy directives, sign letters to foreign dignitaries, or read bills that need to be either signed or vetoed will be short. A president's hours are preciously scarce. Of necessity, only a few leading agenda items, foreign or domestic, can command the president's attention for very long.

U.S. foreign policy is consequently an amalgam of decisions, made not only by the president but also out of the personalities and priorities of his Cabinet appointees and the culture of each government agency. Each of these three elements—the president, his appointees, and the government bureaucracy—plays a role not only regarding what policy is enunciated to the public but, more importantly, what policy is actually carried out.

On matters of foreign policy, the State Department is expected to take the lead role. But the State Department is itself divided into a series of bureaus, each representing a specific region. These regional bureaus are typically populated by experts specializing in the nations that make up each region. U.S. policy formulation on the Middle East falls under the Bureau of Near East and South Asian Affairs. In practical terms, this means that for every "expert" specializing on Israel, there will be some twenty "experts" specializing on the various Arab and Muslim governments of the region. In terms of the corporate culture of this bureau, Near East Affairs has traditionally had a decidedly pro-Arab and anti-Israel tilt. Moreover, the experts and career diplomats who make up the regional bureaus are not replaced or reevaluated with each new president. Presidents may come and go, but the underlying bureaucracy, and its key players, will remain intact. As a consequence, the bureaus tend to preserve their collective culture and policy direction, regardless of who's in the White House.

It should be mentioned that there is one other element within the State Department bureaucracy with potential influence on Middle East strategy: the Bureau of Politico-Military Affairs. The purpose of this bureau is to marry the interests of American foreign policy with American security concerns. In practice, Politico-Military Affairs is much smaller than the regional bureaus and has far less influence than the regional bureaus wield.

The Defense Department and CIA have usually served more of an advisory function in the formulation of foreign policy, reacting to the policy alternatives put forward rather than proposing policy directions of their own. The priorities of these two agencies should be well understood and require little elaboration. The National Security Council (NSC), on the other hand, is less well known to most Americans.

The National Security Council was established under the National Security Act of 1947 and includes the president, vice president, secretary of state, and secretary of defense. It also includes the president's national security advisor, who commands a small core staff. The NSC is really whatever the president in office at the time wants to make of it. In some presidencies the NSC has been merely another forum for all of the affected agencies to express their views. Under others the national security advisor has become the focal point for major policy initiatives.

The most noteworthy example of the latter pattern came under President Richard Nixon, who used his national security advisor, Henry Kissinger, as an emissary for covert contacts with Red China. At the time, official U.S. policy still recognized the government of Taiwan as the legitimate Chinese leadership. But Nixon saw things differently. He regarded the opening of diplomatic relations with communist China as a means to moderate Soviet ambitions. Nixon was also convinced, however, that he could not embark on such an ambitious change in foreign policy if he were to rely on the State Department. In his view, the State Department was a clumsy bureaucracy, prone to inopportune leaks. There were simply too many "experts" in the State Department who might leak or otherwise sabotage his efforts. For this reason, Nixon pursued the opening of relations with China using the offices of his national security advisor. A major U.S. foreign policy initiative was thereby pursued, and ultimately concluded, unencumbered by bureaucratic intrigues.

Nixon's experiments, however, have proven to be the exception. Although the national security advisor has remained an important asset to every president since Eisenhower, most presidents have continued to rely on the State Department as their prime initiator for diplomatic contacts.

From a historical perspective, the State Department has had a decidedly pro-Arab, anti-Israel tilt, which has often been overcome only by direct presidential intervention. The earliest example of this trend came in November 1947, when President Harry S. Truman decided to ignore the advice of his own State Department and ordered that the United States should vote in favor of the UN Partition Resolution, which called for the creation of a Jewish state.[1] When Israeli independence was declared on May 15, 1948, President Truman once again chose to ignore his own State Department's preferences, and at his direction the United States became the first nation to extend diplomatic recognition to the new State of Israel. Secretary of State George Marshall was so vehemently opposed that he reportedly warned President Truman, "If you give this recognition, Mr. President, I may not vote for you in the next election."[2]

The anti-Israel bias in the State Department during the late 1940s had its origins in several wells. Some measure of this bias, however, can be gained from the attitude and actions of one of the early directors of the Near East Affairs Bureau: a career diplomat named Loy Henderson. Originally a specialist on the Soviet Union, Henderson was widely known inside the State Department as "Mr. Foreign Service"—one of the most admired and influential of American diplomats.[3] Henderson was also infected, however, by a virulent strain of antisemitism.

In one diplomatic cable, dispatched during his tenure in Eastern Europe, Henderson would confide, "I am convinced that the Soviet Union realizes that, by and large, international Jewry is an important supporter of it in international affairs."[4] In another cable, in April 1942, Henderson would go further and add his voice to those in the State Department who opposed the easing of U.S. immigration restrictions on Jews. For Henderson, the overriding issue was not the plight of Hitler's victims but rather the prospect that the refugees might be "secret Soviet or Communist International agents."[5] The opposition of Henderson, together with others of like mind in the State Department, ensured that bureaucratic obstacles to immigration—going above and beyond the strict annual quota system—would seal the fate of thousands who waited in vain for visas.[6]

Being assigned to the Near East Affairs office did little to change Loy Henderson's views. In Baghdad, where he was assigned in 1943, Henderson would blame the Jewish community for the anti-Jewish riots that had broken out in the Iraqi capital in 1941, in which over 150 Iraqi Jewish civilians were killed. In Henderson's opinion, the Jews were responsible for their own massacre both because they were "secretly sympathetic to Zionism" and because of "the public dishonesty, profiteering and greed of some of the Jewish merchants who play a leading role in the retail trade."[7] When he was later promoted to director of the Near East Affairs Bureau, Henderson would become one of the most vocal opponents of the creation of the State of Israel, as well as of establishing diplomatic relations with the new state. An admired role model in the foreign service, Henderson offered but one example of the anti-Semitic overtones that pervaded the ranks of the U.S. State Department throughout the first half of the twentieth century.[8]

The pattern and origins of this State Department bias were not lost on President Truman, who related that "the Department of State's specialists on the Near East were, almost without exception, unfriendly to the idea of a Jewish state. . . . Some of our diplomats also thought that the Arabs, on account of their numbers and because of the fact that they controlled such immense oil resources, should be appeased. I am sorry to say that there were some among them who were also inclined to be anti-Semitic."[9]

President Truman understood only too well where the State Department's regional "experts" stood on Israel and the Middle East in general. He also understood that these "experts" constituted a constant challenge to his authority as president: "The difficulty with many career officials in the government is that they regard themselves as the men who really make policy and run the government. They look upon the elected officials as just temporary occupants. Every President in our history has been faced with this problem: how to prevent career men from circumventing presidential policy. Too often career men seek to impose their own views instead of carrying out the established policy of the administration."[10] There was a limit, however, to the degree to which Truman was willing to contest his own State Department. Although he insisted that the United States should vote in favor of the formation of a Jewish state and later extend diplomatic recognition, he also acquiesced to State Department plans for an embargo on U.S. arms sales to Israel.[11]

For the next decade U.S. relations with Israel were polite, but cold. In the early 1950s, under President Eisenhower, the United

States would briefly flirt with the idea of authorizing a token sale of F-86 Sabre fighters to Israel. The proposal was put forward as a means to gain political support for proposed weapons sales to the Arab world. The State Department, however, could never quite bring itself to approve the plan.[12] It would remain for the Kennedy administration, years later, to approve the first weapons sales to Israel, and for the Johnson administration to approve the first sales of U.S. jet fighters.

Throughout the 1950s, American foreign policy in the Middle East was focused on efforts to organize a military alliance of friendly Arab and Muslim nations, as part of America's global effort at containing Soviet ambitions. The Baghdad Pact was the first such attempt at a Western-oriented, pan-Muslim alliance. Founded in 1955, the organization provided for mutual defense cooperation between Turkey, Iraq, Iran, and Pakistan, coordinated by Great Britain. The Baghdad Pact, however, proved fragile from the start. In 1958 Iraq's Hashemite king was overthrown in a bloody revolution. Dragged through the streets of Baghdad, the dead king's corpse came to symbolize the death of the military alliance that bore the city's name. The new Iraqi regime withdrew, and the Baghdad Pact was renamed the Central Treaty Organization in 1959. As a military coalition, however, it had already unraveled.

American policy toward Israel changed only gradually under the administrations of Kennedy and Johnson during the decade that followed. These changes were based on the personal judgments of individual presidents and did not reflect a fundamental shift in the State Department machinery. For the State Department, the vision of creating a coalition of friendly Arab or Muslim nations that could serve U.S. policy interests would continue to be pursued like an elusive mirage.

The first true transformation in the U.S.-Israeli relationship would not come until the Nixon administration. While Nixon's government may have been accused of stalling on the airlift of supplies to Israel during the Yom Kippur War, it was also the Nixon administration that first approved real security assistance, in the form of military grants, to Israel rather than merely selling arms.

The Nixon administration introduced a new vision regarding how a solution to the Arab-Israeli conflict could be reached: the belief that a strong Israel could more easily make concessions at the bargaining table and would also be less likely to invite another Arab invasion. This underlying policy stance has endured throughout every administration, Republican or Democrat, ever since.

U.S. aid to Israel ultimately convinced the Egyptian leadership that another round of Arab-Israeli wars would be futile and that the road to peace led through negotiations in Washington, not the arms merchants in Moscow. Since the United States first began supplying military grants to Israel in 1973, no Arab leader has been successful in forming a war coalition broad enough to invade the Jewish state. But this shift in American policy was not accepted without resistance from some in the State Department.

During a meeting in March 1969, in the midst of the War of Attrition, President Nixon confided in the Israeli ambassador regarding his own frustrations with the Washington bureaucracy: "Some sections of the administration are strenuously opposed to supplying arms to Israel at this time. I won't identify them, but believe me, they have spared no effort in trying to convince me. You can be sure that I will continue to supply arms to Israel, but I shall do so in other, different ways. The moment Israel needs arms, approach me, by way of Kissinger, and I'll find a way of overcoming bureaucracy."[13] Here was the president of the United States, the most powerful man in the free world, acknowledging that he was not the lord of his own house. The bureaucracy had grown too big, and delay is the one trade at which every bureaucracy excels. The solution of this particular administration was a typical Nixon response: bypass the State Department and direct the Israelis to employ Kissinger, his national security advisor, as their direct contact.

The disconnect between presidential policy directives and the execution of that policy was not unique to the Arab-Israeli dispute. Kissinger, for example, cited multiple occasions when the Washington bureaucracy would attempt to pursue its own policy agenda. One noteworthy example was during the disintegration of Pakistani rule over East Pakistan (now Bangladesh) in 1971. In describing the chain of events that eventually led to yet another outbreak of violence, Kissinger would later vent his frustration: "Nixon had ordered repeatedly that we should move Pakistan toward political accommodation through understanding rather than pressure. The State Department had every right to a contrary view: that massive public pressure would make Pakistan more pliable. What strained White House–State relations was the effort by State to implement its views when the President had chosen a different course."[14] U.S.-Israeli relations were clearly not the only sphere where rogue operatives had attempted to carry out their own direction in foreign policy. Nor was the Nixon administration the only presidency to be beset by these problems.

Members of President Reagan's White House staff also reported having to deal with the State Department's corporate bias regarding Israel. Among them was Lt. Col. Oliver North, who was a staff member under President Reagan's National Security Council:

> There was certainly a State Department perspective on Israel. Again, nobody ever said so aloud, but it seemed to me that many officials at State were automatically opposed to whatever it was the Israelis favored. . . . Within the State Department there seemed to be a constituency that actually relished any antagonism that could be fostered between us and the Israelis. Some of this came from a long-standing and barely hidden pro-Arab tilt at State, which I'm hardly the first to notice. Another large chunk, I believe, is the result of an ingrained streak of anti-Semitism in our government.[15]

This State Department tilt, long evident in the Near East Bureau, did not disappear simply because a more pro-Israel president was in the White House.

The underlying State Department bias that may have threatened the Lavi program was not unique to the Reagan administration. Past presidents had also dealt with this phenomenon and had been able to overcome it. Moreover, Israel had many powerful friends in the Reagan administration, including both Secretary of State Alexander Haig and his successor, George Shultz, not to mention the president himself. Beginning with Prime Minister Begin's visit to Washington in September 1981, Ronald Reagan had set the tone for a warming of U.S.-Israeli relations that was to have far-reaching ramifications. Begin was accorded what many have described as the "warmest reception" ever received by an Israeli leader. At the conclusion of their meeting, President Reagan also went a step further than his predecessors and directed that the Defense Department formulate a memorandum of understanding to institutionalize U.S. and Israeli military-to-military contacts and cooperation. It was not a defense treaty, but it went further than any previous administration had. Reagan's decision also came as a shock to Secretary of Defense Weinberger, who had not been consulted in advance and who wanted nothing to do with the idea. Weinberger complied, however reluctantly, and the memorandum that President Reagan had asked for was eventually formulated.[16] In the words of Secretary of State Alexander Haig, "Israel has never had a greater friend in the White House than Ronald Reagan."[17]

Unfortunately, the Reagan administration would also experience its own particular brand of policy adventurism, a process whereby various administration officials would take it upon themselves to manipulate U.S. policy. To a degree that had not been experienced under previous administrations, the various presidential appointees and their supporting staff believed that they were at liberty to pursue their own agendas, ensuring that no pattern resembling a unified foreign policy could emerge. As Jeane Kirkpatrick, Reagan's UN ambassador, described the problem, "There was a real lack of mutual respect and a real lack of what I would call disciplined limits at the top of the Reagan Administration."[18] The Lavi therefore had to contend not only with the traditional State Department bureaucratic bias but also with the internal political squabbles of the individual Cabinet appointees and White House staff members as they jockeyed for position and influence behind the scenes.

Alexander Haig noted multiple incidents of this nature during his tenure as secretary of state. During the 1982 Lebanon War, for example, a resolution was expected to come before the United Nations Security Council that, like so many UN resolutions, was expected to condemn Israel regardless of any facts surrounding the events of the day. However, this particular resolution also threatened to go much further, issuing a Security Council call for international sanctions against Israel, an action that would have amounted to a complete reversal in the course of U.S.-Israeli relations. The real shock to Secretary of State Haig, however, was that this resolution just might pass. By the time that the secretary of state was informed of the contents, it was already on the verge of being approved. Haig was told that President Reagan had already authorized U.S. acceptance of the resolution and, in the words of National Security Advisor William Clark, "We've got the decision and there is no more discussion." Perplexed as to why Reagan would agree to such an out-of-character initiative, Haig confronted the president directly. It was only then that he learned that the recommendation to approve the UN resolution had been made not by the president but by vice president George Bush's "crisis management team." The recommendation had been transmitted to President Reagan with the express understanding that it reflected the unanimous judgment of the senior staff, Secretary of State Haig included. President Reagan, it would seem, had been misled. It was only the personal intervention of Haig, who informed the president that he had not been consulted regarding the resolution and that he was opposed to it in the strongest possible terms, that averted a crisis in U.S.-Israeli relations. With the substance of the resolution laid bare, Reagan ordered that the United States should veto the UN resolution. It was not the last episode, however, in policy-making adventurism in certain quarters of the Washington bureaucracy.

In a similar incident, also during Israel's war in Lebanon, National Security Advisor William Clark had delivered a draft letter for President Reagan to sign, addressed to the Israeli prime minister. The letter called for an unconditional Israeli withdrawal, with no allowances made for the dismantling of the terror bases in Lebanon. Upon learning of the letter's contents, Secretary Haig once again intervened, expressing his disapproval for the one-sided letter. Persuaded by Haig's arguments, Reagan ordered that the letter, which had already been signed, be destroyed. As Haig later lamented, "Far from speaking with a single voice on foreign policy, the administration was becoming a sort of Babel."[19]

George Shultz, who took over the office of secretary of state after Haig stepped down in July 1982, also noticed the "loose cannon" effect that plagued the Reagan administration. Comparing his experiences under President Reagan with his earlier experiences in the Nixon administration, Shultz wrote, "This was a different Washington from the one I had experienced a decade earlier as Secretary of the Treasury. The number of aides that surrounded the President and each of the top appointed officials had ballooned. Staffs of organizations, supposedly following the same administration policy, waged perpetual battle on behalf of—and often without the knowledge of—their principals."[20] There were far too many free agents within the Reagan White House for the administration to ever speak with one voice. This bitter reality would add yet another hurdle that the supporters of the Lavi program would have to overcome.

It had also become clear that the State Department's Near East Bureau would not be the only element in the Reagan administration that was to prove hostile to Israeli interests. Among the first initiatives undertaken by the Reagan White House was a plan to sell five E-3 Sentry AWACS to Saudi Arabia. Capable of detecting aircraft from hundreds of miles away, the E-3 could provide the Saudis with the capability to act as an airborne command center during a future Arab-Israeli war.

It was only natural that the Israeli government would express opposition to such an arms sale and would feel free to voice its disappointment among Israel's friends in the administration and on Capitol Hill. This placed the Israeli government in conflict with a number of Reagan administration officials who were attempting to secure congressional approval for the sale. They included White House chief of staff James Baker, as well as William Clark, who later became President Reagan's national security advisor. Approval for the AWACS sale to Saudi Arabia was ultimately passed in the Senate by only the narrowest of margins. But rather than seeing U.S. and Israeli positions over the sale as a disagreement between friends, Jim Baker and others involved in the lobbying campaign would continue to hold personal grudges against the Israelis for years to come.[21]

U.S.-Israeli relations during the Reagan years were consequently characterized by an internal tug-of-war between various administration voices speaking either in favor of U.S.-Israeli cooperation or against it. At times these policy wars would be manifest in the constant struggle to gain the president's ear. As National Security Council staff member Dr. Raymond Tanter was later to describe, "In Washington, as in any capital, 'access to the throne' is a sign of power. But when policy changes as a consequence of who has the ear of the President last and for the longest period of time, this indicates a flaw in the policy process."[22] At other times the various actors took matters into their own hands, quietly reinterpreting presidential policy to their own ends.

President Reagan, for his part, had entered the White House with a clear vision of where he believed America needed to go. There were two central elements to his national agenda: jumpstarting the American economy by lowering taxes and winning the Cold War with the Soviets. All other issues that arose would command a lower priority. Closer ties between the United States and Israel were certainly a part of the president's larger objectives, but they were not a central goal. Of necessity, the vast majority of his time and attention would be focused elsewhere. In almost every sphere, Ronald Reagan depended on the integrity of his staff members in performing their daily duties in accordance with the policies that he had articulated. As Reagan later explained, "I don't believe a chief executive should supervise every detail of what goes on in his organization. The chief executive should set broad policy and general ground rules, tell people what he or she wants them to do, then let them do it. . . . I don't think a chief executive should peer constantly over the shoulders of the people who are in charge of a project and tell them every few minutes what to do. I think that's the cornerstone of good management: Set clear goals and appoint good people to help you achieve them."[23] In many cases, his staff served him admirably. In others, they would betray him.

That so many members of the Reagan administration felt free to exercise their own policy agenda could only suggest a belief that there would be no ill repercussions for such actions. There was no real fear of censure or reprimand. Vice President George Bush, reflecting on his own observations of President Reagan, reported, "I learned from watching him that he was discomforted by the feuds and the battles between strong willed secretaries or the internal battles on the staff."[24] Rather than intervening to resolve the policy wars, Reagan tended to withdraw from them, expecting his subordinates to sort out their own differences. As Jeane Kirkpatrick later related, "The President hated disharmony and didn't want to hear about it, and he didn't want people telling him about their disagreements or their quarrels or their concerns or coming to him about them—and even enforcing his own decisions if it involved disharmony on the team. He just didn't want to hear about it."[25] Given the ensuing chaos, it was only natural that U.S. relations with Israel would eventually fall prey to these interoffice rivalries.

Secretary of State Alexander Haig, long experienced with the Washington political scene, would later attempt to sum up the nature of this particular disease: "To me, the White House was as mysterious as a ghost ship; you heard the creak of the rigging and the groan of the timbers and sometimes even glimpsed the crew on the deck. But which one of the crew had the helm?"[26] Years later, this same lack of accountability would explode into the headlines during the Iran-Contra scandal. Elements of the president's staff had felt free to create their own policy direction, to the point where the president was not only not consulted in advance but not even informed after the fact. The Iran-Contra affair, however, was only the most visible example of this pattern of rogue policy making that was to likewise threaten the future of the Lavi and that was destined to cast a cloud of doubt over U.S.-Israeli relations.

The release of U.S. export approval for the Lavi contracts for the composite wings and vertical tail was only the first round in the Washington policy battle over the Lavi. The contest, however, was far from over. It would not be long before the next round in this Washington battleground would play itself out.

8. Funding Measures

B y mid-1983, Israeli press releases had begun to reflect a new shape to Israel's air force modernization plans. A production run of three hundred Lavi fighters was envisioned, including sixty two-seat fighters that would double as trainers, with the airplane expected to replace Israel's A-4 Skyhawk and Kfir fighter fleets. Plans called for the first prototype flight to occur on February 25, 1986, with the first production fighter expected to roll out a little over a year later, in 1987. Deliveries for operational service were expected to begin in January 1988.[1]

Lavi performance figures quoted in the press included a sustained turn rate of 13.2 deg/sec when at Mach 0.8 and 15,000 ft altitude and configured for an intercept mission. This compared favorably with equivalent sustained turn rates of 12.8 deg/sec for the F-16A or 11.8 deg/sec for the F-15C at the same altitude and Mach number. The Lavi's maximum instantaneous turn rate, meanwhile, was estimated at 24.3 deg/sec when at this same altitude. Combat weight, in an air-to-air configuration with 50 percent of internal fuel and carrying two heat-seeking missiles, was pegged at 18,695 lb (8,480 kg), providing a thrust-to-weight ratio of 1.10 in air combat. Maximum internal fuel was expected to be 6,000 lb (2,720 kg), with up to 9,180 lb (4,160 kg) of external fuel capacity. Maximum takeoff weight was quoted as 37,500 lb (17,010 kg).[2] Plans were also revealed to develop an all-new pulse-Doppler multimode radar for the aircraft and to equip the aircraft for low-drag, conformal stores carriage. The latter feature was to become crucial for extending the airplane's range and maximizing its penetration speed in the attack mission. It should be remembered, however, that the official figures for combat radius that were being quoted were still pathetically low and almost certainly reflected the earlier, shorter-range, A-4-type role.

This still left the Israeli air force with a requirement for additional aircraft to replace some 130 F-4ES in the long-range attack role. IAI was busily drawing up plans at the time to equip F/A-18 fighters with Israeli avionics to fulfill this requirement, although interest was also expressed in the cranked-arrow F-16XL. There was also a sense of urgency behind these procurement efforts. The Heyl Ha'Avir wanted to replace its entire F-4 fleet by the mid-1990s. Similarly, all three hundred Lavi fighters were expected to be delivered by 1995.[3] That would require a production rate of around forty aircraft per year, more than twice the maximum Kfir production rate of eighteen aircraft per annum. The aggressive delivery schedule was another indication of just how seriously the Israeli military viewed the emerging threat. They had already placed a second batch of seventy-five F-16s on order and were plainly intent on maintaining their edge in the face of the ongoing arms buildup in Syria, Iraq, and elsewhere.

Table 3. Israeli air force, 1995: Early 1983 projection

Aircraft	Number
F-15	50
F-16	150
F-18	100
Lavi	300
Total	600

This however, was where the Lavi ran into the real-world obstacles of weapons systems costs and funding. Modern technology had made weapons systems far more deadly but also vastly more expensive. The arsenals of the great world powers, from the United States and NATO allies to the Soviet Union and the Warsaw Pact states, had all shrunk in absolute terms since the end of World War II.

They were flying fewer aircraft and fielding fewer tanks and fewer warships. This was the general worldwide pattern—except, that is, in the Middle East.

Oil had turned once-impoverished, third world dictatorships into some of the wealthiest nations on earth. Even Arab League members with only limited oil resources, such as Jordan and Syria, received subsidies from kingdoms on the Persian Gulf to fuel their war machines. Likewise, the Soviets had rushed to assert their presence in the oil-rich region, supplying arms at cut-rate prices or even as outright gifts to their client states. The result was that the armies of the Middle East went from fielding hundreds of tanks in the 1950s to fielding several thousand by the 1980s, and from fielding tens of warplanes to fielding well over a thousand. The only nation in the Middle East that did not benefit from this new-found regional wealth was Israel.

The unit flyaway cost for the Lavi had been quoted initially at $10.8 million in 1982 dollars, including $4.75 million for the air-frame, $2.6 million for the engine, $1.75 million for the radar and self-defense systems, and $1.7 million for avionics. This figure compared well with the $17 million unit cost for the F-16. But the Lavi was still anything but cheap. Development and tooling costs alone were estimated at $1.5 billion. By 1983 the Israeli government had already spent $198 million on Lavi development, and it planned on spending another $210 million in that next year alone.[4] Funding was to become the attack jet's most contentious issue.

In the aftermath of the Yom Kippur War the United States had stepped in, not only as Israel's primary foreign arms supplier but also as Israel's benefactor. By 1983, annual U.S. military aid to Israel totaled $1.7 billion, comprising a combination of loans and grants. This aid went to pay for the weapons that Israel received from the United States and, by definition, could be spent only on weapons or services purchased in the United States.

The military aid received by Israel has become a source of controversy for some. Measured in terms of America's global security commitments, American aid to Israel has been a very small fraction of the overall U.S. budget. But whereas U.S. security assistance to Europe or the Far East was measured in terms of U.S. soldiers and weapons systems deployed in their defense, U.S. assistance to Israel was measured purely in arms shipments. The United States did not deploy American armed forces to defend Israel in the same way that it defended Western Europe, Japan, or South Korea, nor was the military and economic aid supplied to Israel on the same scale as the tens of billions that the United States was spending each year to defend Japan or Korea or the hundreds of billions devoted to defending Europe. But while U.S. assistance to Israel was relatively small on the scale of America's global commitments, it had become a progressively larger portion of Israel's defense budget. By 1983 U.S. Foreign Military Sales (FMS) grants to Israel totaled $750 million, or 13 percent of Israel's total defense budget.[5] It was this existing and as yet untapped funding that Defense Minister Arens sought as a means to meet the budgetary needs of the Lavi.

This would not be the first time that an Israeli government had asked permission to devote FMS credits toward an Israeli development effort. A similar request had been granted in 1979. But this prior request had been a one-time grant to complete development of the Merkava tank. It had been a commitment of limited scope and had amounted to no more than $30 million in aid. Applying FMS funds to a jet fighter project would mean devoting hundreds of millions in aid dollars toward weapons development over a multiyear period. It was not that the United States did not already devote millions or even billions to overseas defense spending. But those funds were spent for U.S. basing rights and for maintaining U.S. armed forces overseas. Such funds came out of the defense budget, rather than the foreign aid budget, and rarely stirred up the same controversy. Arens knew that proposing the use of FMS credits to help finance the Lavi would mean fighting yet another political battle in Washington.

To no one's great surprise, Defense Secretary Caspar Weinberger was quick to voice his opposition to applying U.S. FMS credits toward the Lavi. Weinberger explained his resistance by claiming that the airplane was "clearly not designed to have the effectiveness" of its American counterparts.[6] But even if Weinberger had been unaware of the significance that the change in the Lavi engine selection implied, it should still have been obvious that the Lavi was meant to be far more survivable in the attack role than any of its U.S. counterparts. Once again, however, circumstances were to prove that the defense secretary's views were not always in line with those of the president.

Over a period of months, Defense Minister Arens worked closely with his counterpart in the U.S. State Department both to resolve the Lebanon quagmire that continued to entangle both the United States and Israel and to lay the framework for administration support for the Lavi. In October 1983 his negotiations began to bear fruit, with the Reagan administration announcing for the first time that the president was in favor of using existing FMS funds to help finance the Lavi. This announcement emphasized in particular the many Lavi subsystems that were then under development in the United States.[7] U.S. participation in the Lavi program extended well beyond the engine or the wings and vertical tail. As a cost-saving measure, wherever possible, off-the-shelf components were modified for Lavi use, and whenever American components were cheaper and easier to obtain, American companies had been contracted. Everything from the cockpit head-up display (HUD) and the flight control computer to the actuators that moved the control surfaces was to be developed and manufactured in the United States. In all, nearly half of the airplane was to be built in America, with contracts in nearly every state in the union. What had begun as an economic decision, aimed at taking advantage of off-the-shelf components and existing expertise and technologies to save cost, had become a political asset.

The full, formal public policy announcement that Moshe Arens had been campaigning for would be delivered one month later, in November 1983, when Defense Minister Arens and Prime Minister Yitzhak Shamir were in Washington to meet with President Reagan. This would be Reagan's first meeting with Israel's prime minister since Shamir had taken over the mantle from Menachem Begin. The meeting therefore represented a unique opportunity for the administration to strengthen U.S.-Israeli ties and cooperation, following a year of strain during Israel's Lebanon War and subsequent U.S. attempts to broker a cease-fire.

Speaking to reporters on the south lawn of the White House, President Reagan followed up on that day's meetings with a public call for Congress to approve the use of U.S. military assistance funds to develop the Lavi: "We've agreed to take a number of other concrete steps aimed at bolstering Israel's economy and security. These include asking Congress for improved terms for our security assistance to Israel; [and] using military assistance for development of the Lavi aircraft in the United States and for offshore procurement of Lavi components manufactured in Israel."[8]

President Reagan's public endorsement of U.S. funding for the Lavi was essential to seeing this funding signed into law. Politically, Arens could not easily have achieved congressional approval for extending FMS credits to cover such a substantial commitment without Reagan's endorsement. The Lavi had become a truly binational development effort, drawing on the best of both Israeli and American expertise, with the full approval of the White House. The political battle for Lavi funding would thereafter shift from the White House to Congress.

At the same time that Moshe Arens was carrying out his talks with Secretary of State Shultz, he had also launched a parallel campaign to obtain U.S. congressional approval. Approval from both the executive and legislative branches of the U.S. government would be necessary to ensure a sustained commitment for the Lavi.

In order to understand the role that Congress played in the Lavi's development, however, it is essential to understand the roles that Congress does and does not play in America's foreign policy. Under the framework established in the Constitution, Congress plays only a secondary or supporting role in the conduct of foreign policy. Congress may be asked to approve treaties or packages of foreign aid, but the origination of foreign policy and defense initiatives has remained the sole privilege of the executive branch. This is not to say that Congress does not play a crucial role. Aside from its responsibilities to act as a watchdog over the White House, Congress also possesses the all-important "power of the purse": the authority to approve, amend, or reject the federal budget. But Congress can act on foreign and defense policies and budget proposals only after they have been put forward by the White House.

There are some opponents of U.S. support for Israel who would like to claim that American military assistance to Israel stems exclusively from the influence wielded over Congress by the votes and campaign contributions of a small pro-Israel minority. No matter how ludicrous such claims might be, they continue to be raised by the ill-informed and the anti-Semitic. Such spurious claims fail to recognize the purely secondary role that Congress plays in the conduct of U.S. foreign policy. Congress reacts to presidential foreign policy initiatives. It has no foreign office of its own. Instead, it acts as an open forum, where competing representatives must hammer out compromises based on the principle of majority rule. Such an apparatus is hardly conducive to initiating new directions on anything so hotly disputed as foreign policy.

U.S. security assistance to Israel was extended only gradually, over a series of decades, based on the initiatives of individual presidents, not Congress. Had such decisions been made purely on the basis of the preferences of a small pro-Israel minority, as some claim, the United States would have been providing arms to Israel long before President Kennedy's sale of Hawk missiles in the 1960s, and American foreign aid would have flowed to Israel decades earlier than 1973, when President Nixon approved the first grants.

Moreover, it makes little sense to believe that America's small Jewish community, a population that makes up less than 3 percent of the American public, could induce large majorities of congressional representatives to approve budget measures that they did not fundamentally agree with. Surveys have shown that both campaign contributions from pro-Israel political action committees and the percentage of Jewish voters in any particular district tend to be very poor indicators of how a particular representative or senator will vote regarding aid to Israel. A better statistical correlation can be found among those members of Congress who tend to favor a proactive approach to foreign policy.[9] Members of Congress who favor an active U.S. foreign policy, one that includes a foreign aid program and foreign military assistance, are far more likely to vote in favor of aid to Israel than are those with an isolationist agenda.

Fundamentally, aid to Israel is supported by majorities in both the House and Senate because it is seen as money well spent. There is a widespread perception, both inside and outside of Congress, that the majority of foreign aid supplied to most countries has been wasted: it has gone to enrich corrupt dictators or to prop up unpopular regimes. In the case of Israel, however, it has been very clear just where the money was going. Congress only had to count the aircraft and tanks or the victories on the battlefield. In the words of one member of the U.S. House of Representatives, "[Israel] is one of the few nations in the world that knows how to use foreign aid. We have tried so many programs in so many nations that have been woefully unsuccessful, but our programs in Israel have generally succeeded."[10] It should be recalled that, despite supplying far greater annual aid packages to Korea and Vietnam, the United States still had to send American troops to fight wars in those nations. Israel, in contrast, has requested no American troops to defend its borders. For a fraction of the annual cost of equipping and maintaining a single carrier battle group, U.S. assistance has helped Israel to maintain an air force six times the size of an aircraft carrier's complement. Together with U.S. assistance to rebuild Europe under the Marshall Plan during the 1940s and 1950s, aid to Israel is seen as one of the few success stories for U.S. foreign aid.

There is also the issue of popular American sentiment on this subject. A crucial component for understanding congressional support for Israel has been the strong, broad base of support that has existed among the American populace. Opinion polls taken across a period of decades have demonstrated that American popular support for Israel extends far beyond America's small Jewish community and crosses political and geographic divides. Even at its lowest point, during Israel's 1982 Lebanon War, popular support for Israel outpaced sympathy for the Arab states by a ratio of better than two to one in opinion polls.[11] Americans could relate to Israel as a fellow democracy, with a shared history and shared democratic values, in ways that they could not relate to the dictatorships and monarchies of the Arab League.

Arens's cause found an unlikely champion in Representative Charles Wilson (D-TX), whose acquaintance Arens had made while serving as ambassador to the United States. Representative Wilson was by no means a compulsory supporter of Israeli causes on Capitol Hill. He had voted in favor of selling AWACS to Saudi Arabia and in interviews had indicated his hope that support for the Lavi program might persuade the Israeli government to take a more charitable view of Caspar Weinberger's own pet project: to arm and train two brigades of the Jordanian Arab Legion.[12] Wilson, however, also saw support for the Lavi as a means of helping Israel's faltering economy. As Wilson described it, "These people have got their brain power, and that's about all they've got in the way of a natural resource. I thought that assisting the development of the Lavi would be a good way to help them get better at technology that they could export."[13] Whatever his motivation, Wilson agreed to introduce an amendment that would approve the use of FMS funding for the Lavi.

By the time that this amendment reached the floor of the House Appropriations Subcommittee on Foreign Operations, however, it was under the joint sponsorship of the senior Republican and Democratic members of the committee: Congressmen Jack F. Kemp (R-NY) and Clarence D. Long (D-MD). The amendment thus came to the committee with substantial political backing. It also arrived amid a torrent of debate.

Opposition to the Lavi erupted from Northrop, which at the time was attempting to market its own jet overseas: the F-20 Tigershark. The F-20 had been developed as an upgraded version of the F-5E Tiger II, originally designated as the F-5G. It had been developed as part of a program promoted by President Carter to develop a line of low-cost fighters for export to American allies. The concept had been to restrict the sale of America's own frontline fighters to America's closest friends and to offer a separate line of fighters for other nations. Two aircraft were developed under this proposal, both without government funding: the F-16/79, a downgraded F-16A featuring a J79 turbojet in place of the F100 turbofan; and the F-5G, an upgraded version of the Vietnam War–era F-5E.

The Reagan administration, however, had reversed the Carter administration's policies regarding the sale of American jet fighters and offered to sell America's own frontline warplanes to any ally who could afford them. Only the electronics package would differ. Suddenly, no one wanted a second-rate export fighter. Despite this policy shift, Northrop's executives chose to continue pursuing their program, in an attempt to recoup their investment. One of their first steps, as part of their new marketing strategy, had been to rename the airplane the F-20 Tigershark and to then market it as a direct competitor to the F-16.

Northrop consequently claimed that the Lavi, like the F-16, would compete with their airplane for export sales and predicted that if the Lavi went forward, it could cost up to six thousand American jobs due to lost F-20 business. Lavi proponents, meanwhile, countered that the joint U.S.-Israeli airplane would also create between twenty thousand and thirty thousand new jobs in the United States across a variety of aerospace suppliers, from Maine to California. This issue also pitted Northrop against two other American aerospace giants, Pratt & Whitney and Grumman, both of whom had a great deal to gain if the Lavi went forward.[14]

In reality, the Lavi was hardly an export threat to Northrop. Setting aside for the moment that the two airplanes were built with completely different roles in mind, any future Israeli export of the Lavi would have had to obtain U.S. approval. The Israelis had learned this lesson the hard way in February 1977, when the Carter administration killed a proposed sale of twenty-four Kfir fighters to Ecuador. Moreover, even when a ban on Kfir exports was finally lifted, there were relatively few customers for an Israeli-produced jet. By the late 1980s, only three export orders for the Kfir would be announced, with ten going to Ecuador, twelve to Colombia, and a follow-on batch of another thirteen aircraft to Colombia. Proposals for the delivery of twelve Kfir fighters to Cameroon would later fall through.[15] A decade afterward another eleven aircraft would be sold to Sri Lanka—hardly a ringing sales success. All of these orders had also involved the resale of used Israeli air force fighters. No new-production Kfirs would ever be commissioned by any export customer.[16]

To put these paltry few Kfir sales into perspective, consider that by 1983 F-16 export orders had already surpassed 330 aircraft, not including the 390 fighters being coproduced in Europe.[17] Many hundreds more would be sold over the succeeding decades. The Lavi was hardly a significant competitor for Northrop's F-20, or for any other U.S. fighter. Most of the nations that could afford such an airplane were already committed to another fighter. And of those remaining, most were too sensitive to retaliation from the oil powers to consider buying an airplane made in Israel.

Whatever Northrop's pretenses, there was never any competition between the two airplanes. The F-20 was developed primarily as an air-to-air fighter, with almost no ground attack capability. It didn't have the payload or range to match the F-16, much less the Lavi. The F-20 also did not die for lack of development funding. An investment of $1.2 billion had been more than enough to demonstrate the viability of the design.[18] It had died because it couldn't find a customer. By late 1983, when Lavi funding proposals first came before Congress, Northrop was campaigning on Capitol Hill to compel the U.S. Air Force to directly compete the F-20 against the F-16 for annual deliveries. In truth, the Tigershark was an excellent airplane—in the role for which it was designed. But it was no F-16. It didn't have the range, and it didn't have the payload. Congress eventually passed a mandate that required the U.S. Air Force to stage a competition between the F-20 and the F-16 for the role of continental air defense of the United States—a role for which neither aircraft was ideally suited. As studies by the U.S. Air National Guard had pointed out, both aircraft lacked the range and radar capabilities necessary to intercept incoming Soviet bombers and cruise missiles at large distances. The Air National Guard proposed upgrading the F-4 as an inexpensive alternative, which better fit the role. A study by the General Accounting Office would go even further, pointing out that the ideal aircraft for the mission would have been the U.S. Navy's F-14 Tomcat, with the F-15 coming in as a close second.[19] Faced with a congressionally mandated competition over a role for which neither aircraft was optimum, there should have been little doubt that the F-16's advantage in range and endurance was sure to bring it out on top. The air force would officially announce its decision in October 1986, bringing the F-20 saga to a close. Its demise, however, had nothing to do with the Lavi.

For most members of Congress, the question of support for the Lavi was simple to answer. The Israeli government was not asking for an increase in the level of aid that it received, merely for flexibility in how that aid was spent. Add to this the fact that virtually every state in the United States had some contractor that was expected to provide components for the Lavi, and approval for the Lavi funding proposal became relatively simple. On November 10, 1983, the Kemp-Long amendment was approved by the full House of Representatives by a vote of 224 in favor to 189 opposed. The amendment allowed Israel to spend up to $550 million out of the aid that it received toward Lavi expenses: $300 million to cover development costs in the United States and up to $250 million to cover expenditures in Israel.[20] Combined with President Reagan's public endorsement for the program, made that same month, passage by the U.S. Senate became all but assured. Moshe Arens's efforts had paid off. The Lavi had secured the funding necessary to keep the development effort on track. In fact, the amount approved for fiscal year 1984 would exceed the program's requirements, and in the subsequent bill for fiscal year 1985 only $150 million would be set aside to cover development expenses in the United States.

The debate on whether to approve funding for the Lavi would be renewed once again late in 1984, as the House debated a round of spending bills for fiscal year 1985. Representative Nick J. Rahall (D-WV), a Lebanese American and longtime opponent of U.S. aid to Israel, proposed a measure to cancel U.S. funding for the airplane. This time the margin was much wider. The proposal to rescind Lavi funding failed by a vote of 379 to 40.[21] As far as Capitol Hill was concerned, the issue of Lavi funding was settled. If the Israeli government wanted to spend U.S. security assistance on new weapons development, then by act of Congress, it could do so.

Securing a stable source of funding was a vital ingredient in ensuring the success of the Lavi. To this end, it was essential that U.S. Foreign Military Sales credits that had previously been devoted to Israeli F-15 and F-16 purchases be made available for application to the Lavi. To find a place for the Lavi in the U.S. military aid package, Defense Minister Arens had successfully employed a two-track strategy, negotiating with both the executive and legislative branches of the U.S. government to secure the necessary commitments. This effort was no doubt aided by the highly binational flavor of the Lavi subcontracts, drawing as they did on both American and Israeli weapons expertise to achieve the lowest-cost solution. President Ronald Reagan's public endorsement of this funding measure ensured that funding for the Lavi would receive a ready reception within the halls of Congress. It was a stamp of approval that should have established, once and for all, official White House policy. Unfortunately, not everyone in the administration regarded President Reagan's pronouncements as dictating administration policy.

9. The Lion Unveiled

E ven as a second year of funding for the Lavi was being debated by Congress, a political battle of a different sort was taking place in Israel. The war in Lebanon had deeply divided Israel's population. Casualties continued to mount long after Israel succeeded in driving the PLO training camps out of Lebanon. New terrorist groups, funded by Iran and supported by Syria, had taken their place. It was in this atmosphere that Israel entered into new national elections in 1984.

The results of the election were less than decisive. Israel's Likud Party had lost the margin of seats that they needed to maintain their coalition. But Israel's other leading party, the Labor Alignment, had also failed to win a clear victory. Neither could easily form a stable governing coalition with the smaller political parties. The two leading parties therefore reached a compromise, forming a "National Unity Government" in which Likud and Labor agreed to a power-sharing arrangement. Under this agreement, the Labor Party's Shimon Peres would hold the prime minister's office for the first two years of the agreement, while the Likud Party's leader, Yitzhak Shamir, would hold the post of foreign minister. After the two years were up, the parties would rotate these two key positions. The balance of the Cabinet was to be divided evenly between the two parties, giving them an equal number of votes in deliberations. Crucially, under this new agreement Labor Alignment member Yitzhak Rabin was to be the new minister of defense, with Moshe Arens becoming a minister without portfolio. Arens might still have had a vote in the Cabinet, but he could no longer directly oversee the progress of the Lavi. The change also left him poorly positioned to intervene in Washington.

It was not at all clear what the policies of Israel's new defense minister would be regarding the Lavi. Lt. Gen. Yitzhak Rabin had been Israel's chief of staff during the 1967 Six-Day War and had gone on to become a fast-rising political star in Israel's Labor Party. Assigned as Israel's ambassador to the United States during the Nixon years, he had returned to Israel in 1974 to become prime minister. But his time at the helm was short. Public anger over the 1973 war was still roiling and, caught up in a minor controversy, Rabin was pressured to step down.[1] In the next elections the Labor Party would be soundly defeated at the polls.

With regard to his attitude toward the Lavi, the new defense minister was something of a paradox. During his years in the Israel Defense Forces, Yitzhak Rabin had been an architect of some of the earliest proposals for replacing European weapons suppliers with their counterparts in the United States. This did not, however, translate into an equal enthusiasm for developing an independent Israeli weapons manufacturing capacity. At a symposium held at Israel's National Defense College during his years as chief of staff, Rabin had upbraided the chief executives from Israel's arms industries for failing to make efficient use of the resources provided. "We are already in the 1960s," he told them, "and you have been operating for more than 20 years. What have you contributed to the Israel Defense Forces? Nothing!"[2]

The French and British arms embargoes of subsequent years did little to sway Rabin's opinion. Throughout the late 1960s and into the 1970s, Rabin would remain among the most highly placed critics of the Kfir fighter program, preferring instead to see the Israeli government focus on obtaining additional American-supplied aircraft.[3] In 1978, when the Knesset Foreign Affairs and Defense Committee had endorsed the development of a new indigenous fighter, Rabin had been one of only two committee members to cast a vote opposing the resolution.[4] Rabin's opposition to the Lavi, and toward Israeli arms manufacturing efforts in general, was well established.

The Lavi, however, was not without its supporters in the Labor Party. Shimon Peres had played a direct role in the founding of Israel Aircraft Industries and had already come out publicly in support of the airplane. Although Rabin had once headed the Labor Alignment, in 1984 this was no longer true. Whatever reservations Rabin may once have had about the program, he did not express them openly when the new National Unity Government took office. Officially, both Labor and Likud were united on this subject: the Lavi fighter would proceed as planned.

By mid-1985, therefore, the Israeli air force's modernization efforts were in full swing. A decision was expected soon as to which American aircraft would replace the F-4E, and preparations were underway for flight testing of the first Lavi prototypes. Everything appeared to be on course for Israel's air force of the 1990s. Then came the defense cuts.

At the time that Israel's National Unity Government took office, the nation was undergoing an economic earthquake. Decades of extended defense budgets had taken their toll. Defense expenditures had always been a leading element in Israel's national budget. In the aftermath of the 1973 war, however, Israeli defense expenditures had skyrocketed—consuming an average of 24 percent of Israel's gross domestic product during the decade that followed.[5] In comparison, the United States—even at the height of the war in Vietnam—devoted less than 10 percent of its GDP toward defense.[6] The burden on Israel's economy was unbearable, driving budget deficits and inflation to unprecedented levels.

By mid-1985 Israel's monthly inflation rate had reached 28 percent. Life savings could be wiped out in a matter of days, and the cost of groceries or a meal at a restaurant could go up in the time that it took to stand in line to pay. The annual inflation rate was projected to reach 2,000 percent. A cycle of hyperinflation had set in, and something had to be done soon. People were spending their wages as quickly as they were paid, scurrying to spend their paycheck before the value of their wages fell. The Lebanon War had only added to this burden, driving Israel's national budget deficit up to 15 percent of the gross national product.[7] It was this economic crisis, as much as the war in Lebanon, that had brought down the previous Israeli government. And it was this same crisis that threatened to bring down the new governing coalition if drastic steps were not taken.

In July 1985 the Israeli government's austerity plan was unveiled. Wages and prices across the country were frozen, while the shekel was first devalued, and then its exchange rate fixed to that of the American dollar, which was itself on the decline. The plan worked, and inflation did come down. But cutting the budget deficit still remained an imperative.

The amount eventually axed from the defense budget would come to $600 million, out of the 1985 budget alone. Within the Israeli defense industry, sales to Israel's armed forces dropped by over 40 percent from their 1984 levels.[8] At Israel Aircraft Industries, Israel's largest defense contractor, government sales dropped by 16 percent—amounting to a total loss of some $72 million in annual income.[9]

The Israeli air force had to select between the programs that they wanted, and those that they could afford. Among the projects cut was an F-4 replacement. The modified F-18 variant under consideration was too expensive, and none of the other American aircraft that might have fit the role promised to be any cheaper. This problem was compounded by the fact that Israel, as a non-NATO member, had to pay a surcharge to help cover "development costs" on the aircraft that it purchased, a charge that America's NATO allies did not have to pay.

This left the Israelis with an aging, vulnerable fleet of F-4ES that had never been intended for the kind of agile, close-quarters combat that even an attack jet was likely to see in the Middle East. During Israel's extraordinary success over the skies of Lebanon in 1982, in over a year of fighting and out of over eighty air-to-air kills, the F-4 had claimed only one enemy aircraft.[10] Unable to afford a near-term replacement for the F-4E, the Israeli air force would have little choice but to embark on another round of upgrades to keep the airplanes flying. Israel has had a long history of modifying its foreign-built weapons to meet its own needs, and the F-4 had been no exception. But the kind of modifications required to keep the Phantom in service into the twenty-first century would be the most extensive that Israel had yet undertaken. The upgrade program proposed by IAI involved three distinct phases.

The first leg of the proposed upgrade packages was termed the Phantom 2000 and consisted of a complete refit of the airplane's electronics and avionics systems. It was intended to eventually include the retrofit of a Norden radar, derived from the U.S. Navy's canceled A-6F program, with digital processing and a full look-down/shoot-down capability. When finally installed, the system was expected to provide synthetic aperture radar mapping and ground-target tracking, with air-to-air performance equivalent to the F-16C's, and air-to-ground performance that was decidedly superior. In addition, the refit included the installation of a new mission computer: a derivative of Elbit's ACE-3, the Israeli computer that had already been retrofitted into all of Israel's F-16s. A new wide-angle head-up display developed in the United States by Kaiser and offering a 20° vertical and 30° horizontal field of view was also part of the package. Other additions included new multifunction displays, a new communications system, and a complete rewiring of the aircraft, which would cut overall wire weight by 30 percent and reduce the number of wire harnesses from five hundred to three hundred.[11]

But no matter how many avionics systems might be added, they alone could not change the fact that the F-4E was never intended to be a dogfighter. It was this problem that the second phase of modifications was meant to address. It was called the Super Phantom upgrade and centered around replacing the Phantom's J79 turbojets with the same PW1120 turbofan intended for use on the Lavi. In addition to increasing the aircraft's range, the new powerplant would also improve the F-4's thrust-weight ratio, granting an appreciable increase in agility. A standard F-4E had a thrust-to-weight ratio of 0.86 when in an air combat configuration, as opposed to 1.1 for the F/A-18 or 1.12 for the F-16. The Super Phantom upgrade would increase this ratio to 1.04, boosting the sustained turn rate by 15 percent and acceleration by 27 percent at medium altitudes.[12] One observer who witnessed a prototype Super Phantom in a flight demonstration at the 1987 Paris Airshow described the airplane's performance as "a startling display of brute power in a series of vertical maneuvers and tight, high-g turns that were totally out of character for the aging F-4."[13]

The third upgrade phase proposed by IAI, which could be performed either with or without the Super Phantom engine program, included structural refurbishments that would add another two thousand hours of life to each airframe and the installation of a 600 gal (2,270 L) belly-mounted external fuel tank, plus the addition of Kfir-like canards on the air intakes. Overall, the full, three-phase upgrade promised to drastically improve the F-4's performance while reducing the airplane's overall weight by some 1,500 lb (680 kg).[14]

The combined cost of all three Phantom upgrade packages, however, was estimated at $12 million per airplane.[15] It was unlikely from the beginning that all of Israel's F-4s would go through all of the proposed modifications, and although the rewiring and avionics refit were begun as soon as each airplane was brought in for regular maintenance and inspection, it was already clear that the majority of the airplanes would never see anything beyond the phase-one, Phantom 2000 modifications. The loss of a near-term F-4E replacement, however, was potentially a long-term gain for the Lavi.

It was plain that Israel could afford to field only one new fighter model in the 1990s. For air force commander Maj. Gen. Amos Lapidot, the choice of which new airplane to choose was clear. However urgent the need may have been to replace Israel's F-4 fleet, the need to replace Israel's Skyhawks and Kfir fighters was even greater. Neither the Skyhawk nor the Kfir had any margin left for incorporating additional electronic countermeasures. Moreover, with a short-term option for an F-4 replacement gone, it also made more sense than ever to stretch out Lavi production beyond the initial three hundred aircraft then on order. As Lapidot soon revealed, the Lavi was expected to replace not only Israel's A-4 and Kfir fighters but, eventually, Israel's F-4ES as well. The possibility had been raised for extending Lavi production to a total of some four hundred aircraft in all.

Table 4. Israeli air force, 1990, 1995, and 2000: 1985 projections

Aircraft	1990	1995	2000
A-4	120	N/A	N/A
F-4E	140	40	N/A
F-4E/2000	20	60	N/A
F-4E/2000+	2	20	20
F-15	50	50	50
F-16	150	150	150
Kfir	100	20	N/A
Lavi	12	250	400
Total	594	590	620

In order for Lavi production to have been extended, however, a true transformation must have already occurred. The implication of Major General Lapidot's announcement was that the Lavi must have evolved into a very long range attack platform.

The delays caused by Caspar Weinberger's earlier embargo on Lavi contract approvals had set back the timetable for Lavi rollout by six months. However, if the aggressive Lavi production rate initially proposed could actually be achieved, IAI would still be able to deliver four hundred aircraft by the end of the century. IAI's production facilities had just undergone a sweeping modernization program, which included the addition of a new computer-aided system that promised to improve both product quality and the production rate. If the original production goal of three hundred aircraft in seven years' time was attained, then, with the timetable stretched out or not, the Heyl Ha'Avir would still have their F-4 replacement before the year 2000.[16]

It was at this time, while the budget cuts and decisions on Israel's air force were still being made, and long before the first Lavi prototype rolled into view, that the Lavi had to begin proving its worth. As

Israel's only remaining new aircraft program, and under fire from critics in both Israel and the United States, the Lavi had to begin answering its detractors, including charges that it was "clearly not designed to have the effectiveness" of its counterparts elsewhere.

In a nation for which security has become a national obsession, every premium is placed on secrecy. The entire Kfir program, from its inception to the day that the first production aircraft rolled out, was carried out in complete secrecy. There were no preproduction artist's impressions, no photo opportunities at the assembly line. There should be little doubt that only the high degree of American involvement, both technologically and financially, prevented the Lavi from being developed in a similar manner. Unable to keep the project's existence a secret, the Israeli leadership did the next best thing: they disguised its capabilities. Design details were kept in the dark for as long as possible, and performance projections for the PW1120-powered aircraft remained unquoted—until the budget battles made it necessary to roll them out.

This practice became evident in small ways from the very beginning. At the 1981 Paris Airshow, for example, a correspondent from a British aviation journal was led to believe that the Israelis had down-selected to a Lavi configuration that closely resembled the Kfir, complete with side-mounted, variable supersonic inlets and a fixed canard.[17] Within less than two years it would become clear that such a suggestion was grossly erroneous. Yet even when the first sketches for the airplane were publicly released by IAI in 1983, and even as late as December 1984, when IAI released an artist's interpretation for the airplane, the aircraft portrayed continued to bear the influence of the austere A-4 replacement from which it had sprung, with a more simple, squared-off ventral inlet and a nose radome so disproportionally small as to suggest nothing more than a tiny, compact radar of modest means. When the Lavi engineering mockup was unveiled only one month later, in January 1985, however, it displayed the rounded ventral inlet and much larger nose radome that would be featured in the prototype fighters. It also displayed a pair of ventral strakes, surfaces never seen or mentioned prior to the mockup's unveiling. As became evident, the Israeli censors had been releasing outdated drawings and sketches for many months. The true dimensions of the airplane became visible only as the actual hardware was rolled out.[18]

This pattern of omission, and a reluctance to reveal more to the public than was absolutely necessary, extended across the board. It was not until March 1985, for example, barely a month before the inevitable defense cuts, that the outlines of the Lavi flight-test program were made public. It was finally announced that six flying prototypes and one nonflying structural test aircraft were slated to be built. The first two prototypes were to evaluate the airplane's fly-by-wire flight control system and handling characteristics, with the later prototypes assigned to evaluating its avionics systems and mission capabilities. The fifth prototype was expected to be the first aircraft to include the complete avionics suite. More surprising, however, was that the entire test program was expected to be complete after only three years of flight test.[19] That would mean a lot of flying for only six aircraft and three years' time.

It was also not until this point that there was any hint regarding the thought process that was going into the cockpit design, which was expected to make considerable use of multifunction displays, including what was to be the first full-color CRT display to reach production in a fighter aircraft. These were the sort of details that American defense contractors would have capitalized on much earlier to gain some free publicity. In Israel, however, every minute detail was treated as if it were potentially sensitive and of value to the enemy.

As the impending defense cuts began to cast their shadow on Israeli budget planning, still more details surrounding the airplane's electronics suite and production plans would be released. It was emphasized, for example, that in spite of the new cockpit displays, the primary instrument during air combat was still expected to be the wide-angle, holographic head-up display, which was being developed in the United States by Hughes. Controls and switches were to follow the HOTAS (hands on throttle and stick) philosophy, with the goal of simplifying the pilot's workload by placing all switches needed for air combat or ground attack within fingers' reach on the control stick and throttle.[20] At this time it was also announced that the first thirty production aircraft were to be two-seaters, slated to replace Israeli A-4 Skyhawks in operational training.[21] All of these decisions had undoubtedly been reviewed, debated, and ultimately approved many months prior. But only as the defense cuts loomed were the outlines of Israel's flight test and operational deployment goals made public.

These emerging details all pointed toward a far more complex and capable aircraft than had been suggested by the A-4 replacement approved by Ezer Weizman. But the true measure of the Lavi's outlines would not be revealed until June 1985, just days before Israel's defense cuts were publicly announced. The maximum Lavi weapons load had been slowly edging upward over the years, but what came in June was truly a startling revelation. The Lavi development team had determined that, by modifying the wing design, and with a few changes to the fuselage and actuators, they could increase the Lavi's maximum takeoff weight by some 4,500 lb (2,040 kg), to 42,500 lb (19,280 kg). The first two prototypes were already too far down the road in the manufacture of their detail components to incorporate these subtle but powerful changes. They would have to fly with the previous wing. Beginning with the third prototype, however, the Lavi would be capable of carrying sharply increased fuel and ordnance loads.[22]

This alone was remarkable enough. The Block 25 F-16C, which had a slightly higher empty weight and a more powerful engine, was limited to a maximum takeoff weight of 37,500 lb (17,010 kg), which in itself was nothing to sneeze at.[23] But that was not the end of it. The Israeli developers also dropped the fact of how this minor wing and structural modification would affect the Lavi's range: the Lavi combat radius was now estimated to be in excess of 1,100 nm (2,040 km) in a hi-lo-hi attack profile—nearly 50 percent greater than the equivalent range of the F-16.[24]

Any observer at this point, Pentagon expert or Washington novice, should have realized that the Lavi was no longer a short-range attack fighter, nor even a medium-range attack jet, and it was definitely more than just an A-4 replacement. It had become a long-range multirole aircraft far in excess of its peers. What was more, this information was now in the public domain.

IAI had quietly gone about producing a long-range strike fighter to replace not only the A-4 and Kfir but also Israel's F-4 fleet, meeting Israeli air force inventory needs into the next century. It was a transformation that had been ongoing ever since the Lavi development team had changed their engine selection back in 1982. Performance increases of the kind seen on the Lavi, in the span of only four short years of development, are not only unusual— they are unheard of. There was no way that the quoted 244 nm (450 km) combat radius could still have been a serious representation of the Lavi's potential at the time that it was reported in January 1983. With the details of the Lavi's design, deployment, and performance so long cloaked in a veil of secrecy, it ultimately had been the political and budgetary pressures that forced Israel Aircraft Industries' hand and pressed them into revealing them. But with the Lavi's full potential now laid bare, there was one argument that the Lavi developers would not be hearing again: that the Lavi was "not designed to have the effectiveness" of its American counterparts.

10. Inside the Department of Defense

The new revelations concerning Lavi mission capability did little to stem opposition from its critics within the U.S. government. If even the president's own endorsement had been insufficient to tame the rancor of some, unveiling the dimensions of the fighter's capabilities would hardly serve to change their minds. Leading this charge would be Secretary of Defense Caspar Weinberger. Only now, instead of claiming that the Lavi was somehow less capable than its American counterparts, his new line of attack would be that the fighter was too expensive.

A variety of explanations could be put forward to explain Weinberger's unremitting opposition to the Lavi program, not the least of which was his personal rivalry with the program's most visible benefactor within the administration, Secretary of State George Shultz. Shultz and Weinberger had been locking horns for over a decade, ever since their days together in the Office of Management and Budget under President Nixon. For much of his career, Weinberger had been Shultz's unwilling subordinate, forever doomed to walk one step behind. The disdain that each man held for the other often erupted into heated arguments: loud, unruly matches that embarrassed the president and that he seemed powerless to diffuse. President Reagan's arms control chief, Ken Adelman, once described the discomfort of attending these meetings as being reminiscent of, "a double-dating situation if the other couple started fighting about who should take out the garbage."[1] National Security Advisor Robert McFarlane was also dismayed by the rivalry between the two men and offered his own explanation for this contest of wills:

> In Cap's relationship with Shultz, though, there was an undeniable undercurrent of jealousy. For many years, Weinberger had operated in Shultz's shadow. He had been his deputy at the Office of Management and Budget under Nixon; at the Bechtel Group, Shultz had been president, Weinberger general counsel. Now, Cap found himself head of a Cabinet department that was still, in a hierarchical sense, subordinate to that headed by Shultz. Whatever the true wellspring of his hostility to George, the plain truth was that he was always ready to pick a fight, challenge Shultz's position, or oppose State Department strategy at the drop of a hat.[2]

From the day that Shultz had intervened to ensure the release of those initial Lavi development contracts, the airplane would be marked as deserving of Weinberger's unremitting opposition.

On Weinberger's part, there was also a wider pattern of opposition to anything that might be construed as being in Israel's best interests. A variety of arguments or excuses may have been offered, but this pattern had become indisputable. On numerous occasions, Weinberger's own strategic vision, emphasizing closer U.S. relations with the Arab world, had run afoul of Israel's supporters in the United States. There had been, for example, the decision by Congress to deny Weinberger's proposal to train and equip two brigades of Jordan's Arab Legion so that they could act as surrogates to protect U.S. interests in the Persian Gulf. Even Weinberger's natural tendency to align himself with the Arab monarchs, however, still would not have explained his hostile reaction to Israel's raid on Iraq's Osirak nuclear reactor, which had eliminated a grave threat to both Israel and the Arab monarchs. It also would not have explained Weinberger's repeated choice of suspending arms shipments as his preferred tool for shaping Israeli policy. Something deeper was at play here. In the words of Lt. Col. Oliver North, who was a member of President Reagan's National Security Council staff,

Weinberger seemed to go out of his way to oppose Israel on any issue and to blame the Israelis for every problem in the Middle East. In our planning for counterterrorist operations, he apparently feared that if we went after Palestinian terrorists, we would offend and alienate the Arab governments—particularly if we acted in cooperation with the Israelis. Weinberger's anti-Israel tilt was an underlying current in almost every Mideast issue. Some people explained it by pointing to his years with the Bechtel Corporation, the San Francisco engineering firm with contracts in many Arab countries. Others believed it was more complicated, and had to do with his sensitivity about his own Jewish ancestry.[3]

There are many possible explanations for Weinberger's anti-Israel tilt, none of which can be confirmed or refuted. What can be said, however, is that Weinberger's attitude toward Israel was consistent and unremitting. Indeed, so severe and all-encompassing was his bias that it interfered with Weinberger's ability to objectively carry out his duties as secretary of defense.

A striking example of Weinberger's inability to separate his personal bias from the duties of his office occurred in the fall of 1985. In October 1985 four PLO terrorists hijacked the Italian cruise liner *Achille Lauro*, taking hostage numerous American and other passengers. With the lives of American citizens in danger, Weinberger would expressly forbid the Joint Chiefs of Staff from seeking Israeli assistance in tracking or rescuing the passengers aboard the cruise ship. It was a decision that he would never explain. He clearly, however, was intent on owing no favors to the Israeli government. One American citizen among the hostages, Leon Klinghoffer, would die while the U.S. Navy was in the process of preparing its rescue from inadequate facilities in Egypt. Israeli facilities had also been offered and would have been both closer to the hijacked ship and better equipped. The Israeli facilities included sophisticated communications and tracking gear that the Egyptians lacked, as well as the support of the most potent naval force in the region. Weinberger, however, would have nothing to do with such a proposal. The U.S. Navy, which at the time had few warships deployed into the eastern Mediterranean, twice lost track of the cruise ship while preparing a rescue attempt but was prohibited by Weinberger's order from seeking Israeli aid in either tracking or securing the vessel. On both occasions, the location of the hijacked vessel was reestablished only when members of the National Security Council bypassed the defense secretary's prohibition and requested Israeli assistance in locating the *Achille Lauro*. On both occasions, the Israeli navy promptly pinpointed the location, which the NSC then passed on to the U.S. Navy. Sadly, no American rescue operation could be prepared within the limited time and resources available, and the elderly, wheelchair-bound Klinghoffer would be murdered while Weinberger was insisting that the navy prepare the ship's rescue using only Arab-ruled facilities. The hijackers later surrendered to Egyptian authorities, who promptly released them.[4]

Whatever Weinberger's motives for his adversarial attitude toward Israel, it was an obsession that systematically impaired his judgment. Weinberger punished Israel for eliminating Saddam Hussein's nuclear weapons program, endangered the lives of Americans to avoid requesting Israeli assistance to rescue the *Achille Lauro*, and was intent on denying Israel the fighter plane best suited to its defensive needs. The amount of time and energy that Weinberger's office devoted to stalling and attempting to eliminate the Lavi was unparalleled. No similar opposition was voiced to indigenous fighters developed in Europe or the Far East, and Weinberger supported plans to allow the Japanese to develop a locally produced derivative of the F-16. At every turn, Weinberger sought to use the powers at his disposal to oppose Israeli interests. This included using every available measure to kill the Lavi fighter program, even if doing so ran in direct contradiction to President Reagan's endorsement of the program, as had been clearly articulated on the White House grounds in November 1983.

Of course, Weinberger was well aware that his earlier attempts had failed. Further, his previous suggestions that the Lavi was a less capable fighter had been proven erroneous, if not deceitful. His efforts had been undermined, either by the secretary of state, who overturned Weinberger's earlier export suspensions, or by President Reagan, who had endorsed U.S. funding for the program. Attempting to work from inside the president's Cabinet had failed him. What Weinberger needed was a concerted, behind-the-scenes campaign to kill the program. A team of people dedicated to this one goal. And having failed to find technical grounds for canceling the Lavi, Weinberger turned his attention to attacking the program on its financial merits. To do this he would need an accountant, not a defense analyst. He needed someone who would be unwavering in the assigned mission, yet someone who was not so clearly in the pro-Arab camp as to render his campaign easily dismissible.

To lead this new assault, Weinberger selected Dov Zakheim, an assistant undersecretary of defense for policy and resources who held a PhD in economics from Oxford University and who also happened to be an observant, orthodox Jew. An independently ordained rabbi, Zakheim spoke fluent Hebrew and Yiddish, making him an ideal candidate for carrying out a concerted lobbying campaign, both in the United States and in Israel. Moreover, while he admitted that he might have had a sentimental tie to some of the holy sites, Zakheim was ambivalent with regard to his sympathies for the modern Jewish state. Rather, Zakheim avowed that he was part of that segment within the orthodox Jewish community that believed "that there will be a Diaspora until the coming of the Messiah."[5]

Zakheim was briefed regarding his new assignment in March 1985. It was at this time that Fred Ikle, undersecretary of defense for policy and resources and Zakheim's immediate superior, first charged Zakheim to "develop and implement a plan to terminate" the Lavi.[6] The choice of Dov Zakheim as the point man assigned to lead this effort, as well as the terms of reference, were all too telling. Zakheim was not tasked with evaluating Israeli air force needs nor with assessing how those requirements could best be met. He was, after all, hardly qualified for making such an assessment. He was also not charged with evaluating which weapons platform, or combination of platforms, would most economically meet Israel's specific requirements. Such a question was of little interest in the Weinberger Pentagon. Rather, his task was to "terminate" the Lavi program, regardless of Israeli requirements or the financial costs of an equivalent alternative. The expected outcome of Zakheim's assessment had been predetermined by his terms of reference.

In preparation for Fred Ikle's upcoming trip to Israel, which was due to take place in late April, Zakheim's staff prepared two cost estimates for the Lavi. As Zakheim later admitted, these initial projections were short on substance and were assembled purely with an aim to "infuriate" the Israeli leadership. The first of the two projections compared the original cost estimates for the F-15, F-16, and F/A-18 fighters to the final program costs and assumed that similar cost overruns could be expected for the Lavi. Using this approach, Lavi development costs could be projected as high as $3 billion, with production costs of up to $13.9 billion, or twice the Israeli estimates. The second cost estimate was based on developmental, "learning curve" costs that had been experienced by previous U.S. weapons development efforts, and it assumed that similar, unforeseen events would plague the Lavi. By this estimate, the Lavi development costs could be projected as high as $10 billion, or six times the value originally projected. Both of these estimates failed to take into account that many of the underlying technologies for the Lavi had already been developed and matured under previous programs.[7] These initial estimates were also so artificially high that any follow-on estimate, no matter how inflated, couldn't help but appear rational in comparison.

At the end of April 1985 Zakheim accompanied Ikle to Israel to begin the process of campaigning for the Lavi's termination. Their first meeting was with the Lavi program director, Brig. Gen. (Res.) Menachem Eini. To say that Zakheim's report was not well received by the Israeli program team would be putting it too mildly. The reception that Zakheim and Ikle received at the Ministry of Defense was equally cool. Yitzhak Rabin was accompanied at the briefing by Menachem Meron, the Defense Ministry's director general, who was also known to be a solid Lavi supporter. The American pair's presentation to the Israeli air force commander, Maj. Gen. Amos Lapidot, also received a chilly reception.

Not surprisingly, Zakheim's team likewise received few warm greetings from the officials that they briefed at Israel Aircraft Industries. The IAI delegation included former air force commander David Ivry, who had retired from active duty to become IAI's new chairman, as well as Moshe Blumkine, IAI's vice president of engineering. At each destination, Zakheim's team was met with quiet tolerance and suspicion.

The one exception to this trend was at the Israeli Ministry of Finance. Finance Minister Yitzhak Modai had for some time raised concerns that the Lavi fighter program would consume an ever-increasing share of Israel's defense budget as it transitioned to production. However, even Finance Ministry officials who were sympathetic toward Zakheim's objectives pointed out that he needed to assemble a more substantive cost projection if he wished to be taken seriously.[8]

The one concession that the Israeli officials did provide was a verbal agreement from Yitzhak Rabin that the Defense Ministry would cooperate with Zakheim's efforts to produce a more accurate cost review for the program. Armed with Rabin's acquiescence, Zakheim returned to the United States and drew up a list of the data that his office wanted the Israelis to provide.

Zakheim and his team would meet with the Lavi program director, Menachem Eini, two more times over the next several months: once on June 10, when Eini was visiting Washington, and again on July 29, when Zakheim made a second trip to Israel. Needless to say, Zakheim's requests for information were met by Israeli air force personnel with suspicion and, on occasion, hostility. For a nation obsessed with security, even the most mundane details surrounding a weapons system are considered sensitive. Their concerns were much stronger for the kind of details that Zakheim's office was requesting. Among other items, Zakheim requested information on Israel's expected reliability rates for both the Lavi and F-16s in Israeli service.[9] While this information may have been invaluable for Zakheim's cost estimates, it would also have been invaluable to any potential adversary intent on assessing Israeli sortie rates. The Israelis refused this request and others like it.

They similarly refused to provide information regarding the Lavi's expected mission profile, as well as detailed performance targets. Only information that had already been publicly released would be forthcoming. Although Zakheim's office insisted that they needed such information to assess the "probability of design changes," the Israeli air force was not about to release information about the mix of weapons and combat roles that they foresaw as likely in a future war. Similarly, no detailed breakdown of Lavi component weights would be provided.[10]

It was also at this time that the test of wills between Zakheim and his staff, on the one hand, and the Israeli team overseeing the Lavi development effort, on the other, became personal. Program Director Eini in particular resented the intrusion of the American analysts, who arrived with neither a technical nor a combat background and were quite obviously charged with terminating the program that he oversaw. Eini saw this contest through the lens of his experience as an Israeli war veteran, from a nation where all able-bodied men were expected to serve in their nation's defense—all able-bodied men, that is, with the exception of Israel's Arab citizens and the ultraorthodox Yeshiva students.

Following Israel's War of Independence, coming as it did on the heels of the destruction of the centers for Jewish religious study in Europe, the Israeli government had granted deferrals from military service for those young men engaged in full-time religious study. At the time, these deferrals applied to only a few hundred. By the 1980s, however, Israel's population of orthodox, observant Jews had mushroomed, with tens of thousands opting out of military service each year. Like all Israeli citizens, they could vote in national elections and cast their ballots on issues of national importance. But so as long as they remained cloistered in the religious school system, they would not be subject to the draft. Many orthodox Jews did choose to serve in Israel's armed services. But many others chose not to, creating a class of professional students who avoided military service and who, unable to seek full-time employment, remained dependent on government subsidies. It had become a source of friction between Israel's ultraorthodox community and the less overtly religious, "secular" Jewish population that made up the majority of Israeli society. Although the ultraorthodox were a minority, they remained a unified voting bloc that ensured that government support for their religious school systems, as well as the social welfare system that they depended on, would continue. Rather than see Zakheim as merely another mid-ranking official in the Weinberger Pentagon who was attempting to curry the favor of his superiors, Eini instead saw him as yet another orthodox Jew who had not served in Israel's armed forces but who nonetheless felt entitled to make decisions regarding Israel's national security. Before this contest of wills was over, the exchange was doomed to turn ugly.

In September 1985 Zakheim was promoted from assistant undersecretary to deputy undersecretary of defense for policy and resources. By this time over thirty Department of Defense personnel and consultants had been assigned in support of Zakheim's efforts to terminate the Lavi. Zakheim also drew on the State Department's Near East Bureau, which proved to be an eager supporter of his goal, as well as on the American ambassador to Israel, Thomas Pickering, who helped Zakheim to maneuver among Israel's political echelons during his repeated trips there.[11]

The resources placed at Zakheim's disposal in support of this campaign were impressive, although Zakheim still needed to tread lightly where Secretary of State George Shultz was concerned. Shultz had opposed Weinberger's use of pressure tactics, under whatever guise, and had been instrumental in having previous roadblocks to the Lavi lifted. While the Pentagon staff that Zakheim led were in essence running a rogue operation, in direct contravention to stated policy as pronounced by the president, it was nonetheless essential that they at least appear to represent a unified administration stance. There was of course, no way that they could obtain the secretary of state's approval. But they desperately needed him to maintain his silence. The cooperation provided by the State Department's Near East Bureau therefore played a crucial role in keeping the secretary of state at arm's length. As Zakheim was later to acknowledge,

[Shultz] was working closely with Shimon Peres to rescue Israel from the threat of hyperinflation and did not want to complicate this effort with a quarrel over defense economics that Weinberger's department had initiated. Shultz's attitude posed another potential complication for me. While his staff might sympathize with our opposition to the program, and indeed was very much involved in our effort, we somehow needed to have Shultz aboard, if only to maintain a common front vis-a-vis the Israelis. Thus far he had not voiced any objection to what we were doing. I could only hope that his staff . . . would continue to ensure that Shultz not only did not try to quash it, but also would not even intimate to anyone that he had reservations about it.[12]

The Near East Bureau, together with the embassy staff in Israel, were themselves running a dangerous risk in actively supporting Zakheim's efforts. The embassy staff not only walked Zakheim through the Israeli political system during his many trips but also campaigned behind the scenes in Zakheim's absence.[13]

There was ample reason to believe that the long-standing feud between Weinberger and Shultz, over the Lavi program as well as other subjects, could spill out into an open confrontation. The perpetual state of policy war that existed between Shultz and Weinberger had become the stuff of legend among Washington insiders. As White House Press Secretary Larry Speakes would later write, "Strong-willed Cabinet officers like George Shultz and Caspar Weinberger were constantly at odds over foreign policy, leaving the Reagan Administration in a quagmire of feudal bickering on such issues as arms control, U.S.-Soviet relations, the Middle East, Central America, and South Africa. You name it, Shultz and Weinberger would debate it—often in a debilitating public controversy that sent alarming signals of disarray to friend and foe abroad. Our allies, in particular, wondered why we couldn't get our act together."[14] Nor was President Reagan oblivious to the fact that Shultz and Weinberger were at opposite ends of the policy spectrum on virtually every issue. As Reagan observed himself, "Cap Weinberger and George Shultz never got along especially well together. There was always a little chill—a tension—between them. I suspect that it went back to when they were both executives of the Bechtel Corporation in San Francisco. Whatever it was, they didn't see eye to eye on a lot of things."[15]

What made the campaign to terminate the Lavi unique was that Shultz's own State Department bureaucracy not only disagreed with his previous show of support for the program but quietly acted in collusion with the Defense Department team in support of the termination campaign. Long-standing State Department biases had come to the fore. Undermined by his own staff and preoccupied with other matters of state, Shultz would thereafter cease to be a player in deciding policy regarding the Lavi.

Late in 1985 Defense Minister Rabin approved a production plan calling for the delivery of twenty-four to thirty Lavi fighters per year, or a little more than half of the original production goal. The delivery of the first three hundred fighters would need to be stretched out across the next decade. It was an uncomfortable compromise, the result of fiscal realities that the Israeli leadership had to wrestle with. They did not need Zakheim to tell them that their resources were limited. The extended mission capabilities that had been added to the Lavi had inevitably led to an increase in cost. Publicly, the Israelis had earlier released estimates placing the Lavi unit flyaway cost at $14.6 million.[16] More recent internal estimates, however, placed the unit cost at $15.2 million.[17] The Israeli leadership were not oblivious to the costs of the program. But they disagreed with the conclusions drawn by Weinberger and his subordinates. The cost of the Lavi was still substantially less than the off-the-shelf cost that they had been charged for their most recent batch of F-16s, and far less than the cost of developing an existing U.S. airframe into an equivalent attack platform.

In February 1986 Zakheim's office released their final report, claiming that the Lavi unit price had been vastly underestimated by the Israeli government and projecting a much higher unit flyaway cost of $22.1 million per airplane. Unlike the previous estimates, which had contained more speculation than substance, this latest report attempted to add at least a veneer of thought. The report also contended that, even at the new, reduced production rate that the Israeli Defense Ministry had announced, the costs of aircraft production, including initial spares and maintenance, would exceed the $550 million annual spending cap that the Israeli government had established.[18] Moreover, unlike prior Lavi cost estimates, which had been presented in private consultation, this latest report was intended for public consumption from the onset. Zakheim's efforts were no longer a purely behind-the-scenes campaign.

The Israeli government was quick to respond, countering that the report had been biased from the onset. The Defense Department had assumed a labor rate of $45–49 per man-hour, which although a reasonable estimate for wages in the American aerospace industry, was far beyond the $24 per hour paid for skilled labor in Israel. That error alone would have biased the Defense Department report by $2 million per airplane. Other errors, such as overestimating the engine price by $1.5 million per copy and exaggerating the cost of raw materials by $2 million per airplane, had nudged the Defense Department estimate up by another $3.5 million. The Israeli leadership also objected to the maintenance cost estimates. The Defense Department report assumed that there would be as many bugs to work out as there had been for prior, all-new aircraft. The Israeli contention was that, unlike the F-15 or F-16, the Lavi would employ existing, off-the-shelf components wherever possible, which would eliminate much of the maintenance "learning curve." IAI also lost no time in rushing to defend their airplane, pointing out that any Israeli-built airplane would still come out far cheaper than the $32 million unit price tag that Israel had been charged for its first batch of seventy-five F-16A/BS, and cheaper still than the expected price for the follow-on batch of F-16C/DS.[19]

The debate over Lavi program costs had, however, caught the attention of members of Congress. In March 1986 Lee Hamilton, chairman of the House Foreign Affairs Subcommittee on Europe and the Middle East, directed the General Accounting Office (GAO) to conduct an independent review of the program's costs. It would require nearly a year for the GAO to complete its work. When the study was eventually released, it would place the airplane's unit fly-away cost at $17.8 million per fighter on a production run of three hundred aircraft. The GAO had agreed with most of the objections that the Israeli government had raised regarding inconsistencies in the Defense Department analysis.

When budgeting for the procurement of a fighter fleet, however, flyaway cost was only one element. The GAO report also rolled up the cost for initial spares and support activities. At a unit flyaway cost of $17.8 million, the cost of initial spares and support was placed at $10.6 million per aircraft.[20] Significantly, the GAO report projected that the overall program costs would run higher than what the Israelis had budgeted. At a production rate of thirty airplanes per year, the Israelis would exceed the $550 million annual spending cap that had previously been set for the program.[21] Either the annual spending cap would have to be raised or the number of aircraft procured each year reduced.

The emergence of Dov Zakheim's office as the focal point for Caspar Weinberger's efforts marked a new phase in both the overt and the behind-the-scenes campaign to terminate the Lavi. Arguments would no longer be made regarding the "effectiveness" of the Lavi but would instead focus on program costs. Moreover, it would no longer be a haphazard campaign, characterized by the personal pronouncements of the secretary himself, but rather a concerted effort led by a team dedicated to the task. Nor would cost studies be the only tool that Weinberger had at his disposal. Before this campaign was over, Weinberger's rogue offensive to kill a program that had been given the president's own stamp of approval would cross yet more boundaries between the authority of the president and the agenda of his secretary of defense.

11. With the Sky at Stake

D ov Zakheim had not been the first to question how much the Lavi program would cost. As in any democracy, not all Israelis were of the same mind on this matter, any more than all Americans supported every weapons project conceived by the Pentagon. There was, however, a fundamental difference between the debate underway in Israel and the arguments put forward by Zakheim's team. The real substance at the core of the debate was not whether purchasing the Lavi would be more or less expensive but whether Israel could afford to purchase another three hundred jet fighters, of whatever variety. The $550 million per year that had been set aside to cover Lavi procurement costs was capped at that amount to protect other defense programs from cuts. Even at a production rate of thirty aircraft per year, however, the Lavi was all but assured of exceeding this total. The other branches of Israel's armed services were beginning to eye the Lavi budget as either a threat to their own procurement efforts or as a means to restore defense cuts already made. Likewise, Israeli government agencies outside of the military sought to protect or enlarge their own share of the budget at the expense of the Lavi. The Lavi was simply too big of a program to escape debate.

The most vocal Lavi opponents inside of the National Unity Government were Minister Without Portfolio Ezer Weizman and Minister of Finance Yitzhak Modai. Modai was a member of the Liberal Party, one of the two political parties that had merged to form the Likud. A small businessman by trade, Modai was concerned that the Lavi might adversely affect a variety of government commitments. Weizman, meanwhile, had turned from being an advocate of the program to being one of the program's most vocal critics. Weizman had envisioned the Lavi as a small, austere A-4 replacement, not as a long-range, multirole attack jet. As Weizman stated bluntly, "The Lavi is out of control."[1] In August 1985 Weizman and Modai would cast the only two dissenting votes in Israel's Cabinet, opposing continuation of the Lavi program.[2]

The Lavi was also drawing criticism from elements inside of Israel's armed forces who saw the project as draining funds from their own defense priorities. Officers in the Israeli navy were concerned that the Lavi might make it impossible to finance Israel's naval modernization efforts. More importantly, Maj. Gen. Dan Shomron, Israel's deputy chief of staff and the man expected to be the next leader of Israel's armed forces, had likewise expressed his reservations. Shomron made no secret that either the Lavi procurement pace would need to be slashed or the project shelved to protect other elements of Israel's procurement plans.[3] Even within the Israeli air force, the Lavi was not without its critics. Foremost among these was Brig. Gen. Avihu Ben Nun, who was chief of planning for the Israeli armed forces. Ben Nun was widely expected to become the next commander of the Israeli air force, and his opposition added significant fuel to critics' arguments.

Brig. Gen. Ben Nun represented the first of a new generation in Israeli air force leadership. The four previous Heyl Ha'Avir commanders—Mordechai Hod, Benny Peled, David Ivry, and Amos Lapidot—could trace their common experiences back to the time that they had served together in the same Ouragan squadron during the mid-1950s, under the command of Benny Peled. Ben Nun, in contrast, had made his debut in the air force over a decade later, in a Mystere squadron during the Six-Day War. He later went on to serve as the commander of Squadron 69, one of Israel's two original Phantom squadrons. As one pilot remembered Ben Nun from those days, "The most impressive aspect in the squadron was Avihu Ben Nun's dominance. Young, charismatic, and well connected, Avihu emphasized operational standards."[4] By the beginning of the Yom Kippur War, Ben Nun was in charge of strike planning at Israel's air force headquarters. His perspective on that war differed significantly from that of his peers within the leadership of the Heyl Ha'Avir.

In the early 1970s, Col. Ben Nun had been the principal architect of a plan called Tagar (challenge), aimed at eliminating Egypt's missile batteries at the onset of any future war. The plan called for waves of Israeli fighters, equipped with the best available electronic-jamming pods, to sequentially peel back the layers of Egyptian antiaircraft defenses. Like an intricate ballet, the plan required precise timing, tight choreography, and the dedicated attention of the entire air force. A similar plan, code named Doogman V (model 5), had been developed for the Syrian front. Years of training went into demonstrating the tactics that would be necessary to execute these missions. Not all of Israel's pilots, however, were equally impressed by the results.

> These drills were very difficult and complex, and hazardous, too. I am proud of our wonderful air force, which succeeded in accomplishing these elegant maneuvers again and again in training and in war games, and which got out without casualties. Preparation for a SAM attack drill required bookkeeping any accountant would admire, and the actual performance was more courageous and spectacular than any aerial show by the Blue Angels over Oshkosh or anyplace else. Avihu demonstrated to us and to our commanders what a magnificent air force we were. . . . Those drills created in us feelings of enormous satisfaction and great power, but I, and a few of my buddies, felt uneasy about all that. Our argument was that the operational worth of a fighter pilot lay in his being free to maneuver, not locked inside a cohort marching in lockstep to run the enemy over with the weight of our bodies. . . . The real clients—the missile batteries—watched balefully from the balcony. They didn't play our games.[5]

Ben Nun's intricate plans also held one potentially fatal flaw. These plans rested on the assumption that, in the opening hours of a future war, the Israeli air force would be provided the go-ahead to carry out a preemptive attack on the opposing air defense network. As Israel's air force commander, Maj. Gen. Benny Peled, had warned his superiors, "You should know that these plans aren't worth the paper they're written on unless we get permission to strike first."[6] When war finally did break out in October 1973, every available Israeli fighter was desperately needed to supply close air support, in order to stem the tide of the invading Arab armies. Israeli fighter pilots were ordered to fly into the jaws of an undamaged, multilayered air defense network in order to save their country from annihilation. It was this decision, and this battle, that was at the crux of Ben Nun's disagreement with his superiors and predecessors regarding the need for a strike fighter such as the Lavi.

Ben Nun remained convinced that a concerted attack on the enemy's air defenses would have succeeded, had it been implemented as planned in 1973. He was convinced that his approach provided a better, more affordable way to counter the antiaircraft threat than developing a new, dedicated attack jet. Further, he could point to the Lebanon War to demonstrate that, under the right conditions, the Israeli air force could eliminate the missile threat. In Ben Nun's view, the unique qualities of the Lavi were unnecessary.[7] This ran counter to the views of Israel's air force commander at the time, Maj. Gen. Amos Lapidot, as well as against those of his immediate predecessors, who remained convinced that the Lavi was needed precisely because they could not count on Israel's political establishment to authorize a preemptive strike.

Disagreement over the value of the Lavi and the wisdom of pursuing the project in the political and military establishments should not have been unexpected. It was too big of a program to escape debate. In some quarters, such internal debate would be interpreted to suggest that the project was secretly opposed by a majority of Israel's military and government officials. But the reality was something quite different. Despite this raucous process of public policy debate, throughout 1985 and 1986 the Lavi continued to command the support of the leading members of Israel's political and military establishment. The leaders of Israel's two largest political parties, Shimon Peres and Yitzhak Shamir, remained firm advocates. Chief of Staff Lt. Gen. Moshe Levi, like his predecessor Raful Eitan before him, also supported the program. And of course, Israeli Air Force Commander Amos Lapidot could likewise be counted as a Lavi advocate. As Major General Lapidot would argue, "The Israeli air force needs the Lavi. This fighter was designed to answer our operational demands."[8]

Even many of those who had originally opposed the development of an all-new indigenous fighter, such as the former air force commander Benny Peled, had come around in support of the effort once it was underway. To many in Israel's political and defense establishment, it had become evident that having already come so far, the Lavi had become the most economical alternative for meeting Israel's need for a survivable strike fighter.[9]

In January 1986 the first set of composite wings and tail supplied by Grumman were attached to the first Lavi prototype. The little airplane wore the camouflage of a warbird in the making: a patchwork of pale-yellow primer alongside the black finish of composite panels. Its many access panels opened onto empty chambers, with wires bristling from its seams. There were many more months of assembly and testing to go. Yet in spite of its clever disguise, it was already beginning to take on the shape of a warplane. In May the first two prototypes would be rolled into the sunlight for the first time, to undergo static engine tests. The program was coming ever closer to that all-important first flight.

In February Dov Zakheim returned from his latest lobbying campaign in Israel. He immediately set about working on a Lavi alternatives study. Preparing reports, however, was not the only role that Zakheim had. For reasons of export regulation the Israelis had to gain Defense Department approval for the Lavi subcontracts with various U.S. firms. And in Weinberger's Pentagon, it was Zakheim's office that had been assigned to review these contracts. Weinberger could be assured that Zakheim would be anything but impartial.

Having gained the minimal Israeli cooperation needed to complete his report, Zakheim began the process of stalling the Lavi contracts. As Zakheim himself would later acknowledge, "I was deliberately slowing down the American support process by insisting that all Israeli requests for DSAA approval of American support for the Lavi be routed to me before any further action was taken. Once my office received the Israeli requests, we sat on them for at least a week."[10] Delay is the one tactic at which any bureaucracy excels.

Whatever his own reservations might once have been in connection with the Lavi, Defense Minister Rabin did not respond well to bullying tactics, a message that he made clear during a visit to Washington in April 1986. Rabin insisted that the roadblocks be removed. The future of the Lavi program was an Israeli decision, not Weinberger's.[11]

Zakheim followed up with a visit to Israel at the end of May, during which he presented Defense Minister Rabin with two letters. The first of the two had been signed by Secretary of Defense Weinberger and expressed the secretary's opposition to the Lavi program. The second letter had been drafted by the State Department's Near East Bureau and had been signed by Secretary of State Shultz. The State Department letter called on the Israelis to help reconcile the divergent cost estimates produced by the Defense Department and their own Ministry of Defense. Shultz's letter was a far cry from a call for outright cancellation. Indeed, it was little more than a perfunctory request that the Defense Department and Israel's Ministry of Defense reconcile their different estimates. Delivered in concert with Weinberger's more forceful letter, however, it helped sustain the appearance of unity.[12]

The letters did not fully have the desired effect, and Zakheim returned to Washington with little to show. He therefore became convinced that a "tougher go-slow" policy was needed. Halting the Lavi contract approval process outright, however, would be sure to place Zakheim's bureau on a collision course with a wide range of U.S. officials. Secretary of State Shultz had already registered complaints regarding Zakheim's stalling maneuvers. But as Zakheim himself related some years later, there should never have been any doubt regarding where Weinberger's sentiments lay: "Even as the two secretaries reached no agreement, however, we continued to put a stall on Lavi contracts. We were certain that Weinberger wanted to block them all and thought that Shultz ultimately would yield to Defense's position. In any event, Weinberger finally moved unilaterally on June 23, and we braced for the latest Congressional onslaught as word would leak out that we were not permitting any contracts to be implemented."[13] The decision to halt all further contract approvals was made quietly. It would be some weeks, they knew, before Israeli officials realized that the tactics of delay had been replaced by a policy of stonewall obstruction.

In July an additional setback came to the program when it was revealed that the airplane's fly-by-wire computer, under development in the United States by Lear Siegler, had fallen behind schedule.[14] This announcement was pounced upon by Weinberger's office as an after-the-fact justification for the halt in Lavi contract approval that they had already implemented. The Defense Department announced that they had impounded $70 million in Lavi funds while certain Lavi contracts were "under review." The Defense Department impoundment meant that six Lavi contracts that were about to be signed, including one with Lear Siegler to complete work on the flight control system and another with Grumman to modify the design for the Lavi wing, were suspended while Weinberger's office "reviewed" their "technical merit."

Defense Minister Rabin lost no time in pointing out that the window of opportunity for developing an American alternative into an adequate contender for the attack role had long since passed. Israel had twice been turned down in its requests to license produce the F-16, in 1977 and again in 1980. It was simply too late to start fresh on a modifications program for the F-16 and still meet the in-service deadlines set by the Israel Defense Force. Rabin described the Pentagon move as an effort to "get Israel" on the part of "some U.S. agencies" and announced that his office would refuse to even discuss Zakheim's forthcoming report on "alternatives" until the impounded funds were released.[15]

In Washington, the response from Capitol Hill was equally swift. Weinberger's attempts to sidestep the congressional budget process came as a slap in the face to elected officials. Numerous representatives and senators wrote letters in protest to the secretary of defense, as well as to the secretary of state and the president's national security advisor. In one such letter, addressed to National Security Advisor John Poindexter—submitted by Representative Mel Levine (D-CA) and cosigned by seven other congressmen—it was emphasized that "if Israel is to consider alternatives to the Lavi, we believe it should do so of its own accord, and not through coercion. Israel has, thus far, displayed considerable prudence in its use of its FMS funds, and its freedom of choice has always been respected by the United States. We are strongly of the view that this principle should be maintained, both with respect to the Lavi project and to our broader relations with Israel."[16] These letters were purely a warning volley. As the senators and representatives intimated, Congress could take more drastic action if need be.

Congress was not the only branch of government to be appalled by Weinberger's tactics. Secretary of State Shultz was also disturbed by this chain of events and forwarded a memo to National Security Advisor John Poindexter requesting that the White House intervene and order the release of Lavi funds. A draft letter, which had been prepared by the NSC staff and awaited only the president's signature to bring it into legal force, was quietly passed along to Dov Zakheim. The letter would have directly ordered Weinberger to release the Lavi funds. Weinberger sent out word that he would relent and release the impounded funding.[17]

But Weinberger was not quite ready to comply fully, at least not yet. Instead, his office continued to order that the Lavi contracts be held up until the Israeli government agreed to be more "open" in its cooperation. Included in his demands were details connected with some of the Lavi subsystems then under development in Israel. The Israeli government promptly declined Weinberger's invitation.[18]

The issue of the Lavi subsystems, and in particular those elements relating to its mission capabilities and threat avoidance strategies, were particularly sensitive subjects in Israel. In the words of Israel's air force commander, Maj. Gen. Amos Lapidot, "Lavi is tailor made for the air force's needs and, since the Lavi's weapon systems and mission electronics will be largely Israeli made, they cannot be passed on to any Arab air forces, and therefore provide Israel with an ace card in any future combat situation."[19]

The Israelis had particular reason to be cautious regarding what information they might share with Weinberger. During the Lebanon War, after Israeli troops had surrounded the PLO leadership in West Beirut, the United States obtained private assurances that Israeli troops would not enter the city while the United States was negotiating the withdrawal of the PLO. Weinberger, without advising other members of President Reagan's staff, passed this information along to members of the Saudi royal family. The Saudis in turn passed the American assurances on to PLO leader Yasser Arafat, advising him to delay his withdrawal and demand better terms, safe in the knowledge that Israeli forces had promised not to enter the city.[20] The Israeli leadership was not about to make the same mistake again by sharing information with a defense secretary who had already demonstrated his affinity for the Arab monarchs.

It was no surprise that on the Lavi, as on other issues, Weinberger took a stance at odds with Israeli security concerns. What was more disturbing was that the secretary of defense felt free to disregard presidential policy and then—once threatened with presidential intervention—to lie about his intentions so that he could buy additional time to pursue his own agenda.

As staggering as this sorry chain of events was, it was not the first time that Caspar Weinberger had intentionally ignored a directive from his commander in chief. An example of this same behavior had occurred in November 1983, shortly after a suicide bomber had murdered 241 U.S. Marines in Beirut. The CIA had tracked responsibility for the bombing to a militia that was known to have been supported and trained by the Iranian Revolutionary Guards. At the urging of his national security advisor, President Reagan had ordered a retaliatory air strike on the Iranian command and training center, located in Lebanon's Bakaa Valley. The raid was scheduled to occur on November 16.

But the air strike never took place. Weinberger, who had never agreed with sending U.S. peacekeepers to Lebanon, called the raid off. As Weinberger would explain afterward, "I thought it was the wrong thing to do." As for President Reagan, the stunned commander in chief could only mutter, "I don't understand. Why didn't they do it? . . . We should have blown the daylights out of them. I just don't understand."[21] It was truly mind-boggling. The secretary of defense had refused to carry out a directive from his commander in chief. But there would be no bite behind the president's bark. President Reagan just couldn't bring himself to reprimand, much less dismiss, a longtime friend. The murder of American peacekeepers in Lebanon would go unpunished, and American credibility would remain tarnished. Weinberger knew that he would be free to reinterpret or even ignore presidential decisions with which he disagreed. The threat of presidential intervention was therefore not enough to persuade Weinberger to relent and release the Lavi contracts.

In August, however, word leaked out that Bob Kasten, chairman of the Senate Appropriations Subcommittee on Foreign Operations, was preparing an amendment that would have forced Weinberger to release Lavi funding. Unlike the president, the senator would not be swayed by old friendships. Faced with the prospect of congressional intervention, Weinberger at last relented and released the stalled Lavi contracts.[22] When the next budget proposal for military assistance came in September, the Senate Appropriations Committee took the unusual step of including an amendment to the fiscal 1987 foreign military sales budget, which included a stipulation requiring the Defense Department to release future Lavi funds once it was demonstrated that the contracts were legally valid.[23]

In the meantime, the official rollout ceremony for the Lavi had taken place as scheduled on July 21, with the formal unveiling of the first two prototypes at Ben Gurion International Airport. The number-one aircraft was still in its assembly-line coat of yellow primer, undergoing preflight tests. The second prototype, however, wore a full coat of paint, a gleaming blue-and-white warbird anxiously awaiting flight.

The official Lavi rollout ceremony was attended by a delegation of six members from the U.S. Congress. The six representatives and senators took full advantage of the photo opportunity to appear on camera and to point out the Lavi subcontracts that benefited suppliers in their districts. Among the more noteworthy speeches, however, was one by Representative Jack Kemp (R-NY)—who, it will be remembered, had cosponsored the bill approving the use of U.S. FMS credits for the aircraft: "The Lavi is the product of Israeli technical excellence in partnership with U.S. industry and financial support. Actually, the aircraft could have both the Star of David and the Stars and Stripes as its insignia. It is a joint venture in a very real sense with a number of American aerospace companies directly participating. . . . This is not a marriage of convenience. It is a union of spirit and purpose."[24]

Congressman Kemp had already realized what some in the American aerospace industry were only beginning to wake up to. Some 40 percent of the Lavi subsystems and components were under development in the United States and would almost certainly be manufactured in the United States during production. The Lavi truly was a "joint venture," incorporating both American and Israeli technology and American and Israeli funding. And while the Lavi could expect to find few, if any, export customers elsewhere, there was nothing to stand in the way of additional sales to the two partner nations. The Israeli engineers had unwittingly created an aircraft that threatened some of America's most wealthy corporations for the richest plumb of them all: sales to the U.S. Air Force.

IAI was then in the process of negotiating for a U.S.-based partner that could help market the Lavi in the United States and abroad. Talks were underway with both McDonnell Douglas and Grumman Corporation—and it would be Grumman, which was already expected to manufacture the first twenty Lavi wing and tail sets, that would finally sign a coproduction contract in September 1986.[25] The idea was that, should additional orders emerge, a second assembly line could be set up in the United States.

A second production line in the United States could also compete for U.S. Defense Department contracts. With 40 percent of the Lavi already expected to be manufactured in the United States, it would have been a simple matter to substitute American electronics and Grumman-produced fuselage components to bring the percentage manufactured in the United States up to 60 percent, 70 percent, or more. Such an arrangement would have been ideal for Grumman, which had recently lost their contract for the A-6F and which had no new fighter of their own. Such an arrangement would also have been a boost to Pratt & Whitney, which would have produced the engines. Such a joint Israeli-U.S. production arrangement, however, would also have been a potential threat to General Dynamics, the largest defense contractor of them all.

There was little if any chance of the Lavi competing against the F-15 or F-16 in the air superiority role. The Lavi was built as an attack jet first, with air superiority as a secondary role. Some IAI officials had suggested offering the Lavi as a replacement for the U.S. Air Force's T-38 supersonic trainer.[26] However, a replacement for the T-38 was not high on the air force's priority list. The United States was, however, searching for a new close air support and battlefield interdiction jet to replace 713 A-10 and 366 A-7 attack jets. It was in this role that the Lavi would have been best suited. Such a contract bid would also have placed the Lavi in direct competition with General Dynamics' proposed A-16—an F-16 with minor modifications—which was seen as the front-runner to replace the A-10.

The Lavi really wasn't a contender against the F-16, or any other U.S. aircraft, in any other role. It hadn't been built for landing on an aircraft carrier, and the U.S. Air Force tended to emphasize the air-to-air role over air-to-ground operations when selecting its multirole fighters. But as an attack aircraft, in terms of range, payload, and agility, the Lavi clearly had an edge. Only the far more expensive F-15E could have compared with the Lavi in terms of range and ordnance. Nor, for that matter, would an air force purchase of the Lavi have been the first U.S. buy of a foreign-built jet fighter. The U.S. Marine Corps had earlier purchased 102 AV-8A Harriers directly from the British manufacturer, with virtually no U.S. participation. Afterward, McDonnell Douglas had derived an improved version of the airplane, the AV-8B Harrier II. The initial batch of fighters, however, had been delivered with virtually no U.S. content. The Lavi, in contrast, already expected 40 percent of its components to be supplied by U.S. firms, a fraction that could easily have been raised. General Dynamics' anxieties, unlike Northrop's complaints years earlier, were legitimate. They stood to lose several hundred fighter sales to a Grumman-IAI alliance.

As early as October 1985, Pentagon newsletters were beginning to report that at least some Defense Department policy makers were considering the Lavi as a legitimate contender for the USAF's close air support role.[27] Although the Lavi's detractors dismissed these stories as having been "planted" by Israel's supporters, the truth was that the Lavi very much fit the bill of what the U.S. Air Force would need.

On July 31, 1986, Pratt & Whitney's PW1120 engine flew for the first time, aboard an Israeli F-4E Phantom. The airplane flew with one J79 engine and one PW1120, commencing the flight-test program for the proposed "Super Phantom" upgrade package as well as for the engine that would power the Lavi. It's initial assignment was to clear the flight envelope for the PW1120 up to 50,000 ft altitude.[28] The two Lavi prototypes, meanwhile, were undergoing preflight vibrations tests.

In October 1986 yet another new addition to the Lavi was announced: it was now expected to include a helmet-mounted sight and display as part of its production cockpit suite.[29] Two Israeli firms, Elbit and El Op, were then in the process of developing helmet-mounted displays and sights. Development of similar helmet-mounted displays and sights had been proposed before, but the majority of systems had been too large and heavy for use in a high-g fighter application. Most industry observers hadn't expected to see a practical helmet-mounted sight and display on a production fighter until the U.S. Advanced Tactical Fighter entered service a decade later. But the Israelis had already rewritten those plans. The Israeli systems allowed the pilot to lock his missiles onto a target simply by turning his head in the direction of his opponent. They could also display vital systems information directly onto the pilot's visor. Concurrently it was announced that a helmet-mounted sight and display system would also be included as part of the Phantom

2000 upgrade program and that a similar system was already being retrofitted to Israel's F-15 and F-16 fleet. The true magnitude that this addition represented would not dawn on the American aerospace community until half a decade later. Suffice it to say that, once again, the Israelis had redefined the state of the art.

It was also in October that Lear Siegler finally delivered the first set of flight control computers to Israel Aircraft Industries. The Lavi had already missed its target date for a first flight in September. As the Israeli crews worked frantically to install and test the flight control system, Zakheim's office was nearing completion of their alternatives study. The contract delays had cost the Lavi development team precious months.

It was December 31, 1986, when a small, blue-and-white warbird rolled onto the runway at Ben Gurion International Airport with IAI chief test pilot Lt. Col. (Res.) Menachem Shmul at the controls. The airplane was dwarfed beside the jumbo airliners that regularly flew in and out of the airport. But upon the wings of this tiny aircraft rested the hopes and dreams of Israel's aerospace industry and the future shape of its defense plans. A former combat pilot, Shmul had been only a junior officer flying the Mirage in Israel's 119th Squadron decades before, when he had become one of Israel's top four MiG killers during the Six-Day War.[30] His many years as a combat veteran and test pilot had provided him with experience in over forty different types of aircraft. On this day, as he pushed the throttle forward and sent the small airplane thundering down the runway, he was flying a warbird that was truly a breed apart.

In spite of all of the pressure from Caspar Weinberger and the apparatus at his disposal, in spite of all the delays, pressure tactics, and setbacks, at 1:21 that afternoon the Lavi took to the air for the first time. Menachem Shmul brought it up to 5,500 ft, performed a systems check, and then was cleared to bring the airplane up to 12,000 ft altitude and 260 knots airspeed. As an added precaution, the landing gear would remain extended throughout much of this maiden flight. Shmul gingerly brought the airplane through a series of lazy maneuvers, fielding its response. High above the ground, he ran through a sequence of simulated landing approaches, briefly retracting and extending the landing gear. They could afford no mistakes on a project that meant so much. The Lavi performed flawlessly.

Menachem Shmul brought the Lavi back to Ben Gurion International in a long, leisurely approach and landing. Touchdown went without a hitch. As he taxied to the hangar, he was greeted by a jubilant crowd that included everyone from the ground crew and technicians who had serviced the airplane to the many engineers who had designed it and the numerous government officials who had supported the effort. Climbing out of the cockpit, Shmul was doused in the water bath traditional for a first flight. The flight had lasted twenty-six minutes.[31] Despite all the controversy, and in defiance of the efforts of a defense secretary bent on its termination, Israel's winged lion had flown.

12. In the Ministry of Defense

A single test flight was no guarantee of success on the political battlefield. The Lavi would have to prove itself—showing both that IAI could recover from their schedule setbacks and that this airplane's worth went well beyond what any alternative might offer.

The first Lavi prototype, aircraft B-1, underwent its second flight test on January 8, 1987. This mission marked the first time that the landing gear was retracted at takeoff and landing, rather than at high altitude. The aircraft reached an altitude of 20,000 ft (6,100 m) and 300 knots (560 km/h) airspeed during the forty-five-minute flight test.[1] The Lavi continued to reward its proud parents for their years of preparation, delivering handling qualities that were every bit as stellar as had been promised. As the chief test pilot Menachem Shmul would later remark, "You know, the F-16 is a hard airplane to beat for handling qualities, but Lavi beats it. And even the most experienced pilots treat the F-16 with great respect when landing in only a 15 knot cross-wind. It gets very squirrely. But I landed the Lavi from its second flight in a 17 knot cross-wind, no problems. Steady as a rock."[2]

This latest flight test happened to coincide with yet another visit by Deputy Undersecretary Zakheim, who had launched the next phase in his lobbying campaign. Zakheim arrived in Israel on January 4 and spent the next week presenting the results of his alternatives study. The arrival of Weinberger's messenger was, of course, long anticipated. What might have come as a surprise however, was the selection of aircraft that his latest study cast as "alternatives" to the Lavi.[3]

The whole contention behind Zakheim's previous trips had been that the Lavi was too expensive and that cheaper alternatives already existed. Yet the study cited the F-15E, F/A-18, and AV-8B as potential substitutes—all aircraft that by any measure were vastly more expensive. In addition to these three aircraft, the study also proposed the F-16C and under its appendices added the F-20—rounding out an eclectic collection of "alternatives" with very little in common. The F-20 had been designed for the short-range, air-to-air role. As a substitute for a long-range attack aircraft, it was a nonstarter. The AV-8B, on the other hand, had been built around a vertical takeoff and landing requirement, compromising range, speed, and payload in the process. Why this airplane would ever have been included as a Lavi "alternative" was a mystery. As Zakheim would explain, "A fighter was a fighter was a fighter."[4] Once again, Zakheim betrayed his lack of technical acumen. Concepts of mission capability, much less aircraft survivability, never entered into his thoughts. By this line of thinking, one fighter was just as capable as another, the F-15 no more so than the F-20.

The one major concession that Zakheim did bring with him during his latest trip was an agreement that, henceforth, Israel would be designated by the Pentagon as a "strategic ally" and would be able to waive the research and development surcharges that had previously been paid. For the first time, Israel would be accorded the same purchasing privileges as NATO allies, Australia, and Japan.[5] This was a crucial concession. Without this agreement, the cost of purchasing American warplanes would have remained significantly greater, ensuring that none of the "alternatives" had any chance of being remotely cost-competitive. Cost quotes for each of the alternative aircraft were supplied by the manufacturers and included proposed work-share arrangements, under which some fraction of the airframe would have been produced in Israel. All of the quotes were made on the basis of a three-hundred-aircraft purchase.

Table 5. Proposed fighter alternatives

	Lavi	AV-8B	F-15E	F-16C	F/A-18
Flyaway price (millions)	$17.8	$21.4	$27.6	$16.9	$27.0
Length	47.80 ft	46.33 ft	63.75 ft	49.50 ft	56.00 ft
	14.57 m	14.12 m	19.43 m	15.09 m	17.07 m
Height	15.68 ft	11.65 ft	18.47 ft	16.60 ft	15.29 ft
	4.78 m	3.55 m	5.63 m	5.06 m	4.66 m
Span	28.81 ft	30.35 ft	42.81 ft	31.00 ft	34.50 ft
	8.78 m	9.25 m	13.05 m	9.45 m	10.52 m
Wing area	355.7 sq ft	230.0 sq ft	608.2 sq ft	300.0 sq ft	400.0 sq ft
	33.05 m^2	21.37 m^2	56.50 m^2	27.87 m^2	37.16 m^2
Internal fuel	6,000 lb	7,759 lb	13,123 lb	6,972 lb	10,860 lb
	2,720 kg	3,520 kg	5,950 kg	3,160 kg	4,930 kg
External fuel	9,180 lb	8,060 lb	21,645 lb	6,760 lb	6,732 lb
	4,160 kg	3,660 kg	9,820 kg	3,070 kg	3,050 kg
Empty weight	15,310 lb	13,086 lb	31,700 lb	19,100 lb	23,050 lb
	6,940 kg	5,940 kg	14,380 kg	8,660 kg	10,460 kg
Max takeoff weight	42,500 lb	31,000 lb	81,000 lb	42,300 lb	49,224 lb
	19,280 kg	14,060 kg	36,740 kg	19,190 kg	22,330 kg

	pw1120	f402-406	f100-220	f110-100	f404-400
Engine					
Engine thrust					
Afterburning	20,620 lb 91.7 kN	N/A	46,900 lb 208.6 kN	28,000 lb 124.5 kN	32,000 lb 142.3 kN
Military power	13,550 lb 60.3 kN	21,450 lb 95.4 kN	28,740 lb 127.8 kN	16,760 lb 74.5 kN	21,600 lb 96.1 kN
Number of hardpoints	15	7	17	9	9
Payload					
Maximum	>20,600 lb 9,340 kg	13,235 lb 6,000 kg	24,500 lb 11,110 kg	20,450 lb 9,280 kg	17,000 lb 7,710 kg
At max load factor	16,000 lb 7,260 kg	9,200 lb 4,170 kg	N/A	11,950 lb 5,420 kg	13,400 lb 6,080 kg
Maximum load factor	9.0 g	7.0 g	9.0 g	9.0 g	7.5 g
Maximum Mach speed					
At height	1.85	0.93	2.50	2.05	1.80
At sea level	1.20	0.89	1.20	1.20	1.0+
Combat radius					
Hi-lo-hi attack	1,200 nm 2,220 km	480 nm 890 km	1,080 nm 2,000 km	760 nm 1,410 km	575 nm 1,060 km
Air combat	1,000 nm 1,850 km	627 nm 1,160 km	N/A	N/A	400 nm 740 km

Of the options described in the study, only the F-16c came in at a price lower than that of the Lavi, and it was on this aircraft that the majority of attention was focused. Not accounted for in Zakheim's study, of course, was the fact that the cost of modifying the F-16 to fully meet Israeli strike-fighter requirements would have been prohibitive. What the study considered instead was the unit flyaway price for an F-16c in the Peace Marble 2 configuration—the variant under Israel's most recent F-16 order. This cost was quoted as being $14.6 million per airplane, once the usual "research and development" surcharges were waived. This price also assumed that elements of the airplane would be manufactured in Israel, to help contain production costs.

The Peace Marble 2 configuration did incorporate Israeli electronics and was promoted during this lobbying campaign as being "specially tailored" to Israeli needs. What was not clearly stated was that the Peace Marble 2 aircraft had been configured with the attack mission as its secondary, not primary, role. The price tag for an F-16c carrying an avionics suite derived from the Lavi, on the other hand, was estimated by the U.S. Air Force at $16.9 million per airplane on a three-hundred-aircraft purchase.[6] This would also have meant hanging much of the electronic warfare suite externally, on the airplane's pylons. The F-16 had, after all, never been meant to carry such a quantity of electronics gear.

Unlike the Lavi, which carried much of its fuel in the wings, the F-16 had to rely on fuselage space to achieve its fuel volume. This robbed the F-16 of valuable real estate that the Lavi could put to use for additional electronics gear. Integrating the Lavi electronics, and in particular the electronic countermeasures, into an airframe that had not been designed for them would have been a difficult and expensive task. Hanging them on pylons, on the other hand, not only would mean tying up hardpoints otherwise available for weapons but also would have degraded the airplane's agility over the battlefield.

Israel's earlier raid on Iraq's Osirak nuclear reactor, it should be recalled, had been at the extreme limit of the F-16's range. To make this mission possible, the Israelis had exceeded the airplane's recommended takeoff weight and had also stripped the airplanes of all but the most essential electronics gear. This included removal of the electronic countermeasures suite. The Israeli fighters that had staged the raid on Osirak had flown to and from the target effectively naked, with only the element of surprise and a pair of covering F-15s fitted with jamming gear to shield them from the enemy.[7] It had been a gutsy move, driven by desperation, but it was hardly a suitable alternative for a wartime scenario. The Israelis needed an attack warplane with equivalent or better range, without having to strip it of the very electronics gear that could give it a fighting chance of survival.

The off-the-shelf F-16C didn't have the range or payload to replace the Lavi. Of the other candidates proposed under the study, only the F-15E, the most expensive option of them all, was capable of matching the Lavi in terms of payload and range. There was just no equivalent to the Lavi short of starting over again with the redesign of an existing airframe for the attack role. That, of course, would have been even more expensive than completing development of the Lavi.

What was missing from the alternatives report submitted by Zakheim's team was a cost-benefit trade study comparing the mission capabilities of the Lavi to an equivalent mix of off-the-shelf fighters. As Israeli purchasing patterns had already suggested, the most advantageous mix would have derived from a combination of F-15 and F-16 aircraft. Comparing the purchase price for 300 Lavi fighters for example, to a similar purchase of 40 F-15ES and 260 F-16CS, the projected flyaway cost for the fleet of Lavi aircraft would have come in at $340 million less than the cost for the U.S.-built fighters.[8] Moreover, evaluating this alternative airplane purchase on the basis of attack capability over a hostile battlefield, the conclusion can be reached that a fleet of three hundred Lavi fighters would be capable of delivering the same bomb load with 20 percent fewer sorties.[9] On a three-hundred-airplane purchase, the Lavi was the more cost-effective alternative, as well as the most capable attack platform. All of this was lost, however, in the "alternatives" study that Zakheim was peddling. As Lavi chief test pilot Menachem

Shmul commented shortly after the report was released, "I know nothing about politics. Zakheim knows nothing about planes."[10]

Part of the reason that the DoD study had fallen so far short in assessing Israel's strategic needs lay in the fact that preserving Israel's qualitative edge had never been part of the mandate for the Defense Department team. They had been charged with the goal of "terminating" the Lavi. When Dov Zakheim had presented a summary of the alternatives study to Weinberger that past December, the defense secretary had at no time expressed interest in whether the alternatives would satisfy Israeli strategic objectives. As Zakheim himself testified years later, Weinberger's one area of concern had been, "What will the Saudis think?" He had been more worried that the Saudis might be offended than in ensuring that a crucial U.S. ally was capable of repelling another round of aggression. Weinberger became satisfied only when he was assured that none of the proposed alternatives would "radically upgrade" the capabilities of the Israeli air force.[11]

Table 6. Idealized cost and payload trade study on a 300-aircraft purchase

	Lavi	F-15E	F-16C
Flyaway price (millions)	$17.8	$31.1	$17.1
Payload (lb), at max load factor	16,000	20,000	11,950
Quantity	300	40	260
Total cost (millions)	$5,340	$5,681	
Sorties to deliver 100 million lb	20.83	25.60	

Zakheim began this latest round in his lobbying campaign in Israel with a trip to the offices of the Israeli defense minister, Yitzhak Rabin. Zakheim was accompanied on these outings by U.S. ambassador Thomas Pickering, who this time brought with him two identical letters: one addressed to Defense Minister Rabin and the other to Prime Minister Yitzhak Shamir. The letters called on the Israeli government to give the alternatives study serious consideration and were signed, respectively, by Defense Secretary Weinberger and Secretary of State Shultz.[12] Following their briefing with Rabin, the DoD team met with Foreign Minister Shimon Peres and later still with the new finance minister, Moshe Nissim. Like his pre-decessor, Nissim was a member of the Liberal Party, which had merged with Herut to form the Likud. Also much like his prede-cessor in the Finance Ministry, Nissim was concerned regarding the burden of defense spending on the Israeli economy. Finally, Zakheim concluded his rounds in Israel with briefings to Ezer Weizman, Prime Minister Yitzhak Shamir, and finally to Knesset Finance Committee chairman Avraham Schapira. A member of Israel's ultraorthodox community and part of the Agudath Israel religious party, Schapira was not unsympathetic to calls for can-celing the Lavi program. For many in Israel's orthodox religious parties, defense expenditures took a secondary priority, behind the social programs that benefited their communities.

The majority of the ministers, their deputies, and the legisla-tive leaders that Zakheim dealt with had long ago staked out their stance in relation to the Lavi program. The Israeli Defense Minis-try continued to be divided on the issue. But even the support of the chief of staff and air force commander was now tempered by the realization that the Lavi program was not untouchable. As air force commander Maj. Gen. Amos Lapidot acknowledged late in January, "I love the Lavi, but can live without it."[13] For a man who had once described the Lavi as "vital" to Israel's national security, this was a painful admission.[14]

The real issue, as many in Israel were aware, was not whether the Lavi compared favorably on a purchase of three hundred fight-ers, but whether a purchase of three hundred new aircraft was even in the cards. The Israeli defense budget could not main-tain the rates of growth seen during the 1970s and early 1980s. And on a purchase of 150 aircraft or less, the cost-effectiveness of the Lavi began to rapidly erode. It may still have been the more capable attack platform, but it was more sensitive to a cut in its production rates than were its American counterparts, which already had hundreds, or even thousands, of orders behind each airframe. If the press reports are to be believed, it was at this juncture that the commitment of Defense Minister Rabin first began to waiver.[15]

The Lavi alternatives study continued to stir controversy in the month following Zakheim's visit to Israel. As was to be expected on an issue on which so much was at stake, the debate was oftentimes heated, even personal. The air force's program director, in particular, had taken offense at these intrusions into what was ostensibly an Israeli issue. Eini described the study as being "a bit fantastic" and "a sloppy job." On February 26, however, his remarks turned to the principal author behind the study. The fact that Zakheim not only was campaigning against the Lavi but had even attempted to enlist the support of Israel's ultraorthodox religious parties in his effort had particularly galled Eini. Here was an American orthodox Jew, who had never served in Israel's armed forces, attempting to enlist the support of Israel's ultraorthodox religious community, whose members likewise had never served in Israel's armed forces. All this in the name of a campaign to cancel Israel's largest defense program. In one interview, Eini went so far as to describe Dov Zakheim as a "*kipah*-wearing religious Jew, who claims to be motivated by love of Israel, [but who] is in fact causing tremendous damage."[16]

In that moment of indiscretion, the sharp-tempered Eini crossed a line between what might be interpreted as legitimate debate and personal attack. Eini's reference to Zakheim's religious observance would unleash a wave of criticism from throughout Israel's orthodox community, as well as from the orthodox community in the United States. Had Eini been a politician rather than a representative of the Defense Ministry, his remarks probably would have been chalked up as one more ugly political exchange. As a ministry official, however, his remarks were unacceptable. Within a day, Defense Minister Rabin would insist that Eini issue an apology. Months later, again at Rabin's insistence, Menachem Eini would apologize once more, this time personally to Dov Zakheim.

Years of individual careers had gone into the Lavi, and deeply held convictions were coming into play. The debate over Lavi production had come to involve a volatile mixture of national pride and aspirations, mixed together with the ongoing debate over Israel's religious-secular divide. The political battle for the Lavi was sure to turn yet more vicious before it was over.

The second Lavi prototype, aircraft B-2, took to the air for the first time on March 30, 1987. It reached a top speed of 350 knots (650 km/h) and an altitude of 20,000 ft (6,100 m) on its maiden flight. In an unexpected turn of events, it flew for the first time with the very same engine that the first prototype had used in its own maiden flight. The engine had been damaged by ingestion of a foreign object and had been removed for repair before being reinstalled into the second airplane. Among other things, the second prototype had set out to evaluate the airplane's midair refueling system and had been painted with the visual cue markings necessary for the receptacle-and-boom in-flight refueling system commonly used in the U.S. Air Force. Unlike the U.S. Air Force, however, Israel also flew a number of aircraft that employed the probe-and-drogue flight refueling system, which was commonly used by aircraft in the U.S. Navy. The Israeli developers had consequently come up with a detachable refueling probe for the Lavi, allowing them to maintain the use of their existing midair refueling fleet and allowing the Lavi to employ both types of refueling systems.[17]

By the time that the second prototype flew, the first prototype had already undergone a total of twenty-three flights, verifying the flight envelope up to Mach 0.75 and an altitude of up to 43,000 ft (13,100 m). The Lavi was well on its way in a flight-test program expected to total some 1,800 flights between the five flying prototypes.[18]

This early segment of the flight-test program was particularly critical for validating the flight control system. For an aircraft like the Lavi, which relied on its flight control software to keep the airplane flying, there would be two flight regimes of particular concern: low-speed handling at takeoff and landing—where "ground effects" could radically alter behavior—and transonic flight. Takeoff and landing always offered tricky flight conditions, and many experimental aircraft have met tragic ends in this low-altitude regime, including an early prototype of the Swedish JAS-39 Gripen, as well as America's own YF-22. The other region of concern would have been the transonic flight regime, where an airplane can experience significant changes in its control behavior as it approaches Mach 1. Both of these flight conditions were therefore treated by the Lavi flight crew with great respect as they went through the process of fine-tuning the fighter's control laws. It was discovered, for example, that the Lavi's elevons were 20–30 percent more efficient in practice than had been predicted. Adjustments would thereafter be made to the software for the third prototype, which was also expected to employ the revised wing design with additional control surfaces. The prototypes also experienced a pitch-up tendency as they decelerated through Mach 1, from supersonic to subsonic flight—a phenomenon known as "Mach tuck." This behavior was not uncommon among supersonic aircraft and had been predicted in preflight simulations. However, the development team needed actual flight-test data to fine-tune the behavior.[19]

But even while the flight-test program was accumulating hours, pressure to kill the program continued to mount. Israel's defense budget had experienced another $66 million in cuts in 1986. As part of these and earlier cost-saving measures, Israel's standing army had been reduced by over six thousand personnel over the course of a year.[20] The Lavi continued to play a divisive role within Israel's military. By March 1987 the IDF's general staff had evaluated at least one proposal to scrap the program altogether.[21] There was no denying that the Lavi was the best airplane for the job. In spite of the report assembled by Zakheim's staff, there was no one-for-one equivalent for the Lavi within financial reach. As one Israeli F-16 wing commander explained it, "I love the F-16, but the Lavi is the aircraft I really want. Knowing the F-16 and knowing the Lavi, our aircraft is better suited for us, and only this must be the ultimate consideration."[22] It was the opposing view, however—that cost and not performance should decide the future of Israel's air force—that was beginning to gain traction.

In April 1987 Israel's military high command underwent a change in leadership. Lt. Gen. Dan Shomron, who had earlier voiced his reservations concerning the price tag for procuring three hundred new fighters, became the IDF's new chief of staff. The post of deputy chief of staff went to Maj. Gen. Ehud Barak, who had likewise questioned the resources being devoted. In addition, it was only a matter of weeks before Brig. Gen. Avihu Ben-Nun was expected to take the helm as Israel's new air force commander. Ben-Nun remained, as ever, a critic of the Lavi.[23] The messages that Defense Minister Rabin was hearing from Israel's military leadership had turned from a mix of praise and apprehension to sharp criticism of the Lavi's costs.

The Israeli military was faced not only with the budget cuts being made in Israel but also with budget cuts being made in the United States. The amount of aid provided by the United States to Israel had remained at a steady level since 1986.[24] Further, under the Gramm-Rudman Deficit Reduction Act of 1985, Israel had returned $77 million out of the amount approved for fiscal year 1987, as part of measures aimed at balancing the U.S. budget.[25] By the late 1980s, nearly a third of Israel's defense budget came in the form of U.S. security assistance.[26] Israel had several weapons and modernization programs beyond the Lavi that would also demand significant financial resources. The cost of constructing four Saar 5 missile corvettes alone was estimated at over $600 million.[27] Add to that the cost of three new submarines and the hundreds of Merkava main battle tanks that were needed to replenish Israel's aging fleet, and the Lavi program simply could not be allowed to surpass its targeted spending cap of $550 million per year.

Table 7. U.S. security assistance to Israel, 1983–87 (in millions of dollars)

| Fiscal year | Total assistance* | | Lavi funding | |
	Loans	Grants	In United States	In Israel
1983	950	750	**	**
1984	850	850	300	250
1985	N/A	1,400	150	250
1986	N/A	1,800	150	300
1987	N/A	1,800	150	300

Notes: * Includes funding for the Lavi. ** Approval was also granted to apply funding allocated for fiscal year 1984, to cover Lavi expenses from prior years.

In May the Lavi controversy again flared up on Israel's political landscape. It was time to begin making budget decisions for Israel's 1988 fiscal year and to decide whether to sign the first Lavi production contracts. The paperwork for the initial production orders was already being drawn up. But when the issue of Lavi funding came up this time, facing growing apprehension from within Israel's general staff, Defense Minister Rabin proposed that the program be canceled. Instead, he advocated the purchase of an F-16 variant, fitted with Lavi avionics, as the only option within Israel's financial reach.

Despite whatever misgivings he may once have held regarding the program, Rabin had remained an advocate for the Lavi as long as Israel's general staff had supported it. Ever since the option of license producing the F-16 in Israel had been ruled out, and for as long as Israel's military leadership had continued to support the development of a dedicated attack jet, Rabin had been content to follow their recommendations. But Israel's military high command was changing hands, and the new leadership was unwilling to continue Lavi development if it came at the expense of other needs. As the defense minister explained at the time, "With the limits of the budget, it is impossible to go ahead with Lavi development. So, the government has to make a decision with a price tag on it. The Lavi is tailor-made for Israel, the F-16C is not."[28]

By June, the two Lavi prototypes had accumulated over forty flight hours, reaching a maximum speed of Mach 0.9 and a peak altitude of 43,000 ft (13,100 m). The maximum angle of attack had been validated in flight test to 23°. In addition, between 60 and 70 percent of the production drawings had been finalized and released by IAI's manufacturing division, and assembly of the third prototype was well underway. The latter airplane was targeted for a first flight in early 1988.[29] A race was on, between those who wanted to halt the program and those who wanted to carry it too far for it ever to be stopped.

In July Rabin paid a visit to Washington in an effort to win additional concessions from the Weinberger Defense Department, in return for an Israeli agreement to cancel the Lavi. Although Rabin had already agreed in principle to scrap the program, he was virtually alone in the Cabinet. Even his own party's leadership was against him on this issue. Rabin needed to bring back something that might persuade his fellow Labor Party members to come around to his point of view.

Canceling the Lavi's subcontracts would cost anywhere from $400 to $800 million and would mean laying off most of the four thousand employees then working on the program at IAI. With a total of over twenty thousand employees, Israel Aircraft Industries was not only Israel's largest defense contractor but also Israel's largest corporate employer. Those four thousand employees represented a skilled labor pool that would largely be lost if the program was canceled. There would not be enough jobs within Israel's aerospace sector to support them. Rabin argued that it would be an undesirable but necessary sacrifice, pointing out that at other Israeli defense contractors, such as Israel Military Industries, between 15 and 20 percent of the workforce had already been laid off. Nationwide, seven thousand Israeli defense industry workers had lost their jobs in the previous two years alone.[30] This, of course, did little to console IAI or its employees. Selling additional job cuts to his own Labor Party would be an uphill battle. It was therefore essential that Rabin bring something home from his visit.

Weinberger's offices did agree to some of Rabin's requests, including an increase in the amount of military aid that could be spent in Israel, raising the total from the $300 million under the Lavi program to $400 million in the years immediately following cancellation. They also agreed to extend the ongoing program for $150 million in directed offsets for two more years, until 1990. Under the "directed offsets" system U.S. manufacturers were required to maintain a certain minimum value of Israeli-made components in the weapons that they sold to Israel. Unlike most major recipients of U.S. arms, the Israelis did not license produce the weapons locally. Whereas F-16 customers in Europe, Turkey, or Korea, for example, had set up local assembly lines, the Israelis continued to take delivery from the U.S. assembly floor. The directed offsets system was therefore a substitute for local production and was a minimum requirement that Rabin would have to secure if he expected to convince fellow members in the Labor Alignment to vote in favor of canceling the Lavi. In addition, there was agreement that the Pentagon would allow the military aid allocated to Israel to be used to cover expenses associated with canceling the Lavi contracts.[31] Combined, these measures provided Rabin with at least a minimal package of incentives with which to entice his fellow Labor Party members.

However, no commitment was made in the area of providing Israel's aerospace industry with additional programs to minimize the number of workers laid off. Defense Minister Rabin had been looking for U.S. support for the development of the Arrow antitactical ballistic missile system, and he had also hoped that there might be an opportunity for some level of involvement in the U.S. Air Force's Advanced Tactical Fighter program. He received none of these.[32]

During his trip, the Israeli defense minister also expressed an interest in soliciting detailed quotes for a purchase of seventy-five to one hundred off-the-shelf F-16s, to help fill in near-term gaps in Israel's order of battle. The total cost of the aircraft buy was estimated to be $2.4 billion, with first deliveries to begin in 1991.[33] His willingness to accept off-the-shelf airplanes, with minimal effort to substantively improve their air-to-ground performance, confirmed that Israel's incoming air force chief was more interested in receiving aircraft as soon as possible than in whether the aircraft could fill the gap left by the Lavi.

Table 8. Idealized cost and payload trade study on a 150-aircraft purchase

	Lavi	F-15E	F-16C
Flyaway price (millions)	$27.8	$31.3	$17.5
Payload (lb), at max load factor	16,000	20,000	11,950
Quantity	150	25	160
Total cost (millions)	$4,172	$3,583	
Sorties to deliver 100 million lb	41.67	41.46	

Rabin's willingness to settle for only seventy-five to one hundred new airplanes was also the clearest public admission to date regarding the real problem that the Lavi faced: Israel just couldn't afford three hundred new fighters. Not by 1995, and not even by the end of the century. Although the Lavi was the most cost-effective alternative on a buy of 300 aircraft, when the production lot dropped to 150 aircraft or less, that advantage eroded away. In April 1987 the Defense Ministry published a study concluding that on a purchase of 150 aircraft, the Lavi unit price would grow to be 46 to 56 percent greater than the cost for an off-the-shelf F-16c.[34] The American airframe already had over two thousand orders behind it. The Lavi did not. Examining these expenses under a simplified, cost-benefit trade study, the cost of buying 25 F-15ES and 160 F-16cs would come out to roughly $590 million less than an equivalent Lavi purchase of 150 aircraft—after taking into account the lot sizes involved. Moreover, on a purchase of this reduced scale, similar payload capabilities could be obtained by buying the appropriate mix of American fighters. The American aircraft still could not have fully matched the Lavi's capabilities. But looked at in terms purely of payload capacity and cost, a mix of American-made fighters offered a superior alternative.

It had been a painful day of reckoning for many in Israel's defense establishment. However flawed the studies produced by Zakheim's team might have been, there were legitimate reasons to be concerned with the cost of the Lavi program. The Israeli defense minister had been faced with the choice of going ahead with the Lavi, fighting Weinberger's disapproval, and facing the possibility of having to cut back Israel's naval and armored corps modernization plans, or with accepting a smaller, less capable aircraft buy. Ultimately, concerns over cost had won out. At least, that is, in the Ministry of Defense.

13. Broken Wings

Concessions or not, Defense Minister Rabin still faced the daunting task of selling his Lavi cancellation package to the Israeli Cabinet. Yitzhak Rabin could count on the support of only two Cabinet members in his bid to cancel the program: Minister Without Portfolio Ezer Weizman and Finance Minister Moshe Nissim. Nissim, like his predecessor, saw the Lavi as a potential budget buster. In public statements, he estimated that continuing the Lavi program could add up to $2,000 to the tax burden of each Israeli citizen during the next decade.[1] Nissim's, however, was a lone voice from the Likud side of the aisle. The rest of the Likud Party remained firm in their commitment to the program. Even Yitzhak Modai, who had opposed the Lavi during his own term as finance minister, now proposed that the program be allowed to proceed on a reduced scale.

Moreover, Rabin could not even count on the support of his own party on this issue. Once he had been at the head of the Labor Alignment. But those days were long since gone, and Shimon Peres, foreign minister in the National Unity Government, had superseded Rabin as the Labor Party leader. The rivalry between Peres and Rabin was decades old. The two had first clashed in 1960, when, as deputy chief of staff, Rabin had first challenged Peres, who was then deputy minister of defense, over control of Israel's defense budget.

Rabin and Peres would clash again in the months following the 1973 Yom Kippur War, when both men would claim to be the rightful successor for the leadership of the Labor Party. Rabin had won that round, but only narrowly. Peres would remain in the upper echelons of the Labor Party, waiting for his chance to pounce on Rabin's missteps. That opportunity would ultimately present itself, but not before a number of embarrassing leaks were made to the press—leaks for which Rabin would place the blame squarely on the shoulders of Peres.[2] It would be difficult for Rabin to convince Peres to cancel the Lavi, based on the merit of his own convictions alone.

Peres had established himself early on as a vocal supporter of the Lavi program. The program had become far more than just another defense project. It had become a symbol of Israeli technical excellence and pride: proof that Israel, a nation the size of the state of New Jersey, could produce an achievement on par with some of the largest industrial powers in the world. It had also become the largest research and development program in Israel's history. Shimon Peres had himself compared it to the American space program, describing it as a research effort capable of hurtling Israel's high-tech industries into the twenty-first century. And he wasn't far off in his comparison. Viewed in terms of its percentage of Israel's gross national product, the Lavi program was a more monumental undertaking for a small nation like Israel than the moon shots of the 1960s had been for the United States.

The issue of whether to continue the Lavi had become politically charged. A poll conducted in August 1987 had reported that 43.5 percent of the Israeli public favored continuing the Lavi as planned, while 19.6 percent favored continuing at a reduced scale, and only 27.6 percent were in favor of canceling the program. In spite of Rabin's best efforts and his trip to Washington to obtain concessions that might make the project's termination a little more palatable, a vote by Israel's Cabinet to decide on whether to go forward with the Lavi was postponed eight times between May and August 1987.[3]

Caspar Weinberger's Lavi termination team had, however, finally made some headway. Rabin was a valuable ally. Focus now began to shift from a broader lobbying effort toward a more focused campaign. If they could convince Peres in addition to Rabin, then the entire Labor Alignment would fall into line. Moreover, ever since the first fissures had appeared, suggesting that momentum might be shifting, the State Department's Near East Bureau and embassy staff had been able to operate more openly. Success begets success, and what had begun as a rogue operation—stalling contracts and impounding funds in direct contradiction to stated administration policies—could now be performed in the open, with an air of legitimacy. Once Israel's own defense minister had come out in favor of terminating the program, it was difficult to envision anyone in Washington standing in Weinberger's way.

On August 9 the Knesset Foreign Affairs and Defense Committee passed a nonbinding resolution calling for the continuation of the Lavi program. In response, the U.S. State Department took the unusual step of criticizing a vote by a democratically elected legislature and publicly urged the Israeli government to cancel the project.[4] There would be no personal intervention by Moshe Arens this time, no one calling the secretary of state to clear up discrepancies between stated administration policy, as set forth by the president only a few years before, and the manner in which policy was being carried out.

Yet despite the months of debate on the subject, no resolution to the Lavi controversy appeared to be in sight. The majority of Israel's Cabinet remained publicly committed to the program. And Weinberger was becoming impatient. Unable to convince Israel's leadership of the financial merits of canceling the program, Weinberger began instead to leak thinly veiled threats, intimating that, should the Lavi program continue, his office would seek to delay or undermine every other U.S.-Israeli joint effort within his reach. Press reports began to surface detailing how Weinberger's staff was preparing plans to sabotage joint weapons programs ranging from the Arrow ballistic missile defense system to cooperative research in tank armor and radar warning systems for aircraft.[5] Using precisely the same tools of bureaucratic delay and obstruction that his team had previously used to hobble the Lavi, Weinberger was now threatening to retaliate against all U.S.-Israeli weapons programs.

On the night of August 30, with another vote on the Lavi due any day, Ambassador Thomas Pickering delivered a letter to Shimon Peres, urging the Labor Party leader to cancel the program. The letter had been drafted by the State Department's Near East Bureau and had been signed by President Reagan himself.[6]

How much this letter might have been reviewed and scrutinized by other members of the White House and Cabinet may never be known. Certainly Shimon Peres would have been asking these same questions as he read the letter before him. At the time that the letter was written, the White House was still reeling from the Iran-Contra controversy: yet another example of a rogue operation that had gone badly awry. Secretary of State Shultz, among others, had been called to provide testimony before Congress in hearings that stretched from May 5 through August 6. Given the events taking place at the time, Shultz and the leading members of the president's staff would have been heavily distracted. How much scrutiny this particular letter might have received would forever remain unclear.

Peres faced a difficult decision. There was no question that the Lavi was the best airplane for the role. But there was also no doubt that Israel would have to cut its fighter purchases, certainly to no more than 120 new warplanes by the middle of the next decade, regardless of which airplane was selected. Terminating the Lavi would have been a severe blow to an Israeli aerospace industry already reeling from cuts in other programs. Bet Shemesh Engines, the company that was expected to assemble the PW1120 powerplant for the Lavi, was on the verge of bankruptcy and had laid off 569 out of its 1,275 workers. The company had been facing threats of a pullout by Pratt & Whitney, which still owned a 42 percent interest. To head off catastrophe, the Israeli government had recently agreed to sell its own 58 percent share to a private investor and to write off $93 million in company debt. Terminating the Lavi could further cripple the company's chances for survival.[7] Other Israeli firms were equally at risk. But a decision had to be made soon. IAI was awaiting final approval for the production contracts. The papers had already been drawn up and, once they were approved for production, there would be no turning back. The costs of canceling a production contract would rule out termination.

Further reinforcement of the anti-Lavi atmosphere was provided by the summary of purchase options, as presented to the Cabinet by the Ministry of Defense. Rather than having the current head of the Israeli air force lay out the available options, Rabin had instead directed that Brig. Gen. Avihu Ben Nun should be the one to provide the summary. Ben Nun presented the Cabinet with the costs for a truncated production run of a mere eighty Lavi fighters—further inflating the unit price of the aircraft. Options for stretching out the Lavi production run, to perhaps 150 fighters or more across the next two decades, were never discussed.[8]

The combination of opposition to the program from the Weinberger Defense Department, misgivings from Israel's own military leadership, and now an apparent reversal in U.S. presidential policy was ultimately too much. On the day following Ben Nun's presentation to the Cabinet, August 31, 1987, Shimon Peres—a man who had helped to found Israel Aircraft Industries—himself offered up the motion to terminate the program. The final vote was twelve in favor of cancellation and eleven opposed, with one abstention. The vote had followed party lines, with the Labor Party and its allies voting in favor of cancellation and the Likud against. Finance Minister Moshe Nissim was the one Likud defector to vote against the airplane, and Labor's minister of health, Shoshana Arbeli-Almoslino, who had earlier threatened to vote against her own party on this subject, was the one abstention.[9] The Lavi had been officially scrapped.

Finance Minister Nissim declared, "This is a sad day. We took a painful decision. But knowing the situation as I do as Finance Minister, I want to say that this was the decision that had to be made." Minister of Industry Ariel Sharon described the move as "another example of weakness" on the part of the Labor Party.[10]

The public reaction was swift, and far less profound. IAI employees staged angry demonstrations, at one point breaking down a fence at Ben Gurion International Airport, where IAI's manufacturing plant was located, and blocking access to a runway. The demonstrations in Tel Aviv, meanwhile, lasted for three days. In Jerusalem, protesters brought coffins bearing the names "Rabin" and "Peres" to the Western Wall, and only police intervention prevented them from carrying a half-scale model of the Lavi right up to the site of prayer.

One of the few industry voices to come out in support of the government's decision was Al Schwimmer, one of the early founders of IAI: "If we were to get 80 or 90 Lavis, they would contribute nothing to our defense capabilities, and a production run of 80 or 90 aircraft is nothing at all. . . . It's competing with the F-16, of which 3,000 or so will be sold, and even if it were a better aircraft, it's too late. The market for this generation of aircraft is over, and the next generation is going to be a very different type of aircraft." He instead advocated that $100 million per year be set aside to fund the development of a "next-generation" fighter. "Within six or seven years we could have an aircraft that would be in front of the buying cycle rather than behind it. The Israeli air force could support it with a purchase of 250 or 300 aircraft, and we could start to look for export customers."[11]

The vast majority of Israel's aviation officials, however, did not share Schwimmer's enthusiasm. The problem was not that the Heyl Ha'Avir didn't want three hundred aircraft, but that they couldn't afford them. And any future Israeli fighter, even provided that it somehow avoided U.S. involvement and export restrictions, would face the same hurdles in the export market that the Lavi had faced.

The other reason that most Israeli officials disagreed with Al Schwimmer's rosy outlook was that canceling the Lavi was sure to deal a crippling blow to Israel's aerospace industry. Those 4,000 IAI employees whose jobs were threatened included some 1,500 engineers. As IAI president Moshe Keret put it, "The 4,000, most of whom will probably have to go, represents about one one-thousandth of our total population. For the U.S. to have a layoff of such magnitude, more than 220,000 aerospace workers would have to be laid off."[12] IAI engineer Rafi Meir put it even more directly: "The decision closed down aeronautic development in Israel for the next 25 years. For people like us, the alternative employment they will offer us here is not on our level. The decision was taken in a shameful way, a political way, an end-of-the-season sale."[13]

Nor was IAI the only one to be hit. Besides the various Israeli subcontractors, 736 U.S. firms had once held contracts for the Lavi, totaling $750 million in research and development contracts and $4.86 billion in unsigned contracts for production.[14]

Within the Israeli government, the most severe response came from Moshe Arens. The man who had pushed hardest to see the Lavi underway, and who had been instrumental in its evolution from a modest A-4 replacement into the most potent strike fighter of its day, responded with the only form of protest left open to him: on September 2, Arens resigned from the Israeli Cabinet. "The decision to kill the Lavi was a wrong decision, with negative implications," he announced on his departure. "It hurts the best people in the country."[15] An era was over.

At the time of cancellation, the two Lavi prototypes had flown just over one hundred hours in a total of eighty-two flights, opening the flight envelope up to a maximum speed of Mach 1.45 at 41,000 ft and to 540 knots calibrated airspeed at 10,000 ft altitude. Prototype B-1 had been removed from flight status on July 1 to undergo the modifications necessary for installation of the new, redesigned wing and was to have flown with the new wing for the first time in late February or early March of the following year. The qualitative test versions of the PW1120 had been delivered one week prior to the project's termination, together with a total of ten flight control computers from Lear Siegler, seven of which had already been certified as flightworthy. Another two computers were still under assembly when the announcement came through. IAI's long lead-time manufacture for the first production fighters had begun in October 1986, and roughly two hundred employees were already assigned to the airplane's production phase when the program was canceled that August. A total of fifty pilots had been selected and trained to fly the Lavi, with assembly of the first production fighter to have begun in January 1988.[16]

As part of the termination package, Israel Aircraft Industries was expected to receive $100 million per year to continue development of the Lavi avionics systems, for application to other projects. It was estimated that a total of $200–300 million would be needed to complete the development of the airplane's avionics subsystems. In the meantime, Defense Minister Rabin announced a plan to purchase ninety off-the-shelf F-16cs to fill immediate gaps in Israel's force structure.[17]

Israel Aircraft Industries proposed a reduced flight-test program to gain as much data as possible from the aircraft. The proposal would have covered test flights for another two to three years, aimed at flight testing of the first prototype with the new wings, an updated flight control computer, and the full avionics system, plus an additional ten to fifteen flights by the second prototype to open up the airplane's flight envelope. This, however, was strictly a flight-test program and could in no way offer hope to salvage the company's manufacturing capability. In the words of IAI's Lavi project manager, Ovadia Harrari, "Within two or three months at the most, the development team will disperse, either to other industries or to aerospace companies in other countries. After that, there is no way we could reconstitute the team."[18]

Israeli engineers and technicians had already begun shopping around for other jobs. There were reports that some would leave for work in Canadian firms, while others were hired to work on Mirage upgrade programs for the South African government.[19]

In September the Israeli government rejected IAI's proposed flight-test program but did approve $25 million to finish construction of the third Lavi prototype, which was already nearly complete. The plan was to use the aircraft to demonstrate the core avionics package, with additional funding expected to follow. The $25 million would allow IAI to retain three hundred out of the four thousand employees connected with the Lavi program through the end of March 1988, and it would also allow them to retain another three hundred Lavi employees at various subcontractors. The first flight of the third prototype was set for February 1989.[20]

In March 1988 Israel Aircraft Industries made one last attempt to resurrect the Lavi program, formally proposing the airplane to the U.S. Air Force as a candidate close air support fighter to replace A-7 and A-10 fighters.[21] However, with the flight-test program grounded and with no Israeli orders for the airplane, it was too little, too late. In all subsequent air force discussions on candidate CAS aircraft, the Lavi was never mentioned as a contender.

The cancellation of the Lavi, however, was not the end of Israel's woes with the Weinberger Defense Department. Among the joint defense programs that Israel had been working on at the time of the Lavi cancellation was the Arrow antitactical ballistic missile (ATBM) system—meant to counter the growing threat posed by surface-to-surface missiles. The Arrow was at the core of a multitiered Israeli strategic defense program. Weinberger's staff had never missed an opportunity, throughout their Lavi termination campaign, to point out that spending on the Lavi could potentially jeopardize funding for the Arrow missile. A technology evaluation study conducted by the U.S. Strategic Defense Initiative Organization had cited the Arrow, together with Tadiran's command, communications, and control system, as being two of the Israeli strategic defense projects that the U.S. Strategic Defense Initiative stood to make substantial technology gains from.

The technological benefits for the United States, however, apparently meant little to Weinberger. Once the Lavi was canceled, Weinberger's Defense Department remained no more forthcoming toward reaching an agreement on joint Arrow development. Remarked one of Weinberger's officials regarding the Arrow, "Frankly, we have paid our dues for the Lavi."[22] Another Pentagon official, in discussing the views held by the Weinberger staff members, pointed out that "the last thing they want to do is another program with Israel."[23] No agreement on U.S. cooperation on the Arrow program would be reached until December 1987, two months after Weinberger stepped down as secretary of defense.[24]

In the weeks following the cancellation of the Lavi, Dov Zakheim, writing in the editorial pages of the *New York Times*, would contend that the termination package that had been offered by his team had been more than generous and that "no jobs need therefore be lost as part of the cancellation."[25] Whether Zakheim's accounting skills had suddenly gone awry, or whether he thought he might so easily mend fences with an American Jewish community that had widely condemned his role in Weinberger's campaign, may never be known.[26] As soon became evident, however, the resources freed up by the Lavi cancellation would be focused on meeting Israel's defense needs, rather than going toward maintaining a fighter-manufacturing capability that was no longer intended for use.

Israel Aircraft Industries' workforce dropped from 22,000 employees in August 1987 to 17,050 just one year later: a loss of 4,950 employees, or 950 more than had been initially predicted. Moshe Arens continued long after to lament his failure to successfully defend the Lavi. As he was heard to remark a year after the project was killed, "In the aircraft business nowadays it's not enough to design a good product, you must also be an effective lobbyist with the customer and the government. I guess I was not a good enough politician."[27] In another interview, several years later, Defense Minister Arens would describe the decision to cancel the Lavi as "a tragic mistake, a stupid mistake."[28] The cancellation also left Israel without a fighter-production capability and vulnerable once again to the fickle winds of foreign politics. "It was David Ben Gurion's idea [as Israel's first prime minister] to build an aeronautical technology capability in Israel," Arens said. "Some people thought it was outrageous, but remember that Ben Gurion was Defense Minister himself and had the conviction that in the Middle East, if you don't know how to defend yourself, you don't stay alive."[29]

In the early 1990s IAI briefly toyed with the idea of developing yet another, all-new airframe, named the Shahal (biblical lion). As outlined, the aircraft would have been similar to the original Layout 33 concept study, featuring a small aircraft with limited payload capacity—aimed primarily at the export market. The theoretical unit price for the stripped-down aircraft was reported to be roughly a third of the cost of an F-16. Although the project could have built upon Lavi experience, it lacked the range, payload, and survivability that had made the Lavi attractive to the Israeli air force. There was no interest inside the Heyl Ha'Avir for such an airplane, and without an Israeli buy to help cover the development costs, the proposal never left the drawing board.[30]

The Lavi contract termination costs eventually totaled $262.7 million. Of the remaining funding that had previously been earmarked for the Lavi program over the next fiscal year, $87.1 million was devoted to upgrading jet engines in Israel's existing F-15 fleet, $54.1 million went toward completing the construction of the third Lavi prototype, and $26.5 million was allocated toward completing development work on the Lavi avionics package. Program termination costs were equally divided between U.S. and Israeli firms.[31]

As events were to prove, even the modest flight-test program initially approved for the remaining Lavi prototype was not in the cards. When the initial allocation to complete construction of the third prototype ran out, no government funds were approved for a follow-on flight-test effort. IAI instead chose to continue to fund the flight-test phase on its own, using the Lavi as a showcase for its avionics and cockpit upgrade programs. The third prototype was relabeled as the "Lavi Technology Demonstrator" and bore the designation "TD" on its tail, rather than the "B-3" of the original flight-test program. Its first flight came on September 25, 1989, with IAI chief test pilot Menachem Shmul at the controls.

The original test program had cleared the aircraft only to 7.2 g's, but no plans were announced to extend that envelope. The purpose of the technology demonstrator was to provide an avionics test bed, not to develop an operational fighter. To reduce wear on the remaining three PW1120 engines at their disposal, the maximum operating temperature of the powerplant was reduced, a measure that was expected to double their useful lifetime but that also degraded their operational performance. This engine modification reduced available thrust in military power from 13,550 lb (60.3 kN) to just under 12,500 lb (55.6 kN). Afterburning thrust similarly dropped from 20,620 lb (91.7 kN) to 18,600 lb (82.7 kN).[32] The composite speed breaks on the Lavi had also not been fully tested before the cancellation decision came through. Rather than extend the flight-test program to verify their use, IAI chose to bolt them shut.

Plans were announced to install the operational radar, the EL/M-2035, sometime in 1991. The radar had already undergone its initial flight tests on a Boeing 707 electronics test bed but had not yet been demonstrated in a fighter airframe. IAI also planned to add a global positioning system (GPS), an inertial navigation system (INS), and improved multifunction color cockpit displays before the revised flight-test program was completed.[33] But the airplane remained a truncated version of what it was meant to be. One lonely winged lion was all that remained—a testament to all that might have been, and to what nearly was.

14. Jerusalem Takes Stock

For Israel, the story of the Lavi is far more than merely the tale of a failed weapons program. For a nation so small, the development of a modern jet fighter represented a monumental undertaking, with ramifications that extended far beyond its military implications. No program of similar magnitude would ever be undertaken by the Jewish state, either before or since. It is therefore all the more essential that Israel's policy makers take full measure of the chain of events that surround this story.

In hindsight, it can now be said that the first misstep on the part of Israel's leadership occurred in 1980 when efforts were abandoned to obtain approval for licensed production of the F-16 in Israel. At the very least, this option should have been explored one last time in 1981, when the Reagan administration came into office. Although an Israeli fighter derived from the F-16 would not have been able to incorporate all of the innovations seen under the Lavi, the savings in development and production costs would have permitted more aircraft to be fielded. More importantly, from a political standpoint, such an aircraft would have provided a far more elusive target for its political detractors in the United States and elsewhere.

That being said, there was also no way, at the time that the decision was made to launch the Lavi in February 1980, that Israel's leadership could have foreseen the kind of unrelenting political campaign that would be focused against this program. There was nothing in their past experience that could have prepared them for the personal animosity of select administration officials, or for the vulnerability of a cooperative effort of this scale.

The next major milestone crossed by the Lavi program was the decision in 1982 to transform the Lavi from a simple A-4 replacement into a more versatile, long-range fighter-bomber. Proponents of the original design maintained that a smaller, less ambitious program might have been able to avoid the budget ax. But while a Lavi designed purely around the A-4 role may have been cheaper to produce, such a program would have been no more resistant to the personal vendetta that was waged from Weinberger's office. It would also have been more open to criticism from within Israel's air force, where both an A-4 and F-4E replacement were sorely needed. An austere, lightweight fighter could have fulfilled only one of these two roles.[1]

Finally, the question remains open regarding whether the decision made in August 1987 to terminate the program was the right one. This is a question that will probably never be answered to everyone's satisfaction. The central arguments in favor of scrapping the Lavi were the issues of cost and of opposition from the Weinberger Pentagon. Regarding the latter of these two, Caspar Weinberger would leave office on November 23, 1987, less than three months after the Lavi program was scrapped. Had the Israeli Cabinet chosen to continue the Lavi, its production was all but certain to have become an accomplished fact. No one else in the Pentagon, even if they had attempted to mount a similar campaign of obstruction, could have counted on Weinberger's personal friendship with the president to shield them.

However, what the Lavi program truly needed to keep it alive was a larger production run than what Israel could afford. To make the Lavi an attractive alternative in light of Israel's reduced purchasing power in the 1990s would have required additional customers. And in 1987, the only customer that could possibly afford to purchase the minimum two hundred or so additional fighters needed to keep Lavi production costs under control was the U.S. Air Force. With Weinberger out of the way, the door may well have been opened for the Pentagon to view the Lavi in a more rational light.

The Lavi would have fit with America's stated objective to upgrade its close air support and attack fighter fleets. IAI had even taken their first, tentative steps down this road, identifying Grumman to set up a parallel, American production line for the fighter. Like so many things, this subject will remain an unclosed controversy.

To successfully pursue a U.S.-Israeli dual production route, however, the Lavi also needed two other ingredients that were lacking: an Israeli government that was firmly committed to its success, and a defense minister who had the acumen necessary to navigate the U.S. political landscape. While Defense Minister Rabin might have protested publicly over Weinberger's delay tactics, the truth was that he remained ineffectual in getting them lifted. Only after months of delay, added cost, and lost time did the threat of presidential or congressional intervention convince Weinberger to lift his blockade. Rabin's inability to navigate the back halls of Washington stands in sharp contrast to the performance of his predecessor, Moshe Arens, who had succeeded in getting Weinberger's previous blockade of Lavi funding lifted within two days of his first telephone call.[2] Unlike Rabin, Arens understood the underlying tensions and divides that were part of the Washington landscape. Rabin's understanding of U.S. politics, on the other hand, is probably best illustrated by a famous incident that occurred during the Carter administration, while Rabin was prime minister. After a grueling day of talks, President Carter had asked if Rabin would care to join him to listen to the president's daughter, Amy, play the piano. Rabin responded in characteristically blunt fashion: "No."[3]

The Lavi was a unique warplane, born out of the harrowing experience of the 1973 Yom Kippur War: an aircraft intended to survive the most intense air defense arrays in the world and still deliver close air support to soldiers on the front. No other airplane, before or since, has been built around this same scenario. During the 1991 Gulf War, as well as during the Israeli air campaign over Lebanon in 1982, the strategy exercised by both the United States and Israel hinged upon eliminating the opposing air defenses before attempting to provide support to troops on the ground. To place the kind of hostile environment that the Lavi was intended to face into perspective, it should be recalled that in 1982, as part of the nation's stunning aerial victory over Syria, Israel shattered previously held records by knocking out seventeen Syrian surface-to-air missile batteries during the course of a single afternoon. Accomplishing this had required a concerted Israeli effort, combining reconnaissance drones, long-range artillery, and surface-to-surface missiles, as well as radar jamming and strike aircraft.[4] In a full-scale war, however, Israel would have faced an air defense network of over 150 surface-to-air missile batteries on the Syrian front alone.[5] This was the environment that the Lavi was designed to overcome: a scenario in which achieving air superiority would have to take a backseat to delivering the bomb loads needed to slow an armored advance. In 1973, out of necessity, the price for buying that time had been paid willingly, however brutal a toll it might have taken. The Lavi was intended to make that price somewhat less bitter.

Outside of Israel, the depth of trauma felt from the 1973 war has seldom been understood. By the end of the war, over 2,900 Israelis would be listed as either dead or missing in action. This represented nearly one out of every thousand Israeli citizens. America has not experienced casualties of this magnitude since the Second World War, and even then, never so many in so short a period of time. It should not be surprising that, even decades after the fact, the decisions made by Israel's political leadership continue to arouse controversy. There were many senior officers at the time who viewed the Cabinet's decision to refrain from the preemptive option as a fundamental betrayal. Maj. Gen. "Raful" Eitan, who was then the commanding officer in charge of Israel's northern front, was among them:

> It was explained by the late Golda Meir, with other politicians voicing the same line, that a preventative blow was ruled out for political reasons, so that Israel would not be blamed for starting the war. I cannot conceive of any greater folly. When the existence of a nation is in the balance and its military is not mobilized and the mass media are

shut down because of Yom Kippur and there is no possibility of mobilizing the reserves via a public call-up, the political consideration has the lowest possible priority, and the question of what will be said about Israel is of absolutely no importance.[6]

Eitan, of course, was Israel's chief of staff during the formative years of the Lavi's development. He was among those officers who presided over the transformation of the airplane from an austere A-4 replacement into a warplane intended to fight and win under the same scenario that in 1973 had cost so many Israeli lives.

It is often difficult for Americans, who have never lived with neighbors bent on their destruction, who have never known the rain of artillery on their farmlands or the guns of snipers aimed at their city streets, to fully grasp the magnitude of the threat that Israel both has and continues to face. This gulf was something that Moshe Arens had himself grappled with during his term as Israel's ambassador to the United States in the early 1980s. As Arens observed, "It's not easy to get Israel across to the public in the United States because Israel is facing the kinds of problems that people here have never faced. Israel is still fighting for its survival. Most of the issues that face Israel are issues of life and death. You don't have that here, and the depth and severity of Israel's problems are sometimes misunderstood. People look on the Middle East as if it were the Middle West. What they don't understand is that our margin of error is so small. Our physical existence is at stake."[7] It is this precarious position, this small margin for error, that has ensured that the story behind the Lavi remains relevant today, even decades later.

There was a time, during the 1990s, when it appeared as if the road to peace had become inevitable. The Soviet Union had collapsed and the Middle East was no longer a Cold War battleground. The leadership of the PLO, once Israel's sworn enemy, had entered into talks with Israel's government. A war-weary Israeli public eagerly traded away control over ever-widening stretches of territory in the West Bank and Gaza to their PLO negotiating partners in the Palestinian Authority. To some, the days of jet fighters and their pilots, of all the events that had led to the launch of the Lavi and the mission for which it had been built, belonged to a bygone era. In the new world order, the fortunetellers of peace could see no use for the kind of warbird that the Lavi represented. But it all ended with startling clarity, as a new era of violence and terrorism descended.

Despite all of the warning signs, when the negotiations finally collapsed, it would catch both the American and Israeli governments by surprise. Everyone had been convinced that the settlement offered by the Israeli government was too generous for PLO chairman Arafat to pass up.[8] As President Bill Clinton would later relate, "I still had no idea what Arafat was going to do. His body language said no, but the deal was so good I couldn't believe anyone would be foolish enough to let it go."[9] Yet let it go he did, in the most violent of manners. As U.S. envoy Dennis Ross would later observe,

> Rabin and Peres had made a historic choice; Arafat made only a tactical move. . . . There was almost no conditioning of his public for peace. There was never talk of painful compromises for peace. On the contrary, Arafat was telling his public they would get everything, and give up nothing. Even worse, he continued to promote hostility toward Israel. Thousands of Palestinian children went to summer camps where they were taught how to kidnap Israelis. Suicide bombers were called martyrs, even when Arafat would crack down on Hamas and Islamic Jihad. Violence as an instrument was never delegitimized nor given up as Arafat preserved his options. Israelis were held responsible for all ills.[10]

When the peace process between Israel and Arafat's Palestinian Authority broke down in September 2000, it would be followed by a fresh wave of violence that served as a bitter reminder of how little had truly changed. Within days, Israel's capital was under sniper fire, and Israeli buses, restaurants, and hotels became the targets of relentless suicide bombings. Between October 2000 and September 2001 alone, 132 Israeli civilians would die in a total of sixty terrorist attacks—with many more wounded. For the first time since the Six-Day War, the "peace process" had brought terror bases within rifle range of Israel's civilian population.

Israeli soldiers, many of them reservists who had seen service in the Yom Kippur or Lebanon Wars, would be called upon to once again recapture many of the same territories that Israel had surrendered to the Palestinian Authority only a few years before, paying for each mile in costly, street-by-street, door-by-door battles.[11] The pace of the terrorist attacks would abate. The scars left behind, however, would not so easily heal, and the "peace process" would never again take root in the popular imagination of Israel's citizens with the same vigor.

For Israeli families watching the scenes of the suicide bombings on the evening news, the message could not have been more clear, more chilling, or more personal. The debris field where there had once been a bus, a cafe, or a thriving market; the frantic medics rushing to the scene; the stricken faces of the survivors: open wounds were everywhere to be found. In places where there had once been families, the smiles of children, so wide-eyed and full of promise, only devastation was left: a crime scene marked by overturned chairs, tables, and strollers. Where once there had been hope and promise, flesh had been torn from flesh, their stories never to be complete. In the words of the Israeli poet Yehuda Amichai,

> So much death in everything, so much packing and transport,
> so much open that will never close again, so much closed
> that will never open.[12]

The civilian casualties, dead or maimed at the hands of the suicide bombers and gunmen, had not been unfortunate bystanders to the horrors of battle. Quite the contrary: the civilians had been the intended victims. In virtually every instance, the suicide bombers had ample opportunity to observe their surroundings, to see the faces of the men, women, and children whom they were about to murder. They would have every opportunity to seek out the precise spot to detonate their bombs for maximum effect: the center of the bus, the most populated corner of the restaurant, a crowded shopping plaza, or a children's playground.

The aim of the terrorists was not, nor had it ever been, territorial. No amount of territorial withdrawal, no number of "land for peace" initiatives or wishful sloganeering, would placate a blood-thirsty intent of such magnitude. Israel's neighbors had been fed too much anti-Semitic hate to ever accept the existence of an independent, non-Arab, non-Moslem state in their midst. Words written by diplomats in Oslo had less lasting impact than the graffiti plastered across the walls of Gaza. Graffiti that proudly proclaimed, "We knock on the gates of heaven with the skulls of Jews."[13] The attempt to generate peace from the top down had been an unmitigated failure. The groundwork for a lasting peace simply had not existed, nor could it be artificially created among the halls of power in Europe or America. In the words of one PLO terrorist, "The aim was to kill as many Jews as possible and there was no moral distinction between potential victims, whether soldiers, civilians, women or children." Or as another PLO terrorist proclaimed, "The main thing was the amount of blood."[14]

So it was, nearly two decades after the program had been canceled, that the story of the Lavi and the lessons that it contained were endowed with fresh relevance for Israel's leaders. The hatred reflected by terrorists armed with guns, rockets, and bombs was espoused equally by states armed with missiles, tanks, and warplanes. To this day, Israel's survival depends on its ability to either deter or repulse the violent intentions of its neighbors. Far from being a mere footnote in history, the role and need for a warplane like the Lavi would remain as vital as ever.

In the year following the Lavi cancellation, Israel Aircraft Industries' workforce would plummet from 22,000 employees in August 1987 to 17,050 employees one year later.[15] But the layoffs did not end there. By 1990 IAI had shrunk to 16,500 employees.[16] This downward slide would continue to gain momentum, culminating in a corporate-wide loss that totaled $87 million in red ink in 1993 alone, with some $750 million in outstanding debt. Some 77–78 percent of the company's business still came from defense sales, a market that was continuing to dwindle. By 1994 IAI's workforce would fall to fewer than 14,000 employees, marking the firm's lowest point since the 1960s.[17] Faced with defense budgets that were continuing to shrink worldwide, IAI set out upon a corporate recovery strategy that aimed to diversify its portfolio. It would be 1997, however, before IAI could once again report a profit. By the year 2000, 40 percent of the company's backlog would be from the civilian sector, and the size of IAI's workforce would again be on the rebound.[18]

The road to recovery was equally rocky for Israel's other armament industries. Between 1985 and 1990 alone, the number of employees at Israel's nine largest defense manufacturers would drop by some 26 percent, from 62,500 to 46,500 employees.[19] Mergers became common fare throughout the 1990s. The Israeli company El-Op (Electro-Optics Industries) would be bought out by Elbit in January 2000, with Elisra merging first with Tadiran before being absorbed by Elbit in July 2005.[20]

For Israel's air force, the road would be equally rocky. The ninety F-16Cs that had been sought by Defense Minister Rabin proved to be beyond Israel's means, and the official order placed in April 1988 authorized the purchase of no more than seventy-five fighters. This purchase would later be slashed again, to a mere sixty F-16C/D models.[21] As a result, Israel's aging A-4 fleet was asked to soldier on into the twenty-first century.[22]

The cancellation of the Lavi also brought an end to proposals for re-engining Israel's F-4 fleet with the PW1120 powerplant. Setting up a production line for such a small run of engines would have been prohibitively expensive.[23] Other options did remain and were in due course pursued to keep Israel's F-4 fleet viable. At least some of Israel's Phantom 2000s were eventually outfitted with FLIR (forward-looking infrared) navigation and targeting pods. By September 1990 IAI was upgrading Israel's F-4 fleet to the Phantom 2000 standard at a rate of one aircraft per month, with the first dozen fighters already delivered for squadron service. By mid-1991 this overhaul rate had reached two aircraft per month, with twenty aircraft reportedly in service and with some already deployed in combat.[24]

Often described as a "poor man's Strike Eagle," the upgraded F-4s included a holographic head-up display produced by Kaiser Electronics, offering a 30° field of view as well as a complete rewiring of the airplane's electrical systems, two 5 in CRT (cathode ray tube) displays, and a video recorder mounted in a bubble on the leading edge of the left wing. This latter feature allowed the airplane to record bomb damage for postmission assessment. IAI's structural refurbishment was expected to add another fifteen years onto the F-4's useful lifetime. Proposals for incorporating fixed canard foreplanes onto the F-4 were shelved, however. The Heyl Ha'Avir was unwilling to fund the extensive flight-test program that would have been required to validate the high angle of attack and spin recovery characteristics of the revised design.[25]

Following the Lavi's cancellation, Elta continued to develop the various Lavi avionics systems, albeit in a more modular form.[26] Flight testing of the avionics was carried out in phases aboard the Lavi Technology Demonstrator, beginning in the early 1990s. The first twenty-five flights of the Technology Demonstrator were devoted to opening up the flight envelope and toward validating updates that had been made to the flight control software. Following this abbreviated flight-test program, attention was thereafter focused on verifying the performance of the avionics package for future use under other airframes. In each successive phase of flight test, additional avionics elements would be added. No further effort would be expended, however, to develop the Lavi as a weapons platform. Between September 25, 1989, and December 31, 1992, the Technology Demonstrator made a total of 113 flights, accumulating 129 hours of flight time. During this flight-test program, a maximum speed of Mach 1.2 was attained—far less than the Mach 1.8 for which the airplane had been designed, and less even than the Mach 1.45 that had been achieved by the first two prototypes. The airplane did, however, demonstrate a maximum speed at low altitude of 600 knots and a minimum flight speed of just under 80 knots, as well as a 25° maximum angle of attack and a maximum load factor of 8.2 g's.[27]

None of these performance parameters, however, was intended to probe the limits of the Lavi's capabilities. Moreover, as the avionics demonstration wound down and attention was turned to repackaging the Lavi avionics for use on other airframes, the Technology Demonstrator came to be flown less and less often. In all of 1993, for example, the Lavi Technology Demonstrator made only twelve additional flights, adding no more than fourteen hours to the total flight time of the program.[28]

As for the remaining Lavi prototypes, the majority would meet an ignominious end. The B-2 prototype, minus its engine and electronics, was donated to the Israel Air Force Museum at Hatzerim. The B-1 prototype, as well as the airframes for the partially complete number four and five prototypes, were sold as scrap in 1996 and melted down into aluminum blocks. Efforts to keep the Lavi Technology Demonstrator flightworthy remained a private investment on the part of Israel Aircraft Industries.

In the years following the Lavi cancellation, the funding freed up by canceling the Lavi came to be hotly contested between competing modernization and operational needs. A U.S. General Accounting Office study conducted for the 1990 fiscal year, for example, determined that 42 percent of the offshore security assistance funds had been devoted to meeting daily operating expenses, including the costs of fuel, aircraft maintenance, and ammunition. Only 8 percent of the funds would be spent on aircraft upgrade programs, with the balance being devoted to purchasing missiles and unmanned air vehicles and toward procurement and modernization programs for the Israeli army and navy.[29] As Defense Minister Rabin acknowledged, "We hoped to use the funds saved by the termination of the Lavi project for R&D and for financing alternatives to the Lavi. Except that cutbacks in the defense budget and extra expenditures on activity in the territories devoured all the money."[30] The situation was somewhat alleviated when the United States offered to provide a number of older, used F-15 and F-16 aircraft that were in the process of being retired following the 1991 Persian Gulf War. A total of twenty-five early model F-15A/B aircraft and fifty early model F-16A/B fighters were transferred to Israel under this program. All of these airplanes required significant structural refurbishment to extend their useful service life, not to mention an avionics upgrade to bring them into alignment with Israeli standards. The F-16s, for example, were all Block 10 aircraft, with half of them having been withdrawn from Air National Guard or U.S. Air Force Reserve duty. These airplanes had an average of 3,200 flying hours on them, out of a design life of 4,000 hours.[31] Including structural refurbishment and avionics upgrades, each of these F-16s was expected to cost the Israelis between $15 and $16 million before the aircraft could be returned to service. Once the structural refurbishment was completed, however, the useful lifetime of the airframes would be extended from four thousand to eight thousand hours, providing a valuable and inexpensive means for modernizing Israel's aerial arsenal.[32]

Israel's most pressing air force need, however, continued to be the void in its long-range strike capabilities that had been left when the Lavi was canceled. The sixty Block 40 F-16s that Israel had purchased immediately following the Lavi cancellation had only partially fulfilled Israel's strike-fighter requirements. These aircraft had included thirty F-16D two-seat fighters, fitted with extended ventral spines to allow them to carry additional avionics. These aircraft would be fitted with Elisra's SPS-2000 electronic warfare system, which had been derived from the package originally developed for use under the Lavi. All of these fighters were reportedly dedicated to the air defense suppression (ADS) role.[33] Even with these additions, however, these F-16s could in no way substitute for the Lavi in the deep strike role, a mission whose importance continued to be magnified by developments in Iran. Plans were formulated in the mid-1990s calling for the purchase of forty to forty-eight long-range strike aircraft, with both the F-15E Strike Eagle and the F/A-18 identified as candidates.[34]

The F-16, however, was not considered to be a serious contender for this mission. While the Heyl Ha'Avir certainly appreciated its many qualities, the Block 40 F-16 and its predecessors did not have the range that Israeli strategists had identified for their next round of fighter purchases. Yet things had also been changing inside the American defense industry. General Dynamics had sold its Fort Worth division, responsible for the F-16, to Lockheed Martin. The same Fort Worth offices that had once shunned proposals for cooperative development of the F-16 with Israel during the 1970s had begun to see Israeli aircraft orders as essential to keeping the F-16 in production. Lockheed Martin proposed an evolved version of the F-16, the F-16ES (enhanced strategic) as an alternative for meeting Israel's deep strike needs. The new F-16 configuration featured two 500 gal (1,890 L) conformal fuel tanks, mounted on the upper surface of each wing root, as well as provisions for a 600 gal (2,270 L) centerline drop tank. This fuel capacity was expected to increase the strike radius of the F-16 to some 890 nm (1,650 km).[35] The further addition of conventional, wing-mounted drop tanks promised to extend this range even farther. Although not a direct equivalent for the Lavi, the F-16ES was nonetheless an attractive option, providing a long-range strike capability in a much smaller airframe than the F-15E.

When the decision was finally made, however, the proposed Block 50+ F-16 was seen as being too immature to fulfill Israel's immediate needs. In May 1994 a $2 billion deal was signed for the delivery of twenty-five F-15I fighters—the Israeli version of the F-15E Strike Eagle.[36] The new Strike Eagle variant would benefit from the earlier Lavi avionics effort, including Elisra's SPS-3000 radar warning receiver, together with the SPS-2100 integrated electronic warfare package, not to mention the DASH (display and sight helmet) system. Among the innovations that were unveiled with these aircraft was the ability to transfer target coordinates between fighter-bombers using secure data links. This would allow an aircraft that was exiting a target area to relay the location of any untouched targets to fighters that were just entering the scene. This feature added yet another unique element to Israel's strike capabilities that its counterparts elsewhere, including F-15ES flying in the USAF, did not possess.[37]

The Heyl Ha'Avir continued to maintain an interest, however, in the F-16ES configuration. While the payload capabilities of the F-15I were impressive, it was also far too expensive to be fielded in large numbers. By the late 1990s, Lockheed Martin had further refined its concepts for the proposed Block 52+ model of the F-16, demonstrating in flight test that the conformal fuel tanks would have minimal impact on the airplane's handling. In January 2000 Israel closed a deal for the purchase of fifty Block 52+ F-16 fighters, with the new aircraft designated as the F-16I. This Israeli version was expected to feature Pratt & Whitney's F100-229 enhanced thrust powerplant, as well as the conformal fuel tanks of the F-16ES configuration. It also incorporated an avionics suite that relied heavily on development once intended for the Lavi—much of which had also been fielded under the F-15I. The contract was valued at $2.5 billion, with deliveries to commence in 2003. Late in 2001 a follow-on agreement was reached for the supply of an additional 52 F-16I aircraft, to be delivered between 2006 and 2009, bringing the total value of the F-16I purchase to $4.5 billion.[38]

Table 9. Israeli air force order of battle, 1990–2010

Aircraft	1990	1995	2000	2005	2010
A-4 Skyhawk	125	90	80	60	40
F-4E Phantom	135	80	79	60	40
F-4E/2000	10	62	61	60	59
F-15A/B and C/D	48	73	72	71	70
F-15I Strike Eagle	N/A	N/A	25	25	25
F-16A/B and C/D	147	246	243	240	237
F-16I	N/A	N/A	N/A	50	100
Kfir	100	40	N/A	N/A	N/A
Total	565	591	560	566	571

Even before Israel took delivery of the first F-16I, the Heyl Ha'Avir already fielded the largest F-16 fleet of any air force outside of the United States. Unlike all other major F-16 customers, however, Israel had never had an independent assembly floor for the aircraft. It was therefore no accident that the Israeli government sought other means to maximize Israeli industrial participation in the F-16I. Under the terms of the contract with Lockheed Martin, IAI was expected to manufacture a number of the structural subassemblies in the new warplanes, including the wing box structure, the vertical tail, and the conformal fuel tanks. The majority of the Israeli-supplied content, however, was once again in the form of electronic subsystems. Head-up displays would be provided by El-Op, while Elbit was to provide the integrated color display processor, including the software and hardware behind the airplane's digital map system. The airplane's UHF/VHF radio, meanwhile, would be provided by Rafael. And of course, the electronic warfare suite would be of all-Israeli origin. In all, it was anticipated that some $1.4 billion in Israeli hardware would go into the 102 new fighters, amounting to nearly a third of the total contract value.[39]

The one disappointment that the Israelis did experience with these new fighter deliveries, however, was the absence of an Israeli radar. The Heyl Ha'Avir had expressed a preference for incorporating the Lavi's EL/M-2035 radar. The Israeli radar was expected to possess a number of advantages, including better terrain-mapping capabilities and superior multitarget processing. However, the United States was unwilling to share the source codes for the fire control and other aircraft systems with which the Israeli radar system would have to communicate. As a result, the Heyl Ha'Avir had to settle for an upgraded version of the previous F-16C/D radar, the APG-68(v)9, which was expected to feature five times the processing speed of the prior generation in F-16 radars. Elta, meanwhile, continued to work independently toward integrating the EL/M-2035 radar for possible future use.[40]

Taken in sum, the F-16I had come closer than any preceding aircraft to being a direct substitute for the Lavi. More than a decade after the first production Lavi fighters were scheduled to roll off the assembly line, the Heyl Ha'Avir would finally take delivery of a long-range strike fighter that could also retain some measure of agility over the battlefield and simultaneously present a much smaller target than the massive F-15.[41] The F-16I had also included a number of structural modifications aimed at further increasing its maximum takeoff weight from the 48,000 lb (21,770 kg) seen on Israeli Block 40 F-16C/D aircraft to 52,000 lb (23,590 kg) under the F-16I, while retaining the same empty weight of 21,000 lb (9,530 kg) as Israel's previous Block 40 fighters.[42] At long last, the Israeli air force would finally deploy an evolved version of the F-16, optimized for the attack role, something that they had originally requested permission to develop on their own during the 1970s. In combination with Israel's F-15I fleet, the F-16I will provide Israel with the strike radius and survivable attack capability that the Lavi had once been intended to deliver.

The cancellation of the Lavi marked the end of an era. The mid-1980s witnessed the final days of the elevated levels in defense spending that had been maintained ever since the communal shock of the Yom Kippur War. Israeli domestic defense spending, which had peaked at some 30 percent of Israel's GDP in 1975, fell to 12 percent by 1989 and to less than 10 percent by 1994. U.S. security assistance to Israel had also peaked at this time. Although U.S. aid to Israel would modestly increase again at the turn of the century, as a percentage of total Israeli defense spending, U.S. aid had already peaked at 27 percent in 1986, falling to 15 percent of Israel's defense spending by 2008.[43]

The days are long since past when a nation as small as Israel could hope to undertake a weapons program of such magnitude without seeking some form of outside collaboration. It was not a question of technological capability, nor of which airplane was best suited to the task, but rather of economies of scale. The Israeli populace simply could not absorb the costs for the Lavi on their own.

It should be recalled that, with the exception of Sweden's JAS-39 Gripen, and to a lesser extent Taiwan's Ching-Kuo fighter, all of the frontline combat aircraft developed during the 1980s and 1990s were fielded by nations with GDPs that were orders of magnitude greater than Israel's. The GDP of France, for example, which began developing the Rafale at around the same time as the Lavi, was twenty-three times greater than the GDP of Israel during the mid-1980s.[44] The Eurofighter Typhoon, meanwhile, was developed by a consortium of four European nations, which collectively boasted a GDP that was seventy-four times the size of Israel's. Only Sweden, with a GDP that was only four times the size of Israel's, offered a comparable example of a small nation that had successfully developed its own combat aircraft. To accomplish this, however, the Swedes had focused their attention around a fighter requirement that was, of necessity, less ambitious than the survivable, deep strike objectives that had been laid out for the Lavi. The Gripen was not expected to face the same kind of intense antiaircraft environment that Israel contemplated, and the Gripen was aimed at a combat radius that was little more than half of the Israeli target.[45]

Taiwan's indigenous fighter, meanwhile, was even less ambitious in its scope. Taiwan had developed the Chin-Kuo out of necessity, only after the United States had refused to sell additional fighters. The new airplane borrowed as much as possible from its American counterparts, including its AN/APG-67 radar system, which was borrowed from the canceled F-20 program, and an airframe that was designed with assistance from General Dynamics. In terms of its attack capability, the Ching-Kuo was even less ambitious than the Gripen.[46]

The Lavi is likely to remain forever the subject of debate and controversy. Years after it had been canceled, Moshe Arens would describe the Lavi as "Israel's single most ambitious and important technological program."[47] It was all that, and much more. No other Israeli development program, before or since, could rival the Lavi in terms of the workforce and resources dedicated to its completion. With the Lavi died Israel's fighter-manufacturing capability for the foreseeable future. In its wake, there today stands an Israeli arms industry that is smaller, but perhaps politically wiser. Left behind as well is an Israeli defense force that will face the always uncertain future in the volatile Middle East without the Lavi.

15. America in the Mirror

E ven as the tale of the Lavi holds hard lessons for Israel's political and military leadership, so too does it contain lessons for the United States. On one level, the story of the Lavi can be viewed as a case study in how U.S. policies are formulated and carried out: sometimes with and sometimes without presidential approval. It is also, however, a vivid illustration of the competing interests that have alternately nurtured and hindered closer U.S.-Israeli cooperation. For the benefit of both nations, it is essential that the lessons of the Lavi be absorbed by future policy makers.

Caspar Weinberger's behind-the-scenes campaign to kill the Lavi was only one of many rogue operations that were carried out by both high- and mid-ranking officials working behind the scenes in the Reagan administration. The most well-known of these rogue efforts, the Iran-Contra arms-for-hostages scandal, would explode into the headlines early in 1987. Rogue operatives were not unique to the Reagan White House, and many previous presidencies had been handicapped by similar episodes. However, the Reagan presidency in particular appears to have been susceptible to this disease. In the case of the Lavi, this pattern of disjointed policy formulation ultimately had its cost, not only in terms of the billions devoted to a program that was later canceled but also in damage to the U.S.-Israeli relationship. The vacillation between an administration that at first endorsed and promoted U.S. involvement in the Lavi and then subsequently saw a senior Cabinet member campaigning to kill the program could not help but call into question the reliability of the United States as a partner. What was given with one hand could be taken away with the other, and what was stated as policy by a president was not necessarily what would be carried out by his subordinates.

Weinberger's campaign against the Lavi fit into a larger picture of personal animosity toward Israel. Other events, including Weinberger's reaction to the bombing of Iraq's Osirak nuclear reactor and his handling of the *Achille Lauro* hijacking, had long since established Weinberger's credentials. His hostility toward the Lavi was merely one more example in this pattern.

In spite of official support for U.S. involvement in the Lavi program, as publicly voiced by President Reagan in October and November 1983, Weinberger chose to launch a dedicated effort to terminate the program. At no time, however, was an attempt made to assess Israel's security concerns and objectives behind the Lavi or to evaluate the most cost-effective means of meeting those objectives. When his lobbying campaign was met with resistance, Weinberger again turned to his familiar pressure tactics: suspending the approval of contracts and withholding funding already approved by Congress. Even the prospect of a presidential reprimand failed to dissuade Weinberger from his self-appointed agenda. Nothing short of a threat of congressional intervention would persuade Weinberger to relent and release the Lavi contracts and funding.

Weinberger's office was assisted in its efforts by a familiar cast of characters at the State Department's Near East Bureau and in the U.S. embassy in Israel. Working behind the scenes, in contravention of the stated objectives of their own secretary of state, they offered Weinberger's team a valuable lobbying force and seasoned guide into the landscape of Israel's domestic politics. Once Defense Minister Rabin had been convinced to cancel the airplane, the campaign gathered momentum. Few of Israel's friends in the administration or Congress were prepared to raise objections if Israel's own defense minister was not. What had begun as a rogue operation became an established fact. This is a true example of Washington policy making at work, although not quite the model that the Founding Fathers would have had in mind.

This story illustrates several elements of Washington policy making that bear repeating. The first is that a president who gives too free a rein to subordinates who contravene presidential authority will only invite more rogue operations of the same variety. Second is that once a rogue operation succeeds in its objectives, it will almost always become an established part of administration policy after the fact. Few presidents would care to air their dirty laundry and reprimand an appointed official who has just carried out a policy coup.

The loose-cannon effect proved to be an invasive plague throughout the years of the Reagan administration, handicapping the president's ability to form a cohesive foreign policy on more than one occasion. Secretary of State Haig had lamented this phenomenon in a letter to the president in March 1981, pointing out that "members of your personal staff have consistently undermined your stated intention that the Secretary of State be your principal foreign policy adviser."[1] Secretary Haig was neither the first nor the last to note this pattern of behind-the-scenes gamesmanship. In the ultimate twist of irony, during the Iran-Contra affair Weinberger would himself lament that "one or two advisers in the White House . . . had a specific and determined agenda of their own."[2] It was a rather odd complaint, coming as it did from a man who had likewise felt free to circumvent the official White House and Cabinet process—on more than one occasion. Unfortunately, these kinds of internal policy wars had become the norm rather than the exception. As former National Security Council staff member Raymond Tanter observed, "President Reagan was only a part-time captain at the tiller of the American ship of state; consequently, others seized the helm."[3]

In a region as unstable as the Middle East, Israel has been the only sure constant in an otherwise treacherous terrain. In the years preceding President Reagan's election, the most obvious and striking example of this phenomena had come with the fall of the shah of Iran. For decades the Iranian monarchy had formed a central pillar for American strategic planning in the Persian Gulf. The Islamic revolution that catapulted anti-American ayatollahs into power came as a thunderous wake-up call, the underlying significance of which was not lost on the president-to-be: "The fall of Iran has increased Israel's value as the only remaining strategic asset in the region on which the United States can truly rely; other pro-Western states in the region, especially Saudi Arabia and the smaller Gulf kingdoms, are weak and vulnerable. Israel's strength derives from the reality that her affinity with the West is not dependent on the survival of an autocratic or capricious ruler."[4]

President Reagan's first attempt at reinforcing and formalizing U.S.-Israeli strategic ties came in September 1981. Following his first face-to-face meeting with Israeli prime minister Menachem Begin, President Reagan had made a surprise move and directed his secretary of defense to draft a joint memorandum of understanding aimed at officially defining and implementing U.S.-Israeli military cooperation. It was an undertaking that Defense Secretary Weinberger wanted nothing to do with and that he did everything in his power to undermine. The eventual memorandum of understanding drafted by Weinberger's office would be limited in its scope and would be suspended just days after it was signed into effect—over policy differences surrounding the Golan Heights.[5] The following year would see Israel's invasion of Lebanon, where differences over the evacuation of the PLO from Beirut and the timing of Israel's eventual withdrawal would further strain U.S.-Israeli relations.

In 1983, however, U.S.-Israeli relations began to thaw once more, and Secretary of State Shultz launched an initiative aimed at reinvigorating the U.S.-Israeli strategic alliance. President Reagan's public support for funding the Lavi program, as outlined in October and November of that year, would be but one element that would come out of this effort. Prior to this initiative, although there had been routine exchanges between the intelligence agencies of the two nations, no direct military-to-military channel of communication had existed between the United States and Israel. This situation stood in sharp contrast to the routine exchanges that occurred between the U.S. military and its counterparts in NATO countries, Japan, or Australia. Ronald Reagan would change all of that.

As part of this effort, Secretary of State Shultz set about the process of negotiating a revised and expanded memorandum of agreement governing U.S.-Israeli strategic cooperation. The previous agreement, which had been signed under the Carter administration in 1979 and which was far more circumscribed in its scope, was due to expire in 1984. It was this opportunity that President Reagan and Secretary of State Shultz would seize upon to renegotiate both the terms and scope of strategic cooperation between the two nations and to set about formalizing those ties. In so doing, they ensured that the progress made under the Reagan administration would not be lost under future presidencies.

Among the new organizations launched at this time would be the Joint Political-Military Group (JPMG), which first met in January 1984. The JPMG was charged both with defining the terms for future U.S. and Israeli military cooperation and with initiating the practical steps to put that cooperation into effect. The U.S. side of the newly formed body would be led by Rear Adm. Jonathan Howe, director of the State Department's Office for Political-Military Affairs. Also included were representatives of the State Department's Bureau of Near East and South Asian Affairs, as well as the Defense Department and the Joint Chiefs of Staff. This was the first time, it should be added, that representatives from the Joint Chiefs of Staff had ever participated in a direct dialogue with their counterparts in Israel.[6]

The full membership of the JPMG was scheduled to meet twice per year, with the day-to-day responsibility for implementing the group's recommendations to be overseen by a direct military-to-military working committee. The JPMG, together with the military-to-military implementation committee, a Joint Security Assistance Planning Group, and a Joint Economic Development Group, were all formally ratified as official U.S.-Israeli institutions under the final memorandum of agreement signed by President Reagan on April 21, 1988. It was a landmark achievement in the strategic relationship between the two nations that went largely unnoticed. The impetus to create these institutions, however, had come only at the personal behest of President Reagan, and under the persevering hand of Secretary of State George Shultz.[7]

As a direct result of the JPMG's activities, the United States and Israel began to carry out joint military maneuvers and training exercises for the first time in the two nations' history. By September 1989 no less than twenty-seven joint U.S.-Israeli exercises had been conducted at Israeli weapons ranges and training grounds. U.S. Navy forces stationed in the Mediterranean were able to use Israeli training facilities to maintain their readiness. And for the first time, American emergency military and medical supplies were stockpiled in Israel for possible use in the event of a future crisis. Joint medical evacuation exercises were conducted, U.S. warships began to make regular port calls to Israel's Haifa harbor, and joint plans were drawn up for responding to possible scenarios.[8] All of this accomplished by a president whose secretary of defense was cold to the idea of cooperative efforts with Israel.

Table 10. Value of U.S. Department of Defense goods and services purchased from Israel, 1985–90

1985	$180 million
1986	$205 million
1987	$240 million
1988	$480 million
1989	$354 million
1990	$400 million

Among the areas of expanded defense cooperation initiated under the Reagan administration was a series of initiatives aimed at promoting joint U.S. and Israeli arms development and procurement.[9] For the most part, this consisted of the direct purchase of existing Israeli weapons technology for manufacture in the United States. In some instances, however, the level of cooperation went further, with the United States and Israel agreeing to jointly develop and test an all-new weapons system for subsequent purchase by the armed forces of both nations. This pattern coupled Israel's highly sophisticated research and development capabilities with U.S. mass-production capabilities. In the words of former Israeli air force commander David Ivry, "While our R&D capabilities are high, our production requirements are more limited, which can make production lines expensive. . . . Joint ventures with American industry, merging our special R&D capabilities with their advanced production facilities, is certainly one area for fruitful cooperation."[10]

In 1983, prior to Reagan administration initiatives to expand the level of U.S.-Israeli defense cooperation, U.S. arms purchases from Israel had amounted to no more than $9.4 million per year.[11] By the end of the Reagan administration, however, annual U.S. arms purchases from Israel regularly exceeded $300 million, and by 1992 the backlog for U.S. weapons orders in Israel totaled some $1.7 billion. This put American purchases of Israeli arms on the same scale as similar U.S. arms purchases from Britain and Germany.[12] This may not sound news making in itself, until we take into account that by the mid-1980s the entire Israeli gross domestic product was only one-twenty-second the size of Great Britain's, or one-twenty-eighth that of West Germany.[13] Israeli military know-how, refined in the crucible of war, had set the value of Israeli arms expertise far beyond what its small size might suggest.

Ronald Reagan had embarked on his presidency with a number of clearly stated objectives in mind, among them being the goal of strengthening the U.S.-Israel alliance. As he had stated shortly before taking office, "During these critical years to come, one measure of the United States' credibility will be how faithfully it retains its friendship with Israel. We must change from shifting, unpredictable policies to firm dependable ones."[14] As president he was partially successful in achieving this aim and partially unsuccessful. The suspension of arms deliveries following Israel's raid on Iraq's nuclear weapons facilities was one example where the president's own stated objectives became lost in a befuddled policy-making process that somehow saw Saddam Hussein as a U.S. ally. The behind-the-scenes campaign to terminate the Lavi was yet another example. Obviously, the relationship between the two countries has survived these and other storms. Nonetheless, the perceived reliability of the United States as a strategic partner is an essential ingredient to foster future cooperation, whether in weapons development or otherwise. The events surrounding Weinberger's campaign to cancel the Lavi, among other missteps, did anything but foster trust. Quite the opposite: they suggested that when an American president pledges American cooperation and support, even his own administration may not necessarily carry that policy out.

As a small nation under constant threat from its neighbors, Israel has placed a premium on its security and on its war-fighting capabilities. U.S. cooperation with Israel in the sphere of arms development has therefore not only served the purpose of enhancing Israel's deterrent posture, and its ability to take risks at the negotiating table, but has also provided the American armed forces with access to the collective wisdom of the most seasoned armed forces of the past half century. By 1987, 54 percent of all U.S. funding that had been set aside to evaluate foreign weapons systems for possible purchase by the United States would go toward evaluating Israeli-developed arms.[15] Israel had become more than another source of fresh ideas for fleshing out America's vast arsenal; instead, time and again, Israel had proven to be a more vital, more innovative source for advanced technology than all other U.S. allies—combined.

The burden of providing for national security has forced Israeli development teams to seek out methods for stretching their limited resources. In spite of the protests from Weinberger's offices over the Lavi program's cost, the reality was that in the Lavi the Israelis had succeeded in developing a frontline fighter for a fraction of the cost that a similar development effort would have required in the United States or elsewhere. The entire Lavi development program, including flight testing, was estimated by the U.S. General Accounting Office to total no more than $1.90 billion, in fiscal year 1985 dollars.[16] Adjusting for the effects of inflation, the original f/a-18 program, in contrast, had cost some $3.38 billion to develop, in equivalent 1985 dollars.[17] Or to take an example from outside of the United States, the Japanese fs-x, developed out of the existing f-16 airframe and adjusted into terms of 1985 dollars, would cost Japan a total of $2.31 billion to develop, with a projected flyaway cost of $40 million per airplane.[18] It was no small wonder that the United States' armed forces were evaluating the use of so many Israeli weapons systems by the end of the Reagan era. Israeli-developed arms had proven to be competitive with those of their American and European counterparts not only on a performance basis, but equally so on a cost basis.

The reasons behind Israel's success in the sphere of weapons development were simple and obvious: the Israelis focused their attention on developing those aspects of each weapons system that were truly unique and potentially game changing. Whereas a typical U.S. weapons development effort would be directed to redesign and optimize every detail component, the Israelis would routinely reapply existing experience and technology where possible, focusing instead on those few, unique elements that would endow their product with a maximum advantage over its peers or adversaries. It was a practicality, born out of the experiences of a small nation with limited resources and decades of bitter war-fighting experience.

Several missteps in U.S. policy and judgment were made throughout the development of the Lavi, setting aside for a moment the manner in which U.S. policy on this subject was decided and carried out. The first error in judgment was made when the United States refused to extend licensing privileges to Israel for the manufacture of the F-16. Developing a derivative fighter from the basic F-16 design offered the most economical means for meeting Israeli defense requirements. Further, any Israeli refinements, built around the basic F-16 airframe, could easily have been rolled back into the U.S. production line, providing the United States with additional opportunity to benefit from Israeli combat experience.

That having been said, once the decision was made to refuse Israel this option, the United States should have supported the Lavi development effort wholeheartedly, as the best remaining means for meeting Israel's specific defense needs. What was lacking, unfortunately, was willingness on the part of the U.S. Defense Department leadership to make the most out of the situation at hand. The Lavi offered the U.S. Defense Department a rare opportunity to expand the defense capabilities of the United States as well as those of Israel. There was no room in the U.S. defense budget to develop a dedicated close air support and attack platform along the lines of the Lavi. Interest in replacing the A-10 with an "A-16" version of the F-16 was lukewarm, and plans for such a replacement were eventually shelved in the 1990s. When U.S. troops entered the Gulf War in 1991, and again when they were sent into Afghanistan in 2002, it was the venerable A-10 that was still being called upon to provide close air support for U.S. soldiers on the ground. Slow, vulnerable to surface-to-air missiles and antiaircraft artillery, the A-10s could be sent into combat only after the area had been thoroughly cleared of antiaircraft threats. Instead of campaigning to kill the Lavi, the secretary of defense should have been seizing the opportunity to use U.S. foreign-assistance funding to develop a close air support platform suitable for meeting both U.S. and Israeli tactical needs. It was an opportunity to take advantage of funding that the Defense Department would not otherwise have had access to. The Israelis had succeeded in developing a superb attack platform, at a fraction of the cost that a U.S. prime contractor would have required. At a time when the only all-new U.S. fighter development effort centered on the dedicated air-to-air role, the United States should have been sizing up the Lavi as an opportunity to expand its own stable of combat aircraft while keeping costs under control. Unfortunately, the defense secretary in office at that time had neither the imagination nor the temperament to view the Lavi as a potential opportunity rather than as an adversary.

Weinberger's inability to think outside of his own preconceptions and narrow terms of reference was a constant impediment throughout much of the Reagan presidency, affecting a variety of defense and foreign policy issues. Another classical example of this occurred in November 1985, when President Reagan was expected to meet with Soviet premier Mikhail Gorbachev in Geneva. This summit meeting was seen by both the president and his secretary of state as the payoff for Reagan's hard-line defense policies. The United States had brought the cash-strapped Soviet Union to the negotiating table for the first serious strategic arms reduction talks in over a decade. For the first time, the Soviets had shown a willingness to cross their traditional red lines and negotiate terms for a far-reaching, verifiable nuclear weapons reduction pact. Weinberger, however, was unable to readjust his thinking to take advantage of this new opportunity and remained adamantly opposed to the summit. Unable to convince the president to cancel the meeting, Weinberger instead wrote Reagan a sternly worded letter of warning—which was then leaked to both the *New York Times* and the *Washington Post*, just days before the summit was scheduled to begin. President Reagan's Cabinet members and White House staff understood all too clearly that the letter had been intentionally leaked with Weinberger's tacit approval.[19] There was no other rational explanation as to why Weinberger would have penned such a letter. All of the arguments that Weinberger voiced had already been aired numerous times during Cabinet meetings months in advance. As Secretary of State Shultz would observe, "Weinberger's letter must have been written and leaked deliberately to hamstring the President and sabotage the summit."[20] Unable to achieve his aims through legitimate means, Weinberger had once again turned to behind-the-scenes stratagems and rogue operations.

Nor was this the only occasion when Weinberger's inability to readjust to changing realities or find common ground within the Reagan White House had caught the attention of his fellow Cabinet members. During one particularly heated policy discussion, after Weinberger had launched into one of his infamous monologues, Secretary of State George Shultz lost his patience, left his seat, and exited the room. Before he took the final step into the hallway, however, Shultz paused momentarily at the door to deliver one last, parting remark to his fellow Cabinet member: "You know, it's pointless to try to do business with you, Cap. You don't analyze things. You take stances. If you're going to govern, you have to listen and analyze and figure out the right thing to do. But you don't ever do that Cap."[21] Weinberger's inability to seek common ground, to see U.S.-Israeli security cooperation as an asset that could expand on U.S. defense capabilities rather than as a burden that he should forever seek to cast off, meant that the cancellation of the Lavi would become a tragic loss for America as well as for Israel.

Ronald Reagan had entered the White House with the preservation of Israel's national security as a core element of his personal convictions. Despite all of the controversy that surrounded the Lavi and whatever disagreements had taken place during his administration, President Reagan's views on this subject never wavered. As he would write years later, "I've believed many things in my life, but no conviction I've ever held has been stronger than my belief that the United States must ensure the survival of Israel. . . . My dedication to the preservation of Israel was as strong when I left the White House as when I arrived there, even though this tiny ally, with whom we share democracy and many other values, was a source of great concern for me while I was president."[22] It is sad to consider that President Reagan's own stated objectives could be so undermined by bureaucratic infighting among the respective government agencies and presidential appointees.

The "loose cannon" phenomenon that eventually killed the Lavi was a constant drain on President Reagan's legacy. It affected U.S. relations with Israel and U.S. foreign policy in general and ultimately left a stain of scandal when the Iran-Contra affair finally began to unravel. As Reagan's ambassador to the United Nations, Jeane Kirkpatrick, would later observe, "What was missing was follow-through. The President would make decisions three, four, five times, and they would never be implemented. . . . What was missing was the President saying 'Now do it, or do it this way. Cut it out. Don't do that.'"[23]

Ronald Reagan achieved great strides under his administration, including the expansion of U.S. and Israeli defense cooperation, restoring America's deterrent posture throughout the world, and ultimately bringing down the great Soviet juggernaut that had cast its shadow across the globe for decades. We can only wonder at how much more could have been achieved had his vision been allowed to take its natural course and had his appointees and the career civil servants who labored under them remained loyal to the president's objectives, rather than to their own policy agendas.

We will never know what might have happened had the Israeli Cabinet chosen to continue the Lavi program in August 1987. Within a matter of weeks, Defense Secretary Weinberger would step down, and the way might well have been cleared for the Lavi to truly become a collaborative U.S.-Israeli effort, rather than a source of friction. The Lavi was America's loss, not only Israel's, leaving us to forever wonder at what might have been.

1. A Lavi logo from Israel Aircraft Industries, as popularized at the height of the development effort. (Author's collection)

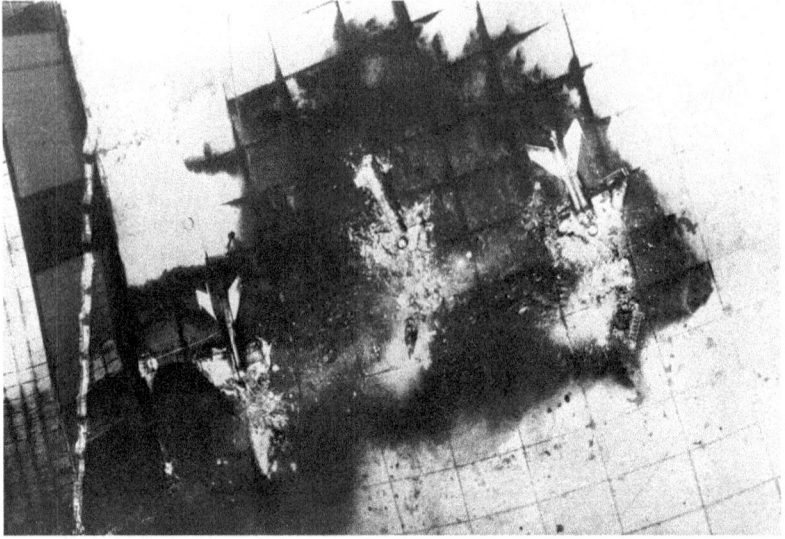

2. Airpower played a decisive role in the 1967 Six-Day War, beginning with the destruction of the Egyptian air force. Depicted are the burned-out remains of three Egyptian MiG-21s, as viewed from an Israeli fighter-bomber. (GPO)

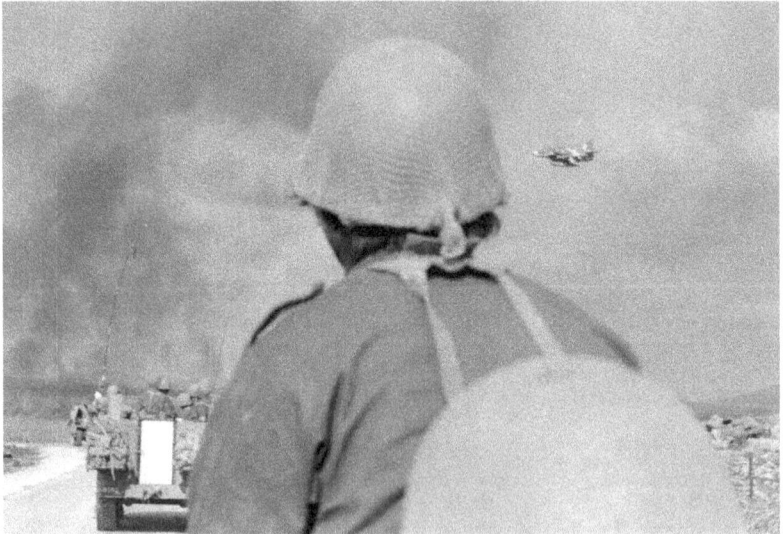

3. An A-4 Skyhawk provides air cover to Israeli troops on the Golan Heights during the Yom Kippur War. The Skyhawk squadrons would experience severe losses from enemy SAM batteries. (GPO)

4. From left to right are IAI director Al Schwimmer, Defense Minister Shimon Peres, and Prime Minister Yitzhak Rabin at the public rollout ceremony for the Kfir in April 1975. (Moshe Milner, GPO)

5. A Kfir roars overhead at the unveiling for the canard-equipped Kfir C2 in July 1976. The black-and-orange triangles on the wings were intended for ease of recognition, to avoid friendly fire accidents. (Yaacov Saar, GPO)

6. The YF-16 and YF-17 prototypes in a rare joint photograph. The Israeli air force followed the development of both programs with keen interest. (USAF)

7. One of Israel's first F-16AS is greeted at an official welcoming ceremony in July 1980. (Yaacov Saar, GPO)

8. Prime Minister Menachem Begin (*left*) is accompanied by the air force commander Maj. Gen. David Ivry (*right*) as he tours the Israeli F-16 squadron responsible for the Osirak nuclear reactor raid. (Chanania Herman, GPO)

9. From left to right: Moshe Arens, Prime Minister Menachem Begin, and chief of staff Lt. Gen. "Raful" Eitan prepare for a press briefing on the Osirak nuclear reactor raid. (Chanania Herman, GPO)

10. A prototype f-16xl puts its extensive weapons load on display. Proposed to the usaf as a deep strike platform, the f-16xl eventually lost out to the f-15e. Despite Israeli interest in the type, it never reached production. (usaf)

11. Japan's f-2 was another derivative of the f-16, featuring a stretched fuselage and an enlarged wing—offering additional payload and range—as well as a stronger, two-piece canopy. (usaf)

12. Defense Minister Moshe Arens meets with Secretary of Defense Caspar Weinberger. Although the two seldom saw eye to eye, Defense Minister Arens was at least on better speaking terms with the secretary than his predecessor was. (DoD)

13. President Ronald Reagan meets with Prime Minister Yitzhak Shamir, Defense Minister Moshe Arens, and Secretary of State George Shultz in November 1983. (Yaacov Saar, GPO)

14. President Reagan addresses the press corps on the White House lawn on November 29, 1983, when he first calls upon Congress to approve the use of FMS funding to assist in developing the Lavi. (Yaacov Saar, GPO)

15. Technicians install components into the engineering mockup of the Lavi in July 1985. (Herard Reogorodetzki, GPO)

16. The engineering mockup was used to test the fit of various electronic, fuel, and hydraulic systems, prior to the assembly of the prototypes. (Herard Reogorodetzki, GPO)

17. Air force commander Maj. Gen. Amos Lapidot points out features of the Lavi cockpit for Prime Minister Shimon Peres in July 1985. The engineering mockup can be seen in the background. (Chanania Herman, GPO)

18. Dov Zakheim (*right*) meets with Prime Minister Yitzhak Shamir. Secretary of Defense Caspar Weinberger is in the background. (Chanania Herman, GPO)

19. The official rollout ceremony for the first two Lavi prototypes in July 1986. (Nati Harnik, GPO)

20. At the time of the rollout ceremony, the first prototype was undergoing preparation for first flight and had not yet been painted in its flight test colors. The second prototype, shown here, was therefore rolled out for the official welcoming. (Nati Harnik, GPO)

21. The number-one Lavi prototype is prepared for a flight test in February 1987. (Nati Harnik, GPO)

22. The number-one Lavi prototype in flight test in January 1987. (IAI, GPO)

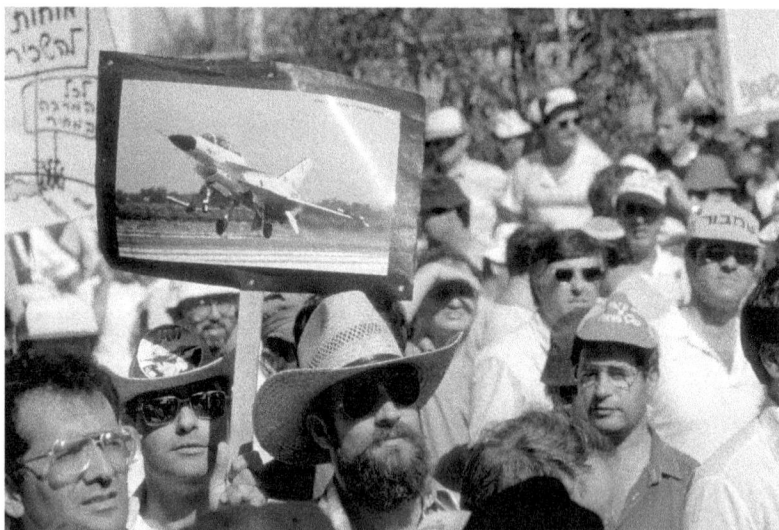

23. Protesters march outside of the prime minister's office in Jerusalem, condemning the cancellation of the Lavi program. (Maggi Ayalon, GPO)

24. Angry protesters near IAI's manufacturing facility in Lod set fire to tires and block access to the airport following the Lavi cancellation decision. (Maggi Ayalon, GPO)

25. Introduced over a decade and a half after the Lavi cancellation, the F-16I finally offered the kind of deep strike capability that the Lavi was once intended to provide. (USAF)

26. The Lavi Technology Demonstrator makes an appearance during an Independence Day open house—the last member of its breed. (Ziv Koren, GPO)

27. Despite being a much larger airplane, the Chengdu J-10 betrays its kinship with the Lavi.

APPENDIX NOMENCLATURE

General

A: aspect ratio, $A = b^2/S$

A: [appendix 4] regression coefficient for airplane weight

A_{max}: [appendix 7] maximum airplane cross-sectional area, minus the inlet capture area

a_0, a_1: [appendix 7] empirical coefficients for Oswald's efficiency

B: [appendix 4] regression coefficient for airplane weight

B: [appendix 5] bandwidth of the jammer antenna

b: wingspan

C: [appendix 5] the camouflage factor, or the minimum value of the jam-to-signal ratio, (J/S), at which the aircraft is still hidden from a hostile radar

C_D: drag coefficient, $C_D = D/qS$

C_{Dmin}: minimum drag coefficient (equivalent to C_{Do} for a symmetric drag polar)

C_{Do}: zero-lift drag coefficient

C_L: lift coefficient, $C_L = L/qS$

C_{Lmax}: maximum lift coefficient

C_{Lmin}: lift coefficient at the minimum drag coefficient, C_{Dmin}

$C_{L\alpha_{wb}}$: the wing-body lift-curve slope

$C_{L\alpha_c}$: canard lift-curve slope

C_{Lah}: horizontal tail lift-curve slope

c_j: thrust specific fuel consumption

c_r: wing root chord

c_t: wing tip chord

$\bar{c}$: the wing mean aerodynamic chord; for a straight, tapered wing, this value is given by: $\bar{c}=\frac{2}{3}c_r(1+\lambda+\lambda^2)/(1+\lambda)$

D: drag

e: Oswald's efficiency constant

g: Newton's constant, $g=32.174\,\mathrm{lb_m\,ft/lb_f\,s^2}$

G_j: [appendix 5] gain of the jammer antenna, in the direction of the receiver

G_r: [appendix 5] gain of the receiver radar antenna

$\bar{h}_c$: vertical separation between the canard and wing, $\bar{h}_c=h_c/\bar{c}$

(J/S): [appendix 5] jam-to-signal ratio

K_c: correction factor for Oswald's efficiency, to account for canard effects

K_m: correction factor for Oswald's efficiency, to account for Mach number effects

L: lift

(L/D): lift-to-drag ratio

l_c: axial distance between the quarter-chord of the wing mean aerodynamic chord and the canard mean aerodynamic chord

l: airplane length

n: airplane load factor in g's

P_j: [appendix 5] power of the radar jammer

P_r: [appendix 5] power of the hostile radar

P_s: specific excess power

q: dynamic pressure, $q=\rho v^2/2$

R: airplane range

R: [appendix 5] distance between airplane and tracking radar

R_B: [appendix 5] radar burn-through range

S: the wing reference area

S_c: canard area

S_h: horizontal tail area

sm: static margin

T: the available thrust

(T/W): thrust loading, or thrust-to-weight ratio

v: airplane velocity

W: airplane weight

W_E: airplane empty weight

W_f: final airplane weight, at the end of each mission segment

W_i: initial airplane weight, at the beginning of a mission segment

W_{TO}: airplane takeoff weight

(W/S): wing loading

x_c: the distance from the airplane center-of-gravity to the canard quarter chord location

x_h: the distance from the airplane center-of-gravity to the horizontal tail quarter chord location

$\bar{x}_{ac_A}$: location of the airplane aerodynamic center, as measured in units of the wing mean chord, $\bar{x}_{ac_A} = x_{ac_A}/\bar{c}$

$\Delta\bar{x}_{ac_b}$: shift in the wing-body aerodynamic center, due to the fuselage

$\bar{x}_{ac_c}$: distance to the canard aerodynamic center

$\bar{x}_{ac_h}$: distance to the horizontal tail aerodynamic center

$\bar{x}_{ac_w}$: location of the wing aerodynamic center

$\bar{x}_{ac_{wb}}$: location of the wing-body aerodynamic center, $\bar{x}_{ac_{wb}} = \bar{x}_{ac_w} + \Delta\bar{x}_{ac_b}$

$\bar{x}_{cg}$: location of the airplane center of gravity, as measured in units of the wing mean chord

α: angle of attack

λ: the wing taper ratio, $\lambda = c_t/c_r$

ρ: ambient air density

σ: [appendix 5] the airplane's radar cross section

$\dot{\psi}$: airplane turn rate

Derivatives

$\frac{de_c}{d\alpha}$: upwash at the canard due to the wing

$\frac{de_h}{d\alpha}$: downwash at the horizontal tail due to the wing

$\frac{de_w}{d\alpha}$: mean downwash on the wing due to the canard

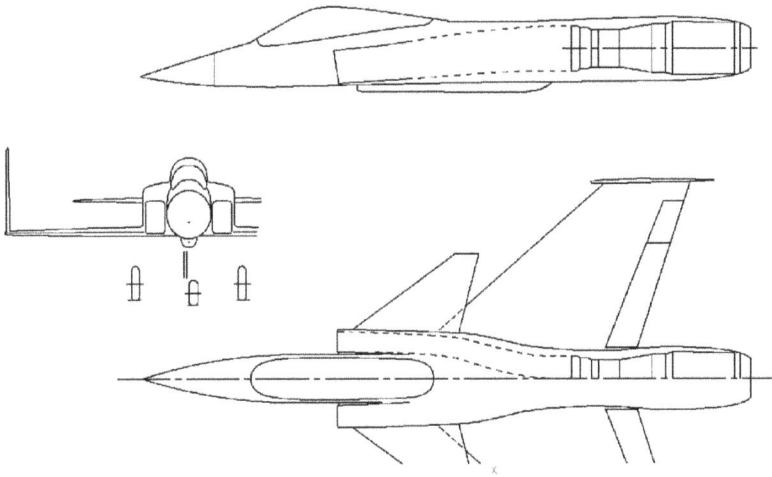

Fig. 1. A single-engine fighter from an IAI concept drawing dating back to 1973—at a time when the Kfir was still under development. This and other IAI concept studies were described in detail by S. Tsach and A. Peled in *Proceedings of the 16th ICAS*.

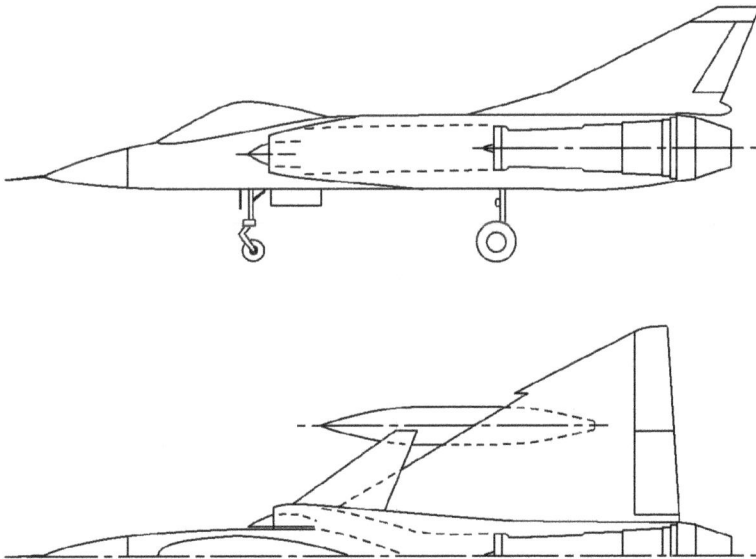

Fig. 2. Another IAI single-engine concept sketch—this one dating from 1974. The influence of IAI's Kfir experience is obvious.

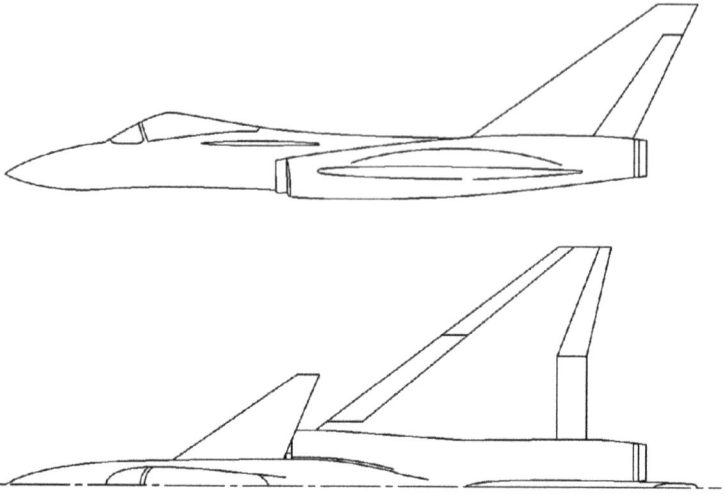

Fig. 3. By the mid-1970s, much of IAI's attention had turned toward twin-engine fighter studies. The concept shown was labeled Layout 26.

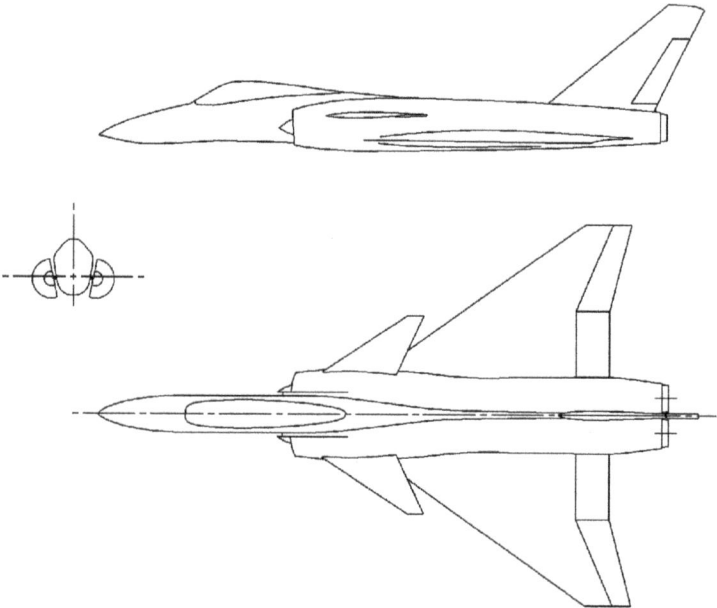

Fig. 4. The concept shown here is Layout 34. This configuration shared the wing geometry of the early Layout 33 studies, but with an axisymmetric, supersonic inlet.

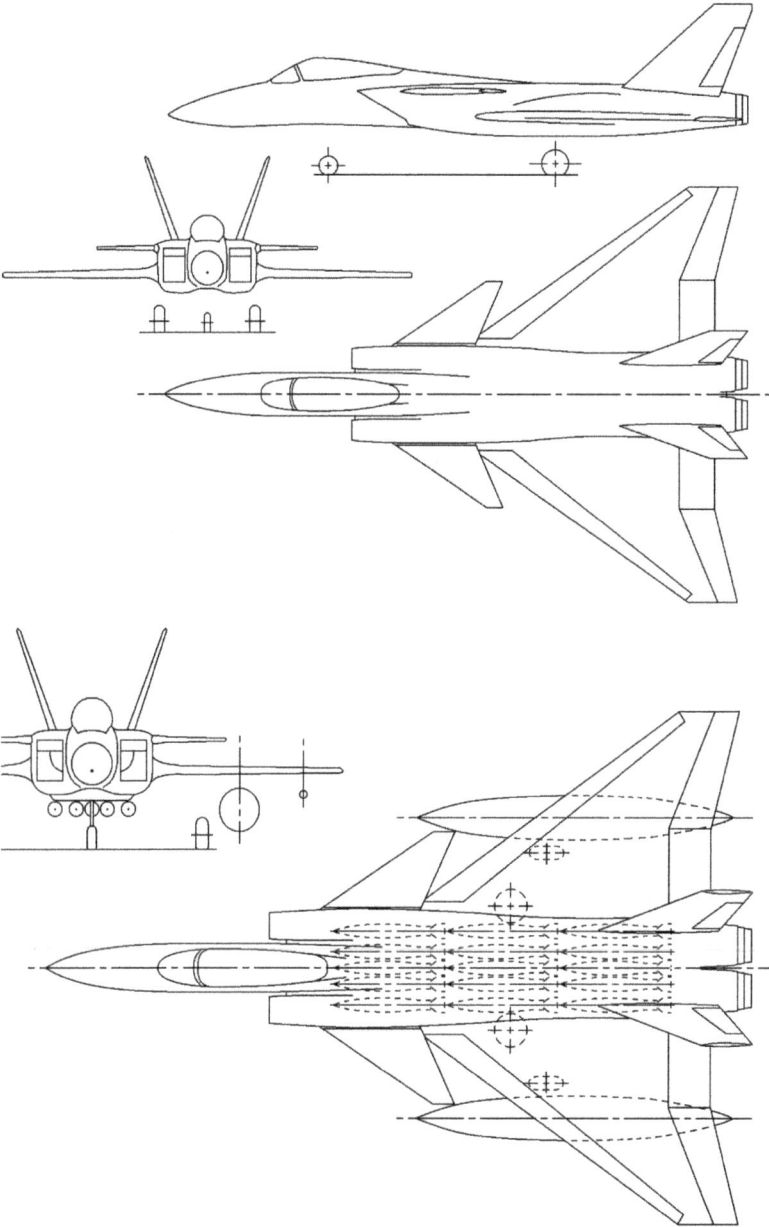

Figs. 5 and 6. Many of IAI's concept studies during the mid-1970s were focused on a large, multirole twin-engine proposal. The configuration shown represents different phases of the Layout 28 design study, which was the subject of considerable interest.

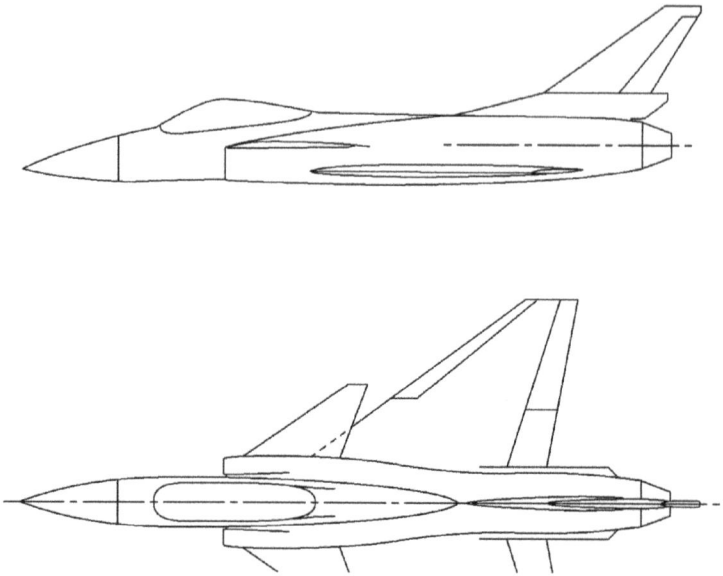

Fig. 7. A variation on the early Lavi trade studies featuring side-mounted inlets. Both the side-mounted and the ventral inlet offered low distortion at high angles of attack, but the ventral inlet proved to be lighter.

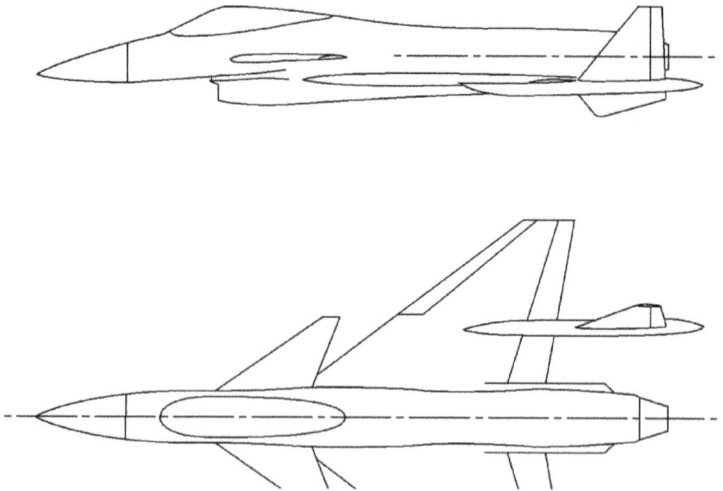

Fig. 8. One of the more unusual configurations evaluated was the tail boom design. Although the configuration had promise, it was heavier than the conventional alternatives.

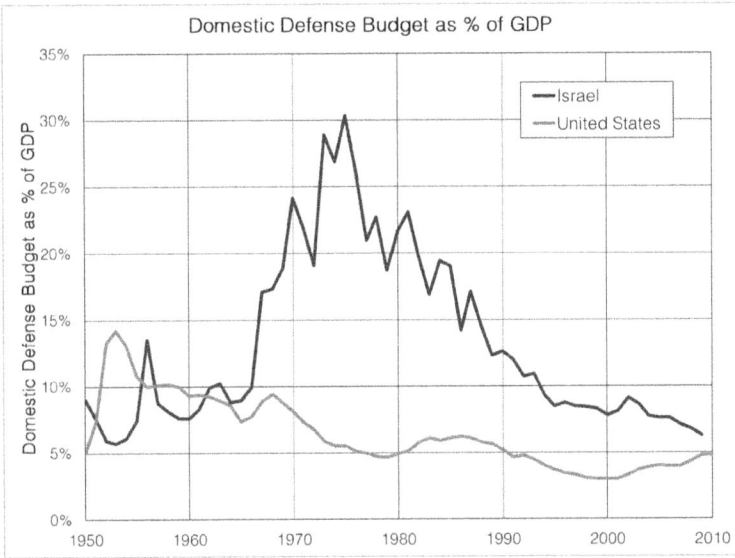

Fig. 9. As a percentage of Israel's GDP, Israeli domestic defense spending reached its peak following the Yom Kippur War, before declining toward a more sustainable level. Data assembled from Central Bureau of Statistics, *Defence Expenditure in Israel*; U.S. Office of Management and Budget, *Fiscal Year 2013 Historical Tables.*

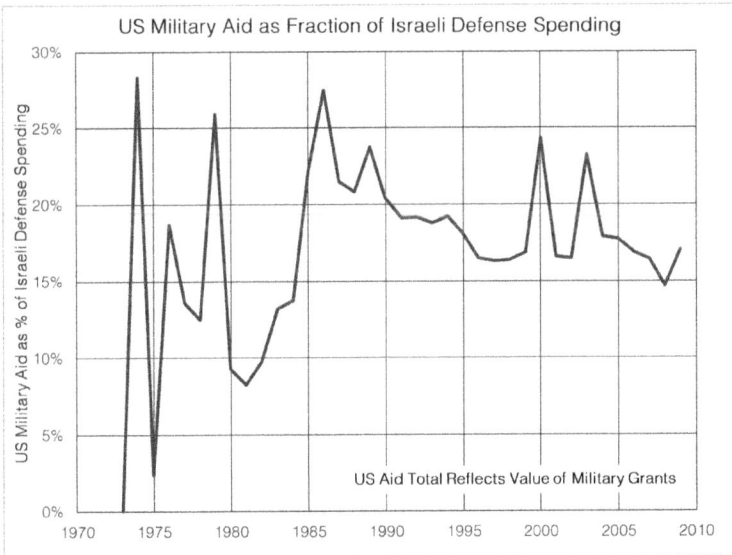

Fig. 10. U.S. military aid to Israel had plateaued by the mid-1980s, before declining during subsequent decades. Assembled from Sharp, *U.S. Foreign Aid to Israel.*

APPENDIX 1

Aerodynamics and a Philosophy for Design

Aerodynamics encompasses far more than how sleek an aircraft appears in pictures or how much drag it generates in flight. The aerodynamics of an airplane play an integral role in everything from handling and control to its turn rate and a host of related performance measures.

This particular segment of the text is not intended to delve into the more obvious aerodynamic features of the Lavi, whose function should be obvious to anyone familiar with aircraft. It is assumed that most readers will already be aware of what an elevon is, what an aileron does, or that a ventral engine inlet will assure a supply of undistorted air at high angles of attack. Instead, this appendix will focus primarily on that one aerodynamic feature of the Lavi that has been the most often poorly understood, if not misunderstood, even by many of those within the industry: the canard-delta combination.

Few features of modern fighter design have been more poorly understood by the general public than has the canard. Too many see the choice of a canard arrangement as being a reflection of stylistic preference—as if it were an article of clothing that the developers had chosen to accessorize with, rather than being the calculated engineering trade that it truly represents. In recent decades, canards have featured prominently in designs from Europe to the Far East, yet their value has remained strangely contested. Some have even gone so far as to argue that a canard design is likely to inherit higher induced drag penalties, due to the challenges of providing trim authority across the entire flight envelope, and that canards should therefore be abandoned.[1] There were defining reasons, however, that led the developers of the Lavi, and others, to choose the canard configurations that they did.

The Delta Connection

Many of the early jet fighters to first explore the application of a canard did so not so much out of a desire to explore a novel control surface geometry, but rather because they were attempting to alleviate shortfalls in the delta-wing configuration that they were already contemplating. From the 1950s onward, it had been recognized that a delta-wing configuration afforded certain advantages that made it attractive for some applications. The delta wing provided the maximum wing area possible, within the constraints on wingspan that many high-performance aircraft have had to wrestle with. This wing area, in turn, provided the airplane with the potential for superior lift, and as a result, with superior turn rate capabilities. The compact delta-wing geometry also offered a deeper wing root, providing for greater structural efficiency and a lighter-weight design. Added to this was the benefit of having a large, ready-made fuel tank, as well as a convenient location for hanging stores. Finally, the delta wing afforded excellent supersonic performance, with superior supersonic lift-to-drag characteristics, leading the delta wing to be embraced by bombers and fighters alike during the 1950s. Aircraft such as the B-58 Hustler, XB-70 Valkyrie, and Dassault Mirage III heralded the delta wing as the shape of the future. These were, at least, the theoretical advantages.

In practice, however, the delta wing also suffered from a number of shortfalls. In order to rotate the airplane at takeoff, the delta wing needed to produce a tail-down force with its elevons—producing negative lift at precisely the moment when the airplane most needed to be adding lift. The result was seen in disappointingly long runway requirements for a wing of such large area. The spanwise lift distribution of the delta wing was also suboptimal, with too much of the lift being produced near the root of the wing and much less near the tips. This distribution detracted from the subsonic aerodynamic efficiency and hence the lift-to-drag ratio of the airplane. While the delta wing appeared to be promising on paper, it often failed to deliver on all of its theoretical potential.

These shortfalls were what drove many of the earliest innovators to experiment with a canard configuration. Among the first was Sweden's Saab, which would embrace a canard design for their Viggen fighter. Its developers had been struggling with how to wring additional short runway performance out of a fighter compact enough to take off and land on stretches of remote highway. This dispersed basing scheme was an integral part of Sweden's airfield survivability concept. On the one hand, a delta-wing design seemed a natural choice when faced with the tight geometric restrictions imposed by a narrow, semiprepared runway. On the other hand, the extended runway requirements that came with a conventional delta-wing configuration were prohibitive. With the addition of a canard, however, the delta-winged Viggen was able to take full advantage of the lifting capabilities of its substantial wing area without the need for a downward elevon force at takeoff. The result was a fighter of compact dimensions and superb short-runway performance.

As was soon recognized, however, the canard also had the effect of taming a variety of performance characteristics associated with the delta wing—allowing a delta-wing design to take maximum advantage of its superior wing area and potential lifting surface. It was this phenomenon that ultimately led the Israeli developers of the Kfir to add a canard to their design—beginning with the flight of the first Kfir c2 prototype in February 1976. The Israeli developers added their canard to counteract the performance shortfalls that they were experiencing as they attempted to evolve the air-to-air Mirage III design into a multirole fighter-bomber. Adding the canard recovered much of the performance that had been eroded, increasing the airplane's sustained turn rate by 11 percent and its instantaneous turn rate by 13 percent.[2] Although the canard had, in this example, been added to ameliorate the deficiencies of an existing design, it was this same kind of benefit that would lead later developers to fully embrace a canard configuration.

A Tale of Two Families

Canard aircraft can be divided into two families of design philosophy: close coupled and long coupled. Most canard-equipped fighter aircraft fall into the former category. All of the civilian canard-equipped aircraft and a few of the fighters fall into the latter. The difference between the two is even greater than what their respective names might suggest.

All lifting surfaces—wings, canards, and horizontal tails alike—produce both an upwash and a downwash. This pattern of circulation is part of how they produce lift. The wing or control surface will produce an upwash ahead of the airfoil and a downwash behind it. For a conventional wing and tail arrangement, this means that the horizontal tail will produce a modest upwash on the wing, while the wing will produce a significant downwash on the tail. Similarly with a canard design, the wing will produce an upwash on the canard, and the canard will produce a downwash on the wing. It is this interaction that the designers of a canard configuration will seek to either maximize or avoid when selecting their arrangement.

Close-coupled canard designs are developed with the intention of leveraging this canard-wing interaction to optimize the aerodynamic performance of the canard-wing combination. This design philosophy is reflected in such aircraft as the Israeli Kfir and Lavi, the Swedish JA-37 Viggen and JAS-39 Gripen, and the French Rafale. Members of this family of design tend to position the canard in close proximity to and somewhat above the wing.

Long-coupled canard designs, on the other hand, attempt to minimize the canard-wing interaction. Examples of this approach include the various homebuilt designs developed by Burt Rutan and the Piaggio P180 Avanti, as well as the X-31 technology demonstrator and the Eurofighter Typhoon. Aircraft such as these will tend to position the canard as far away from the wing as practical, often locating the canard below the plane of its wing. As the existence of these two divergent families of design should suggest, there is more than one reason why a developer might choose to adopt a canard design.

Aerodynamic Authority

For airplanes like the x-31 and Eurofighter Typhoon, the canard provides an aerodynamic control surface that retains its authority at elevated angles of attack, under conditions where a conventional horizontal tail becomes progressively less effective. High angles of attack, of course, are an essential part of how a jet fighter is able to generate lift and turn the aircraft during an engagement. Consider for a moment that an airplane that is undergoing a 9 g turn is asking the wings of that airplane to provide a lifting force equal to nine times its weight. The airplane is able to perform this extraordinary feat primarily by increasing its angle of attack (AoA or "alpha"). The ability of a jet fighter to achieve and maintain control at these high-alpha conditions is therefore crucial to its success.

The secret to maintaining control at these high-AoA conditions is not in the ability to create a pitch-up moment but in the ability to generate a pitch-down moment, to prevent the airplane from diverging into uncontrolled flight. For an aircraft with a horizontal tail, this pitch-down moment must be provided by an ever-increasing incidence angle—causing the horizontal tail to stall much earlier than the airplane's wing. Once stalled, the horizontal tail is no longer effective at producing lift, and the only way that it can still produce a restoring moment to return the airplane to level flight is through drag. At even higher AoA conditions, the horizontal tail will approach a 90° incidence angle—at which point the airplane enters "deep stall" and has insufficient control authority to return to level flight. On the F-16, for example, this occurs just beyond 50° AoA. In stark contrast, the canard on the x-31 retains aerodynamic authority all the way up to 85° AoA—well beyond the point where the wing of the airplane has stalled.[3] The practical result is that the canard of such airplanes as the x-31 and Eurofighter Typhoon can be sized substantially smaller than the horizontal tail seen on the F-16 or other conventional aircraft. This results in a lighter structure, with less wetted area and lower drag than a conventional tail design could afford—in addition to superior aerodynamic authority in the post-stall flight envelope.

Close Coupled

There is, however, another set of reasons why a canard configuration might be adopted: the canard-wing interactions of a close-coupled design. The objective of the close-coupled canard and wing is to optimize this interaction effect, to produce a canard-wing combination with superior aerodynamic characteristics. This interaction is by no means an act of simple addition. The aerodynamic center of the airplane is shifted farther forward than what might be suggested from the size of either the wing or canard on its own.[4] This nonlinear effect is what makes a close-coupled canard-wing combination so difficult to design—and potentially so rewarding.

One of the most well-known components of this canard-wing interaction involves the phenomenon of vortex shedding. In a close-coupled canard-and-wing design, the tip vortices from the canard will trace their way across the upper surface of the wing, energizing and stabilizing the tip vortices produced by the wing. The interaction of the two will cause the canard vortices to move inboard, while the wing vortices will move outboard, relative to a canard-alone or wing-alone configuration. These tip vortices create a suction that helps to keep the airflow of the wing attached at high angles of attack. The effect of the canard is to stabilize the tip vortices produced by the wing—permitting the wing to achieve higher angles of attack without experiencing flow separation, and in turn allowing the wing to produce more lift.[5] This interaction is not without its repercussions. The stall characteristics of the wing will tend to become sharp and sudden, with its handling remaining steady right up until stall occurs. This interaction, however, increases the maximum AoA and lift available to the airplane, and in an age of fly-by-wire control systems, there are other means that can be used to warn the pilot that he is approaching the envelope's edge.[6]

This is not, however, the only canard-wing interaction that is of potential importance in the design of a close-coupled configuration. The interaction of the canard downwash on the wing also alters the span-wise lift distribution across the wing. It reduces the amount of lift produced at the wing root and increases the lift at the wing tip. In doing so, the net lift distribution will migrate toward a more elliptical lift profile—improving the aerodynamic efficiency of the wing and, by extension, improving the airplane's lift-to-drag ratio.

The reasons why this lift distribution should be so important should be obvious to anyone familiar with the classical drag polar:

$$C_D = C_{Do} + C_L^2/\pi A e$$

(1.1)

The drag coefficient, C_D, is a nondimensionalized expression for the overall drag of the airplane that comprises the sum of two elements: the parasitic or skin friction drag, C_{Do}, and the induced drag or drag due to lift, expressed by the $(C_L^2/\pi A e)$ term. Notice from equation 1.1 that the induced drag is related to the lift coefficient squared divided by the aspect ratio, A, and the Oswald's efficiency, e, where the aspect ratio is defined by the wingspan squared divided by the wing area:

$$A = b^2/S$$

(1.2)

As should be evident from equation 1.1, drag will increase as the airplane's lift increases, but it will increase less rapidly for airplanes with a larger aspect ratio, A, or a larger efficiency constant, e. For a fighter, the physics of high-speed flight and maneuver mitigate against a large aspect ratio. An enhanced aerodynamic efficiency, on the other hand, is still a commodity to be sought after.

The highest Oswald's efficiency factor that is theoretically possible will occur for a wing with an elliptic lift distribution. A classic example of this principle in practice is the World War II British Spitfire, with its elliptic wing planform—selected for precisely this reason. An elliptical wing planform, however, is impractical for a transonic or supersonic aircraft. An unswept wing would experience transonic "drag rise" at a much lower Mach number, decreasing its practical cruise velocity. Designing a close-coupled canard configuration that emulates a net elliptical lift distribution, however, is possible. This was yet another reason why many developers came to embrace the canard-delta combination.

Achieving the most out of the Lavi wing and canard, however, was not as simple as combining an arbitrary canard with an arbitrary wing. To truly optimize this lift distribution, the Lavi wing and canard had to be tailored to each other and to the specific flight conditions intended for the airplane. This meant that particular attention also had to be paid to the individual airfoil section characteristics. The Lavi development team had to fine-tune their wing cross section, and wing sectional twist, to maximize the performance enhancement provided by the canard. This marked yet another deviation between the Lavi and prior generations of jet fighter design. Previous Western fighter aircraft, including both the F-15 and F-16, had relied on NACA airfoil sections developed during the 1940s and 1950s to define their basic wing-section geometry. The Lavi, in contrast, took full advantage of the aerodynamic advances that had been developed over the intervening decades to develop a three-dimensional wing definition that was tailored to transonic flight. Advances of this kind had already made their mark on the civilian aircraft market, where "supercritical" wing sections—which delayed the onset of transonic drag rise—had already improved efficiencies and increased cruise speeds for the latest generation of business jets and airliners. The Lavi, however, had to carry this technology one step further, to integrate a canard with a supercritical wing. In all, a total of fifty airfoil sections would be used to define the Lavi wing, each selected with the aim of increasing the critical Mach number of the airplane and allowing for the maximum reduction in induced drag.[7]

Design and Aerodynamic Prediction

Every aerospace magazine in the business, from the professional journals to the weekly news magazines to the popularized monthlies, has by now had its fair share of dazzling images generated by computer-driven flow simulations. They are almost always displayed in bright colors, with flashy streamlines or pressure contours, and we are always told with confidence that this image represents the flow at such-and-such a speed, at this-or-that altitude. What the uninitiated are often unaware of is that without meaningful calibration against a similar aircraft or missile geometry, either in wind tunnel or flight test, the flashy picture is little more than an over-zealous guess. The computer images represent a model of how we suspect the flow might behave. It might be correct. It might also be little more than an expensive cartoon. In either event, that suspicion alone is never enough on which to risk tens of millions in development cost, much less a pilot's life.

The modern computer age has brought about a revolution in computational fluid dynamics (CFD). It is now possible to assemble complex mathematical models that can predict airflow characteristics over a wide range of conditions. But not over all conditions, or at all times. Unlike the finite element models that are commonly used for structural analyses, the world of computational fluid dynamics is filled with complex interactions and nonlinear phenomena, such that no one computational model can adequately capture the whole of nature's tapestry. The simulations must always be calibrated against experimental and flight-test data. Even then, they remain valid only for that narrow range of conditions and geometry against which they have been properly calibrated. The computer and computational fluid dynamics are therefore tools, not magic wands. They make possible a series of optimization cycles that would have been prohibitively expensive to explore in flight test. They still rely, however, on informed interpretation and experimental verification.

To provide preflight validation of their CFD results, the Lavi development team, like every generation of aeronautical engineers since the Wright Brothers, turned to wind tunnel models. Israel Aircraft Industries had at their disposal their own 4 ft subsonic wind tunnel to provide the initial test data needed to correlate their computer predictions against physical observations. Scale models of the Lavi were repeatedly tested, equipped to take measurements of aerodynamic pressures and hinge moments, helping to verify the behavior of the control surfaces and the feedback gains that would later become part of the flight control software.[8] Even then, once the Lavi did enter flight test, the flight envelope was explored cautiously, probing for the unexpected surprises that were certain to turn up.

There would always be phenomena that neither the computer model nor the subscale wind tunnel tests could predict. In flight test, for example, the Lavi elevons proved to be more effective than had been predicted by either the wind tunnel or CFD results. This phenomenon, at around Mach 0.95, became coupled to a higher than expected static margin, with the aircraft proving to be some 3 percent more stable at these flight conditions than had been anticipated from preflight modeling. The two effects combined to produce a pitch oscillation across this flight condition, which had to be rectified by readjusting the feedback gain for the elevons. Once the flight control logic was suitably corrected, the pitch oscillations ceased to be a subject of concern. It was, however, another reminder that no amount of simulation, whether on the computer or in the wind tunnel, could substitute for a dedicated flight-test program.[9]

Cousins, Not Siblings

At the time that the Lavi was under development, there were a number of fighter aircraft on the drawing board that would share the Lavi's choice of a canard-delta combination. These would include the Swedish JAS-39 Gripen, the French Rafale, and the Eurofighter Typhoon. This trio would later be joined by China's Chengdu J-10, rounding out a string of canard-delta fighter configurations that would enter service at the turn of the century. Despite superficial similarities, however, each of these aircraft had been driven by a slightly different combination of design objectives, which had led them to emphasize different elements of the canard-wing combination.

Alone among these aircraft, the Eurofighter Typhoon had selected a long-coupled canard-delta configuration that sought to minimize the effect of the canard on the wing's performance. Much like the experimental X-31A demonstrator, the Typhoon embraced a classical approach to maximize its air-to-air agility, which included minimizing wing loading and maximizing the airplane's thrust-to-weight ratio. In this application, the attraction of the canard stemmed from its ability to maintain control authority at high angles of attack, well beyond the limits of stall.

The remaining canard-delta fighter configurations, on the other hand, had all incorporated a close-coupled canard configuration, although the relative canard size and degree of aerodynamic enhancement being sought differed from one airplane to the next. There were a variety of reasons why each of these aircraft had selected a canard-delta combination. For the Swedish air force, in particular, the ability to shorten the airplane's takeoff and landing distance, providing the potential for operation out of remote runways, was a decisive factor.

Alone among these aircraft, however, the Lavi had been optimized not for interceptor performance but for its capabilities as a fully loaded attack jet. It was not that air-to-air performance was not important for the Lavi. Quite the contrary. In the words of Maj. Gen. Amos Lapidot, "Air-to-air combat, the dogfight, is the major area of a modern air battle."[10] It should be recalled that these words came from a man who, before he had taken over the reins as Israel's air force chief, had been personally responsible for overseeing the development of the Lavi from an austere A-4 replacement into a long-range, multirole attack jet. In an arena as heavily saturated with missiles and fighter jets as the Middle East, even an attack jet could not expect to avoid a close-quarters dogfight.

But the Lavi had the added challenge of being an attack jet first, in addition to its air defense responsibilities. It had to be able to travel great distances with heavy payloads and still be able to defend itself from opposing air defenses. Obtaining the maximum benefit from its close-coupled canard-delta design was therefore central to the strategy behind the design of the Lavi. To achieve these objectives, the Israeli developers had focused on a design with a larger, more closely coupled canard than that found under any of its contemporaries. Even the Chengdu J-10, for all of its similarities to the Lavi in other respects, had been designed with a smaller and less closely coupled canard.

Projecting from the published, experimental data to assess the effects of the canard on aerodynamic performance, the majority of the canard-delta fighter arrangements developed to date, including the Rafale, the Gripen, and the J-10, could expect to see roughly a 10 percent improvement in their aerodynamic efficiency (or Oswald's efficiency) as a direct result of incorporating a canard. The experimental HiMAT configuration would have achieved a slightly greater benefit, with roughly a 20 percent improvement in its aerodynamic efficiency. Alone among these aircraft, however, the Lavi would have far exceeded the 20 percent mark. In a clean configuration, in level flight, the Lavi was projected to have a subsonic Oswald's efficiency in excess of unity, a product of a dedicated effort to maximize the range that could be obtained out of such a small airframe.[11]

The aerodynamic design of the Lavi was not a chance occurrence, nor was it merely a predecided preference ingrained into Israel's design community. The decision to select a canard-delta configuration had been based on a solid understanding of the risks and the benefits of such a design. As with all of the other aircraft to select a canard-delta combination, the Lavi development team had been influenced by the potential enhancements to agility and high angle of attack performance that such a configuration could offer. They had also, however, been influenced by the potential to lower their induced drag and, as a result, to vastly improve on the range of their small fighter-bomber. The Israeli developers had been informed by decades of research that had preceded them in the realms of transonic aerodynamics, aeroelastic tailoring, and canard-delta interactions. Most importantly, however, their design had been informed by precisely what it was that the Heyl Ha'Avir expected from this warplane.

. . .

The Chengdu J-10: The Lion's Chinese Cousin

There has been a fair degree of confusion surrounding the Chengdu J-10 (Jian-10) and its relationship to the Lavi. Enough details have emerged, however, to paint at least a partial picture.

The J-10 was developed during a period of relatively cordial relations not merely between China and Israel but also between China and the United States. It was during this same period, for example, that both Israel's IAI and Britain's GEC-Marconi were engaged in an open bidding war to supply China's first AWACS. When the winning contract was finally awarded to IAI in July 1996, the Clinton administration would register only the mildest of protests.[1] Washington was

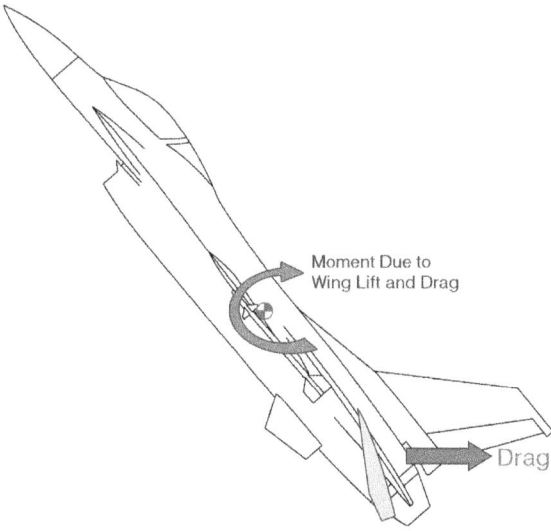

Fig. 11. At elevated angles of attack, a horizontal tail will become stalled well before the airplane's wing. Once this happens, the only restoring moment that the tail can produce will be through added drag.

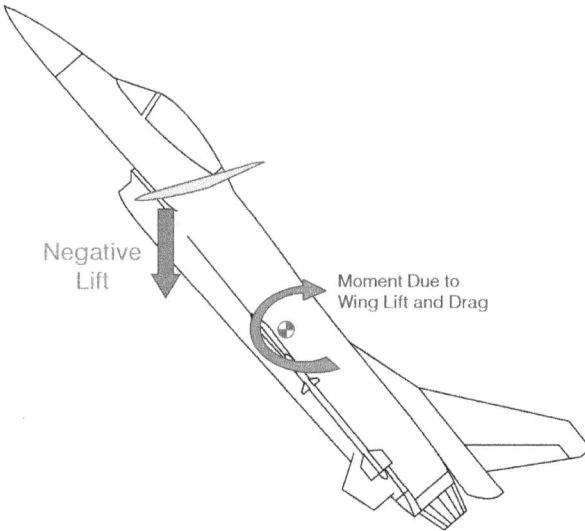

Fig. 12. In contrast to the horizontal tail shown in figure 11, a canard will retain aerodynamic authority even at very high angles of attack, allowing it to exert a restoring moment through negative-lift force.

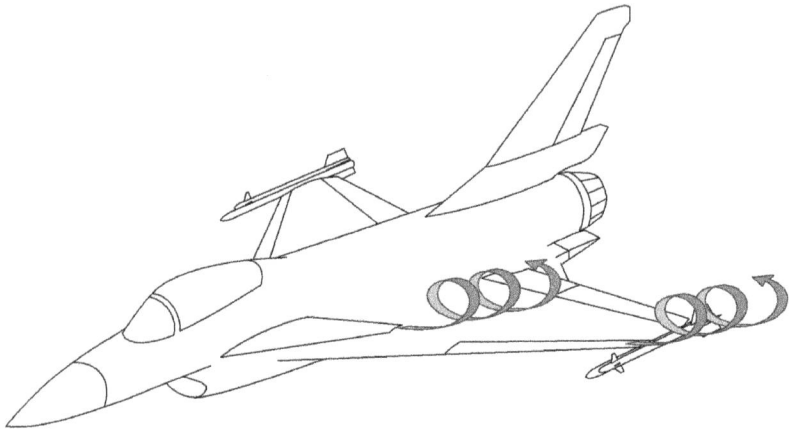

Fig. 13. In a close-coupled design, the canard tip vortices will energize both the wing boundary layer and the wingtip vortices.

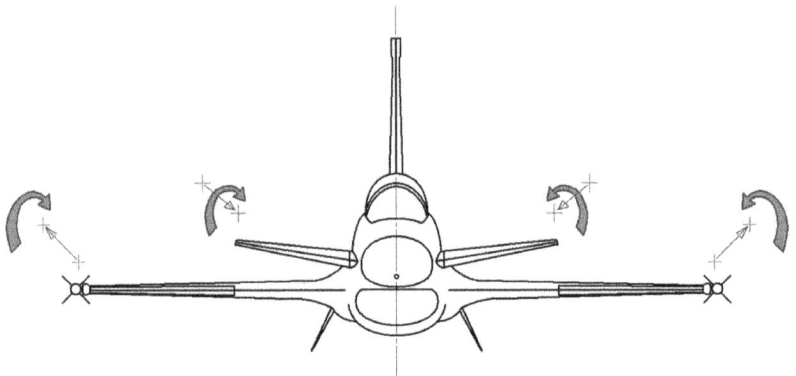

Fig. 14. This canard-wing interaction will tend to shift the wingtip vortices upward, and outward, into a higher energy state. This has the effect of delaying the onset of vortex breakdown and boundary layer separation, helping to maintain lift at elevated angles of attack.

not yet apprehensive regarding China's intentions and still sought to engage China as a strategic counterbalance to Russian ambitions in the Far East.

Israeli involvement in the J-10 appears to have begun at around the same time that China first opened diplomatic relations with Israel in January 1992.[2] In much the same way that Lockheed's Fort Worth Division had been contracted to provide the aerodynamic and structural foundation for Taiwan's Ching-Kuo fighter, Israeli contractors were similarly engaged to provide the aerodynamic and structural outlines for the J-10. The Israeli influences on the J-10's design are unmistakable: a close-coupled, canard delta arrangement; a single-engine fighter featuring a ventral engine inlet; twin ventral strakes; and an area-ruled fuselage. Despite these and other similarities, however, the Chengdu J-10 was also not the same airplane as the Lavi.

In developing an outline for Chengdu to follow, the Israeli consultants had to take into account both their customer's specific objectives and the limitations imposed by China's manufacturing facilities. Whereas the Lavi had featured extensive use of composite structures to reduce its empty weight, China's industrial base was not yet prepared to produce aerospace-quality composite components on a reliable basis. The inevitable result was a heavier, all-metal airframe that also lacked the advantages of aerodynamic tailoring that composites could provide. Structurally, the wing had more in common with the earlier Kfir than with the Lavi. Moreover, whereas the Lavi had been able to rely on a state-of-the-art, American-made engine, the Chinese had at their disposal only Soviet-developed engines. The Chinese ultimately selected the Russian-produced AL-31F for their new airplane, a much larger engine than the Lavi's PW1120. Of necessity, the AL-31F would mandate the development of a much larger airframe. Based upon analysis of photography publicly available to the West, the J-10 is estimated to weigh in at some 21,460 lb (9,730 kg) empty weight, with a 490 sq ft (45.5 m²) wing area.[3] This places the J-10 empty weight at nearly 40 percent greater than that of the Lavi. According to published reports, China eventually closed on a contract for the delivery of three hundred AL-31F engines from Russia to support initial production of the new fighter.[4]

The J-10 remained, however, something of a stray raven, tossed by the winds of fate to roost among a flock of gulls. In an era when airpower has increasingly been at the forefront of modern force projection, China's political leadership has continued to downplay its role.

Official policy statements continued to emphasize the role of the People's Liberation Army Air Force (PLAAF) in providing "indirect support" to the Chinese ground forces, rather than being at the cutting edge of their fighting capability.[5] This lack of appreciation for the breadth of capabilities that a modern air force can afford in a combined-arms environment has been only further hampered by the lack of status that the Chinese air force has enjoyed throughout the history of the People's Liberation Army. It was not until 1985, for example, that the Chinese air force finally had a commanding officer who was himself a career aviator. All prior Chinese air force chiefs, in contrast, had been army generals, appointed to keep a watchful eye over the PLAAF.[6]

The Chinese-Israeli romance out of which the J-10 was born faded during the latter 1990s, as the United State grew more apprehensive in the wake of a series of espionage scandals. The most visible manifestation of this chill in Israeli-Chinese relations came in July 2000, when, at the behest of the United States, the Israeli government announced that it would cancel the sale of the AWACS aircraft to China. The sale, which the Clinton administration had once tacitly accepted, had come to be vocally opposed by Washington. In the words of one U.S. Air Force official, "We knew about the China AWACS deal years ago and nobody complained. Early in the Clinton Administration the U.S. cozied up to China on all sorts of things, including missiles and satellite technology transfers. Now things have changed, and nearly every politician in Washington is opposed to any technology going to China."[7] Israeli involvement in the J-10 program appears to have been curtailed at around this same time, with Russia stepping in to market Soviet-developed avionics systems to supply production versions of the airplane.[8]

According to reports issued by the U.S. Department of Defense, the J-10 completed its developmental trials in 2004 and was introduced shortly thereafter into operational service. Defense Intelligence Agency estimates project that some 1,200 J-10 fighters will eventually be produced.[9] It nonetheless remains to be seen, however, whether the PLAAF will yet overcome its historical doctrinal dogmas and take full advantage of the capabilities that a multirole strike fighter might afford.

1. David A. Fulghum, "Israel Builds China's First AWACS Aircraft," AW&ST, November 29, 1999, 31.

2. Goldstein, China and Israel, 105–25.

3. John Golan, "Piercing the Dragon's Veil: Sizing-Up China's J-10 Fighter," Combat Aircraft, no 9 (November 2006): 20–25.

4. Shambaugh, *Modernizing China's Military*, 261.

5. Mulvenon and Yang, *People's Liberation Army as Organization*, 369.

6. Mulvenon and Yang, *People's Liberation Army as Organization*, 355.

7. David A. Fulghum, "Israel Backs Off China AWACS Sale," *AW&ST*, July 17, 2000, 45.

8. Douglas Barrie, "Chinese Air Force in Throes of Cultural Revolution," *AW&ST*, November 4, 2002, 55–56.

9. U.S. Office of the Secretary of Defense, *Military Power of the People's Republic of China*, 4.

APPENDIX 2

Stability and Control

Aircraft stability and control grew to be recognized as a distinct and separate discipline only after decades of airplane design experience—much of it punctuated by spectacular failures. As aircraft entered the jet age and encountered the added complexities of transonic flight, the importance of stability and control would only grow, further heightened by the emergence of "fly-by-wire" technology. It was no accident, therefore, that the Lavi development team devoted a significant share of their resources, and flight-test time, to ensuring that this key design element would be thoroughly mastered, and validated in flight.

Relaxed Static Stability

The stability of an aircraft is measured in terms of its "static margin": the distance separating the airplane center of gravity from the airplane aerodynamic center, measured as a percentage of the wing mean geometric chord.

$$\bar{x}_{ac_A} - \bar{x}_{cg}$$

(2.1)

The traditional rule for both civilian and military transport aircraft was that for an airplane to be regarded as "stable," the static margin should never be less than 10 percent. For fighter aircraft, where agility is essential and where the pilot is expected to be devoting his full attention, this objective was often relaxed. Historically, successful fighter aircraft were usually designed with a static margin of around 5 percent. Never, however, prior to the age of micro-electronics, was the static margin allowed to wander unrestrained into the negative regime.[1] An airplane with a negative static margin would rapidly become uncontrollable and unfit to fly. No amount of pilot skill could keep up with the rate at which small perturbations could destabilize the airplane.

In order to understand why this should be so, consider first the case of a statically stable aircraft—where the aerodynamic center is located behind the center of gravity. Let us assume for the moment that the airplane is properly trimmed for level flight, with the control surfaces counteracting the natural tendency of the airplane to pitch downward. Now consider how such an airplane reacts to a gust of wind that causes the nose of the vehicle to pitch upward by a few degrees. The increased angle of attack will increase the lift experienced from the wing. Because the airplane is statically stable, with the aerodynamic center located behind the center of gravity, this increase in lift will produce a downward pitch moment, restoring the airplane to level flight. Similarly, if a gust of wind were to produce a downward aircraft pitch, the decreased angle of attack would result in a decrease in lift, resulting in a pitch-up moment, restoring the airplane to level flight. For a properly damped system, all of this would occur naturally, with minimal intervention from the pilot.

Now consider a statically unstable aircraft, one with its aerodynamic center located ahead of its center of gravity. Like the stable aircraft, this airplane can use its control surfaces to trim the vehicle for level flight. As with the stable aircraft, a gust of wind that caused an increased angle of attack would translate into an increase in lift. But because the aerodynamic center would lie ahead of the center of gravity, this would result in a pitch-up moment. Rather than returning on its own to level flight, the statically unstable airplane would continue to pitch further upward. A similar phenomenon would take place following a gust of wind that caused a pitch-down event. The decrease in the airplane angle of attack would decrease the lift, causing a further nose-down pitch moment for the unstable aircraft.

Flying a conventional airplane is much like carrying a deep bowl with an egg in the bottom across a kitchen. Although small perturbations might cause the egg to roll partway up the side of the bowl, gravity would tend to naturally bring the egg back toward the center. Provided that proper care and attention are exercised, there is no reason that this should not be a routine task. Flying a statically unstable airplane, on the other hand, is more akin to turning the bowl upside down and balancing the egg on the outside of the bowl's curved surface while attempting to walk across a room. While it may be possible to master this feat with much care and practice, it will never become routine, and most likely quite a few good omelets will be spoiled before the trick can be properly mastered.

All of this changed, however, with the explosion in computer technology that was heralded in the early 1970s. The miniaturization of electronics allowed for the construction of computers that could cope with the rapid control response necessary to fly an unstable airplane and yet were small enough to fit onboard. All the pilot had to do was tell the computer what motion he wanted, using the same control stick and pedal inputs that he had always used, and the computer would make the adjustments necessary to keep the airplane in level flight. The computer could make adjustments to each control surface at an unprecedented rate, allowing for the previously forbidden, negative static margins to become possible.

The first production jet fighter to take advantage of this technology was the F-16, which became the first to incorporate "relaxed static stability" (RSS). As such, it was also the first production airplane to be built with a computer-actuated, "fly-by-wire" control system. Without the new electronics the airplane would have been unflyable. The impetus for pursuing this technology came from the improved responsiveness that such a system afforded. A fighter with relaxed static stability would be naturally prone toward a rapid pitch-up motion, a feature that could be translated directly into improved responsiveness and dynamic turn rate. There were, however, a series of trade-offs that had to be made when pursuing this route. Such an airplane would be forever dependent on its fly-by-wire software to keep the airplane flyable. There was also a trade-off to be made between trim drag and static instability. In theory, the more unstable the fighter, the greater the improvement in the dynamic pitch response. But this instability came at the cost of an increase in the trim drag necessary to keep the airplane in level flight. A balance was therefore needed.

Although computer technology had matured in the preceding decade, the development of the flight control software necessary for the Lavi was by no means a trivial task. Numerous aircraft have been lost to flight control systems that have gone awry. The most notable examples are the loss of Sweden's first JAS-39 fighter proto-type and the crash of America's YF-22. In the case of the JAS-39, a relatively minor miss in the flight control software led to the total write-off of the first prototype, which lost control during a routine landing and was last seen cartwheeling end over end down the runway. The United States similarly lost a YF-22 prototype when the flight control system overcorrected for gusty crosswinds on landing, leading to a porpoise-like effect, with the airplane pitch-ing alternately up or down as it sped above the earth. The airplane made a belly landing that resulted in the write-off of the airframe. In both instances, the pilot was able to walk away from the acci-dent, but they remained vivid reminders of just how difficult it is to accurately predict the in-flight behavior of a real airplane across all possible flight conditions.

The development of the Lavi flight control software began in 1981, with the first set of preliminary control laws becoming avail-able for evaluation in mid-1983. To test and fine-tune the flight con-trol software, a team of four Israeli air force pilots, together with six test pilots from IAI, were assigned to support the software develop-ment effort. All ten pilots were experienced combat veterans, some possessing degrees in aeronautical engineering, while others were graduates of test pilot school. All of the IAI pilots were also active-duty reservists. In the three and a half years prior to the first flight of a Lavi prototype, a total of 835 simulated flight hours would be accumulated, using a combination of fixed and motion-based sim-ulators. In addition, the flight control software for the Lavi landing and approach routines would also be flight-tested aboard Calspan's NT-33 flying test bed.

Refining and validating the Lavi's flight control software was an exhaustive process, treated with all the seriousness and attention to detail of a combat operation. Each simulated flight was conducted with a team of two control systems engineers, a flight-test engineer, a pilot, and a senior control law engineer who would supervise each simulation. Each test began with a presimulation briefing to review the objectives of the upcoming flight, and each test was followed up with a postsimulation debriefing, typically lasting more than three hours. In this manner, the Lavi flight control software was fine-tuned for each element of the aircraft mission, to the maximum degree possible prior to actual flight test.[2] It was an exhaustive approach, but one that paid off with excellent aircraft handling characteristics and without the loss of a single Lavi prototype during the subsequent flight-test program.

One of the spin-offs of this software development process was the development of an algorithm for the automated recovery of a statically unstable aircraft from deep stall, a phenomenon that—although rarely encountered—could prove fatal to an ill-prepared pilot. For a modern fighter, deep stall will occur at low airspeed and extreme angles of attack, where the pitch control surfaces become ineffective. The standard recovery technique is to rock the airplane in a pitch-up, pitch-down motion until the control surfaces are again effective. The Israeli-developed, automated algorithm was able to coordinate this maneuver, fine-tuning the rocking motion to reduce the recovery time. The Israeli-developed algorithm was demonstrated to reduce the altitude lost from the 10,000 ft required for a manual recovery to only 3,000 ft for an automated recovery. This same software would later be adapted for service on Israeli F-16s.[3]

How Unstable?

Some insight into the Lavi design strategy and performance objectives can be obtained by comparing the static margin of the Lavi under a particular set of payload and flight conditions to the static margin of the earlier F-16 under those same conditions. To perform these comparisons, a series of hand calculations will be applied, relying on approximate, empirical methods to offer insights into trends and design trade-offs that might not otherwise be accessible.

When developing the Lavi flight control system, the Israeli team defined three principal payload configurations that they would need to design their software around: the "hobo" configuration, employed for long-range strike missions; the "cluster bomb" configuration, for shorter-range close air support and attack missions; and a lightweight, air-to-air fighter configuration. In the nominal "hobo" configuration, the Lavi was expected to be equipped with two external fuel tanks, a set of infrared targeting and navigation pods, two 2,000 lb (910 kg) bombs fitted with precision guidance kits, and two air-to-air missiles on the wingtip rails. This configuration was expected to move the Lavi center of gravity toward its aft-most extreme. The more heavily loaded "cluster bomb" configuration, on the other hand, was expected to include an array of bombs mounted beneath the fuselage, shifting the airplane center of gravity farther forward. Finally, in the short-range air-to-air configuration the Lavi was expected to carry a minimum of two heat-seeking air-to-air missiles, mounted on the wingtip rails. Like the "cluster bomb" configuration, this payload geometry was expected to result in an airplane center of gravity that was shifted toward its forward extreme.[4]

In the air-to-air configuration, the Lavi was reported to have a static margin of -5 percent.[5] Comparing this to a hand-calculated, approximate value for an aircraft with 50 percent internal fuel (3,000 lb or 1,360 kg fuel) and two AIM-9L air-to-air missiles, the empirical methods would yield an estimated static margin of -4 percent. This compares reasonably well with the literature value, confirming that the hand calculation should provide an accurate indication of trends in static margin shift under different payload configurations. Using these same methods, a hand calculation for the F-16C with a similar payload produces an estimated static margin of -2 percent. This value is very similar in magnitude to that for the Lavi. Any edge in dynamic response that the Lavi might have had under these conditions would have been primarily a function of its lower wing loading and the benefits of its canard-delta planform—not an outgrowth of a reduced static margin.

In the "hobo" configuration, on the other hand, the Lavi center of gravity was expected to shift much farther aft, increasing the degree of static instability. Published sources quote the Lavi static margin under these conditions to be as low as -15 percent.[6] Carrying out a similar, empirical hand calculation for a Lavi aircraft with maximum internal and external fuel, two wingtip missiles, infrared targeting and navigation pods, and two 2,000 lb (910 kg) smart bombs, the estimated static margin comes out to be -14 percent. Once again, this is in fair agreement with the literature value. A similar hand calculation for the F-16C, however, carrying a similar payload, suggests a static margin of -7 percent.[7] In other words, the evidence suggests that the Lavi experienced a far broader variation in its static margin, across all practical payload configurations, than was evident in the earlier F-16 design. This would have made the job of the Lavi stability and control software team that much more challenging, since they had to be able to handle a much wider range of conditions. It also, however, meant that in the long-range attack configuration the Lavi would have partially offset the effects of increased drag and inertia due to the external payload, with a decrease in the aircraft static margin, which would have helped to improve the dynamic response of their design. Whatever advantage the Lavi might have had over contemporary fighters when in a clean, air-to-air configuration would only have been magnified when comparing alternative designs for a fighter loaded with bombs. The Lavi was an attack jet by design, not by chance. This was a reality clearly demonstrated time and again in the trade-offs selected by the Lavi development team.

The Control Configured Vehicle

The Lavi development team had selected a design featuring a delta-wing configuration, with a large wing area. The additional wing area provided more space for weapons carriage, increased the available fuel volume, and also improved the turn rate of the fighter by reducing the wing loading. As a side effect, however, they had also chosen a wing that, under ordinary circumstances, would have been highly sensitive to gusts, crosswinds, or other aerodynamic disturbances. At low level, such perturbations would typically have made flying such an airplane uncomfortable, at best.

The Lavi flight control computer, however, was also programmed with a special "low-level flight mode" that took advantage of the responsiveness of the airplane's fly-by-wire control system to dampen out such disturbances.[8] A foreign fighter pilot who was allowed a brief flight test in the Lavi Technology Demonstrator would later remark that he had been "struck by the low buffet levels" that he had experienced in the Lavi, particularly in comparison to other delta-winged fighters that he had flown.[9]

The Lavi fly-by-wire control system had also gone a step beyond its predecessors, making the Lavi one of the first production fighters to become a truly "control configured vehicle." As Nissam Ebel, the Lavi deputy project manager, explained, "It's a very ambitious design. The ccv design uses aircraft shaping to achieve optimum flight performance for any given flight conditions and this is optimized by the close-coupled canard-wing design, for which we used our Kfir experience."[10] Whereas on the F-16 fly-by-wire technology had been implemented to make a statically unstable aircraft flyable, on the Lavi the technology had been applied to open the door to flight characteristics that had previously been unthinkable for a conventional fighter. A great deal of the groundbreaking work into ccv possibilities had been made by the experimental F-16 AFTI, a modified F-16 with a pair of ventral canards, which provided an added level of attitude control. This experimental fighter had become known for its unconventional flight capabilities, including the ability to point its nose off-axis from the plane of flight, allowing it to capture targets that would otherwise have been outside of the envelope for its weapons systems. ccv technology was the next logical step in fly-by-wire technology, and one that would no doubt have provided the Lavi with a few new surprises for its opponents.

Where Software Meets Metal

The Lavi flight control system was tasked with melding Israeli-developed flight control laws with American-made computers and actuators to produce a union between theory and physics that could successfully fly the airplane. The Lavi primary flight control system consisted of four digital computers, produced in the United States by Lear Siegler, which together could adjust each of the airplane's nine control surfaces up to seventy times per second. The four separate computers added a layer of redundancy, ensuring that a damaged or malfunctioning computer would not in itself result in the loss of the airplane. Moreover, even if all four digital computers were to become inoperative, there would also be two analog flight control computers to serve as a backup.[11] This philosophy of employing multiple layers of redundancy was employed throughout the design of the Lavi flight control apparatus.

The flight control computers were connected to three angle-of-attack sensors and to four rate gyros for each of the airplane's three axes (pitch, yaw, and roll). Even the servo-actuators that drove the Lavi's primary control surfaces were quad-redundant. The Lavi flight control computers, in turn, were assembled into two "packages," each containing two digital and one analog computers. Each of these computer assemblies was then located at different sites in the airplane, to further protect the system against possible combat damage.[12] No chances could be taken with a system so crucial to the pilot's well-being.

Moreover, as the Lavi transitioned from subsonic into supersonic flight, the stability of the airplane and the effectiveness of each control surface could be expected to change radically. The Lavi's fly-by-wire control system offered the opportunity to fine-tune all of the fighter's nine control surfaces to match the flight conditions at that moment.

The Transonic Domain

There is sometimes a misperception that because a fighter is described as being "supersonic" it must spend a significant portion of its time at supersonic speeds and, consequently, that maximum speed should be the supreme indicator of fighter performance. In reality, little could be further from the truth. In going from subsonic to supersonic flight the zero-lift drag coefficient of most aircraft will more than double. Consequently, the vast majority of the fighter planes in the world today can neither reach nor sustain supersonic flight without using an afterburner. The afterburner, of course, eats fuel at an alarming rate, vastly eroding the potential range of the fighter. Equally important from the viewpoint of a pilot in a maneuvering engagement is that for a given g-load, increasing flight speed into the supersonic realm also translates into an equally dramatic decrease in the available rate of turn, with a concurrent increase in the turn radius. That is why a fighter executing a 4 g turn at Mach 0.8 at 15,000 ft altitude (turn radius of 5,560 ft or 1,690 m) can potentially avoid and outmaneuver a missile capable of attaining 30 g but traveling at Mach 3 (turn radius of 10,420 ft or 3,170 m). The turn radius, for any missile or aircraft, will increase with the square of the speed, due to centrifugal effects. When all of the foregoing factors are tallied together it should become obvious just why most "supersonic" aircraft will actually spend so little of their time at supersonic conditions.

Consequently, the Lavi was designed as a "low supersonic" fighter, with a design maximum Mach number of 1.85, as opposed to Mach 2.3 for the Kfir or 2.02 for the F-16.[13] This value is similar to the 1.80 design Mach number of the U.S. Navy's F/A-18. Throughout most of its lifetime, whether in a dogfight or penetrating enemy air space to strike a target, the Lavi would be flying in the transonic flight range. Supersonic flight was not the Lavi's primary objective.

Transonic flight conditions are distinguished from their subsonic kin by the compressibility effects that become ever more prevalent factors in the airplane's stability, control, and performance. Even though the airplane may not be flying at a supersonic speed, at transonic conditions the local Mach number across some regions of the wing and fuselage will exceed the sound barrier, creating an effect known as "drag rise." The transonic speed range typically extends from around Mach 0.7 up through Mach 1, its lower limit depending on the individual airplane design. Moreover, this transition from fully subsonic to fully supersonic flight will also drastically alter how the airplane's control surfaces function. In subsonic, low-speed flight, the aerodynamic center of the wing will typically be located at or near the quarter-chord location, as measured at the wing mean aerodynamic chord. As the airplane transitions through the transonic speed range, however, the aerodynamic center will gradually shift aft, until at supersonic conditions, it will begin to approach the half-chord location. This effect will drastically alter the airplane's static margin and, as a consequence, the behavior of its control surfaces.

There are also other, equally dramatic changes that take place during this transition from subsonic to supersonic flight. As the airplane approaches ever more closely to the sound barrier, the small, local shock wave that will appear across the surface of each wing will transition back, until it finally reaches the wing trailing edge when the airplane passes through Mach 1. During this transition, the shock wave will at some point come to rest above the various hinged control surfaces on the wing or elevator, with the potential to substantially reduce their effectiveness. It is this phenomenon that led to so many catastrophic failures during the early days of jet aviation. It was not the supersonic shock wave or increasing air pressure that left so many of these attempts scattered across the terrain in a field of debris: it was the loss of control that occurred as these aircraft transitioned from subsonic to supersonic flight.

Even in today's world of sophisticated electronics and fly-by-wire control systems, the transonic flight regime can still pose unique challenges and surprises. In that narrow zone between Mach 0.9 and Mach 1, where airplane stability and control surface effectiveness can radically change, there remains an element of the unknown that only flight test can fully illuminate. Even phenomena that are well understood and are anticipated in advance can occur at an uncertain Mach number, with an unexpected impact on control system response. These were all issues that the Lavi flight control software would have had to directly address, and where the Lavi's fly-by-wire control system could optimize the airplane's response.

Supersonic Flight

Although the Lavi was expected to spend only a small fraction of its time at supersonic conditions, it was nonetheless essential to ensure that these excursions were carried out with minimal impact on fuel consumption while providing the maximum control authority for the pilot. As was described previously, between subsonic and supersonic conditions, the aerodynamic center of the airplane would shift aft, toward the wing half-chord location. This shift in the aerodynamic center would lead to an increase in the static margin of the airplane. For an airplane featuring relaxed static stability, however, the static margin would already have been shifted forward of a naturally stable condition, when at subsonic flight speeds. Most aircraft that are statically unstable at subsonic conditions will become stable at supersonic conditions, while an aircraft that was already stable at subsonic conditions could expect to become even more stable in supersonic flight. The latter airplane would need to exert ever-greater control surface deflections to trim the airplane in level flight. In terms of both control authority and trim drag, a fighter with relaxed static stability would therefore have a clear advantage at supersonic conditions.

But the Lavi had an additional card to play in supersonic flight: its canard-delta combination. The potential advantages of a canard configuration in supersonic flight had been recognized decades before by Grumman Corporation, which produced the U.S. Navy's F-14 Tomcat. The F-14 incorporated a set of small, retractable canards known as "glove vanes," which were buried inside of the leading edge of the wing root. The glove vanes would extend automatically to reduce trim drag at conditions above Mach 1.4. Grumman had also, however, explored the benefits of carrying this concept a step further. In a series of preliminary design studies conducted during the early 1980s, engineers at Grumman concluded that, in supersonic flight, a canard fighter configuration held the potential to increase the lift-to-drag ratio of an airplane by as much as 30 percent compared to a conventional wing-and-tail arrangement.[14]

To understand why this phenomenon occurs, it should be recalled that in subsonic flight an aircraft with relaxed static stability will have a negative static margin, while in supersonic flight its static margin will typically become positive. For a conventional wing and tail configuration, this means that to trim the aircraft in subsonic flight, the horizontal tail must exert an upward force, inducing a pitch-down moment to keep the airplane level. For a statically unstable aircraft in subsonic flight, the horizontal tail will consequently contribute to the overall lift of the fighter. Similarly, for this same reason, in subsonic flight the Lavi was intended to exercise its elevons as its primary trim surface, exerting an upward trim force and contributing to the overall lift of the airplane.

This relationship becomes reversed, however, at supersonic conditions, when the airplane's aerodynamic center shifts aft and the fighter becomes stable. Under these conditions, a horizontal tail would need to exert a downward force to trim the aircraft, reducing the airplane's lift-to-drag ratio. The canard on the Lavi, in contrast, would exert an upward trim force, contributing to the overall lift. At supersonic conditions, it is only natural to find that the canard design would provide a significant improvement in lift-to-drag ratio. By relying primarily on its elevons to provide trim force in subsonic flight and relying on its canard to provide trim in supersonic flight, the Lavi was able to take advantage of the best of both worlds, maximizing its lift-to-drag ratio throughout the flight envelope.

Although in terms of its top design Mach number the Lavi was expected to be slower than many of its predecessors, in terms of its cruise speed, the Lavi was expected to leave them in the dust. The Lavi would have been one of very few aircraft to possess a supersonic cruise capability when in its clean configuration.[15] That is, it was expected to be able to reach and sustain supersonic flight without resorting to the use of an afterburner. Aircraft in this category were able to achieve this feat either by virtue of an extraordinary thrust-to-weight ratio—as was the case for the Typhoon and the F-22—or by substantially reducing their supersonic wave and trim drag, as was the case for the F-16XL and Lavi. Although this capability was expected to be of only marginal operational utility to the Lavi, it does underscore the degree to which the Israeli development team had succeeded in minimizing the airplane's drag and maximizing its ability to perform long-range strike missions. Stability and control had not been a mere sideshow for the Lavi. They had been a central element contributing to its success.

Conclusions

The development and optimization of the Lavi flight control software constituted a long, arduous process, demanding the dedicated attention of an experienced team of engineers, technicians, and pilots. Many hours of simulation would need to take place, long before the first airplane ever left the ground.

For a modern combat aircraft to be successful, aerodynamic design must go hand in hand with stability and control. The two must become inseparable if a development team expects to create an aircraft that not only flies, but flies well.

. . .

Aerodynamic Center

The calculation of aerodynamic center and, by extension, aircraft static margin, can be a complex and daunting task. Although textbook methods do exist, they lack the fidelity necessary for detailed design, much less that needed to write the control logic behind the fly-by-wire software of a modern jet fighter. They do, however, provide the basis for insights into trends and for comparisons between aircraft. It is in this fashion that these methods have been applied here.

The following equation constitutes the formulation used in this text for assessing the aerodynamic center for both the F-16C and the Lavi. It differs from most textbook formulations in that it more fully accounts for the interactions between the canard and wing.[1]

$$\bar{x}_{ac_A} = \frac{\bar{x}_{ac_{wb}} + \frac{C_{L_{ac}}}{C_{L_{awb}}}\left(\frac{S_c}{S}\right)\frac{\left(1+\frac{d\varepsilon_c}{d\alpha}\right)}{\left(1-\frac{d\varepsilon_w}{d\alpha}\right)}\bar{x}_{ac_c} + \frac{C_{L_{\alpha h}}}{C_{L_{awb}}}\left(\frac{S_h}{S}\right)\frac{\left(1-\frac{d\varepsilon_h}{d\alpha}\right)}{\left(1-\frac{d\varepsilon_w}{d\alpha}\right)}\bar{x}_{ac_h}}{1 + \frac{C_{L_{ac}}}{C_{L_{awb}}}\left(\frac{S_c}{S}\right)\frac{\left(1+\frac{d\varepsilon_c}{d\alpha}\right)}{\left(1-\frac{d\varepsilon_w}{d\alpha}\right)} + \frac{C_{L_{\alpha h}}}{C_{L_{awb}}}\left(\frac{S_h}{S}\right)\frac{\left(1-\frac{d\varepsilon_h}{d\alpha}\right)}{\left(1-\frac{d\varepsilon_w}{d\alpha}\right)}}$$

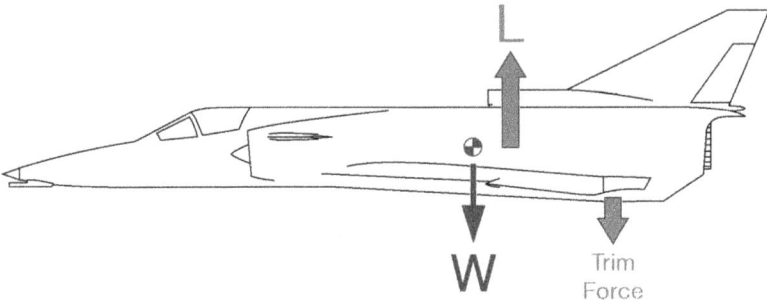

Fig. 15. An airplane with a positive static margin will have its aerodynamic center located behind its center of gravity.

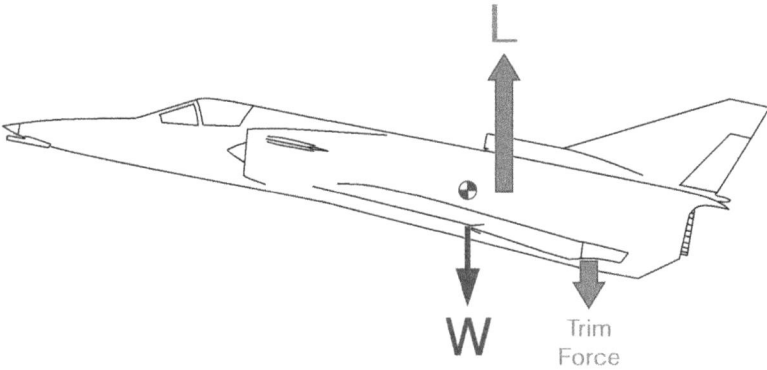

Fig. 16. For a conventional airplane, a small perturbation that increases the angle of attack will also increase airplane lift, producing a restoring moment.

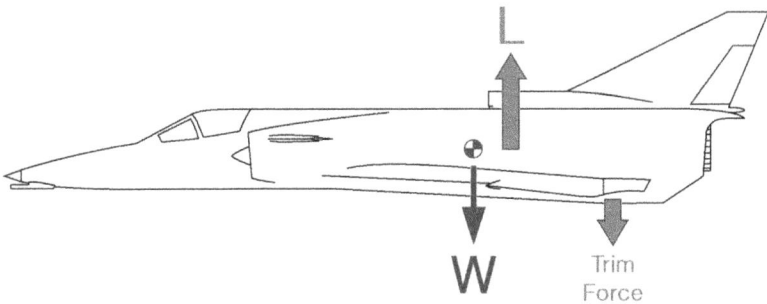

Fig. 17. The restoring moment due to the increased lift will return a trimmed, statically stable aircraft to level flight without direct pilot intervention.

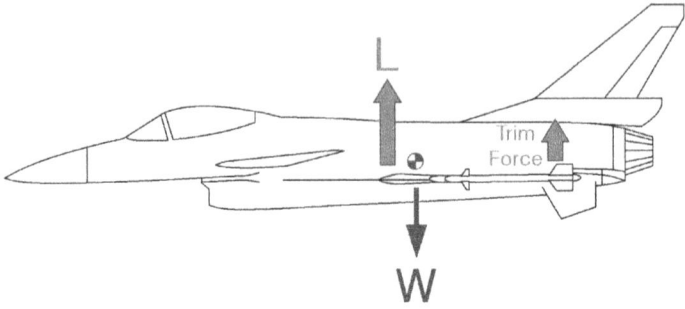

Fig. 18. An airplane with relaxed static stability will have its aerodynamic center ahead of the center of gravity, producing a negative static margin.

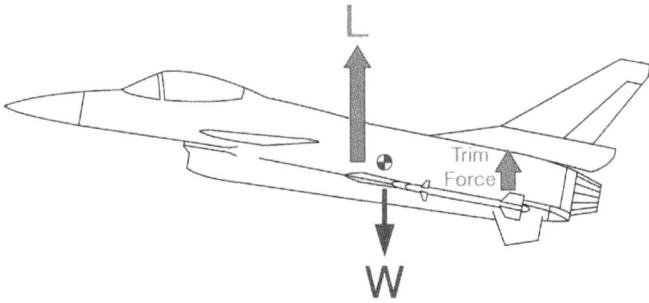

Fig. 19. A statically unstable airplane will also experience an increase in lift associated with an increased angle of attack. Only here, the added lift leads to divergence.

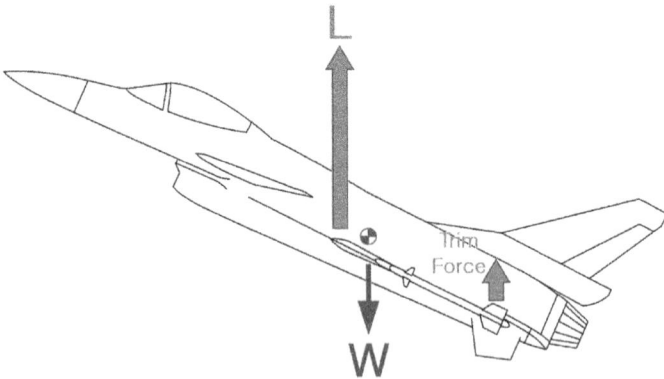

Fig. 20. Without intervention by the flight control software, a statically unstable aircraft would continue to diverge from level flight.

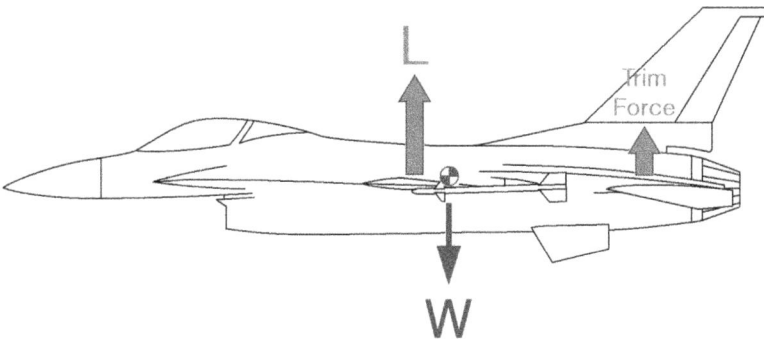

Fig. 21. In subsonic flight, for a statically unstable aircraft with a conventional wing and tail arrangement, the horizontal tail would need to exert an upward trim force in order to keep the airplane in level flight. This would enhance the airplane's subsonic lift-to-drag ratio.

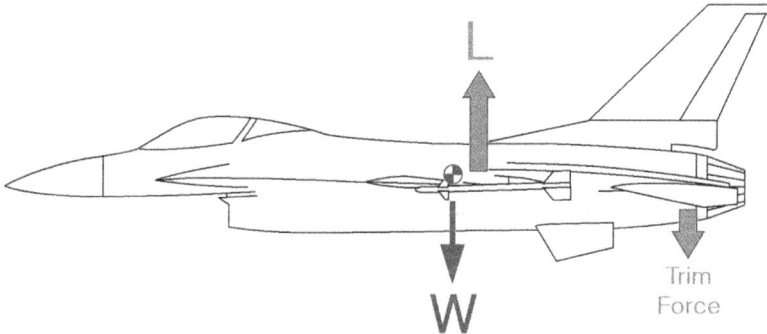

Fig. 22. In supersonic flight, the aerodynamic center shifts aft, and the airplane becomes stable. The horizontal tail must now exert a downward force in order to trim the airplane, reducing the overall lift-to-drag ratio.

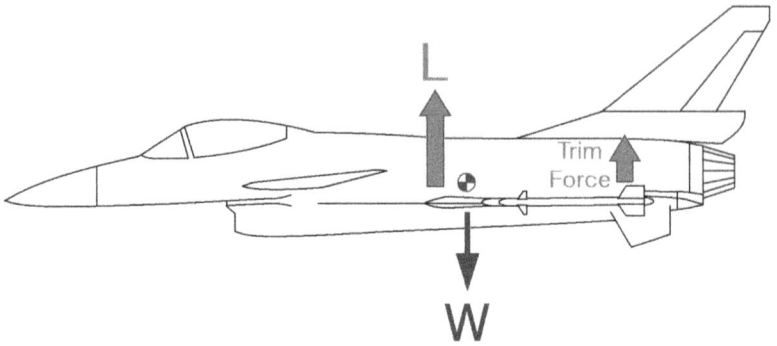

Fig. 23. In subsonic flight, the Lavi was expected to rely primarily on elevon deflection to provide the trim force necessary to maintain level flight. This elevon trim force would add to the overall lift of the airplane and increase its lift-to-drag ratio.

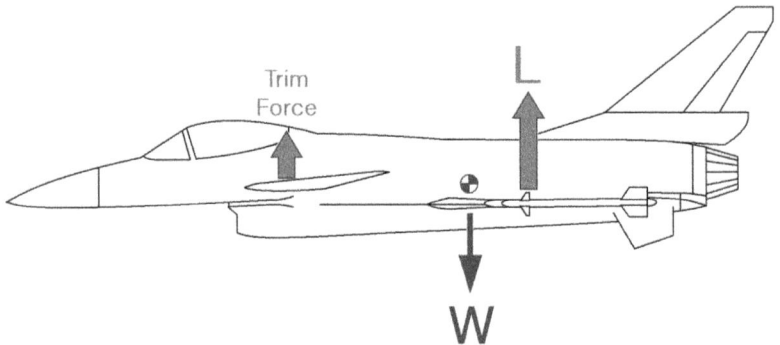

Fig. 24. In supersonic flight, the Lavi was expected to rely primarily on an upward trim force from its canard to sustain level flight. This upward canard trim force would enhance the airplane's supersonic lift-to-drag ratio.

Some of the values required for this calculation are well-understood quantities, which can be approximated with a fair degree of confidence using either analytical or empirical means. Items such as the location of the wing aerodynamic center and lift curve slopes for the wing, tail, and canard, for example, can be estimated in a direct and straightforward manner. This is not true, however, for the downwash and upwash gradients or for the shift in aerodynamic center due to fuselage effects. Most of the published material for estimating these latter values was developed for use with configurations featuring a relatively high aspect ratio, as compared to those typically seen on jet warbirds such as the F-16 ($A = 3.2$) or the Lavi ($A = 2.3$). Many of the estimates made for a jet fighter, therefore, will need to be extrapolated from the available data.[2]

In drawing the comparisons used in this book, analyses were conducted for the Lavi and for the F-16C Block 30 aircraft. All of the estimates reported in this appendix were approximated for a flight condition of Mach 0.80.

1. Levy, *Prediction of Average Downwash Gradient.*

2. Hoak and Fink, USAF *Stability and Control* DATCOM; Roskam, *Airplane Design,* pt. 6, *Preliminary Calculation;* Roskam, *Airplane Dynamics and Automatic Flight Controls.*

APPENDIX 3

Airframe and Structure

In the design and construction of an airplane, the objective of the structural design team is to achieve the desired capability within the minimum airframe weight. Every pound that can be shaved off from the airframe is one more pound that can be carried in payload or fuel. The Lavi was expected to take full advantage of the latest in materials technology and manufacturing techniques to achieve this. Making the most out of that technology, however, still had as much to do with the skill and care exercised by those applying it as it did with the technology itself.

A Conventional Airframe with an Unconventional Approach

The contributions the U.S. aerospace industry made to the Lavi's construction were numerous and covered a wide variety of applications. They ranged from items such as the wings and vertical tail, built by Grumman, to brakes and tires purchased from Goodyear.[1] But whereas the overall contribution of American industry to the Lavi accounted for some 40–45 percent of the airplane, American industry was responsible for only 30 percent of the airframe.[2] Airframe manufacture is, after all, the traditional reserve of the prime contractor.

The Lavi fuselage was constructed in three separate assemblies, each of which was assembled within its own production jig before they were joined together. The tail-most section housed the engine and also included the airbrakes, as well as attachments for connecting the vertical tail and the ventral strakes. The central section was taken up largely by fuel tanks and the flight refueling system, while the forward section housed the cockpit and most of the electronics. Once all three sections were joined the wings were added, connecting to fittings on the center and tail fuselage sections.[3] Taken together, it was a fairly conventional approach to jet fighter assembly.

Where the Lavi assembly process differed from those of its predecessors, however, was in the manner in which it had taken advantage of a fully integrated computer-aided design and computer-aided manufacturing (CAD/CAM) system. This technology allowed for the development, flight-test, and production phases of airplane assembly to be condensed into one continuous effort. Prior to the advent of integrated CAD/CAM software, prototypes would typically be assembled on "soft" or "engineering" tooling: tools and assembly jigs prepared specifically for building the prototypes and that relied on a pool of highly specialized technicians and mechanics to exercise. This was a time-consuming process, requiring that production drawings be transferred from engineering to the prototyping lab, then back to engineering to incorporate changes or corrections. Only after this prototype process had been completed would the final blueprints be passed along to the manufacturing division, responsible for building the production airplanes. Since the team that built the prototypes was seldom made up of the same technicians and mechanics who would assemble the production airplane, mistakes would be repeated that should have been corrected in the prototyping phase.

The Lavi was among the first aircraft that were able to take advantage of advances in computing technology to streamline this process. By integrating the design and production phases of the development process through the use of integrated software, the need to transfer the drawings to a specialized prototyping team could be avoided. Software advances allowed for parts to be visualized before production, checked for fit, and then passed directly from the design software to the manufacturing tool designers and machine programmers. Beginning with the very first prototype, the center and rear Lavi fuselage sections were built entirely by

IAI's manufacturing division on production tooling—the same tools and assembly jigs that were expected to manufacture and assemble production jet fighters. Only the forward fuselage section, which was still undergoing revisions to the electronics suite, would be constructed on soft tooling by the engineering division. What was more, beginning with the third prototype, the responsibility for this fuselage section was also transferred to manufacturing. In other words, the airframe of the third Lavi prototype represented exactly what the production Lavi fighter was expected to be, right down to the tooling used to manufacture and assemble it.[4] This approach not only saved money, by eliminating most of the soft tooling and specialized personnel, but also saved time, since the prototype and production phases could more easily be condensed into one smooth continuation from one to the other.

The Composite Contribution

Among the most important structural contributions to the Lavi was the incorporation of composite materials into the wings, vertical tail, canards, ventral strakes, and air brakes. A total of 22 percent of the Lavi structural weight was expected to be made up of composite materials.[5] This was in contrast to earlier aircraft such as the F-15 and F-16, where composites composed only 2 percent of the structural weight, and the F/A-18, where composites made up 11 percent of the structural weight. The Lavi belonged to a new generation of materials technology, a herald of trends to come. The F-22 Raptor, for example, was similarly expected to incorporate a total of 24 percent composite materials by weight.[6]

Composites are manufactured, and behave, quite differently from their conventional cousins. Fiber composites such as those employed on the Lavi owe their unique advantages to the unusual behavior of brittle materials that have been drawn or spun into fibers. These brittle fibers will actually behave as if they were much stronger than that same material would be in its bulk form. This is a consequence of the low volume of the fiber, which leads to relatively few flaws per unit length. Without those flaws, many of the most brittle of materials—including graphite—will actually exhibit greater tensile strength than would steel, aluminum, or titanium alloys.[7]

By the time that the Lavi was developed, graphite fibers had already displaced boron and other alternatives as the preferred fiber for most aerospace composite applications. Graphite forms the fiber component of "graphite epoxy" composites. A typical graphite fiber will measure eight microns, or eight one-thousandths of a millimeter (about three ten-thousandths of an inch) in diameter. These tiny fibers are what actually carry most of the load in the finished component, while the matrix, the material in which the fibers are embedded, is expected to keep the fibers aligned.

Various manufacturers have experimented with employing thermoplastics in place of the traditional epoxy resin that is used in most aerospace composite applications—with mixed results. Thermoplastics, unlike epoxies, can be reheated and reshaped after the part is formed, either to alter the original shape or to repair damage. Epoxy, on the other hand, is a thermosetting resin. The curing process forms a three-dimensional, inter-branching molecule. Once formed, such a matrix is permanent. It cannot be reheated or reshaped without destroying its properties. On the positive side, however, thermosetting composites tend to display a greater tolerance for the elevated temperatures of supersonic flight, conditions where their thermoplastic cousins begin to become soft and deform. It is this combination of strong and relatively inexpensive graphite fibers with the durability of epoxy resin that has made graphite epoxy far and away the most favored composite material in aircraft construction.

Graphite epoxy is sold commercially in many forms, as befits its wide variety of applications. For less demanding, nonaerospace roles, short whiskers of graphite may provide sufficient strength. In aircraft applications, however, graphite epoxy is usually produced in plies with continuous, unidirectional fibers embedded into a partially cured epoxy matrix. These individual plies are referred to as "prepreg," or "preimpregnated," and can be purchased in either a ply, warp sheet form or in a roll similar to tape. For maximum benefit, it is essential not only that the fibers be continuous but that they be oriented in the same direction. It is this combination that provides composite components with both their strength and their unique anisotropic character.

Because it is the fibers that provide the composite component with most of its load-bearing strength, this unidirectional orientation provides a ply that is much stronger and more stiff along one direction than in any of the others. To form a part, plies of pre-preg are typically layered one atop another, over a mold shaped in the form of the finished surface. For a large structural member, such as the skin on a wing or canard, this mold will typically be open, or single-faced. Smaller parts can be formed with a closed-mold process. The mold will need to be covered with a vacuum bag throughout the curing process, to prevent voids or air pockets from forming. The entire apparatus, including the mold, composite plies, vacuum bag, and all, will then be inserted into an autoclave, which will subject them to elevated pressures and temperatures to cure the resin. Temperatures can reach up to 450 °F (230 °C), with pressures of up to 10 atmospheres to achieve a final, fully cured component. If done correctly, the end product should be both stronger and lighter than an equivalent titanium or aluminum part.

To assemble components into larger structures, individual composite subcomponents can also be co-cured, or bonded to form a lighter overall structure than could be achieved using fasteners. The wing of Japan's F-2 fighter provides an example of this approach in practice. Co-curing, however, also heightens the threat of delamination, one of the reasons that led the Lavi development team to employ a more conventional scheme, relying on fasteners to assemble the Lavi wing.

Delamination will forever be the single greatest threat to any composite structure. Any holes in a composite part, whether for fasteners or access panels, will need to be reinforced. Similarly, the leading edges of composite wings, canards, and vertical and horizontal tails will need to be protected by an aluminum or titanium metal sheath, to alleviate the threat of impact damage. Any site where there is an edge will be at increased risk for delamination and will need to be reinforced or protected accordingly. Repairs of composite components likewise will need to take into account these unique characteristics. Whereas in a metal structure, holes and other damage can typically be repaired with a riveted metal patch, a composite structure will more commonly require a "wet lay-up patch"—a new layer of composite laminate that is cured into place and becomes part of the structure. During its early flight-test program, for example, the first two Lavi prototypes recorded at least ten instances in which there was some degree of damage to their composite structure: from minor nicks and dents that required no repair to damage to the canard and vertical tail that required the application of a wet lay-up patch.[8]

The real key to constructing a successful composite component, however, always comes back to the anisotropic character of the individual plies. Any given ply of unidirectional graphite epoxy prepreg will always be much stiffer in one direction than in any other. By alternating the orientation of these plies as they are layered to form a component, it becomes possible to control and customize the characteristics of the eventual product. An all-moving stabilizer, such as a canard, for example, will experience primarily torsional loads and would be built primarily from plies oriented at a plus-or-minus 45° orientation (with the reference axis for ply orientation being in the span-wise direction). A hinged control surface such as an elevon or aileron, on the other hand, would be made primarily from plies oriented in the 90° direction. It was this process of ply orientation and buildup that made composites such an attractive alternative for the Lavi.

Unlocking the Anisotropic Secret

All of these elements of composite component construction were well known and had been successfully incorporated into fighter designs long before the Lavi. Aircraft such as the F-15, F-16, and F/A-18 had already employed composite skins on their vertical and horizontal tails. Applying technology of a similar nature was likewise no great leap for Israel Aircraft Industries, which already had experience with producing composite components for missiles and drones and which would successfully apply that same experience to produce the composite canards, ventral strakes, and airbrakes for the Lavi. The degree of refinement that went into making the Lavi wing, however, was of a different category. The Lavi was among the first aircraft to take advantage of aeroelastic tailoring to enhance and optimize the efficiency of its lifting surfaces. This was a technology that had not been available until the late 1970s.

Any wing, no matter what it is made of, will bend and flex under aerodynamic loads. The idea behind aeroelastic tailoring was to coax that bending to contribute in a positive manner, so as to enhance the airplane's lift-to-drag ratio at those flight conditions of most interest. Like any wing, an aeroelastically tailored wing will present a slightly different airfoil cross section at different flight conditions and different wing loadings. Unlike a conventional wing, however, the aeroelastically tailored wing will provide its most desirable aerodynamic cross section when the airplane is at actual flight conditions (usually cruise), rather than when the airplane is sitting on the ground with no aerodynamic loads. Moreover, by taking advantage of the anisotropic behavior of the composite plies, an aeroelastically tailored wing can also resist much of the structural bending and twist that a conventional wing would undergo during high-g maneuver, providing superior lift-to-drag ratios and turning capability during a dogfight. At both ends of the spectrum, therefore, whether in level cruise or attempting to outmaneuver an opponent, the aeroelastically tailored wing offered a marked improvement in performance over its conventional kin. The ability to achieve this degree of structural refinement was developed only in the latter 1970s—too late to benefit the F-15, F-16, or other fighters of that era. To achieve this effect required both a more detailed understanding of the behavior of composite materials and a more refined knowledge of the aerodynamic loading on the wing. These mathematical models, in turn, needed to be coupled with the appropriate computational capabilities to make optimization possible. These kinds of computer resources were only beginning to become available during the early 1980s.

This was why the Lavi wing and vertical tail, unlike the other composite components that went into the Lavi, were assigned to an American company already experienced in the art of aeroelastic tailoring. In a traditional composite structure, it is generally understood that for every ply that is added with a given orientation, there should be another ply that is oriented in the opposite direction. If one ply of prepreg is given a 45° orientation, for instance, it is understood that there has to be a ply with a -45° orientation, in order to achieve a component of uniform stiffness and behavior. In order to apply aerodynamic tailoring, however, the wings and vertical tail of the Lavi would need to break this rule. Knowing when and how to violate conventional layup procedures would become key to achieving the final design.

The Lavi wings and vertical tail were therefore assigned to the experienced composites team at Grumman Corporation. Grumman, in turn, would make use of a U.S.-developed computer code known as FASTOP (Flutter and Strength Optimization Procedure), which had been developed in the late 1970s. This code was intended to converge on a minimum-weight ply arrangement, which would meet specific aeroelastic and loading criteria. This was the same computer code that Grumman had previously used to design the wings for the x-29 technology demonstrator, and without which the x-29 would never have been possible.[9] In the case of the x-29, this technology had been essential to providing the necessary stiffness to prevent the experimental airplane's forward-swept wings from tearing off in supersonic flight. In the case of the Lavi, this same technology was expected to improve the airplane's lift-to-drag ratio at both cruise and maneuvering conditions, maximizing the airplane's combat radius as well as its ability to outperform an opponent in an air-to-air engagement. Israel Aircraft Industries estimated at the time that it would have set back the entire Lavi program by at least eight months, were they to attempt to duplicate this aeroelastic tailoring expertise on their own.[10]

The Lavi development team had originally envisioned an all-composite wing structure for the Lavi, featuring all-composite spars that would have been co-cured with a composite skin. Such an approach would have eliminated the need for fasteners altogether and would have resulted in what was theoretically the lowest weight structure. This was also, however, too much of a stretch for the state-of-the-art at the time. The initial co-cured test articles constructed by Grumman failed during static ground tests, resulting in a change in direction early on in the wing design.[11] The wing structure that was eventually developed for the Lavi would consist of a composite skin covering a series of metallic wing spars, which were in turn attached to the fuselage at eight points. The optimization of this structure was accomplished in three distinct phases. It began with an initial series of sizing iterations, aimed at meeting an "effectiveness" criterion that balanced the wing's performance across a range of flight conditions. This optimization sequence was followed by a set of buckling iterations that verified the ability of the structure to resist both global and localized buckling under all load combinations. Finally, a set of ply sizing iterations were carried out, to optimize the effectiveness of the hinged control surfaces. In all, a total of 102 flight conditions were specified by IAI, against which Grumman was expected to optimize the Lavi wing structure.[12]

Design for Attack

All of this brings us to the issue of just how the structure of the Lavi fit into the overall picture of the fighter's performance. This was where the high-technology glitter and promises left off and some cold, hard decision making had to take place. Oddly enough, in terms of both its mission and structural design philosophy, the Lavi probably owed more kinship to the A-4 Skyhawk, the airplane that it was intended to replace, than it did to the F-16, against which it was so often compared. It is easy to undervalue today, in an age of supersonic airlines and electronic wizardry, just what it was that the design team at Douglas's El Segundo plant had achieved in the A-4 Skyhawk. The A-4 program began in 1951, with the first flight of "Heinemann's Hot Rod" taking place on June 22, 1954. In 1954 the A-4 not only met the U.S. Navy's requirements for a carrier-based attack aircraft but exceeded them as no other warplane has before or since. It was 125 mph (110 knots or 200 kph) faster than what the U.S. Navy had asked for, could carry twice the bomb load

100 mi (160 km) farther, and weighed in at half the gross weight specified.[13] The A-4 was a truly astonishing feat of aircraft design. It was therefore only natural that the Lavi, by virtue of its own mandate as an attack platform, would be destined to follow in the same pattern set by its predecessor of so many decades before.

What had been the secret behind the A-4? A new, super-secret engine perhaps? A revolution in materials technology? No, it was intelligent design, and what is known in the aircraft business as "structural synergism." The load paths of the airplane were intentionally designed to minimize the number of heavy frames and bulkheads required, by concentrating the load-carrying members and payload attachment points onto the fewest number of bulkheads and spars that Mother Nature would allow. Structural synergism is the art of making one structural member do the work of two or more, and Douglas's chief aircraft designer, Ed Heinemann, had been among the very best at applying this art. In the case of the A-4, the engine was situated on top of the wing torsion box, allowing common spars to support the wing, fuselage, and engine loads. Furthermore, since the A-4 development team had also selected a delta-wing design, most of the necessary fuel volume could be stored in the wing, cutting down on the size of the fuselage required. To complement this effort, the bare minimum in structural materials was applied throughout the aircraft: just enough to get the job done, and no more. The A-4 rudder was a case in point, comprising nothing more than a thin sheet of metal supported by externally mounted ribs. It was a practical, minimum weight solution, not a cosmetic one.

The Lavi was, in many respects, the logical extension of these same lines of thought, applied to a supersonic design. Like the A-4, it was designed to be an attack aircraft first. Like the A-4, its maximum takeoff weight was significantly more than what its empty weight might have suggested. A comparison with the Lavi's contemporary counterpart, the F-16, should help to illustrate this effect. The original F-16A Block 10 and 15 aircraft, which included the first batch of seventy-five fighters delivered to Israel during the early 1980s, had boasted an empty weight of 15,140 lb (6,870 kg), with a maximum takeoff weight of 35,400 lb (16,060 kg). The early F-16C variants, meanwhile, including the Block 30 aircraft delivered to Israel in the mid-1980s, increased the airplane's empty weight to 16,790 lb (7,620 kg) to allow for a higher maximum takeoff weight of 37,500 lb (17,010 kg). The more recent Block 40 F-16Cs, which went into production in 1990, would further increase the maximum takeoff weight of the fighter to 42,300 lb (19,190 kg). However, this came at the expense of an even higher empty weight, which was increased to some 19,020 lb (8,630 kg).[14] Throughout its evolution, the F-16 had gradually been asked to increase its available bomb load, sacrificing structural empty weight, thrust-to-weight ratio, and wing loading in the process. The Lavi maximum takeoff weight, it will be recalled, was expected to be some 42,500 lb (19,280 kg), with an empty weight of 15,310 lb (6,940 kg).[15] In other words, the Lavi delivered a maximum takeoff weight in excess of the Block 40 F-16 model, but at an empty weight that was little more than that of the Block 15 aircraft. In terms of its ability to carry fuel and bomb load, the Lavi far outstripped the "state of the art" of its day.

Manufacturers are usually pretty cagey about handing out details on component weights for their aircraft. However, these are also one element of an airplane design that are relatively straightforward to estimate using empirical means and that can be determined within a fair degree of confidence by using past experience as a guide. For purposes of making comparisons here, the Lavi will be benchmarked against the Block 30 F-16C.

Comparing projections for the Block 30 F-16C fuselage weight to the Lavi fuselage weight, a first approximation would suggest that the Lavi fuselage structure was roughly 5 percent lighter than the fuselage for the F-16C. The fuselage weight for the two aircraft was therefore very similar—a startling revelation, considering that the Lavi was intended to achieve a maximum takeoff weight that was 13 percent greater than the Block 30 F-16C. It should be kept in mind that the Lavi fuselage, like that of the F-16C, was of conventional aluminum construction. There were no fancy composites here.

A similar approximation for wing weight, however, would suggest that the Lavi wing came out to be some 32 percent lighter than that of the F-16C. Some of this difference was no doubt due to the incorporation of composites technology. By far the greater influence, however, was the differences in wing configuration between the two aircraft. The reason was simple: the Lavi had been built around a delta wing design, with a substantially greater chord length at the root. Even assuming that the thickness-to-chord ratio of the Lavi wing was not so very different from that of the F-16C, the Lavi wing root thickness would have been over 30 percent greater, leading to a far more stiff and sound structure.

An airplane wing will be supported by a series of span-wise spars that will serve as the primary load-carrying members of the wing structure, and which are essentially I-beams in their cross section. As every engineering student should already know, the load-carrying capacity of an I-beam will increase as the cube of its height. A delta wing such as that on the Lavi was therefore naturally more stiff and easier to build than the thin, trapezoidal wings found on such aircraft as the F-16 or F/A-18. It would require fewer spars to carry the same load, and those spars could be of lighter construction as well. The end result was a wing structure that weighed significantly less, even for a wing that happened to be a little greater in area than the F-16, and which was expected to carry greater payload. The physics behind this wing configuration had been equally true when Ed Heinemann had designed and built the first A-4 Skyhawk, choosing a delta wing design, just as the Lavi development team would settle upon decades later.

The selected Lavi wing design also saved weight in one other way: by providing an ideal site for storing fuel. By way of rough comparison, the F-16's trapezoidal wings comprise a fuel capacity of around 1,290 lb (590 kg), or about 19 percent of the F-16C's total internal fuel volume. The Lavi wing fuel capacity comes out to around 3,250 lb (1,470 kg), or 54 percent of the total internal fuel. Not only did storing additional fuel in the wing free up valuable fuselage space for other pressing needs, but integral wing fuel tanks were also inherently lighter than the fuel tanks and bladder cells that would otherwise have been added to the fuselage. The choice of a delta wing was not only an aerodynamics decision but one that carried structural ramifications as well.

Coupled with the weight reductions afforded by the delta wing design was an all-around effort to trim off excess pounds wherever possible. It began with how the landing gear and engine were installed to take advantage of the same bulkheads and frames as the wing. Even the ejection seat did not escape attention and was accordingly pared down from the 290 lb (130 kg) for the standard Mk. 10 Martin-Baker model to 260 lb (120 kg) for the Lavi.[16] That the Lavi could outperform its rivals in the United States and elsewhere should not have been surprising. By the time that the first Lavi prototype flew, it had already been over fourteen years since the first F-15 had lifted off the ground and nearly thirteen years since the first YF-16 was airborne. Technology had changed. But that the Lavi outperformed them to the degree that it did was due to some carefully thought-out decisions and some very clever packaging.

The Lavi ultimately outperformed its contemporary "counterparts" as an attack jet because it was an attack jet first, and not as an afterthought. In a very real sense, the Lavi was far more than a mere replacement for Israel's aging A-4 fleet. It was the successor to the legacy of the A-4: as big of a leap over the supposed "state of the art" in attack aviation in 1986 as the A-4 had been to the U.S. Navy's request for proposal in 1954. The Lavi demonstrated what could be accomplished if the attack mission was set out as a priority in fighter-bomber development, rather than added on after the airplane entered service.

· · ·

Lavi Component Weights

For purposes of comparison, component weight estimates were projected for both the Lavi and the F-16C Block 30 aircraft. Those assembled for the Lavi are summarized here. Some of the Lavi component weights were available from literature sources. This includes weights for the Lavi electronics system, ejection seat, and engine.[1] Similarly, published values were available for the combined weight for the Lavi wing and tail structures.[2] The majority of the component weight values, however, had to be estimated using empirical methods.[3]

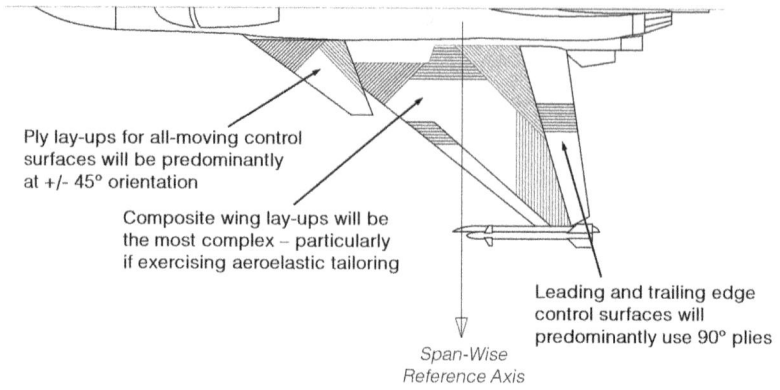

Ply lay-ups for all-moving control surfaces will be predominantly at +/- 45° orientation

Composite wing lay-ups will be the most complex – particularly if exercising aeroelastic tailoring

Leading and trailing edge control surfaces will predominantly use 90° plies

Span-Wise Reference Axis

Fig. 25. Composite ply lay-up patterns.

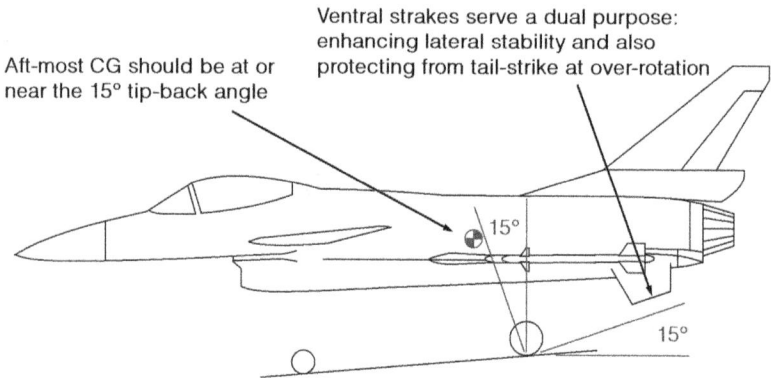

Ventral strakes serve a dual purpose: enhancing lateral stability and also protecting from tail-strike at over-rotation

Aft-most CG should be at or near the 15° tip-back angle

15°

15°

Fig. 26. Airplane tip-back criteria. Good design practice will ensure that the aft-most center of gravity will lie at or near a 15° angle from the rear landing gear. This prevents over-rotation while also minimizing the control surface hinge moments at takeoff.

Table 11. Lavi weights summary

	Pounds	Kilograms
Structure		
Wing	1,917	869
Canard	360	163
Vertical tail	220	100
Fuselage	3,497	1,586
Engine section	115	52
Nose gear	200	91
Main gear	855	388
Powerplant group		
Engine	2,940	1,334
Air induction system	403	183
Wing fuel tanks	193	88
Fuselage fuel tanks	298	135
In-flight refueling system	57	26
Propulsion system	200	90
Fixed equipment		
Flight controls	1,064	482
Instruments	94	43
Electronics	1,300	590
Electrical system	535	243
Armament	211	96
Air conditioning	552	250
Furnishings	260	118
Auxiliary gear	40	18
Total	15,311	6,945

An essential ingredient in any successful component weight projection is the availability of actual aircraft component weight values, from similar aircraft, against which to calibrate the empirical tools. Detailed component weight values were drawn from the published literature for both the F-15A and F/A-18A and were employed here to calibrate the component weight projections for both the F-16C and the Lavi. These values were further refined by correcting the individual component weights to match the known empty weight totals for each of these aircraft. In the case of the F-16, empty weight values were readily available from a variety of literature sources. In the case of the Lavi, published sources place the airplane's empty weight at 15,310 lb (6,940 kg).[4] This value is further corroborated by comparing it to commonly quoted values for the airplane's thrust-to-weight ratio. The Lavi thrust-to-weight ratio was quoted elsewhere to be 1.07 when in an air-to-air configuration, carrying two heat-seeking missiles, and with 50 percent of internal fuel.[5] Accounting for the weight of the missiles, fuel, pilot, and cannon shells, this thrust-to-weight value confirms the Lavi empty weight quoted above.

An appraisal of the accuracy of the final weight values can be made by applying the weight estimates together with projected locations for each component's center of gravity to determine the aft-most center of gravity in an operational aircraft. This will require the addition of operational weights and center-of-gravity values for such items as fuel, weapons load, and the pilot. For a well-designed aircraft, the aft-most center-of-gravity position will be defined by a 15° tip-back criterion, which is typically targeted as a safety margin to prevent over-rotation during takeoff and landing. For the F-16C component weight projections, the aft-most center-of-gravity location would translate into a maximum tip-back angle of 15.9°. For the Lavi, the aft-most center-of-gravity projection would lead to a tip-back angle of 14.1°. Both of these values are within the expected margin of error for the individual component weight and center-of-gravity approximations, adding further confirmation for the validity of these estimates.

1. Peter Hellman, "The Fighter of the Future," *Discover*, July 1986, 68; David M. North, "Lavi TD Cockpit Reflects Pilot's Combat Experience," AW&ST, March 25, 1991, 46; "Specifications: U.S. Gas Turbine Engines," AW&ST, March 18, 1991, 133–35.

2. U.S. General Accounting Office, *Foreign Assistance: Analysis of Cost Estimates*, 20.

3. Roskam, *Airplane Design*, pt. 5, *Component Weight Estimation*.

4. Lorell, *Use of Prototypes*, 53.

5. John Farley, "Vision of the Future," *Flight International*, January 23–29, 1991, 22.

APPENDIX 4

Propulsion and Defining the Mission

To minimize both weight and drag, the airframe and its engine must fit together like a hand to a glove. Once selected, the engine choice will typically remain fixed throughout the lifetime of an airplane. Only a rare few programs will have the resources to integrate an all-new engine late in their life cycle. Selecting the appropriate engine is therefore among the first, critical design decisions that must be made during the preliminary phases of jet fighter development.

When concept studies for the Lavi began, three jet engines were named as candidates for the new airplane: General Electric's F404-GE-400, Pratt & Whitney's F100-PW-220, and Pratt & Whitney's PW1120.[1] All three were low bypass ratio turbofan engines. It was the PW1120, of course, that would eventually win this contest. This selection process, however, offers its own insight into the airplane it was intended to power.

The Language of Propulsion

Many of those who are otherwise well versed in the aeronautical sciences are often unfamiliar with either the inner workings or the evolution of this one, central component at the heart of the "jet age." A jet engine is at once both elegant in its apparent simplicity and awe-inspiring in the raw power that it can harness. Few feats of modern technology are quite as impressive as a jet engine in full afterburner. But the simplicity of the jet engine's thermodynamic cycle belies the underlying mechanical complexity that makes it all possible.

Conceptually, a jet engine consists of only a handful of distinct parts: a fan or compressor, which compresses the air; a burner, which adds fuel to produce heat; and a turbine, which extracts energy from the hot exhaust, providing the shaft horsepower necessary to drive the fan and compressor. There are, of course, many other elements that must also be present for the engine to function: an inlet system that captures air; a starter-generator that rotates the engine at start-up and provides electrical power during flight; bearings and an oil lubrication system; and an exhaust nozzle. Fundamentally, however, the overall arrangement of the jet engine remains deceptively simple.

A jet engine produces thrust from the differences in both pressure and velocity between the air at the inlet and the air at the exhaust. At first appearance, it is an elementary process. Yet the practicalities of developing this theory into a working arrangement are such that the number and complexity of the detail components quickly multiplies. When all of the individual airfoils, air seals, and fasteners are totaled, it is not unusual for a jet engine to comprise a greater number of components than are to be found in the entire airframe—control surfaces, bulkheads, fasteners, and all.

Whereas the Israeli government had the option of purchasing most of the Lavi airframe and electronics components either at home or abroad, no such alternative existed for the engine. Multiple Israeli firms may have laid claim to some experience in the design or manufacture of airframe components, electronics, and software—but none had experience in the design and manufacture of a complete, modern jet engine. Bet Shemesh Engines, which was expected to assemble the Lavi engine locally, had experience with the manufacture of select engine components. They could also assemble jet engines. But they could in no way be expected to either design or produce all of the components that went into a modern jet fighter engine. Indeed, very few companies in the world could lay claim to such expertise.

In the Western world, there are only four jet engine manufacturers which have experience with the development of a modern fighter engine: Rolls-Royce in the United Kingdom, Snecma of France, and GE Aircraft Engines and Pratt & Whitney in the United States. Virtually all of the fighter aircraft flying in the Western world today utilize an engine produced by one or more of these four. Both the Tornado and the Eurofighter Typhoon, for example, employ engines produced by a partnership that leveraged the experience of Rolls-Royce for the design of key components. Japan's F-2 and Sweden's JAS-39 Gripen, meanwhile, both employ American-designed engines developed by General Electric.

On the other side of the Cold War divide, there are of course the Russian engine manufacturers, who have likewise accumulated considerable expertise. They have succeeded, however, in competing with their Western peers only by sacrificing engine durability to achieve competitive thrust-to-weight ratios. Russian engine overhaul intervals are typically measured in hundreds of flight hours. Western overhaul intervals, in contrast, are today measured in thousands of hours.

A case in point is provided by India's Light Combat Aircraft (LCA), launched in 1983. Later relabeled as the Tejas, the LCA was envisioned as a showcase for Indian technical achievement, with little or no foreign involvement. This included the development of a new jet engine—the Kaveri—intended to be produced locally by India's Gas-Turbine Research Establishment. Thus began a saga of trials and failures that was to last for over two decades. India's Kaveri quickly ran into difficulties in its high-temperature core. The airframe for India's first LCA prototype was rolled out in November 1995. Its engine, however, was still nowhere to be seen. When the first aircraft finally flew in January 2001, it was with a U.S.-supplied F404 engine. By that time, only four Kaveri test engines had been produced, none of which was reliable enough to power a single-engined prototype.[2]

The development of a new jet fighter engine, for a nation with little or no jet engine design experience, would have constituted a far greater task than the development of the airframe or electronics. The Israeli government wisely chose to build the Lavi around a proven U.S.-developed powerplant, as did Sweden for its JAS-39 Gripen, and Japan for its F-2 fighter.

But while it was improbable that Israeli industry could expect to develop their own jet engine, up until relatively recently, it had not been implausible that they might seek to manufacture most, if not all, of the essential components that went into whichever engine they selected. Israeli industry had been able to reproduce the French Atar engine for Israel's Nesher fighters, for example, using little more than the blueprints. Similarly, Israeli industry had likewise provided many of the key components that went into the J79 and J52 engines that had powered Israel's fleet of F-4, Kfir, and A-4 fighters. By the early 1980s, however, the possibility of this pattern being repeated had become remote. The latest generation of fighter engines incorporated unique manufacturing technologies that Israeli industry could not reproduce. To understand why this was so, some minimal appreciation needs to be obtained for how the modern jet fighter engine evolved and for how this latest generation of engines differed from its predecessors.

The Evolution of Jet Propulsion

During the early days of jet aviation, it seemed as if everyone wanted to be in the jet engine business. Airplane manufacturers like Curtiss-Wright and Lockheed had their own jet engine divisions. Steam turbine houses like Westinghouse would successfully design and market engines to the U.S. Navy. One by one, however, virtually all of these early competitors would disappear from the scene. Those unwilling or unable to invest the resources needed to continually evolve and perfect their technology fell by the wayside, leaving only a select few contenders.

For the first three decades of jet engine evolution, the leading developmental milestones for the industry centered around compressor system performance and stability. Higher overall compression ratios promised to improve fuel efficiency as well as thrust. Maintaining compressor stability throughout this process, however, became an ever-more-challenging endeavor. Lockheed's L-1000 jet engine never progressed beyond the prototype phase.[3] West-inghouse, which had jumped into an early lead with the design of the J30, the first all-new turbojet to be designed in the United States—failed to deliver on their promised performance for the J40. Westinghouse would subsequently exit the jet engine busi-ness, never to return.[4]

Those developers who remained were the ones that were will-ing to devote the necessary resources to constantly improve and challenge the limits of their product. The strategies that they developed for improving compressor performance and for deal-ing with compressor instability live with us today. Pratt & Whit-ney introduced the first two-spool engine into flight test in 1951, in the form of the J57.[5] Rolls-Royce pioneered turbofan engines with the Conway's first flight in 1955, a technology that Pratt & Whitney would go on to bring to commercial success with the JT3D in 1959.[6] General Electric would introduce the first vari-able compressor vanes with the J79 in 1955.[7] Each of these inno-vations would find its way into every high-performance engine that followed.

Collectively, the innovations described up until then had made the design and development of a modern jet fighter engine far too daunting of a task for a company with limited experience to contemplate. They did not, however, prevent companies such as Israel's Bet Shemesh Engines from becoming a supplier of key components for these early jet engines. All of the necessary tech-nologies that went into producing them had been within their grasp. The next round in jet engine evolution, however, would change that.

Whereas the preceding milestones in the quest for ever-improved performance had been characterized by advances in compres-sion systems technology, the next round of developments would be characterized by advances in "hot-section," or turbine, tech-nology. This is not to say that advances were not still being made elsewhere. But the defining elements of this next round of jet engine evolution would be centered about the hot-section tech-nology that allowed burner temperatures to soar without melting the turbine airfoils upon which the compressor, and indeed the entire engine, relied.

The first fighter engine to herald this new era had been Pratt & Whitney's F100-100. The F100 had been the first jet fighter engine to employ powdered metal forging technology in its turbine rotor. Under this technique, the forgings for the disks that held the spinning blades were produced from a fine metal powder, which was heated under extreme pressures to produce an alloy microstructure with superior strength and high-temperature performance.[8] This allowed turbine rotors to operate at "cooling air" temperatures that could exceed 1,000 °F (540 °C).

In parallel with this revolution in rotor alloys was an equivalent revolution in turbine airfoil design, spearheaded first by directionally solidified airfoil alloys and later by single crystal alloys. Prior to this new generation in alloy technology, the weakest link in the creep life for turbine blades had been the grain boundaries between the individual crystals that made up each casting. Beginning in the late 1960s, however, succeeding generations of blade alloys would seek to either minimize or eliminate those grain boundaries, producing turbine airfoils with markedly improved creep performance.

The original F100-PW-100 engine had incorporated directionally solidified alloys, wherein the metal crystals that made up the blade were oriented along the span-wise axis of the blade.[9] The directionally solidified airfoil alloys used in the early F100 engines were followed by single crystal alloys, which eliminated completely the grain boundaries within the blade castings, further boosting creep resistance. Originally developed for use in Pratt & Whitney's commercial jet engines, this single crystal technology was introduced into the F100 as part of the Improved Life Core that led to the F100-PW-220 engine.[10] The Improved Life Core consisted of a series of improvements intended to extend the longevity of the various F100 engine components, together with a digital electronic engine control that eliminated the stall-stagnation problems that had plagued early models.[11] This same core was likewise incorporated into the PW1120 engine. Similarly, GE's F404 engine also made use of single crystal blade alloys to achieve higher burner temperatures and improved engine performance and life.[12] Taken together, the materials technologies that went into each of the three Lavi candidate engines represented a significant leap beyond anything that had been seen before.

These same manufacturing technologies also ensured, however, that Bet Shemesh could never hope to manufacture the key hot-section components that went into the Lavi engine. Both the powdered metal forging technology that went into the disks and air seals and the single crystal casting techniques that went into the turbine airfoils required specialized manufacturing capabilities. At best, Bet Shemesh might hope to manufacture components for the fan, compressor, or nozzle section of the Lavi engine, and they could assemble completed engines using kits supplied from the United States. In this sense they could "license produce" the Lavi engine, assembling a combination of local, Israeli-produced compressor components and American-produced hot-section hardware. They could not, however, hope to manufacture the entire engine on their own. The technology behind the manufacture of a modern jet fighter engine had simply evolved too far for the uninitiated to produce all of the many components that went into the final product.

Birds of a Feather

The three Lavi candidate engines that the developers had to choose from were closely matched in terms of the technology that the engines employed. Each represented a generation of advancement beyond what could be found in the prior family of engines that powered the majority of Israel's fighter fleet, including the J52s that equipped Israel's A-4 Skyhawks and the J79s that powered Israel's F-4E and Kfir fighters. Perhaps the easiest way to illustrate the impact of this evolution in technology is to draw a comparison between the earlier, J79, engine that had powered the Kfir and the capabilities of these newer jet engines, which were candidates to power the Lavi.[13]

Table 12. Jet engines compared

		J79-11E	F404-400	Lavi candidate engines PW1120	F100-220
Weight		3,855 lb	2,310 lb	2,848 lb	3,108 lb
		1,749 kg	1,048 kg	1,292 kg	1,410 kg
Maximum envelope	Diameter	39.1 in	35.0 in	40.2 in	46.5 in
		99.3 cm	88.9 cm	102.1 cm	118.1 cm
	Length	208.7 in	159.0 in	161.8 in	208.0 in
		530.1 cm	403.9 cm	411.0 cm	528.3 cm
Thrust	Afterburning	17,900 lb	16,000 lb	20,620 lb	23,830 lb
		79.6 kN	71.2 kN	91.7 kN	106.0 kN
	Military power	11,900 lb	10,608 lb	13,550 lb	14,670 lb
		52.9 kN	47.2 kN	60.3 kN	65.3 kN
Specific fuel consumption	Afterburning	1.97 lb/h/lb	1.85 lb/h/lb	1.86 lb/h/lb	2.16 lb/h/lb
		55.7 mg/Ns	52.4 mg/Ns	52.7 mg/Ns	61.2 mg/Ns
	Military power	0.84 lb/h/lb	0.81 lb/h/lb	0.80 lb/h/lb	0.72 lb/h/lb
		23.8 mg/Ns	23.0 mg/Ns	22.7 mg/Ns	20.4 mg/Ns
Thrust-to-weight ratio		4.6	6.9	7.2	7.7
Fan/compressor stages		17	3 / 7	3 / 10	3 / 10
Turbine stages		3	1 / 1	2 / 1	2 / 2
Overall pressure ratio		13.4	24.0	27.0	24.8
Airflow rate		171 lb/s	142 lb/s	178 lb/s	225 lb/s
		78.0 kg/s	64.0 kg/s	81.0 kg/s	102.0 kg/s

To begin with, all of the Lavi engine candidates were turbofans, in contrast to the earlier J79, which had been a turbojet. The turbofan bypassed a portion of the air around the core, making for a more thermodynamically efficient design, reducing fuel consumption, and increasing range. Moreover, while the J79 had been the very first jet engine to employ variable incidence vanes into its compressor, it had also been a single-spool design. Each of the Lavi candidate engines, on the other hand, employed both variable incidence compressor vanes and a two-spool configuration. In combination with advances in compressor aerodynamics, this two-spool approach allowed each of the Lavi candidate engines to achieve a higher overall pressure ratio, using fewer fan and compressor stages. The J79 had required a total of seventeen compressor stages to achieve an overall compression ratio of 13.4—as measured between the pressure of the outside air and the pressure that was fed to the burner. The PW1120, on the other hand, was able to achieve an overall compression ratio of 27.0 using a combination of only thirteen fan and compressor stages.[14]

There were also other technology advances that had been made between the engines of the J79-era and the three engine candidates from which the Lavi development team had to select. The J79 had employed a cannular burner design incorporating a separate mixing "can" for each of its burner nozzles. The F100, PW1120, and F404 each employed an annular burner that was smaller in both length and cross-sectional height. As mentioned previously, however, the greatest technological advancement that this new generation of engines embodied was in their turbine hot-section technology.

To understand the impact of this revolution in turbine materials technology, consider that the maximum burner temperature achieved by the J79-GE-17 used in the F-4E Phantom had measured in at a highly respectable 1,700 °F (925 °C). The F100-PW-100, on the other hand, had been able to boast a maximum turbine inlet temperature of up to 2,565 °F (1,405 °C).[15] It had been no accident that the F100 had so outclassed its predecessor. The combination of compressor performance and a revolution in turbine hot-section technology had all but guaranteed that this new generation in jet fighter engines would offer substantially increased thrust-to-weight ratios and lower fuel consumption.

The net result of these technological advances can best be seen in the thrust-to-weight ratios provided by each engine. The J79 had achieved a maximum thrust-to-weight ratio of 4.6 at takeoff conditions, which was considered to be highly respectable for a jet engine of that era. Each of the Lavi candidate engines, on the other hand, boasted a thrust-to-weight ratio in excess of 6.9—an increase of 50 percent. In practical terms, these engines therefore offered an opportunity to improve both the airplane's thrust-to-weight ratio and its range beyond anything that prior generations could envision.

Fundamentally, the three Lavi engine candidates were much more alike than they were different. They each employed many of the same technological advances and achieved similar fuel consumption rates and thrust-to-weight ratios. Any differences that each engine might have enjoyed in these respects were inconsequential compared to their differences in rated thrust. And they were clearly different in terms of thrust, from the 16,000 lb (71.2 kN) produced by the F404-400 to the more than 23,000 lb (102 kN) produced by the F100-220. The developers tasked with recommending the preferred engine alternative for the Lavi were therefore faced with choosing not between different levels of engine technology or efficiency but between three different levels of engine thrust. To understand why the Lavi engine selection took the course that it did, we must look to the preliminary design and sizing process.

Engine Selection and Airplane-Engine Sizing

Most jet fighters will begin their genesis as a "request for proposal" (RFP) issued by the government or air force that is exploring the development of an all-new airplane. This RFP will comprise two distinct parts: the expected performance demanded from the new airplane and a selection of mission profiles that it is expected to carry out. The performance component of the RFP will include such parameters as minimum climb rate, minimum rate of turn, maximum takeoff distance, supersonic speed requirements, and so forth. The mission definition, meanwhile, will typically comprise multiple mission profiles, each of which will include details regarding the required payload, the minimum range, and the altitude and Mach number projected for each leg of the mission. The RFP may also include dimensional requirements, specifying the maximum allowable aircraft dimensions and weights.

Once the request for proposal is in the contractor's hands, the design process begins with preparation of a preliminary estimate for just how big the aircraft will need to be by evaluating both the aircraft performance requirements and its mission objectives, in parallel. Each performance goal can be related to a range of possible thrust-loading (thrust divided by weight) and wing-loading (weight divided by wing area) combinations that satisfy the individual criteria. Taken together, these performance criteria define an acceptable solution space that meets the design intent for the RFP. These performance relationships are typically plotted in a graph-like fashion, relating thrust loading to wing loading, to create a "constraint diagram." The design that is ultimately selected from within this range of possible alternatives will usually be the one that requires the lowest thrust-to-weight ratio while still meeting all of the performance goals. Few customers will want to pay for a larger airframe or engine than what they absolutely require.

None of these performance trade studies, however, will directly size the airplane. The same performance objective, in terms of turn rate, takeoff distance, climb rate, or what have you, could just as easily be achieved by a small airplane as by a large one, provided that the thrust loading and wing loading remain consistent. What ultimately sizes the airplane, therefore, will be not the raw performance criteria but the mission requirements that go with them.

Table 13. Lavi as sized to its engine candidates

		F404-400	PW1120	F100-220
Maximum thrust, T_{max}		16,000 lb	20,620 lb	23,830 lb
		71.2 kN	91.7 kN	106.0 kN
Weights	Max takeoff weight, W_{TO}	32,980 lb	42,500 lb	49,120 lb
		14,960 kg	19,280 kg	22,280 kg
	Empty weight, W_E	11,720 lb	15,310 lb	17,830 lb
		5,320 kg	6,940 kg	8,090 kg
	Max internal fuel	4,590 lb	6,000 lb	6,990 lb
		2,080 kg	2,720 kg	3,170 kg
	Max external fuel	7,120 lb	9,180 lb	10,610 lb
		3,230 kg	4,160 kg	4,810 kg
Wing area, S		276 sq ft	356 sq ft	411 sq ft
		25.6 m^2	33.0 m^2	38.2 m^2
Combat radius	Hi-lo-hi	970 nm	1,150 nm	1,320 nm
		1,800 km	2,130 km	2,440 km
	Lo-lo-lo	580 nm	670 nm	790 nm
		1,070 km	1,240 km	1,460 km

A mission profile analysis consists of "flying" a theoretical airplane from takeoff, through each leg of its mission, all the way through to landing. In each successive phase of the mission analysis, airplane weights and fuel consumption will be tabulated and the weight of fuel consumed in that mission leg will be subtracted to arrive at the initial weight for the next leg in the mission. Through an iterative process, this analysis will settle on the minimum airplane size that is capable of carrying out the complete mission.

The Lavi mission profiles would have included close air support, interdiction, point air defense, and long-range strike roles. Performance requirements would have included turn rate, rate of climb, and takeoff distance, among other objectives. The airplane weight that was eventually settled upon would have represented the smallest fighter that could fulfill all of these roles.

While we do not know all of the details surrounding the original Lavi mission and performance requirements, we do know the final design point. Based on this information it is possible to project the takeoff weight and wing area for an equivalent Lavi-type strike fighter, built around the F404 or F100 engines, that would fall on the same location on the constraint diagram. We can also take this analysis one step further by using empirical weight estimation techniques to project the associated empty weight for each of these airplanes. As projected, each of the above-mentioned airplanes would fall upon the same point on the constraint diagram and would satisfy the same performance curves. Where each airplane would differ would be in its size, payload, and the distance it could travel.

When the Lavi engine selection was changed in 1981 from the F404 to the PW1120, it was not changed because the Lavi constraint diagram had somehow shifted. There was no indication that the Israeli air force had fundamentally changed their objectives behind the airplane's targeted climb rate, speed, or any other performance parameter. What had changed was its mission profile. It had gone from being a medium-range attack jet to being a long-range strike fighter. A back-of-the-envelope calculation would therefore suggest that switching engines from the F404-400 to the PW1120 would have increased the Lavi's available payload by over 4,400 lb (2,000 kg). Furthermore, this increased payload capability could also be translated directly into an increase in fuel capacity, permitting an airplane built around the PW1120 to achieve nearly a 20 percent increase in its hi-lo-hi combat radius, given the same payload.[16] The advantages of building the Lavi fighter around the PW1120 should be clear. The PW1120 offered an opportunity to significantly increase the airplane's payload and range. What may not be so clear at first glance is why this same principle was not carried one step further, with the F100 chosen in place of the PW1120 to produce an airplane with even greater payload and range capabilities.

In simple terms, selecting the F100 would have required a greater investment, in return for added range and payload that were not deemed necessary. The F100 could have increased the maximum airplane takeoff weight by up to 15 percent. But it would also have increased the empty weight by approximately 16 percent, increasing the airframe price along with it. Every extra ounce in empty weight would translate into extra raw materials and extra man-hours spent in its construction. Selecting the F100 would also have resulted in increased maintenance and operating costs. The PW1120, it should be recalled, had been derived as a simplified cousin to the F100, with fewer parts and with ease of maintenance and reduced spares costs specifically in mind.[17] From a cost-benefit standpoint, selecting the F100 simply hadn't made sense.

Moreover, a fighter built around the F100 would also have produced a larger target. In order to meet the required performance demands while at the same time increasing the aircraft size and empty weight to take full advantage of the added thrust, an F100-powered aircraft would have had to increase its wing area in concert with its takeoff weight. That's a 15 percent increase in wing area, or a 15 percent increase in the size of the target that the enemy would have to shoot at. For an attack jet, minimizing the airplane's size could be crucial to its battlefield survivability. During the 1991 Gulf War, for example, it became painfully evident that the larger aircraft were at a decided disadvantage when it came to avoiding opposing antiaircraft fire. During this conflict U.S. Air Force F-15E

Strike Eagles proved to be 74 percent more likely to be damaged or destroyed by antiaircraft fire than were F-16C fighter-bombers, while flying some of the same strike missions.[18] The difference between a small strike aircraft that was difficult to spot and shoot at and a much larger airplane that drew more than its fair share of surface-to-air missiles and antiaircraft artillery could be the difference between life and death.

When the PW1120 was chosen over the F404 in 1981, it was a decision that had come with a cost. According to a financial analysis prepared in May 1981 by the economic advisor to the Israeli Defense Ministry, on a production series of four hundred airplanes, the unit flyaway cost for a Lavi built around the PW1120 could be expected to be 6 percent greater than if the aircraft had been built around the smaller F404.[19] This was a price that the Israeli developers were willing to pay to meet their objectives for this warplane. They were not, however, willing to pay more for an extra margin in range or payload that didn't fit their needs. The PW1120 won out over the F404 and F100 because it was the right engine for the job. It wasn't necessarily the biggest, nor was it the cheapest. In fact, it was the least amount of engine that could still perform the task. But when it comes time to award a contract and pay the winning contender, being the best fit for the role becomes the highest form of praise.

The PW1120: The Anatomy of Pratt's Little Winner

The PW1120 was a company-financed derivative of Pratt & Whitney's highly successful F100 engine. The objective had been to take advantage of the F100's proven performance and maintenance record to come up with a reliable powerplant targeted at the variety of lightweight fighters that were under development during the early 1980s. The concept was to make it simpler, cheaper, and easier to maintain than the original F100.

The F100 had itself evolved considerably from its initial operational service in the F-15A. Like most new high- performance engines, the F100 had experienced its share of growing pains. Early editions of the engine had encountered compressor stall-stagnation problems that had required years of intense effort to resolve. A compressor stall, much like the stall on an airplane wing, occurs when flow begins to separate from one or more compressor airfoils. When this stall phenomenon persists and spreads to adjacent compressor airfoils, it can lead to stagnation, resulting in a loss of engine thrust. This problem was ultimately resolved by incorporating a digital electronic engine control, which could modulate the afterburner and engine exhaust nozzle to prevent flow disturbances from progressing to stagnation.[20] The PW1120 that went into the Lavi was expected to benefit from this same experience.

The other major hurdle that the early F100 engine models had to overcome was an unexpectedly high wear-out rate, due to the expanded range of operation that this new generation of jet engine had made possible. Previous generations of fighter engines had measured their life purely in terms of engine operating hours. "Hot time," or the hours at military or maximum power, had been assumed to be the only relevant maintenance parameter when the U.S. Air Force had defined their requirements for the early F100. But the unprecedented thrust-to-weight ratio afforded by the F100 had made fighter maneuvers possible in the F-15 and F-16 that hadn't been dreamt of previously. Pilots were constantly adjusting the engine throttle, spooling the engine up and down as they put the aircraft through routines that had once been unthinkable. Each up-and-down throttle adjustment ate into the life of the engine. Under the original design requirement for the F100, the engine had been expected to experience 3,000 hours of operation between major overhauls, consisting of 525 hours at maximum power, and a projected 1,765 thermal-mechanical fatigue cycles. By November 1979, however, the U.S. Air Force would report that for every 2,000 hours of engine operation, they were projecting only 235 hours at maximum power, but with an estimated 10,360 thermal-mechanical cycles.[21] The original F100 specification had failed to capture the true magnitude of thermal-mechanical fatigue. It was an oversight that had led Pratt & Whitney to develop the Improved Life Core for the F100, incorporating new designs and more advanced materials technologies to extend the life of the engine components. Coming out of this experience, the F100 had grown to become one of the true landmark engines in jet fighter history. In the words of Gen. Benjamin N. Bellis, director of the F-15 System Program Office, "Over the 15 years since we started the F100 development program, it still is the highest performing engine in the world, with corresponding fuel efficiencies. It has a better operational record in the USAF inventory than any other fighter engine."[22]

The PW1120 shared the same extended life core and digital engine controls as the F100-PW-220, which was the most advanced version then available for the F100.[23] This shared core included the high-pressure compressor, the burner, and the high-pressure turbine, which together gave the PW1120 a 60 percent parts commonality with the F100 engines that already powered much of Israel's F-15 and F-16 fleet. Where the two engines differed was in their fan, their low-pressure turbine, and their afterburner.

Some sources have erroneously described the PW1120 as a "turbojet derivative" of the F100, in reference to its very low bypass ratio.[24] A look at an engine cross section, however, should make it apparent that a portion of the fan air was indeed bypassed around the compressor and turbine, making the PW1120, by definition, a turbofan. In the F100, however, virtually all of the bypass air was remixed with the turbine exhaust before that air entered the afterburner. Under the PW1120, with its much smaller bypass ratio, much of the available bypass air would be used to cool the nozzle liner before being reintroduced into the exhaust stream.[25] This arrangement had two beneficial effects. It increased the degree of aerodynamic isolation between the fan and the afterburner, making it less prone to stall-stagnation events. It also made the design of the afterburner that much easier, since the afterburner would only have to deal with a single stream of hot turbine exhaust air, rather than a mixture of hot exhaust and cool fan air, as experienced in the F100.

The PW1120 had a redesigned three-stage fan, which incorporated an electron beam welded titanium rotor drum, a technology that was then under development for Pratt & Whitney's PW1128 technology demonstrator. The engine also incorporated a new, single-piece fan case, a feature that was expected to reduce both part count and engine cost.[26] This new fan, in turn, was driven by a single-stage low-pressure turbine, as opposed to the two-stage low-pressure turbine found in the F100. In addition, the PW1120 employed a new, simplified afterburner design, with five fuel injection rings in place of the more complex system of seven rings found on the F100. The PW1120 borrowed its most critical, high-temperature components directly from the proven F100 design, leaving Pratt & Whitney free to redefine the remaining elements of the engine, with an eye toward reducing cost and complexity.

There remains, however, one crucial question still to be answered surrounding this engine: why did the PW1120 fail to catch on with additional customers? The PW1120 offered proven core operation at a reduced life cycle cost. It had once been a prime contender to power a host of international fighter projects, from Sweden's JAS-39 Gripen to India's LCA to Yugoslavia's Novi Avion, and even a proposed Chinese fighter.[27] Moreover, the PW1120 was the only engine on the market that was suitably sized to replace the J79 turbojet in the massive F-4 Phantom inventory still at large—a prospect that both the Israeli and German air forces considered to be a serious possibility.

In spite of this array of potential buyers, however, all of these aircraft either selected a different engine or were canceled. The Chinese and Yugoslav fighter programs disintegrated under political pressures, while Sweden chose the F404 engine and India chose to pursue its own indigenous development program.[28] The ultimate reason that the PW1120 never caught on, however, is the same principle that had led to its selection for the Lavi: each prospective buyer selected the least amount of engine that would fulfill both the mission profile and the performance criteria for its program. With the exception of the Lavi, all of the international fighter projects then under development envisioned a far less demanding mission profile, requiring less range and less payload than what Israel had specified. These other aircraft had all been envisioned as relatively short-range fighters and had emphasized the air-to-air mission rather than air-to-ground as their primary role.

As for proposals to re-engine the F-4 with the PW1120 powerplant, once the Lavi was canceled there was no longer an open production line for the new engine. A case in point was Israel's post-Lavi Nammer (tiger) fighter project. The Nammer was proposed as an export fighter that could be based around either a remanufactured Mirage or Kfir airframe. It was expected to feature an avionics suite derived from the Lavi, including the Elta EL/M-2032 pulse-Doppler radar. The Kfir fuselage was expected to be stretched for the new airplane to afford more fuel capacity, while a variety of engine alternatives were proposed, including the much smaller F404. Moreover, mindful of past frustrations in obtaining export licenses for U.S.-supplied engines, Israel Aircraft Industries selected the latest version of the French Atar engine to power their prototype Nammer on its maiden flight in 1991—the first French jet engine sale to Israel since the weapons embargo announced by Charles de Gaulle in 1967. At 15,830 lb (70.4 kN) thrust, the new Atar engine offered poorer performance than the Kfir's existing J79. However, the French engine would also be free of U.S. export restrictions. The PW1120, meanwhile, was never considered an alternative.[29] When the Lavi was canceled in August 1987, the fortunes of Pratt & Whitney's PW1120 died with it.

. . .

Aircraft Empty Weight Projections

As part of any initial airplane sizing process, a method needs to be in hand for projecting the relationship between the airplane's empty weight and its maximum takeoff weight. This is typically accomplished by means of an empirical regression relationship.[1]

The generic regression relation employed here for conceptual Lavi sizing studies was drawn from studies in the open literature for a fighter-type aircraft:[2]

$$\log_{10} W_{E} = (\log_{10} W_{TO} - A)/B$$

where

$A = 0.5091$
$B = 0.9505$

J79-GE-17

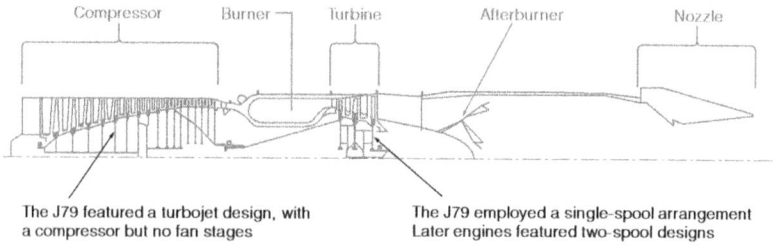

Compressor | Burner | Turbine | Afterburner | Nozzle

The J79 featured a turbojet design, with a compressor but no fan stages

The J79 employed a single-spool arrangement Later engines featured two-spool designs

Fig. 27. The J79, which powered the F-4, Kfir, and other aircraft, was among the last turbojet engines to reach the field.

F100-PW-220

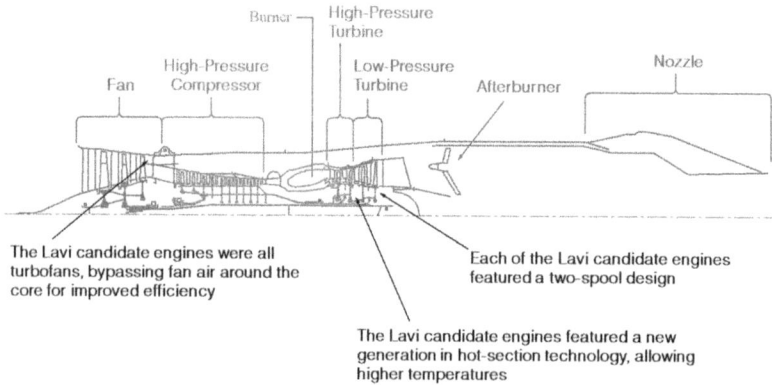

Burner | High-Pressure Turbine

Fan | High-Pressure Compressor | Low-Pressure Turbine | Afterburner | Nozzle

The Lavi candidate engines were all turbofans, bypassing fan air around the core for improved efficiency

Each of the Lavi candidate engines featured a two-spool design

The Lavi candidate engines featured a new generation in hot-section technology, allowing higher temperatures

Fig. 28. Pratt & Whitney's F100 inaugurated an era of afterburning turbofan designs that have dominated the jet fighter industry since the 1970s.

F100-PW-220

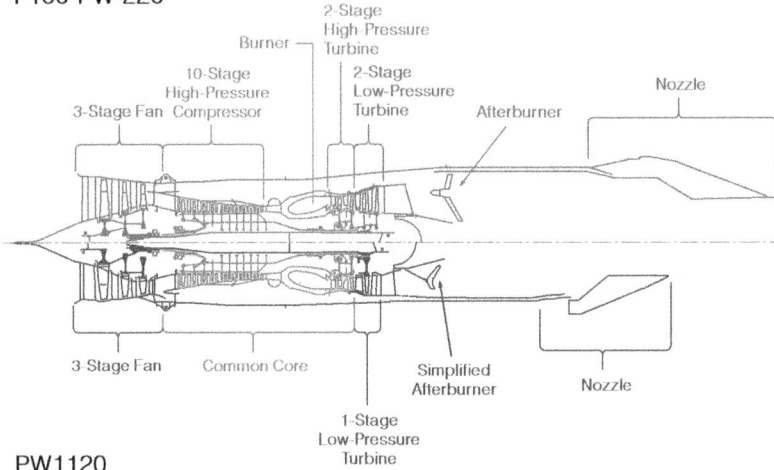

Fig. 29. The PW1120 shared the same high-temperature core with its F100 predecessor.

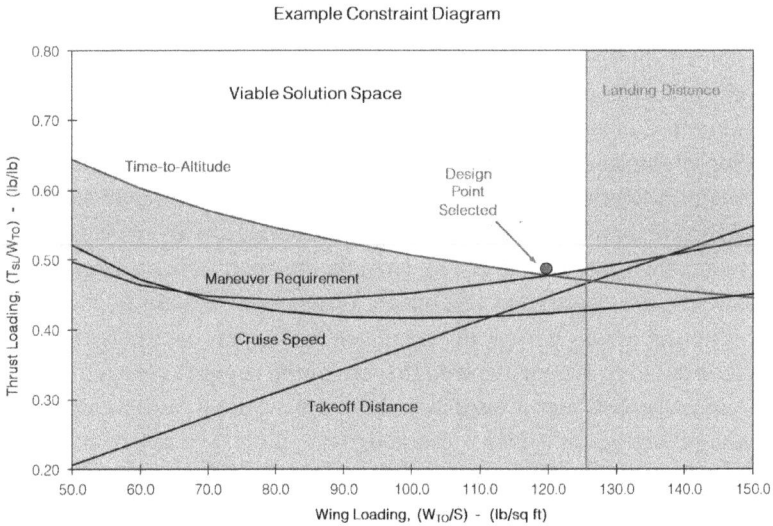

Fig. 30. Constraint diagrams illustrate the solution space available for new designs. The lowest-weight alternative, however, that meets all requirements will invariably be the most affordable.

This regression was based upon a wide range of fighter aircraft, many of them built for very different roles from that of the Lavi. For this reason, this general equation must be adjusted based upon the particulars of the Lavi design. Using the Lavi empty weight of 15,310 lb (6,940 kg), described previously, and a maximum take-off weight of 42,500 lb (19,280 kg), the adjusted coefficients come out to be:

$$A_{new} = 0.6506$$

$$B = 0.9505$$

This corrected equation was used to make empty weight projections for a Lavi-type fighter, as built around the F404 or F100 engine alternatives.

Of course, the design point for the Lavi lies at a considerable distance from that of the typical empty and takeoff weight combinations characterized by the generic regression relation shown above. As should be expected for an airplane that was optimized for the attack role, the Lavi boasts a considerably higher takeoff weight in relation to its empty weight.

To improve our confidence in the revised regression relationship described here, we might consider how this relationship would compare against another delta-winged attack jet, such as the A-4 Skyhawk. With an empty weight of 10,450 lb (4,740 kg), the A-4F had a normal takeoff weight of some 24,500 lb (11,110 kg) when flown in carrier operations. For land-based operators, however, the maximum approved takeoff weight was 27,420 lb (12,440 kg), an impressive feat for so small an airframe. Moreover, the A-4F was produced decades before composite technology was available. The Lavi, on the other hand, was expected to comprise 22 percent composite components by weight.[3] Composite components are typically 15–25 percent lighter than their all-metal counterparts. For an airplane the size of the A-4 with a structure that was 22 percent composites by weight, this would have amounted to a weight savings of between 390 and 715 lb (180 to 320 kg), or an empty weight of between 10,060 and 9,735 lb (4,560 to 4,420kg), for the same maximum takeoff weight.

For an airplane with a maximum takeoff weight of 27,420 lb (12,440 kg), the generic fighter and attack aircraft regression line quoted directly from the literature would suggest an empty weight for the A-4F of some 13,600 lb (6,170 kg). This estimate is some 30 percent higher than what the A-4F actually weighed, and roughly 37 percent higher than what would be expected for an A-4F that incorporated composites technology.

The regression line adjusted to fit the Lavi design point, however, would suggest an empty weight of 9,650 lb (4,380 kg) for an airplane with an equivalent maximum takeoff weight: at the lower limit of the range that might be expected from an A-4F built with a composite wing and tail structure. Remarkably, a regression line adjusted to fit the Lavi design point is not only representative of a modern, canard-delta strike fighter but also provides an exceptionally good preliminary weight estimate for a wide array of delta-winged attack jets, across a broad range of possible takeoff weights. This comparison also tells us that the Lavi and A-4 Skyhawk are in many ways much more similar to each other than either was to the purely air-to-air fighters that make up the bulk of the data points used to achieve the original, uncorrected regression line.

1. Raymer, *Aircraft Design*.

2. Roskam, *Airplane Design*, pt. 1, *Preliminary Sizing of Airplanes*.

3. "Honing the Defenses with Updates," *AW&ST*, December 2, 1985, 80, 84, 88.

· · ·

Estimating Range

A variety of elements come into play when performing a mission profile evaluation. Included in this mix is the airplane's drag polar, the mission that is being performed, and the thrust and fuel consumption provided by the engine.

The mission profile studies carried out in this appendix were focused on evaluating the maximum limits of range performance. To achieve this would mean that the entire mission would need to be carried out without resort to an afterburner. An allowance was made for five minutes at Mach 0.80 at low altitude over the target zone, as well as for a twenty-minute fuel reserve at the end of the mission. The majority of time, however, would be spent at cruise conditions, whether at high altitudes (hi-lo-hi mission) or low altitudes (lo-lo-lo mission). This would be where the majority of the fuel consumption would take place, making it essential that the mission be carried out at the optimum flight speed.

The mission profiles described here closely follow outlines published by the U.S. Naval Test Pilot School.[1] The relationships supplying fuel burn across each leg of the mission, in turn, are provided from a

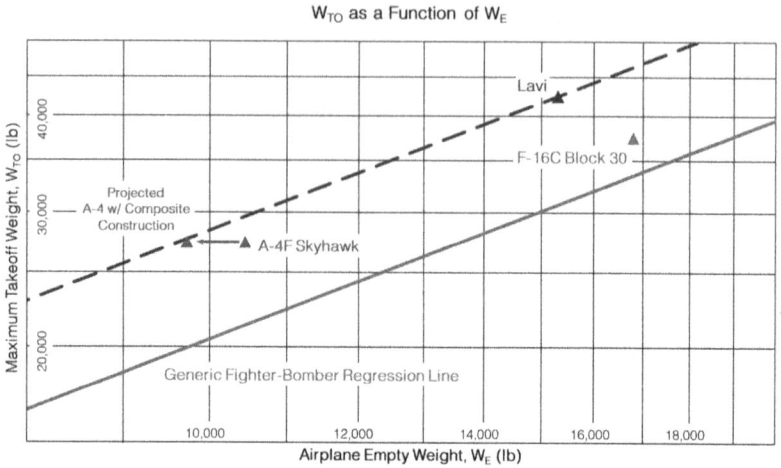

Fig. 31. A regression line relation for weight estimation—adjusted to match the Lavi—also turns out to be an excellent predictor for the empty weight of another dedicated strike jet, once the weight savings from composite technology has been taken into account.

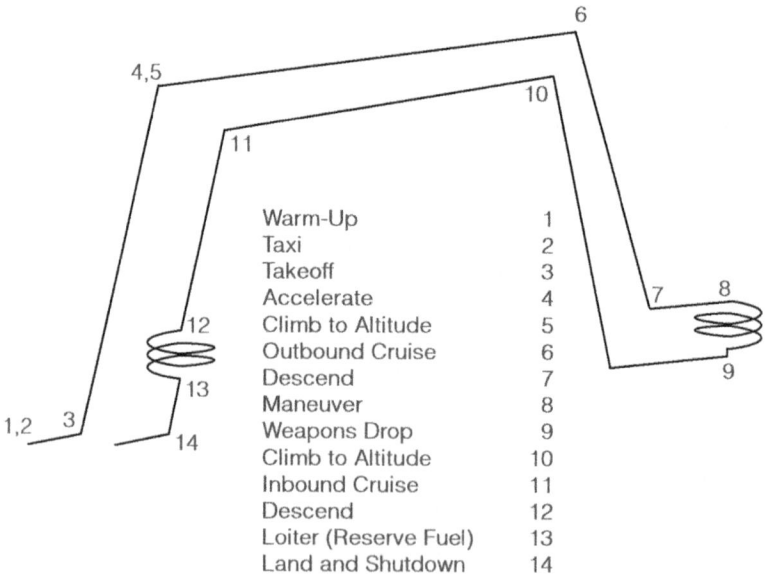

Fig. 32. Aircraft sizing stems from a combination of performance analyses and mission range studies: analyzing fuel burn by breaking the mission down into small segments.

variety of engineering tools, including approximations for fuel burn during takeoff and landing, as well as more elaborate calculations for fuel burn during climb, maneuver, loiter, and cruise.[2]

Finally, at a minimum, a rudimentary estimate needs to be available for the specific fuel consumption of each engine under investigation. Engine performance parameters are typically quoted by the manufacturer for sea level static (sls) conditions, at both military (non-afterburning) and maximum (afterburning) power settings. Reasonable estimates for performance at other conditions can therefore be projected from these values, provided that the proper software is applied. For the purposes of the analyses performed here, projections were carried out by the aedsys (aircraft engine design system) software, produced by the American Institute of Aeronautics and Astronautics. More robust commercial software packages are also available for performing this task. However, aedsys provides a relatively simple tool that meets the more minimal needs of the conceptual design calculations performed here. Note that since, for these mission profiles, the vast majority of the fuel burn takes place at the cruise condition (where thrust matches drag), it was not necessary to precisely match engine performance at the extremes of the envelope. This makes it much easier to utilize off-the-shelf software, with relatively few additional assumptions regarding the limits of engine performance.

1. Gallagher, Higgins, Khinoo, and Pierce, *Fixed Wing Performance.*

2. Roskam, *Airplane Design*, pt. 1, *Preliminary Sizing of Airplanes*; Mattingly, Heiser and Daley, *Aircraft Engine Design.*

APPENDIX 5

Avionics, Electronics, and the Man-Machine Interface

Aircraft electronics have played an ever-increasing role in how warplanes perform their mission, as well as in their cost. Avionics systems were expected to account for 30–35 percent of the Lavi unit cost, as compared to only 10 percent of the unit cost of the Kfir. Early cost estimates for the United States' Advanced Tactical Fighter (ATF) similarly projected that avionics would account for 40 percent of the unit flyaway cost of the F-22. When maintenance, upgrades, and repairs are added in, avionics expenditures have become the single biggest area of investment for a modern fighter program.[1]

Untangling the Labyrinth

The Lavi avionics suite was a maze of interlocked American and Israeli-made subsystems. At the heart of the avionics package, however, was the mission computer: the ACE-4. The ACE-4 was supplied by Elbit, based on prior experience with Elbit's ACE-3 mission computer, which had equipped Israel's F-16C fleet and which had also made its way into Israel's Phantom 2000 upgrade program.[2] The basic ACE-3 had featured 64 kB of memory and was capable of internal bus cycle times of up to 550 kHz. The ACE-4 was expected to improve on its predecessor, featuring a more modular design with a basic memory of 128 kB organized into two modules, which could be expanded to up to 2.0 MB of memory. Processor performance was expected to be in excess of 600 kHz.[3]

These values might appear, at first glance, to have been eclipsed by subsequent generations in home and office computers. But there is more than just the elapse of time at play here. By conventional measures of performance, military electronics consistently lag behind their counterparts in the civilian consumer electronics market. This appearance is deceiving, however. Consumer electronics are not required to endure the rigors of combat. No armed force could afford to wait while soldiers on the ground, air, or sea attempted to reboot wayward computers. The perceived "lag" between civilian and military electronics reflects the difference between developing a product that is minimally acceptable for the consumer market and developing one that is reliable enough to risk someone's life in its application.

As important as the strides in expanding the memory and speed of the Lavi's mission computer may have been, minimizing its space and weight was an equally urgent priority. New and emerging technologies were employed to keep the Lavi computers light and compact—including surface-mounted device (SMD) memory boards, an approach whereby the circuitry that drives the computer is imprinted directly onto the individual circuit panels. This concept was by no means unique to the Lavi. The technology had already been applied in consumer electronics ranging from television sets to microwaves. The Lavi SMD cards, however, were among the first that could withstand the harsh environment of a jet fighter. According to Western military standards, or "mil specs," electronics devices for combat aircraft must be able to operate across a grueling range of conditions, including temperatures that can be anywhere from -67 °F to 257 °F (-55 °C to 125 °C). It is difficult to imagine a home or office computer that would be expected to operate equally well in the deep freeze or the oven. Criteria such as this were a large part of the reason for the perceived "lag" between military and consumer electronics. Elbit had been among the very first companies to develop SMD cards capable of withstanding this temperature range. This breakthrough, in turn, allowed them to vastly reduce the size of the Lavi mission computer, from the 30 lb (14 kg) of the ACE-3 to only 11 lb (5 kg) for the ACE-4. The technology also saved on maintenance time. With its built-in diagnostics capability, faulty computer boards could be identified at the press of a button and replaced within seconds.[4]

But this was but the tip of the electronics mountain. As prime contractor, it was up to Elta, IAI's electronics division, to piece together an avionics suite that would cover a full spectrum of computational roles and sizes. Moreover, the system needed the flexibility to be easily updated to handle new missions and changes to the battlefield. Take the mission data system, for example, which centered around a memory cartridge developed by Israel's Rada Electronics. It allowed the entire terrain and threat update for each mission to be loaded into the computer in the mere seconds it would take to replace one cartridge with another.[5] It was this kind of forethought that had to go into the Lavi from the beginning, if it were to become the kind of survivable and reliable fighter that the Israeli air force needed.

The task that Elta faced was truly monumental. They were expected to integrate both Israeli- and American-made components to create a system that could be easily expanded to meet new threats but that also had a useful lifetime of fifteen to twenty years with minimal modification to its core architecture.[6] As Lavi deputy project manager Nissam Ebel explained, "For sheer computing power the Lavi is way ahead of anything now flying."[7]

Another way to look at it is to recall that the F-16A, once nicknamed the "Electric Jet," had originally carried an electronics package that weighed in at some 700 lb (320 kg). The Lavi, with all of the advances in electronics miniaturization that it incorporated, was expected to have an avionics suite weighing in at 1,300 lb (590 kg).[8] Everything from the fire-control radar to an elaborate electronic countermeasures suite had to squeeze into that one small airframe. In all, over one hundred computers from a variety of manufacturers came together to form the Lavi avionics package. It was this daunting task that led Elta to attempt a feat that had never before been performed: to build an avionics suite that went beyond being a mere collection of independent components to become an integrated whole—from the software on up.[9]

The Lavi was to be the first jet fighter to fly with a fully integrated, software-driven avionics suite. All of the fine details surrounding how each avionics component functioned were to be imbedded into the software, rather than being tied to the physical hardware. To make this concept yield its maximum reward, however, every computer on the Lavi would need to speak the same language—something that prior generations of jet fighter had failed to do.

To fulfill this requirement for a common avionics programming language, Elta selected Jovial (Jules' Own Version of the International Algorithmic Language), which had been evolved specifically for application to aircraft avionics systems under the direction of the U.S. Air Force during the 1970s.[10] The U.S. armed forces, however, had subsequently abandoned the use of Jovial in favor of Ada—a programming language that by government decree was intended to fulfill all government programming needs, from aircraft and missile electronics to paycheck issuance and cost accounting. Israel, however, had no such mandate, and Jovial was selected over Ada as the more mature language.

What IAI needed, however, was not just a unifying programming language but also a new approach to software development—an all-inclusive vision that could replace the piecemeal efforts of the past. They found their approach with Dr. David Harel at the Weizmann Institute of Science. It was Harel who had first developed the "statecharts" method as a formal process for visually analyzing the interaction between different software and hardware modules. It was this approach to computer network design that allowed Elta to successfully integrate the various computers.

The end product endowed the Lavi with several unique features. One of the advantages was that it allowed for graceful degradation of the avionics system in the event of combat damage or component failure. Tasks that had once been assigned to a damaged computer could be rerouted or reassigned to another. The method also helped to alleviate the limitations in computer processing power that have always been the bane of the avionics engineer. A scientist working in an earthbound lab can always build a bigger computer. On an airplane, both weight and space are severely limited. The statecharts method allowed the airplane to maximize the use of the available computing power by defining the tasks most critical to each phase of the mission and assigning them priority in computer processing time. Rather than being a disparate collection of unrelated hardware modules, each acting in isolation, the Lavi avionics suite was intended to act as a single computer network, executing a common task.[11]

The object-oriented programming approach of statecharts also allowed the Lavi avionics package to be easily modularized—which would facilitate later efforts to upgrade individual elements or to apply components from the Lavi to other applications. The top-level, avionics control system, for example, was divided into four modules: a configuration controller, which monitored subsystem health and made corrections for damaged submodules; an operational controller, which fed information to the pilot; a slaving controller, which allocated sensor resources on the basis of mission needs and priorities; and a subsystems translator, which provided feedback between the top-level control system and the subsystems. This architecture also had the added benefit of cutting down on unnecessary "chatter" between the modules.[12]

The "statecharts" method, perfected as it was for use on the Lavi, was also one of the fighter program's successful spin-offs. IAI reportedly used the method on at least eight other avionics integration projects during the 1980s, and in 1984 Harel packaged the method into a stand-alone, commercial software package known as Statemate. The computerized version of the method offered three different sets of graphic displays: one demonstrating subsystems interaction; one for viewing data flow; and another providing a physical view of both hardware and software components. Among the earliest overseas customers of the Statemate package would be McDonnell Douglas, which utilized it to integrate the avionics suite for the F/A-18E/F Super Hornet.[13]

Radar: Eyes for the Lion

At the same time that the first pair of Lavi prototypes were making their maiden flights, flight testing for the Lavi radar was already underway aboard a Boeing 707 flying test bed.[14] The Lavi radar was a pulse-Doppler unit, developed by IAI's Elta division. The Doppler effect is a phenomenon that occurs whenever a wave-type signal interacts with a moving object. In this case the signal is a radar wave that is being reflected by another airplane or from objects being tracked on the ground. The effect of this relative motion is to alter the frequency of the signal. If the object is moving toward the observer, the signal will become compressed, resulting in a shorter frequency. If the object is moving away from the observer, the signal will become stretched, giving it a longer frequency. An example of this from everyday experience is the sound of a train whistle as it goes by. As the train approaches, the sound waves will be compressed, resulting in a higher-pitched sound. As the train speeds away, the sound waves will be stretched out, resulting in a lower-pitched sound. What set pulse-Doppler radar technology apart from its predecessors was its ability to "listen" for these shifts in pitch among the echoes that it received. These shifts would tell the radar not only where a moving object was located but also how fast it was moving.

Pulse-Doppler radar first appeared on fighter aircraft in the early 1970s. Older radar types, such as the radar sets on the F-4E or Kfir, could determine a target only in terms of direction and distance. The real handicap for these earlier radars, however, was that radar returns from aircraft approaching at a lower altitude would be lost in the clutter from the ground. These earlier radar systems were blind to any aircraft flying below them. Pulse-Doppler radar changed all of this. To a pulse-Doppler radar, which looked for frequency shifts, any moving object would stand out like a beacon, making it possible to track low-flying targets.

Elta's first pulse-Doppler radar set was the EL/M-2021, which was offered as an option on export versions of the Kfir and was flight tested in Israeli F-4Es. The Lavi radar, however, was an all-new unit, which built upon this experience. The EL/M-2035 was constructed in four modules: the antenna, the transmitter, a radar processing unit, and a low-power radio frequency system. The flat, planar antenna was designed for minimal sidelobe propagation, cutting down on extraneous signals that could alert opposing air defenses. Moreover, like all Lavi avionics, the radar was meant to be self-adapting: reacting on its own to changes in the electronic countermeasures that it encountered.[15]

The EL/M-2035 featured separate modes for each of the fighter's roles. In the air combat mission the radar would be operated in a track-while-scan mode, with automatic target acquisition. The radar also featured special dogfight modes for terminal engagement, including boresight, slew, scan, and single-track options.[16] Reports suggest that, in terms of overall range, the Lavi radar was intended to operate at shorter distances than the APG-68 radar of the F-16C. However, in terms of its resolution and the number of separate aircraft that it was to be able to simultaneously track and engage, it was to be without peer. The radar's IFF (identify friend or foe) system was also all-Israeli in origin, an important point when both Israeli and Arab air forces were otherwise deploying American-made fighters.[17]

In the ground attack role, the Lavi radar could employ beam-sharpened ground mapping, with "expand" and "freeze" options to provide the pilot with detailed radar images of specific areas. In this mode, the radar would also be capable of picking out moving targets on the ground and would provide target range data. For antishipping duties the radar had a separate sea-search mode. As with all of the Lavi avionics, the radar also included a built-in self-test capability, and radar operation was software driven to allow it to adjust and grow.[18]

The radar was one of the few Lavi avionics systems, moreover, to be built with a stand-alone capability from the onset. It was intended from the beginning to have a life beyond the Lavi, finding its way into retrofit packages for a number of fighters. Development of the radar therefore continued even after the Lavi's cancellation, culminating in the flight test of the prototype radar on the Lavi Technology Demonstrator in late 1991.[19]

Following the cancellation of the Lavi program, Israel Aircraft Industries redirected their energies toward incorporating elements from the Lavi avionics into their selection of fighter upgrade packages. IAI announced three different upgrade packages for the F-5, for example, tailored to the means and goals of each customer. The most basic package consisted of a few modern avionics systems and cockpit displays. The more advanced upgrade packages featured an all-new avionics suite, including an electronic warfare system, as well as the EL/M-2032 radar—which had borrowed generously from Elta's experience with the Lavi. The third, and most comprehensive, package also added a helmet-mounted sight.[20]

Four years after the Lavi was cancelled, IAI would win a contract to upgrade Chile's sixteen F-5ES with a comprehensive avionics suite, featuring a new head-up display and mission computer, as well the EL/M-2032 radar. The cost for this upgrade package was reportedly $5 million per airplane.[21]

A few years later, IAI would win a contract to upgrade MiG-21s for the Romanian air force. This upgrade program included the installation of the EL/M-2032 radar on twenty-five air defense fighters and the installation of an Elta-made, range-only radar on seventy-five close air support and attack fighters, as well as on board ten trainers. The upgrade program also included a new weapons management system, Elisra's SPS-20 radar warning receiver, a mission computer produced by Elbit, color cockpit displays, a head-up display from El-Op, and the DASH helmet-mounted display and sight. The total upgrade program for all 110 Romanian fighters and trainers was reportedly valued at $300 million.[22]

Israeli radar technology did not stand still with the EL/M-2032 and 2035, however. Nearly two decades after the Lavi was cancelled, Elta's first AESA (active electronically scanned array) radar system for fighter applications would take to the air aboard IAI's 737 flying test bed. AESA technology promised to double the effective detection range for the next generation in radar systems: replacing older, mechanically scanned antennae with a fixed array of transmitting and receiving modules. This technology also allowed for more individual targets to be tracked and could combine track and scan functions in simultaneous operation. The EL/M-2052 also was designed to be a plug-in replacement for Elta's earlier EL/M-2032 and 2035 radars—utilizing the same power supply and computer connections as its predecessor. Had the Lavi reached production, the upgrade path for its radar system would have been a natural step in its continued evolution.

Electronic Warfare: A Roar as Fierce as Its Bite

Coming out of the 1982 Lebanon War, reports began to filter out of surface-to-air missiles veering wildly away from their intended Israeli targets to explode in empty air—as if chasing some unseen ghost. Whispers were circulated of "self-defense jammers," in a solemn nod to the shadowy world of electronic warfare—a world in which Israeli developers had become renowned.[23]

This was the reason why the Lavi, in spite of all of the electronics miniaturization that was applied, carried nearly two times the electronics payload of the slightly heavier F-16. Ever since the harsh lessons of the 1973 Yom Kippur War, which found the Israeli air force poorly equipped to deal with the antiaircraft environment of the modern battlefield, the Israeli arms industry had been tasked to deliver the most advanced radar countermeasures that the world had yet known. But they also knew better than to rest on past laurels. Said one Israeli electronic countermeasures (ECM) expert concerning the Lavi, "We'll have a few new tricks up our sleeves."[24]

The Lavi electronic warfare suite was expected to be a fully internal, integrated system. The demand for internal mounting placed significant constraints on the size and weight of the computer processors, transmitters, and receivers but was also the only way to ensure the kind of 360°, all-around coverage that the Israeli air force demanded. This was to be a fully automated system, linking the functions of radar warning, processing, and both active and passive countermeasures into one unified system that could conduct its mission without the need for pilot intervention.

An electronic warfare suite such as that on the Lavi would have consisted of several distinct components, all of which had to function in unison. The first line of defense for any ECM system begins with an array of radar warning receivers that provide detection for any possible attack. Once a threat was identified, the resources of the airplane would need to be marshaled by a power management system, which would assign priority to each task and deploy the airplane's resources accordingly. The system would also need to carry a battery of expendable decoys. Finally, there would need to be an array of radar jammers and deceiving transmitters with which to respond to hostile radar or missiles.

The radar warning receiver (RWR) was the first link in this chain. The warning receiver not only consisted of multiple antennae with which to pick up radar signals but also included a signals analyzer, which could sort through the different radio waves. It needed to identify which signals were hostile, which direction they came from, and how far away the opposing transmitter happened to be. Furthermore, the RWR not only had to sort out hostile radar signals from the background noise but also had to be able to determine the type of radar and what mode the radar might be in: searching for targets, tracking the airplane, or actively guiding a missile. To help it in performing this task, the receiver's computer would include an onboard library of signal types and radar modes. Furthermore, it had to be able to perform this analysis at breathtaking speed. In addition to radar warning receivers, a modern aircraft would also have had a missile launch warning receiver, designed to detect the electromagnetic signature associated with the launch of a hostile missile. Analyses from all of these different warning systems would then be fed into a central countermeasures computer and power management system, which would subsequently decide on the appropriate course of action.[25]

One of the most severe limitations that any ECM system would face was the limited electrical power that is available on board an airplane. For this reason alone, a power management system was a must. An ECM suite that did not assign priority to near and present dangers would instead attempt to jam every radar that it detected. Such a system would very quickly become overloaded and useless.

Once the electronic threats to the aircraft had been detected and prioritized, the ECM computer would then select which course of action to take. If a missile had already been launched at the airplane, for example, the pilot would need to be notified and expendables would be deployed. These "expendables" would include flares and chaff. The idea behind the flare was to imitate the infrared signature of the engine's hot exhaust, providing an alternative target for heat-seeking missiles. Chaff would act similarly as a decoy for radar-guided missiles, distributing a cloud of reflective metal strips. In addition to deploying flares or chaff, the ECM suite on the Lavi would have had two other options with which to respond. These were the trades of jamming and deception.

Radar jamming requires that the jamming aircraft be able to identify the hostile radar frequency and the direction of the signal and be able to emit enough noise, or static, to mask the airplane's location. Quantitatively, the ability of the jammer to blind or confuse a hostile radar can be measured by the jam-to-signal ratio, which can be expressed mathematically as

$$\frac{J}{S} = \frac{P_j B G_j}{P_r G_r} \left(\frac{4\pi}{\sigma} \right) R^2$$

(5.1)

The key elements in this equation are the ratio between the power of the jamming antenna and the tracking antenna, (P_j/P_r), and the range between the hostile radar and the airplane, R.

Equation 5.1 should highlight some of the pitfalls of radar jamming. The power available to the antenna being jammed is almost always far greater than that available to the radar-jamming device. The only practical way to achieve a jam-to-signal ratio that is large enough to successfully hide the airplane is if the range term in this equation remains sufficiently large. Otherwise the airplane will be within the "burn-through range": the range at which the radar echo from the airplane is sufficiently large for the hostile radar to identify it. This range can be calculated by

$$R_B = \left(\frac{P_r G_r \sigma C}{P_j B G_j 4\pi} \right)^{1/2}$$

(5.2)

where C is the camouflage factor—the minimum value of the jam-to-signal ratio, (J/S), at which the aircraft is still hidden.[26]

Keeping the aircraft beyond this burn-through range sounds fine on paper but is highly impractical for an attack jet expected to deliver close air support. Jammers also require a tremendous amount of power, as equations 5.1 and 5.2 should clearly indicate. In addition, certain missiles are designed to home in on jamming signals, such that turning on a jammer could very well place the airplane at greater risk. In modern practice, jammers can be employed only sparingly. In fact, traditional radar jammers were not what the Israeli ECM experts were known for. What they were renowned for, on the other hand, was being the undisputed masters of radar deception.

The objective of radar deception techniques is not to blind the opposing air defense radars but to provide them with misleading signals that disguise the airplane's direction, distance, or velocity. The radar deceiver accomplishes this either by producing false radar echoes or by modulating the original radar return from the airplane. Radar echoes can be modified in one of four ways: by altering the time at which the echo appears to be received, the amplitude of the signal, the apparent frequency, or the phase.[27]

To give a better idea of how this works, it may be helpful to consider an example of one such technique. One of the more simple is a method known as "range-gate pull-off." Upon determining that the airplane is being tracked by a hostile radar, the ECM computer will begin to produce a deceiving signal that coincides with the radar echo of the airplane. The strength of this deceiving signal is increased until the tracking radar has locked on to the deceiving signal, and not the airplane. At this point, the deceiving signal is delayed, little by little, so that eventually the narrow window or "range-gate" of the tracking radar is no longer scanning for the airplane in the correct location. The deceiving signal can then be turned off, making it appear to the tracking radar as if the airplane had just vanished from the sky. The hostile radar must then go back from its tracking mode into its search mode and attempt to reacquire the target.[28]

The real advantage of radar deception is that it requires far less power than jamming. It can also be applied against multiple hostile radars at the same time. This is where the power management routine of the airplane's ECM computer would come into play. Each deceiving signal will require only a fraction of a second to broadcast, allowing multiple hostile radars to be monitored and each deceived in turn. Each hostile radar signal has to be sorted out and identified as to radar type and operating mode before a deceiving signal is produced that must precisely mimic the characteristics of an actual radar return. The advantages of this kind of a self-defense system should be obvious. It is for this kind of electronic counter-measures expertise that Israeli manufacturers have become known as among the best in the world.

The radar warning receivers for the Lavi were supplied by Elisra. The majority of the ECM suite, however, was built by Elta. Among the features included in this system was the ability to load new mission warning and countermeasures parameters on the flight line, before each mission, in a matter of seconds. The entire system also had to be damage resistant, with multiple, redundant sub-systems and backup computers capable of taking over the role of components damaged in combat. The power management routine for the system was therefore incorporated as part of the central avionics software package—allowing it to be updated or modified as the battlefield changed.[29]

To construct this feat of electronic miracles Elta utilized microwave integrated circuits, with a microwave motherboard and plug-in radio frequency modules. The use of plug-in modules gave the system the ability to be expanded or modified as the battlefield threat evolved throughout the years. Coupled to this was a logic and processing core consisting of dense complementary metal oxide semiconductor (CMOS) gate-array components.[30]

It was the responsibility of IAI's Elta division, as the prime contractor for the package, to integrate the different components that made up the Lavi electronic warfare suite into one coherent weapons system. This meant integrating the radar warning receiver supplied by Elisra with Elta's active missile warning system, together with an ECM transmitter supplied by Rafael. Elta would later apply this Lavi experience to develop a pod-mounted ECM package named Cerberus that would be supplied to the German air force. Cerberus, like the Lavi ECM suite, employed a digital radio frequency memory (DRFM) system to accurately record and then retransmit threat radar signals. Equivalent capabilities did not exist in Europe, which was why the German government had turned to Israeli ECM manufacturers when the United States had declined to grant an export license for an equivalent U.S. system.[31] It was this kind of technology that set the Lavi ECM suite so far ahead of its peers.

The Man-Machine Interface

Despite the profusion of electronic wizardry, the builders of the Lavi avionics system never lost sight of the reason behind all of their efforts: the man who sat in the cockpit. Even the most sophisticated avionics suite would be counterproductive if all it did was bombard the pilot with raw information. It was in the cockpit that all of the components of the avionics suite had to come together and perform under the guidance of a human hand.

The design of the Lavi cockpit began with the pilot's working environment. How much room would he have? Could he reach all of the vital switches with ease? Did he have good visibility? Would he feel comfortable flying this machine?

Pilot visibility has always been paramount to the survival of a combat aircraft, and the Lavi would be no exception to this. The Lavi canopy was situated to provide an 80° field of view over each side of the fuselage, with a 180° field of view from the front, looking down over the nose radome, to the back.

Following the advice of Israeli fighter pilots who would be flying the airplane, it was decided to reject the side-mounted control stick seen on the F-16 and France's Rafale, in favor of the more traditional center-mounted stick. The pilots preferred the flexibility of being able to operate the stick with either hand in an emergency. The stick was also provided with a limited degree of movement to allow proper feedback to the pilot, unlike the fixed, pressure-sensitive control stick of the early model F-16A. Movement of the Lavi control stick was set at up to 3.3 in (8.4 cm) aft from the neutral position and up to 2.0 in (5.1 cm) forward and to the sides. The rudder pedals were likewise allowed a limited degree of movement, with up to 0.5 in (1.3 cm) of motion forward or back.[32]

It has long been established that a pilot's ability to sustain high-g loads without experiencing blackout can be enhanced by reclining the pilot's seat. This arrangement helps prevent the pilot's blood from rushing to his legs under the g-forces of maneuvers. This same principle had been applied to the F-16, which had a seat inclination of 30°—among the most severe of any fighter flying.[33] After consulting with Israeli pilots, however, IAI came to the conclusion that while a highly reclined seat made sense for an air superiority fighter, for an attack jet a less severe inclination would be preferred—settling on a seat inclination of 18° for the Lavi.[34]

Similar care was paid to the Lavi cockpit controls, which adhered to the HOTAS (hands on throttle and stick) design philosophy for placing all of the essential controls directly on the throttle and stick. The idea was to keep the pilot's eyes on the target, not in the cockpit hunting for a switch. Buttons for missile lock-on and release, together with the trigger for the 30 mm cannon, were all located on the Lavi control stick. The head-up display was arranged so that the pilot could transition from navigation, to intercept, to air-to-ground, to the air combat mode, simply by toggling a single switch on the throttle, beneath his left thumb. Move the switch up, and the fighter was in dogfight mode. All of the multifunction displays, as well as the head-up display, would adjust automatically. Move the switch to the center position and the airplane would enter the intercept mode. Move the switch down farther and the displays would be reconfigured for ground attack. Moving the switch back from ground attack to the center position would bring the pilot into the navigation mode. Even nose-wheel steering for taxiing across the runway was controlled by a button on the stick.[35]

In keeping with ongoing trends toward a more electronic, or "glass," cockpit, the Lavi replaced many of the traditional mechanical dials with multifunction displays. The Lavi cockpit featured two monochrome CRT displays, a single full-color CRT display, and two smaller, full-color liquid crystal displays. Conventional dialed instruments were still available for backup, but the CRT displays were intended to be the principal in-cockpit instruments. Each of the CRT displays measured 5 in (12.7 cm) across, with a high contrast ratio and a special high-resolution, dynamic focus feature. All of the displays were of Israeli manufacture, with a resolution of 525 by 875 lines and a 30 Hz frame rate. The full-color display also had to overcome the added hurdle of generating colors bright enough to be clearly seen, even against the glaring sunlight of high altitude.[36]

Providing a variety of bright, colorful displays, however, was not nearly enough. The displays and instruments needed to allow the pilot to keep his eyes out of the cockpit once the enemy had been engaged. The ordnance release pattern, for example, was preprogrammed at the beginning of each mission. And however impressive the full-color display might have been, its true effectiveness lay in an intelligent use of each of its seven available colors to relay the maximum amount of information in a single glance. Navigation routes, for example, were displayed in green, with the locations of over fifty airstrips programmed into the system. Tactical information, on the other hand, would be displayed in orange and red. Ultimately, all three cockpit displays needed to work in concert. While the right-hand, color display was providing tactical and navigational data, for example, the center display was expected to provide radar mapping images, and the left-hand display provided weapons status.[37]

Once in air combat, or upon entering hostile airspace for a bombing mission, the pilot's principal source of information would become the head-up display. The wide-angle holographic HUD unit for the Lavi was developed in the United States by Hughes. It provided vital statistics on the airplane's speed and altitude, as well as targeting information. Four different panels of information were available, with critical flight updates provided to the pilot using a computer-synthesized voice. The fact that the canopy of the Lavi was built in two pieces, like that of the F-15 or F/A-18, allowed the HUD display to be sized significantly larger than had been possible on the F-16—where the HUD had to be able to withstand the airplane's slipstream during an ejection. Constructing the canopy in two pieces, with a forward supporting frame, also allowed for a canopy that was lighter than that found on the F-16. The Lavi canopy, made from stretched acrylic, measured some 0.18 in (4.6 mm) thick. The single-piece F-16 canopy, on the other hand, had to measure in at 0.36 in (9.1 mm) thick to meet similar load requirements.[38] Similar considerations would lead the Japanese to select a two-piece canopy configuration for their F-2.

Perhaps the most radical addition to the Lavi cockpit, however, was a helmet-mounted display and sight. Had it entered production, the Lavi would have been the first Western fighter to include such a system as part of its original avionics package, rather than as a retrofitted add-on.[39] The objective behind these helmet systems was twofold: to project basic HUD-type flight information directly into the pilot's field of view, and also to train the airplane's sensors and weapons systems under the direction of the pilot's head movements. Two competing helmet-mounted display and sight systems would be unveiled by Israeli firms during the Lavi development program: one developed by Elbit and the other by El-Op. Both units were publicly unveiled shortly after the Israeli government announced that a helmet-mounted display was expected to become part of the Lavi avionics suite. The concept behind a helmet-mounted display and sight was not new to the Lavi. Several nations had explored these concepts during the preceding decade. The Israeli systems, however, marked the first time that both of these technologies—the helmet display and the weapons system sight—had successfully been brought together into an operational package.

The earliest attempts at fielding a helmet-mounted sight had actually taken place in the 1970s, when the U.S. Navy and Marine Corps fielded their Visual Target Acquisition System (VTAS) on some five hundred F-4 Phantom fighters. Unlike the Israeli systems of the 1980s, VTAS was a helmet-mounted sight, but without a display. First deployed in 1973, the U.S. Navy system was withdrawn from service in 1979 due to disappointing performance. Built by Honeywell, the system suffered from chronic reliability problems. Part of the difficulty lay in the fact that the VTAS system, unlike its successors in the 1980s, was built around the radar-tracking system of the airplane, rather than that of the missile. This proved to be a crude and unreliable combination. The pilot could never be completely sure that the missile had actually located the desired target.[40]

Following the withdrawal of VTAS from service, the United States continued to toy with the idea of a helmet-mounted sight, as well as with the possibility of combining a sight with a helmet-mounted display. As had been evident for some time, the ideal way to present critical information to the pilot would be to project it directly in front of his eyes. The first cockpits to put this idea into practice were those of American assault helicopters, beginning with the Apache's helmet sight and electronic monocle. These helicopter systems, however, were unsuitable for fighter aircraft, being both too heavy for high-g maneuvers and too fragile to survive a pilot bailout at speeds in excess of 600 knots (1,100 km/h). Beginning in the 1980s, the U.S. Air Force had therefore invested millions into government labs that attempted to adapt this technology. The helmets that were produced under this "supercockpit" program, however, proved to be even larger and more cumbersome than those already deployed aboard helicopters. These helmets attempted to do everything at once, combining a wide field of view with a full array of holographic display functions. The result was a laboratory curiosity that was completely impractical.[41]

In the intervening years, however, the Soviet Union succeeded where the United States had previously failed, successfully deploying the first generation of practical helmet-mounted sights—relying on the seeker system of the missile, rather than the airplane's radar to acquire targets. The Russian developers also took this technology one step further, combining a helmet-mounted sight with a new generation of heat-seeking missiles that featured an astonishing rate of turn and high off-boresight target acquisition. The implications of this combination will be discussed in appendix 6. For now, let it be said that the potential lethality of this new combination would not be appreciated by American defense planners for nearly a decade. What the Russians had still not been able to do up to that time, however, was to combine a helmet-mounted sight with a helmet-mounted display.

The Israelis, for their part, had likewise begun development work on helmet-mounted sight and display technology during the 1970s, but they focused on a phased approach to bring technology to the battlefield as individual elements matured. Rather than attempting to develop a helmet display that could do everything that a head-up display could already do, the Israeli developers began by integrating a reliable helmet-mounted sight, then added a rudimentary display and target cueing system, and finally went on to expand the field of view for their display only after they had already proven the previous technology in operational service. Elbit was the first Israeli firm to go public with their success, unveiling their product and seeking overseas orders beginning in early 1986. Within a year the Elbit system would be followed by a competing design from El-Op, and a little bit later by an experimental American unit developed by Kaiser—the latter of which entered flight test in mid-1987.[42]

The Elbit system was known as DASH, or the "display and sight helmet." The helmet projected HUD-type symbology directly onto the pilot's visor, which was chemically treated to reflect light in a narrow band of green wavelengths. To track head movements and cue the missile seeker, the helmet was fitted with magnetic sensors. Among the key selling points behind the Elbit system was the ease with which it could be retrofitted to existing aircraft.[43] This was an essential demand for the Israeli air force, and one that would have given the DASH system a leg up for use in the Lavi. By the time that it was publicly unveiled in 1986, the DASH system was already operational across a number of Israeli F-15 and F-16 squadrons. As part of their phased strategy for technology introduction, the initial Generation 1 DASH system had been deployed without the visual display, to provide an immediately available, helmet-mounted sight. These units would eventually be superseded by a Generation 2 DASH system, which added a limited helmet-mounted display. The more advanced Generation 3 DASH helmet would reach operational service in 1996, featuring an improved, 20° field of view for projecting images onto the visor. Head tracking was reported to be accurate to within 0.6°, while the entire helmet, optics package and all, weighed in at only 3.3 lb (1.0 kg), not including the oxygen mask.[44] Having already been established under Israel's F-15, F-16, and F-4E fighter fleet, the DASH system would undoubtedly have had the inside track for incorporation into the Lavi.

The Lavi also had the option of incorporating the competing El-Op helmet, however. The El-Op system was named HADAS (helmet airborne display and sight). Although no official announcement was ever made confirming the identity of the helmet system for the Lavi, El-Op made no secret of their ambition to make the Lavi the poster child for their system.[45] The HADAS unit transferred display information along fiber-optic cables to holographic elements located on the right side of the helmet. The display provided a 30° horizontal and 26° vertical field of view, within which it could display stroke-written flight data, or raster video data from infrared targeting or navigation sights. Helmet movement was monitored using a camera, mounted above and behind the pilot, which tracked a special pattern painted on top of the helmet. Using this system, helmet movements could reportedly be tracked to within a tenth of a degree. In mid-1987 El-Op would announce a teaming arrangement with the American firm Bendix to help market the system overseas.[46]

The Israeli government would disclose relatively few details regarding its own flight-test or operational experience with either of the two helmets. However, we can gain a good idea as to just what kind of an edge these helmets were intended to provide using similar flight-test experience from the U.S. armed forces. Over the ensuing two decades, the U.S. Air Force and U.S. Navy would explore a number of helmet-mounted display and sight options, including the Agile Eye and Agile Eye Plus systems developed by Kaiser, as well as the Israeli DASH system.

Kaiser began work on its own helmet-mounted sight and display system in 1983, finally teaming up with McDonnell Douglas' electronics division in 1987 to launch a flight-test program. The original Agile Eye featured a 12° field of view for projecting flight information and was followed by the Agile Eye Plus— which entered flight test in 1989—featuring a 20° field of view. The latter system could also display infrared images for use in night attack operations, in a manner similar to Israel's Generation 3 DASH system.[47]

In flight tests simulating air-to-air combat, the Agile Eye was reported to improve pilot kill-to-loss ratios by over two to one when flying against aircraft that were not similarly equipped. The Agile Eye was able to achieve this superior kill ratio by providing the pilot with an earlier lock-on to his target. This ability was demonstrated both in conjunction with infrared-guided missiles, such as the AIM-9M Sidewinder, and with radar-guided missiles.[48]

Beginning in October 1998, the U.S. Air Force and U.S. Navy also began similar flight trials with Elbit's DASH helmet system, reporting similar gains in air-to-air target acquisition. Of equal significance, however, was that equivalent improvements were also reported in the acquisition of ground-based targets. In trials on board U.S. Air Force F-15s and U.S. Navy F/A-18s, the DASH helmet-mounted sight was demonstrated to improve target acquisition times by a factor of five during simulated ground attack missions.[49] In one rare interview, an Israeli F-15I pilot alluded to similar Israeli experience: "The most important thing that DASH gives us is 'line of sight.' We can cue the radar or targeting pod to track or lock any air or ground threat that we can see. We don't have to work the sensors, we just look out, see the target, and designate it."[50] The edge that such a first-lock, first-shot capability can provide should be obvious. Moreover, it was an edge that the Israeli air force had both grasped and implemented into operational service more than a decade before their counterparts in the United States or Europe.

Despite this and other flight-test experience, the U.S. Air Force declined to retrofit a helmet-mounted sight and display into their existing fighter fleet at that time. The reasons behind this reluctance can be traced to competing funding priorities as well as to a philosophical difference in air combat tactics between the U.S. and Israeli armed forces. Among other differences, the U.S. Air Force tended to place less emphasis on visual-range, dogfight-type encounters than did the Heyl Ha'Avir. Since before the Vietnam War U.S. air combat doctrine had emphasized the presumed role of the beyond visual range, radar-guided intercept. The potential benefits of a visual-range, helmet-mounted sight and display did not therefore register as a high priority.

Nonetheless, the U.S. armed forces were still interested in developing a helmet-mounted display and sight for application on future aircraft. Kaiser was therefore funded to develop a system for eventual integration with the U.S. Navy's F/A-18E/F Super Hornet, as well as for the U.S. Air Force's F-22 Raptor. Kaiser, for their part, readily recognized their own limitations, including their lack of experience in fielding such a system in an operational environment. They therefore turned to the one developer that had already accumulated operational experience with the integration of these systems: Israel's Elbit. Together, the two companies formed a "joint venture" named Vision Systems International, drawing from the best features of both the Agile Eye and DASH helmet-mounted systems. After examining the advantages and disadvantages of both designs, it was decided to select Elbit's Generation 3 DASH helmet as the more mature system from which to form a starting point for future development work.

The new operational system, slated for introduction on board U.S. fighters at the turn of the century, was initially designated as the "Generation 4" DASH helmet. The new helmet was expected to introduce a number of further innovations, including a more modular approach to its design. Previous editions of the DASH helmet, for example, had required separate helmets with different visors for day and night operation. The new helmet, in contrast, was expected to use a replaceable visor to fulfill the two roles. The new helmet was also expected to include a camera system that would record the pilot's field of view, in much the same way that existing gun cameras recorded the view from the head-up display. Measures were also taken to shave off additional weight from the helmet and to further improve on the accuracy of its head-tracking system.[51]

The new helmet system was eventually relabeled as the Joint Helmet-Mounted Cueing System (JHMCS) and was first introduced into U.S. service aboard the Navy's F/A-18E/F Super Hornet. The Super Hornet was also the first U.S. warplane to employ the system in combat, demonstrating the versatility and air-to-ground potential of the system in the skies over Afghanistan and Iraq. In actual, wartime application, the JHMCS quickly proved its worth, allowing U.S. Navy pilots to more accurately and rapidly designate ground targets for attack. The improvement in target acquisition time was enough to convince the U.S. Navy to expand their procurement plans and install two such units into each of their F/A-18F fighters. In a two-seat application, the helmet system allowed the weapons officer to survey the battlefield and designate targets, which the pilot could then easily locate and maneuver to engage.[52]

The helmet-mounted sight and display represented one more area of Israeli technical expertise that the U.S. armed forces would take advantage of in the decades following the Lavi's demise.[53] The innovation that the Israeli design team had displayed in the Lavi cockpit was not the result of chance. It was a reflection of the priority that the Heyl Ha'Avir had always placed on the human element and their approach to each new technology as another means to accentuate their pilot's capabilities. In the words of former Israeli air force commander Ezer Weizman, "The Israeli air force was created by men and weapons—in that order; men are the most important, and their weapons help them to express themselves."[54]

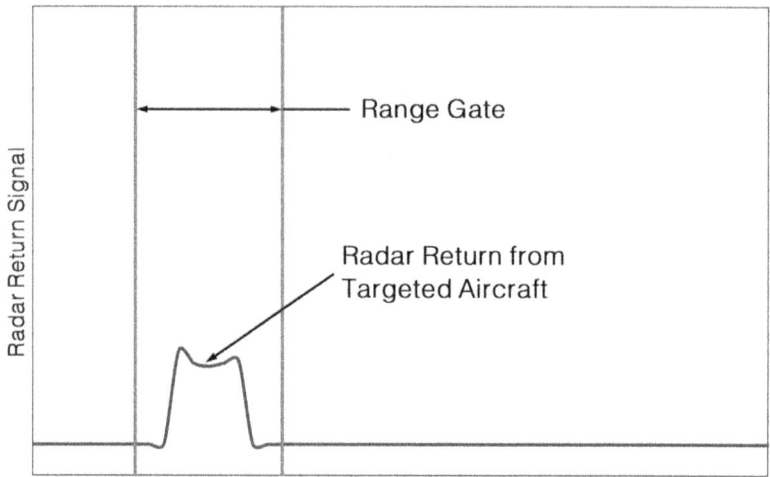

Fig. 33. The range gate pull-off technique begins when the airplane's self-defense system determines that an enemy radar is actively tracking the airplane.

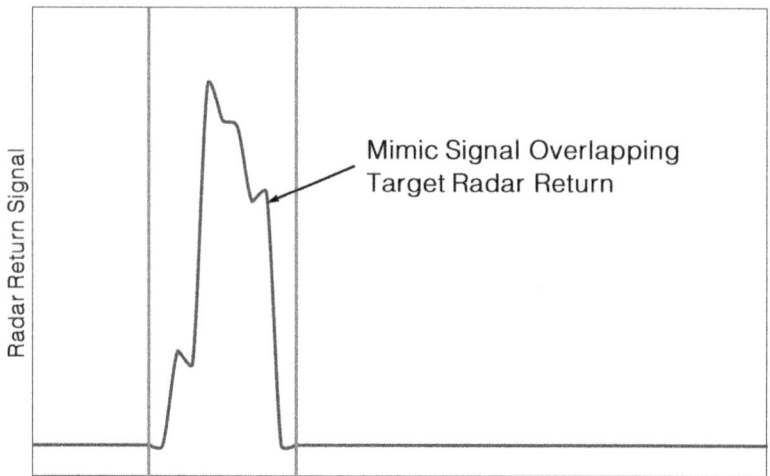

Fig. 34. The electronic countermeasures suite will subsequently broadcast a mimic signal with a stronger intensity than the original radar return.

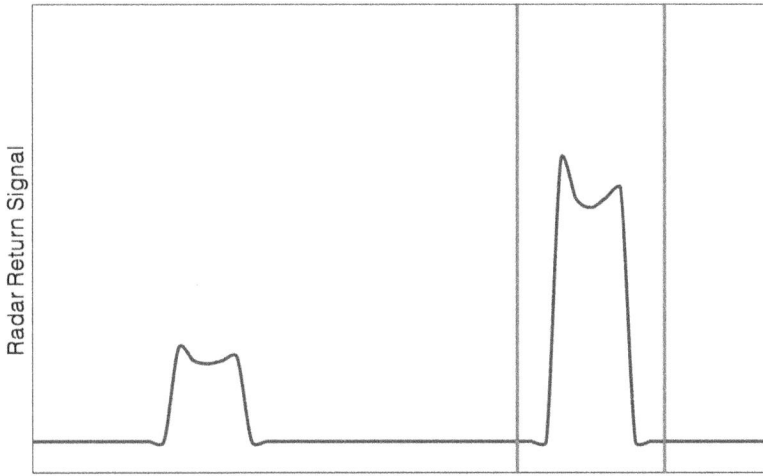

Fig. 35. Gradually the mimic signal is delayed so that the tracking radar loses its fix on the original radar return.

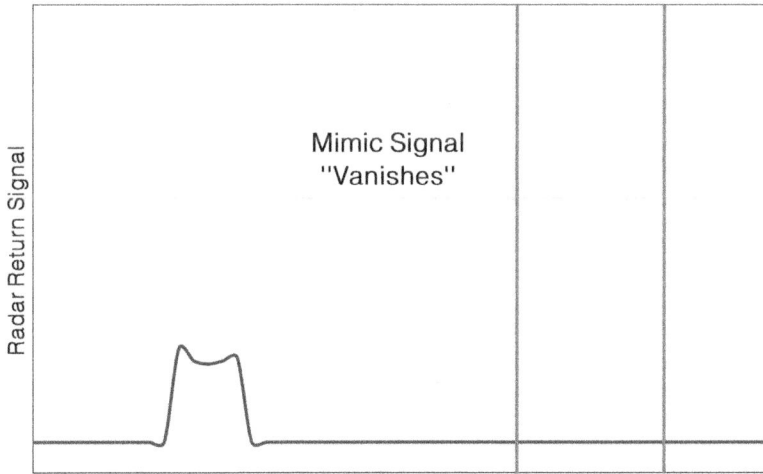

Fig. 36. Finally, the mimic signal is turned off. At this point the tracking radar's "range gate" has completely lost the original radar return and must reenter the search mode to find the target.

Fig. 37. The Lavi cockpit. (1) wide-angle holographic head-up display (HUD); (2) up-front control panel (folds down during flight); (3) tactical situation display–color multifunctional display (MFD); (4) radar display–monochrome MFD; (5) stores management system–monochrome MFD; (6) control stick (switches for weapons targeting and release); (7) throttle control (switches for selecting flight mode); (8) backup buttons for selecting flight mode; (9) color liquid crystal display (LCD) engine gauges; (10) color LCD fuel gauge; (11) conventional backup instruments; (12) compass; (13) master warning lights; (14) detailed warning lights.

APPENDIX 6

Armament and Combat

Today, when modern fighters can carry a bomb load that rivals that of World War II bombers, the different roles that a fighter might be called upon to perform has been multiplied manyfold. Airpower has become a decisive element in the outcome of war. It is all the more important, therefore, to remember that each of these attendant roles is still a separate mission, with its own inherent demands and perils. A multirole fighter cannot be expected to perform all roles equally well and will of necessity be designed with an emphasis on some roles at the expense of others. That the Lavi was meant to be an attack jet first and an air-to-air fighter only second has already been noted. But even among attack jets there are a variety of different missions and objectives to be fulfilled.

Tactical and Strategic Bombing: Different Missions

Although the line between tactical and strategic strike missions tends to be blurred in the minds of many, each of these roles tends to place a slightly different set of demands on the airplane. Tactical strike roles are those missions aimed at directly destroying the enemy's armed forces. This includes close air support, which targets enemy troops already on the front lines, as well as interdiction missions, which target enemy formations behind the front lines. Strategic bombing missions, on the other hand, target the enemy's military and industrial infrastructure. Arms factories, command centers, port facilities, or even the electrical power grid might all be considered strategic targets.

The Lavi was built with the tactical strike role as its first order of business. It had a secondary capability as a strategic strike aircraft, just as it had a secondary role as a point air defense fighter. All of these roles were important, and each had its place in Israel's order of battle. But it was the tactical strike mission that remained central throughout the design of the Lavi.

To better appreciate just what it was that the Lavi was intended to be, it may help to take a closer look at what the Lavi was not. To this end, there is much to be learned by examining a modern, dedicated strategic strike aircraft like the F-117 Nighthawk. The most obvious difference, of course, is the incorporation of stealth technology under the F-117. The Nighthawk was the first stealth aircraft to reach production. Rather than relying on electronic countermeasures to ensure its safety from opposing missiles, the Nighthawk relied on "stealth": minimizing its radar return to the point where conventional radar systems could no longer detect it. But there were many more differences between the two airplanes than merely their strategies for battlefield survival.

The F-117 Nighthawk was built around the singular role of strategic strike, rather than as a multirole strike platform such as the Lavi. Since most of the targets that the Nighthawk was intended to hit were small, single-point objectives such as command centers and communications networks, bombing accuracy was of the utmost importance, while bomb load capacity was secondary. To this end, the F-117 was designed to carry two precision-guided 2,000 lb (910 kg) bombs, and nothing more. No additional bombs, no cannon, and no air-to-air missiles.

The criteria for building a successful stealth aircraft are strict and unyielding. Among these criteria is the mandate that all weapons must be carried internally. Just one protruding bomb would return enough of a radar echo to make all the millions invested in stealth materials an exercise in futility. This was why the F-117 was designed with strategic attack not only as its primary role but as its only role. It could not carry sufficient bomb load to make a dent in the tactical arena. The first attempt to develop a stealth aircraft for a tactical strike role—the U.S. Navy's A-12 Avenger II—resulted in a miniature bomber, with a wing area of more than 1300 sq ft (120 m²) and a takeoff weight of more than 59,000 lb (26,800 kg).[1] The A-12 would have made for a very large target over the battlefield, an airplane hardly suitable as a close air support jet. It would eventually be canceled as overbudget and overweight. It proved much easier to build a successful strategic-strike stealth platform, such as the F-117, than to build a stealth aircraft for the tactical strike role.

Israel, unlike the United States, could never afford to maintain a handful of specialized aircraft dedicated to a single, narrowly defined mission. The Lavi development team had been expected to prioritize among the many missions that they would face—building an airplane around the most vital of these roles but one that could still fulfill any of the others. Of necessity, the balance that they struck would emphasize the tactical strike role above all others.

Although the F-117 certainly collected its fair share of media attention, the small size of the eventual Nighthawk fleet gave testimony to the relative emphasis that the U.S. Air Force likewise placed on the strategic and tactical strike roles. The United States did not cease to procure additional F-16 or F-15E aircraft just because "stealth" had arrived. This pattern became further evident in U.S. wartime experiences during the 1991 Gulf War. At the time that Operation Desert Storm was underway, much of the media attention would focus on the strategic bombing campaign, with "smart bombs" and riveting video images captured by precision-guided munitions. In terms of media coverage, the smart bombs easily won the day. But in this frenzy for up-to-the-minute coverage, and given the media's appetite for fresh images, the public was rarely made aware that the overwhelming majority of bombs dropped over Iraq in 1991 had been unguided munitions, dropped by less glamorous warplanes. Guided munitions had made up only a small fraction of the U.S. inventory.

In the aftermath of the 1991 Gulf War, Greenpeace International would recruit William M. Arkin, a former U.S. Army Intelligence officer, to evaluate the damage, accuracy, and effectiveness of the coalition bombing campaign in Iraq. Arkin would be provided by the U.S. Air Force with a list of 295 strategic bombing targets that had been attacked during the air campaign and would be able to directly observe 153 of these sites.

What Arkin reported back was that although the strategic bombing campaign had been highly accurate in destroying its designated targets, it had made very little impact on the outcome of the war. The Iraqi commanders had anticipated that their primary command and communications centers would be bombed and had dispersed their personnel and equipment before the war began. When Arkin visited the bomb sites, he reported finding Iraqi troops reinstalling computers and communications gear that had supposedly been destroyed when coalition bombs had struck the emptied buildings weeks before.

It was Arkin's assessment that it was the tactical bombing campaign—the physical destruction of the Iraqi war machine and troop formations—that had been pivotal to the successful outcome of the war. In particular, he warned against using the success of guided munitions in destroying empty command centers as justification for pouring dwindling defense resources into aircraft that could "do a triple somersault but can't carry the massive amount of bombs you need to win a war."[2]

Arkin's observations merely reinforced the U.S. Defense Department's own wartime planning. Although precision strikes against Iraqi command and control centers may have received the lion's share of televised coverage, the reality was that the vast majority of the wartime sorties had been devoted against Iraqi troops and weapons systems. Out of a total of 34,980 air-to-ground strikes carried out during Operation Desert Storm, 23,430 had been targeted against Iraqi ground forces, with another 2,000 targeted against the Iraqi air defense network and 1,460 aimed against Iraq's Scud missile batteries. A further 2,990 strikes had similarly been directed against Iraq's airfields.[3] Over 85 percent of all allied air strikes had therefore been targeted against Iraqi soldiers, artillery, missile batteries, or air bases. This was the reality of warfare, no less true in 1991 than it had been in 1941. Defeating an enemy on the battlefield demanded that the majority of resources be devoted to destroying the ability of their adversary to fight. Disrupting the enemy's command and control infrastructure took on a secondary priority.

The defense planners in Israel's Heyl Ha'Avir had learned this same lesson many years before, and many times before, but never so clearly as in the 1973 Yom Kippur War. The strategic bombing role was still critically important to Israel. But as the 1973 war had so painfully made clear, the survival of a nation could hinge on the ability to halt, slow, or destroy regiments of tanks and infantry while the reserves were in the process of being called to the front. That, of course, required tactical airpower.

Arming the Lion

In its primary roles of interdiction and close air support the Lavi would typically have carried a bomb load of Mk-82 500 lb (230 kg) bombs, Mk-83 1,000 lb (450 kg) bombs, or Mk-84 2,000 lb (910 kg) bombs. Although not as glamorous or headline grabbing as the precision-guided smart bombs that received so much attention during the 1991 Gulf War, these so-called dumb-bombs could be extraordinarily accurate when delivered by a properly equipped airplane and a well-trained pilot. It should be recalled that Israel's 1981 Osirak reactor raid had been carried out using these same unguided Mk-84 iron bombs and that out of sixteen bombs released, fifteen had scored a direct hit on the reactor dome and core chamber. That reactor dome had measured only 50 ft across.[4]

The key to delivering an iron bomb accurately lies in the airplane's targeting and release mechanism and in the pilot's skill and experience in using them. Precision guidance systems can be installed either in the airplane or on the bomb. The difference is that when they are installed on the bomb, the guidance system is lost when the bomb is released. This was why smart weapons historically commanded ten times or more the price tag awarded to their unguided counterparts. Up until the introduction of JDAM (joint direct attack munition) kits during the late 1990s, even the United States, with all of its resources, had been unable to afford an inventory dominated by guided weapons.[5] It was therefore imperative to the developers of the Lavi that the new airplane be able to deliver unguided bombs, and deliver them accurately.

The Lavi was intended to carry its weapons load on a total of fifteen hardpoints, including two wingtip missile rails, plus six underwing hardpoints and another seven under the fuselage. A total of 16,000 lb (7,260 kg) could be carried at the maximum load factor of 9 g's. This external payload could be expanded further, to over 20,000 lb (9,070 kg) where need be, although with a reduced maximum g-limit.[6]

The traditional means for carrying iron bombs and other munitions had been to hang them on pylons under the wings, and the Lavi would certainly have had access to this alternative. Conventional pylons, however, would also have significantly increased the airplane's drag, decreasing not only the fighter's range and speed but also its agility over the battlefield. It was for this reason that the Lavi was intended to carry its weapons load semiconformally whenever possible. The United States had experimented with this same concept on the F-16XL. In tests conducted by the U.S. Air Force, an F-16XL carrying fourteen Mk-82 bombs semiconformally was shown to produce 35–45 percent less stores drag than the same aircraft produced when carrying twelve Mk-82s on conventional pylons.[7] The engineers at IAI achieved a similar degree of success by combining semiconformal weapons carriage with aeroelastic tailoring to reduce stores-induced wing flutter, a combination that promised to decrease the stores drag on the Lavi by up to 50 percent.[8]

In the close air support role the Lavi would most likely have operated on internal fuel alone. Goals for target penetration speeds were reported as being 538 knots (996 km/h) when armed with eight Mk-117 750-lb (340-kg) bombs, or 597 knots (1,106 km/h) when armed with two Mk-84 2,000 lb (910 kg) bombs.[9] To put this into perspective, the F-16As that carried out Israel's Osirak reactor raid had delivered their bombs flying at 480 knots (890 km/h) over the target zone.[10] A penetration speed of 597 knots was significantly greater than what could be achieved by contemporary strike jets, suggesting a very clean aerodynamic design. At low altitude on a hot day, with temperature averaging 103 °F (39 °C), 597 knots would translate into a penetration speed of Mach 0.87. That's right on the edge between the subsonic and transonic flight regimes, where the drag rise as the airplane approaches supersonic velocity begins to eat away at aerodynamic performance. This objective could have been realized only by a very clean aircraft, featuring extraordinarily low stores drag.

For targets at longer ranges, such as on certain interdiction missions, the Lavi would have had access to up to 9,180 lb (4,160 kg) in external fuel. An attack mission for the Lavi could very easily have meant traveling hundreds of miles in a lo-lo-lo attack profile to reach Iraqi tanks as they crossed into Jordan or Syria. It could also mean flying even farther in a hi-lo-hi profile to wipe out a Libyan or Iranian arms depot.

In addition to the stalwart iron bomb, the Lavi would also have had access to a variety of more specialized weapons. Rocket pods had been in use in Israel since the Sinai War of 1956, when they had proven their effectiveness against opposing bunkers. Similarly, Israel had first demonstrated its proficient use of runway-cratering "dipper" bombs during the 1967 Six-Day War, when it had crippled the airfields of Egypt and Syria during the opening hours of the war. Israel also produced its own cluster bombs, which scatter small bomblets, or submunitions, across a wide area. Together with the U.S.-supplied AGM-45 Shrike antiradiation missile, this combination proved devastating to the Syrian surface-to-air missile batteries in the Lebanon War of 1982. It was later reported that Israeli strikes on the Syrian missile batteries were carried out in two waves, with Shrike missiles used to first suppress the Syrian radars, while follow-on aircraft moved in to attack the missile launchers using cluster bombs.

The Israeli air force also deployed several versions of the U.S.-supplied AGM-65 Maverick air-to-surface missile, for use in an antiarmor and antifortifications role. It had been rumored that Israeli-modified versions of the Maverick were so accurate that some had even been deployed without their usual high-explosive warhead, allowing kinetic energy alone to destroy the target.[11] Although this approach might at first seem to be counterintuitive, such a specialized weapon might well have been called for under those scenarios where opposing military targets were in close proximity to civilians.

Occasionally there was also news of more specialized, Israeli-developed air-to-surface weapons. There has been word, for example, of a special antiarmor missile, designed to penetrate the armor of a tank by diving down directly onto the turret from above, where a tank's armor is thinnest. And there was also the fabled Luz 1, reported to be an Israeli-developed, TV-guided missile similar in concept to the Maverick, reportedly deployed in Israeli service since 1977.[12] Such programs usually remained part of a black netherworld: some of them no doubt real, some only imagined. Only when the Israeli developers had completed their work and were seeking export customers did these "black" programs ever become public knowledge. An example of this can be seen in the story of the Popeye, an Israeli-developed, air-launched missile that was first revealed to the public in 1986 when it was offered for sale to the U.S. Air Force.

The Popeye would be redesignated as the AGM-142 Have Nap by the United States, which first procured the weapon for the U.S. Air Force in 1987. Originally developed by Rafael, the Israeli Defense Ministry's government-run development center, the Have Nap was intended for use on Israeli F-4E fighter bombers, as well as for subsequent service on the Lavi. The Have Nap was developed as a long-range, precision strike weapon, intended for use against high-priority, well-defended targets.

The AGM-142 weighed in at some 3,000 lb (1,360 kg), measuring 190 in (480 cm) long and 21 in (53 cm) in diameter, with a 750 lb (340 kg) high-explosive warhead. The original Have Nap had a range of up to 50 nm (90 km). The Have Nap was intended to follow a preprogrammed flight profile, using its own inertial navigation system, with either a visual or infrared imaging seeker for terminal guidance. In U.S. Air Force flight tests, the Have Nap recorded a 94 percent hit probability against targets as small as an office window. In fact, during testing, the missile's imaging infrared seeker was able to pick up and guide the missile to score a direct hit against nighttime targets, at twice the range at which equivalent U.S. infrared seekers could operate. When the Lavi needed to carry out a precision, strategic strike mission, it would most certainly have had the tools with which to do so.

Up until the Israeli government offered the missile for sale to the United States, however, even the existence of such a weapon had been a closely guarded secret. The Israeli manufacturer first offered the missile to the United States in 1986. In November 1987 the U.S. Air Force would approve a contract for the purchase of eighty-six AGM-142 missiles, to be manufactured under license in the United States by Martin Marietta. A second batch of thirty-two missiles was ordered for delivery in 1992. The missile would be deployed initially on U.S. B-52 and FB-111 bombers. It was estimated that procuring the Have Nap from Israeli developers had saved the U.S. armed forces half a billion dollars in research and development costs.[13] Even the existence of this weapon, however, would likely have remained a strict state secret had the Israeli developers chosen not to market the weapon to the United States.

The Popeye was followed into service by the Popeye 2, a slightly smaller version of the same missile that reduced the launch weight from 3,000 to 2,500 lb (from 1,360 to 1,130 kg). The new configuration was reportedly deployed by Israeli F-16 squadrons, with the U.S. Air Force purchasing an additional thirty missiles built to this new, Have Lite standard in 1993. The Popeye 2 also reduced the unit cost for the missile from $850,000 to $750,000, making it an increasingly attractive alternative when compared to the $2.7 million per unit price tag that was projected for Northrop's AGM-137 Tri-Service Standoff Attack Missile (TSSAM).[14] Israel's Rafael development center has since gone on to develop yet another version of the missile, powered by a ramjet rather than by a rocket motor, with an even lower launch weight and an effective strike range of over 170 mi (310 km).[15]

At the other end of the air-to-ground weapons spectrum, in terms of both size and complexity, was the SPICE (smart, precise impact, and cost-effective) family of guided bomb kits. Intended as a strap-on modification package for standard 1,000 or 2,000 lb bombs, the SPICE system included a folded wing that deployed after bomb release, as well as a precision guidance system. Although similar in concept to the American JDAM kits, the SPICE system differed in that it offered greater glide range—by virtue of the deployable wing—as well as greater accuracy. Whereas the JDAMs relied on a combination of inertial navigation together with a global positioning receiver, the SPICE system also added an electro-optical seeker. This allowed the pilot or weapons officer in the releasing airplane to guide the bomb during its final moments. The SPICE bomb kits were developed by Rafael and offered an intermediate capability that spanned the gap between conventional JDAM kits and fully powered missiles such as the Have Nap.

In addition to both tactical and strategic strike missions, the Lavi was also intended to perform antishipping duties against opposing naval fleets. In this role the primary armament of the Lavi would have been the Gabriel antishipping missile. The Gabriel was first developed by IAI as a sea-launched antiship weapon for use by the Israeli navy. Beginning with the third generation of the missile, however, an air-launched variant was also available, equipping Israeli F-4, A-4, and Kfir squadrons. The Gabriel III featured an active radar guidance system and a 330 lb (150 kg) warhead. Total missile weight was 1,320 lb (600 kg), with a range of over 32 nm (59 km).[16] Its successor, the Gabriel IV, was at one time funded as a joint effort between the U.S. and Israeli navies, before U.S. interest in the program waned at the end of the Cold War.[17]

The Lavi was therefore intended to carry out a wide variety of missions, against a wide array of targets. Israeli arms manufacturers had succeeded admirably in providing the tools that would go along with each mission.

The Air-to-Air Arena

At any time, under any mission, the Lavi might be pressed into engaging an enemy fighter in air combat. For this reason the Lavi was to be fitted with its most basic air-to-air weapons complement at all times: a pair of heat-seeking missiles and a 30 mm cannon. This choice of armament was not by chance. Rather, it was a reflection of many decades of combat experience, from the one air force with more air-to-air experience than any other air arm of the jet age.

The Lavi was intended to carry a single 30 mm cannon, located at the root of the airplane's left wing.[18] This weapon was most likely intended to be a French-designed DEFA 552, which was already locally produced to arm Israel's Kfir fighters. The Heyl Ha'Avir had always preferred the penetrating firepower of the 30 mm DEFA over the higher rate of fire afforded by the 20 mm Vulcan cannon used in U.S. warplanes. This was most likely a reflection of the emphasis placed on the ground attack role, where a 30 mm round offered greater armor-piercing potential. Nonetheless, the cannon was by no means limited to targets on the ground, even in a missile age. It was reported that in Israel's aerial victory over Syria in 1982, six of the Syrian fighters shot down had been victims of Israeli cannon fire.[19] The Israelis were not about to dispense with such a useful and reliable instrument.

By the time that the Lavi program was launched, however, the heat-seeking missile had already come into its own as the primary weapon of choice for Israel's fighter fleet. This stood in contrast to Israel's earlier wartime experiences in 1956 and 1967, when the Heyl Ha'Avir had possessed no meaningful missile arsenal. The French-supplied missiles at Israel's disposal at that time were notoriously unreliable, even in comparison to their American- or Soviet-produced counterparts. Every one of the air-to-air kills that Israel had scored during the Six-Day War had been accomplished with cannon. Moreover, even the United States, which at the time had a far more diverse and plentiful missile supply, had reported mixed experience. In Vietnam, for example, the cannon had still accounted for a third of all airplanes shot down.[20] Beginning with the War of Attrition in 1969, however, the statistics for air-to-air kills began to shift in favor of the guided missile and, in particular, in favor of heat-seeking missiles. Missiles went from accounting for none of Israel's air-to-air kills during the 1967 Six-Day War to accounting for 30 percent of all kills during the War of Attrition, 70 percent of kills during the Yom Kippur War, and over 90 percent of kills by the 1982 Lebanon War.[21]

At the time that the Lavi program was initiated, Israel's inventory of heat-seeking missiles already included the latest in both

American- and Israeli-made heat-seeking weapons: the American AIM-9L Sidewinder and Israel's Python 3. Both the AIM-9L and the Python 3 made up for many of the shortcomings of earlier heat-seeking missiles—which had been restricted to attacks from behind an opposing aircraft, where they could zero in on the hot engine exhaust. Both featured an all-aspect infrared seeker, allowing them to home in on an opposing aircraft from any angle, by zeroing in on the warm surface of the airplane's skin. The Python 3, which was first revealed to the public in 1981, was slightly larger than the AIM-9, weighing in at 267 lb (121 kg) to the AIM-9L's 191 lb (87 kg). It was also, however, reported to be more agile and to have a more sensitive seeker.[22] By the time that the Lavi development program had turned that fateful corner in 1982 and headed down the road toward becoming a more versatile, longer-range fighter, these two heat-seeking missiles already formed the backbone of Israel's air-to-air weapons arsenal. Within a few years, however, the winds of change could already be felt. The impetus for this transformation would come not from within, from U.S. or Israeli weapons development labs, but from the threat posed by the latest generation of air-to-air weapons being fielded by the Soviet Union.

By the mid-1980s, the Soviets had begun fielding their first generation of helmet-mounted sights, right around the same time that the Israelis had similarly introduced their first generation of DASH helmets. These Soviet systems lacked the helmet-mounted display capabilities that the Israelis were then in the process of perfecting, but they also added one crucial complement to the helmet-mounted sight that had hitherto been overlooked: the addition of a high off-boresight, heat-seeking missile. The Soviet R-73 air-to-air missile, code named the AA-11 Archer by NATO, was first fielded in 1985, featuring a significantly wider field of view for its infrared seeker than was available under previous Soviet missiles. What made the AA-11 so lethal, however, was that it not only allowed the pilot to more rapidly acquire a target—when used in conjunction with a helmet-mounted sight—but that it was also capable of maneuvering at an extraordinarily high turn rate, right from the moment that it left the launching fighter's missile rail. This capability enlarged considerably the envelope from which the aircraft could fire a missile and still expect to achieve a successful kill.[23]

The impact of this development was largely lost on the U.S. armed forces at the time. It was not, however, lost on Israel's armed forces. Whereas the U.S. Air Force and U.S. Navy had long emphasized the importance of the beyond visual range (BVR) radar-guided intercept, the Heyl Ha'Avir had continued to focus on the role of the dogfight as a central element in both their training and their air combat doctrine. The Soviet combination of a helmet-mounted sight with a highly agile dogfight missile had the potential for granting Israel's adversaries a distinct advantage in these future, close-quarter air-to-air encounters. Israel's air force leadership would therefore waste no time in correcting this deficit.

At the same time that the Lavi program was in full swing, Israel launched the development of a new high off-boresight heat-seeking missile, to regain the technological edge over the R-73. Like its predecessors, this missile-development program was carried out in complete secrecy and would not be unveiled to the public until well after the Python 4 had already entered operational service in 1993. The Python 4 was slightly lighter than its Python 3 predecessor, weighing in at some 235 lb (107 kg), although it retained the 6.3 in rocket motor that had been used under previous Israeli missile designs. Although many of the details behind the Python 4's performance remain classified, it is widely acknowledged that the Israelis went well beyond the kill envelope afforded by the Soviet AA-11, with a larger field of view as well as a higher missile turn rate and better resistance to countermeasures.[24]

In contrast to the Israeli reaction to Soviet missile developments, the U.S. military failed to recognize the true nature of this threat until after the fall of the Berlin Wall and the collapse of the Soviet empire. Only after the United States received its first, up-close demonstrations of the edge that such a system could potentially afford—during exchange and training exercises with former East German MiG-29 squadrons—did it finally recognize the "missile gap" that it had unwittingly allowed the Soviets to create.

In training exercises between German MiG-29 and U.S. F-16 fighters, the German pilots were able to fire the first shot in virtually every close-quarter engagement. American F-16s were reportedly able to outmaneuver the MiG pilots following that first shot up to 60 percent of the time, but that all-important first kill opportunity consistently went to the MiGs.[25] According to U.S. industry sources, American fighters armed with the latest versions of the AIM-9 Sidewinder, facing a dogfight with an opponent armed with the Soviet AA-11 Archer, were expected to win only one out of every fifty dogfight engagements.[26] The American F-15 fared even worse in these exercises. As Eugene Adam, who at the time was a McDonnell Douglas fellow in charge of pilot-vehicle interface, would explain, "The MiG pilot could acquire targets in 30 times the volume of the F-15, and the exchange ratio was also very high. The MiG was overwhelming." Gen. Ronald W. Yates, then commander of the U.S. Air Force's Material Command, described this air-to-air deficit in even more chilling terms. As Yates summed it up, in a visual range scenario, facing an opponent with a high off-boresight missile capability, "he's going to kill you. If he can see you, you're dead."[27] Only after this experience did the United States finally acknowledge the leap that Israel's Python 4 represented over contemporary U.S. heat-seeking missiles. As Lt. Cdr. Don E. Gaddas, the U.S. Navy's air-to-air missile requirements officer, acknowledged, the Python 4 "totally outclasses" its U.S. counterparts.[28]

Following these revelations, the United States finally launched the AIM-9X program, with the goal of producing a new generation of Sidewinder missile that could match the rapid turn-rate capabilities of the Python 4 and AA-11 systems. Two U.S. contractors, Raytheon and Hughes, were selected to develop competing designs, with the less expensive Hughes missile eventually coming out the victor. The American design was expected to replace the traditional Sidewinder heat-seeking sensors—which used a rotating mirror to scan the sky and focus light onto a set of detector elements—with a focal plane array, a technology that was expected to provide better resistance to countermeasures. However, the decision was also made to retain the existing 5 in diameter Sidewinder rocket motor, even though it was acknowledged that the Python 4, with its larger, higher-energy motor, would still have an advantage over its U.S. counterpart in terms of both acceleration and range. This short-coming in the Sidewinder missile was acknowledged by air force general Mike Loh, chief of Air Combat Command, who confirmed that "there's a significant number of conditions where the rocket motor will run out of steam before it gets to the target."[29] Raytheon had even proposed adapting the existing Python 4 rocket motor to extend the envelope for the new Sidewinder missile. This offer, how-ever, was declined. Moreover, the AIM-9X was not expected to enter production until 2003, more than a decade behind the Python 4. Despite the abysmal performance of American fighters during sim-ulated engagements against German MiG-29s, the United States would allow this missile shortfall in the dogfight arena to persist for another decade, turning down Israeli offers to sell the Python 4 to the United States as an interim measure. It was a telling deci-sion, and one that underscored the differences in air combat phi-losophy between the U.S. and Israeli armed forces.

Both the U.S. and Israeli armed forces had access to much of the same historical evidence. The two, however, had drawn radi-cally different conclusions regarding what this experience meant. Within the U.S. military, the BVR, radar-guided intercept had taken on a hallowed place in the pantheon of official air combat doctrine. The United States had therefore not reacted with the same degree of urgency to the deployment of the Soviet R-73 dogfight missile, even after firsthand experience convinced it that the new helmet-mounted sight and high off-boresight missile combination would place American aircraft at a distinct disadvantage. Instead, in keep-ing with official combat doctrine, the U.S. leadership continued to insist that the majority of future aerial engagements would be decided far beyond visual range, where longer-range, radar-guided missile capabilities were expected to win the day.

The Israeli air force, on the other hand, had continued to empha-size the centrality of dogfight training, in the conviction that future air battles would continue to be decided in close-quarter combat. Both the Lavi and the Python 4 were products of this philosophy. In the case of the Lavi, despite the fact that it was developed with the attack role primarily in mind, it was also developed with the belief that an attack fighter needed to be able to outmaneuver potential adversaries both to and from the target. The Lavi was built with the understanding that, to be survivable, an attack jet required both the necessary electronic countermeasures to penetrate enemy airspace and the agility to outmaneuver enemy fighters. In this respect, the U.S. and Israeli armed forces emphasized very different elements in their order of battle.

The American romance with the beyond visual range intercept actually dated back to the 1950s, when the radar-guided missile was still in its infancy. The idea of being able to intercept Soviet fighters and bombers from well beyond the lethal radius of their own missile armament had great appeal to American war planners. It conceivably allowed a numerically inferior U.S. military to whittle down the far larger inventory of Soviet fighters and bombers. This fixation on the concept of the BVR intercept, however, would persist long after it had been largely debunked by America's wartime experience in Vietnam.

There were a number of elements that led to the disastrous outcome of those earliest attempts at BVR war fighting in the skies over Southeast Asia. American rules of engagement called upon the U.S. pilots to make positive identification of their targets before releasing any missiles. Electronic identification techniques were still in their infancy at the time, and in the crowded and contested skies over Vietnam, the Americans could ill afford to be shooting down their own aircraft. The result was that by the time the U.S. aircrews had confirmed the identity of their targets, they were already within visual range, facing a dogfight scenario for which they were poorly equipped.[30] Added to this was the poor reliability of early versions of the Sparrow, with fewer than 10 percent of all Sparrow missile firings resulting in a successful kill over Vietnam. The early versions of the Sparrow proved to be particularly vulnerable to humidity, and the radar tracking system often became confused by ground clutter. Even when everything worked as advertised, North Vietnamese pilots aptly demonstrated that a forewarned fighter could easily outmaneuver the missile.[31] For American pilots, it was a painful experience. Within the U.S. defense establishment, however, the conclusion reached was that conditions had not yet been right in Vietnam to adequately exercise the BVR option. Official U.S. doctrine continued to maintain that future conflicts would be dominated by BVR weapons.

For their part, the Israeli armed forces had also never abandoned the radar-guided missile. On more than one occasion it was suggested that in a combat air patrol mission the Lavi was indeed intended to have its own BVR-intercept capability.[32] The Israelis had not, however, emphasized the role of BVR weapons as the centerpiece of their air combat strategy.

At the time of the Lavi development program, Israel already possessed an inventory of radar-guided AIM-7 Sparrow missiles, which equipped Israeli F-4E and F-15 squadrons. However, at 514 lb (233 kg) the Sparrow was a much larger missile than either the Sidewinder or Python, and it could not be accommodated by the wingtip missile rails of most fighters. It remains highly doubtful that the Lavi was ever intended to carry the Sparrow.

A far more likely scenario was that this Lavi BVR capability would have revolved around the long-awaited AIM-120 AMRAAM (advanced medium-range air-to-air missile), which was then under development in the United States. The AIM-120, unlike the Sparrow, had its own active guidance radar, freeing the launching fighter to take whatever evasive or offensive action was necessary once the missile was released. It was also significantly lighter than the Sparrow and, at only 345 lb (156 kg), could be accommodated by most existing wingtip rails. The Israelis ultimately would buy the AMRAAM during the 1990s, reportedly to equip their F-15 squadrons. This same missile was also available for use on the F-16 and would have been the most likely BVR weapon to equip the Lavi.

Yet this reliance on a U.S.-supplied BVR missile that was still an ongoing development effort throughout the 1980s only serves to illuminate yet another puzzle. Over the years Israeli arms manufacturers had developed Israeli counterparts in virtually every major category of air-launched weapons. From cluster bombs, to antishipping missiles, to antiarmor missiles, to heat-seeking air-to-air missiles, Israeli examples of all of these weapons were already in production long before the Lavi was launched. Yet throughout the 1980s and 1990s, there was still no sign of a radar-guided air-to-air missile under development in Israel.

Technologically there was nothing to stand in the way of an Israeli-developed BVR weapon. If they had wanted to develop a radar-guided air-to-air missile for the Lavi, they could easily have borrowed much of the necessary technology and experience from previous Israeli radar-guided weapons, including the Gabriel III antishipping missile and the Barak I surface-to-air missile.[33] Just as the American armed forces had placed a relatively low priority on the development of a high-agility heat-seeking missile, the Israelis had similarly placed minimal emphasis on developing their own BVR missile.

It was not until 2001 that Rafael would unveil Israel's first radar-guided air-to-air missile. As was subsequently revealed, this new weapon had been quietly under development since the mid-1980s, a weapon that was nearly two decades in the making. It was still, however, not expected to reach operational service with the Heyl Ha'Avir until 2002. Built using some of the same components that went into the Python 4, the export version of this new radar-guided weapon was named Derby. The Derby weighed in at 260 lb (118 kg) and was reported to have already been delivered to its first export customers by the time that it was unveiled to the general public.[34] The development program for this missile, however, had stretched out far longer than any similar development cycle for past generations of Israeli-developed, air-launched weapons. Evidently, the development of this radar-guided weapon had not been given the same sense of urgency within Israel's defense establishment as had the heat-seeking missiles being developed during the same time. Indeed, by the late 1990s, at a time when the United States was developing the AIM-9X to provide it with a capability comparable to the earlier Python 4, the Israelis were already developing their own next generation of heat-seeking missile, the Python 5. This new generation of weaponry was expected to feature an even longer range, as well as additional resistance against countermeasures.[35] In other words, in approximately the same amount of time that the Derby had been developed, the Israelis would develop two generations of heat-seeking missiles: the Python 4 and the Python 5. The radar-guided Derby was simply not given the same status within Israel's list of priorities.

There were a number of factors that might explain this pattern. Whereas the Python 4 and 5 promised to deliver capabilities that went well beyond what their American counterparts could provide, the same could not be said for the Derby. Other than its lighter launch weight and slightly lower price, the Derby had little to recommend it that was not already available from the AIM-120 AMRAAM. Then, too, radar-guided missiles represented a more substantial financial investment than their shorter-range, heat-seeking cousins. By 1990 the projected AIM-120 unit price totaled some $500,000 per missile, or about ten times the cost of a single Sidewinder.[36]

There were other reasons, however, for the Israelis to assign priority to their heat-seeking, rather than their radar-guided, missiles. In the latter 1980s the USAF's AMRAAM Project Office assigned Col. James Burton to conduct a study into the historical effectiveness of various air-to-air weapons systems during actual wartime experience. Colonel Burton studied the 407 known air-to-air missile kills that had been catalogued since 1958, as well as all known air combat engagements made since that time, neglecting only those that had occurred during the 1967 Six-Day War and the 1971 Indo-Pakistani War. The latter two engagements, of course, had involved air forces with limited inventories of air-to-air missiles and were therefore omitted. In particular, Colonel Burton concentrated his attention on the total of 2,014 missile firings made during actual wartime scenarios, particularly those made in Vietnam and during the 1973 and 1982 Arab-Israeli wars. The conclusions of this study would run in stark contradiction to over three decades of American defense expenditures and official air combat doctrine.

Colonel Burton discovered that out of over 260 fighters shot down by Israel during the 1973 Yom Kippur War, only 5 fell to the radar-guided Sparrow, in a total of 12 Sparrow missile firings. What was more, all 5 of those successful radar-guided kills had been made within visual range. In fact, out of a total of 632 Sparrow missiles fired in all wars studied, only 73 actually destroyed their targets. That made for an 11 percent kill rate. By comparison, out of some 1,000 Sidewinder missile firings, 308 had scored kills, for a 30 percent kill ratio.

What was more startling, however, was that out of all of these wars, and all of the air-to-air engagements examined, there were no more than four missile kills made from beyond visual range. Two of these kills had been made by American F-4s fighting in Vietnam. The other two had been made by Israel, which, according to Colonel Burton's findings, went after those two BVR kills specifically to appease U.S. pressure to validate American air combat doctrine. Colonel Burton's survey concluded that the beyond visual range kill had played no significant role in the outcome of any air war to date.[37]

Colonel Burton was not the only one to ring alarm bells from inside the Pentagon. In a separate U.S. Defense Department study, which examined all known air combat losses between 1975 and 1985—including aircraft lost to surface-to-air as well as air-to-air weaponry—it was determined that 90 percent of all recorded aircraft kills had been made by heat-seeking missiles.[38] The heat-seeking missile had repeatedly proven itself to be the most reliable and lethal air-to-air or surface-to-air weapon of the modern jet age.

It was not until the 1991 Gulf War that conditions were finally ideal for demonstrating the true potential and merits behind the beyond visual range intercept. Out of a total of thirty-eight air-to-air kills scored by coalition aircraft during Operation Desert Storm, sixteen could be credited to missiles fired from beyond visual range, a true milestone in the evolution of air combat weaponry.[39] Finally, the U.S. Air Force had a conflict they could point to that justified over three decades of official doctrine, and billions of dollars in spending.

Yet, out of all the available coalition aircraft that took part in Operation Desert Storm, only the F-15 Eagle had the necessary electronic sophistication to be authorized to engage targets from beyond visual range. The rules of engagement outlined by the U.S. military dictated that only aircraft that could positively identify their targets, using two independent means, would be allowed to engage from beyond visual range. It was not enough to know that an approaching aircraft was "unknown." It had to be confirmed as a hostile aircraft before it could be fired upon. Among coalition fighters, only the F-15, with its sophisticated suite of electronics, could meet these stringent criteria.[40]

In contrast to these very strict rules of engagement, American surface-to-air missile batteries, including the Patriot missile batteries operating in both the 1991 and the 2003 Iraq wars, had no such requirement. As a result, in 2003 two coalition aircraft would be mistakenly shot down by Patriot missiles: an RAF Tornado and a U.S. Navy F/A-18. Although excuses would be made that the coalition aircraft had strayed outside of their assigned flight zones and that their IFF systems were likely damaged by Iraqi antiaircraft weapons, the reality was that the Patriot missile batteries had identified both aircraft as "unknown" targets. The Patriot missiles lacked the sophisticated electronics that the F-15 employed to ensure the identity of opposing aircraft. An "unknown" target was presumed to be hostile.[41] The painful lesson for the advocates of beyond visual range interception should have been stark and crystal clear: BVR weapons can be safely employed only under closely controlled circumstances, where the identity of a potential target is confirmed, not presumed.

The implications of this reality would have been well known to the Israeli planners who developed the Lavi. The Israeli air force employed both the F-15 and the F-16 and was already familiar with the individual strengths and weaknesses of each. As a strike aircraft, the Lavi electronics were focused on the air-to-ground role, not the air-to-air role. In its primary mission, the Lavi would rarely have been afforded the opportunity to employ a beyond visual range weapon. The Lavi was expected to penetrate enemy air defenses, not to engage enemy fighters that were not an immediate obstacle to its primary mission. When the Lavi did encounter hostile aircraft, it would almost certainly have been at close quarters, in a dogfight scenario. The Lavi's heat-seeking missiles would therefore have constituted the most lethal air-to-air armament that it could possibly employ. The very limited array of air-to-air scenarios where the use of BVR missiles might possibly be contemplated were better left to Israel's existing arsenal of F-15 fighters.

Israel also operated out of a far more restricted swath of airspace than the United States had enjoyed over Iraq. Israeli warplanes scrambling to intercept a potentially hostile target could easily find themselves within visual range of their adversary long before they left Israeli airspace. The realities of defending a small nation within a limited amount of airspace had been a problem that Israeli pilots had grappled with for decades. In the words of one Israeli Mirage pilot, "At fifty thousand feet, in a supersonic Mirage, I can fly only north and south; otherwise, I'd be out of the country in a matter of seconds. You can see on one side Cyprus, Turkey—on the other Iraq and Sharm el-Sheikh. You have no trouble spotting the Suez Canal. But your own country is very difficult to see; it's under the belly of your plane. You have to turn around and look back to see it. You become very aware of its smallness."[42]

Israel's precarious position was further complicated by the proliferation of the same or similar warplanes in the inventories of the various Arab air arms. In 1973 concerns over the possibility of fratricide had led the Heyl Ha'Avir to deploy their Mirage and Nesher fighters in a high-visibility color scheme, featuring bright-orange triangles on the surfaces of each wing. The Israelis needed to ensure that their own aircraft would be easily distinguishable from Mirage fighters flown by Libyan or Egyptian pilots. By the time that the Lavi was under development, this identification problem had been further complicated by the deployment of F-15 fighters by both the Israeli and Saudi air forces and by the deployment of the F-16 in both the Israeli and the Egyptian services. In this environment, the use of a beyond visual range weapon could be contemplated only under a very narrow set of circumstances.

The 1991 Gulf War did not fully settle the debate surrounding the presumed supremacy of the BVR missile in future air-to-air engagements. The Iraqi air force had not attempted to contest air superiority against coalition warplanes but sought instead to preserve their strength for use in a postwar scenario. Many of the Iraqi aircraft shot down had been in the process of fleeing to Iran. The Gulf War had been an ideal testing ground for the BVR concept. It had not, however, convincingly made a case that the age of the dogfight was over. Despite the overwhelming numerical and technological advantage enjoyed by coalition warplanes, some 60 percent of all coalition air-to-air kills were nonetheless made within visual range. Even under ideal circumstances, close-quarter air combat was destined to remain an essential element of future engagements.

The choice of air-to-air weapons selected to arm the Lavi had therefore been no accident. The Heyl Ha'Avir had intentionally focused their development resources on the heat-seeking missiles that would afford them the highest probability for a successful kill.

APPENDIX 7

Performance and Bringing the Pieces Together

For the Lavi, as a multirole fighter with an emphasis on the attack role, two competing sets of requirements would have shaped the final design. On the one hand, the Lavi needed to have the range and payload necessary to complete its primary missions as both a close air support and long-range strike aircraft. This was a demanding enough objective in itself. It was also necessary, however, to endow the fighter with sufficient agility both to evade enemy air defenses and to successfully engage opposing fighters in its secondary, air defense role.

Range and Payload

The Lavi's two distinct attack objectives would have formed competing cornerstones for measuring its success. The close air support mission would have emphasized payload capacity, rather than range. The long-range strike role, on the other hand, would have emphasized the strategic reach of the airplane, demanding that the fighter be capable of targeting destinations as far away as Libya or Iran.

To understand how this balance was achieved requires some minimal appreciation for the Breguet range equation:

$$R = (v/c_j)(L/D)\ln(W_i/W_f)$$

(7.1)

As should be evident from this relationship, a number of elements held out the potential to extend the Lavi's combat radius.

Obviously, an engine with lower specific fuel consumption, c_j, would have a ready means for achieving an expanded combat radius. Fuel consumption, however, was not an element that the Lavi developers could further evolve at will. Engine choices were limited to the off-the-shelf options.

Greater range could also be achieved if a higher cruise velocity, v, could be maintained. This could be realized in practice, however, only if the airplane's critical Mach number could somehow be increased—something that would require a very clean aerodynamic design that delayed the onset of transonic drag rise. As discussed previously, the Lavi's conformal weapons carriage and aerodynamic shaping were intended to provide precisely this advantage.

Also in evidence under the Breguet range equation is the impact of aerodynamic efficiency, which would directly affect the airplane's lift-to-drag ratio, (L/D). The aerodynamic efficiency of the Lavi was enhanced first and foremost through an optimized canard-delta configuration, which sought to achieve the maximum lift-to-drag ratio possible from a compact design. This canard-wing interaction allowed an airplane with a relatively low aspect ratio and a more highly swept wing to achieve a lift-to-drag ratio that rivaled those of its more conventional, higher aspect ratio cousins. More importantly, it allowed the Lavi developers to seek improvements in lift-to-drag ratio at the same time that they optimized their wing sweep to achieve a higher cruise Mach number.

A rough calculation, calibrated against experimental data, would suggest that the addition of a canard allowed the Lavi to increase its lift-to-drag ratio by nearly 7 percent at cruise conditions. Taking into account the collective measures employed to decrease the Lavi's drag, and to increase its lift-to-drag ratio, it is projected that the Lavi should have achieved an 11 percent greater lift-to-drag ratio at cruise, compared to an F-16C with a similar payload.[1]

Added to this mix was the incorporation of area ruling, which delayed the onset of drag rise, as well as the incorporation of composite wing technology, which lowered the airplane's skin friction and drag coefficient. Taken together, these measures not only permitted the Lavi to achieve higher cruise speeds and greater range but would also have increased the fighter's penetration speeds at low-altitude conditions, in the close air support role.

Based upon published capabilities for the two respective aircraft, it is estimated that the Lavi's optimum cruise speed, in a hi-lo-hi mission profile, armed with two 2,000 lb (910 kg) bombs, would have occurred at approximately Mach 0.89, compared to Mach 0.76 for a similarly armed F-16C. Taken in combination, these elements allowed a small airplane to boast a hi-lo-hi strike radius that was 50 percent greater than a similarly armed Block 40 F-16C. Achieving this degree of success had required an integrated, team effort, requiring the cooperation of multiple engineering disciplines. In the words of airplane designer Ed Heinemann, the chief engineer behind the A-4 Skyhawk decades before, "No single person could do it all."[2]

Air Combat Maneuver

As important as the strike role was to the Lavi's success, it also had to be able to perform equally well as an air-to-air platform. This requirement would place a slightly different set of demands on the airplane, mandating that a careful balance be struck between the fighter's competing objectives.

Unlike range or payload calculations, for air combat performance there are multiple measures that attempt to portray which airplane might have an advantage. In general, these metrics will fall into one of two categories: measures of agility, or the ability to out-turn an opponent; and measures of acceleration. Most fighter designs tend to be biased in favor of either one or the other.

Three principal components collectively determine the majority of airplane performance measures, air combat included: the airplane's thrust-to-weight ratio; the airplane's wing loading, or weight divided by the gross wing area; and the airplane's overall aerodynamic effectiveness, typically measured either by Oswald's efficiency or in terms of the airplane's lift-to-drag ratio.

Constraint analysis charts plotting the airplane's thrust loading against its wing loading were introduced previously in appendix 4. Lacking any other knowledge of a particular airplane's aerodynamic characteristics, this relationship is probably a good place to begin when exploring relative aircraft capabilities. All other things being equal, instantaneous turn performance will be superior for an airplane with a lower wing loading, while the advantage in acceleration will go to the airplane with the higher thrust loading. Classical dissimilar air combat is centered on just such a contest: between one airplane with an advantage in thrust loading and an opponent with an advantage in wing loading.

The Lavi, as an airplane built primarily around the attack role, could not expect to possess an advantage in both thrust loading and wing loading and yet still expect to meet its primary mission objectives. The added weight of the oversized engine that would have been necessary to secure an advantage in thrust loading would also have made the achievement of the Lavi's range objectives unthinkable. The developers of the Lavi therefore biased their design toward providing an advantage in wing loading: endowing their creation with superior instantaneous turn rate at the expense of acceleration and climb capabilities. To understand how these pieces fit together, we will therefore need to arrive at a better understanding of both the calculation and the measurement of agility.

Measuring Agility

The two most commonly employed measures for air combat agility are sustained turn rate and instantaneous turn rate. In the traditional, textbook setting, the sustained turn rate would be calculated directly from the airplane's drag polar, as described previously:

$$C_D = C_{D_0} + C_L^2 / \pi A e$$

(7.2)

This equation can be rearranged in terms of the maximum load factor, n, that the fighter is capable of sustaining when airspeed and altitude are held constant:[3]

$$n = \left\{ \left[\frac{(T/W)}{(W/S)} \cos \alpha - \frac{q C_{D_0}}{(W/S)^2} \right] \pi A e q \right\}^{1/2} + (T/W) \sin \alpha$$

(7.3)

Given this maximum, sustained load factor, the associated turn rate, $\dot{\psi}$, would be provided by

$$\dot{\psi} = \frac{g}{v}(n^2 - 1)^{1/2}$$

(7.4)

On the surface, these equations would appear to provide a relatively direct and easily accessible path for estimating an airplane's sustained turn rate. In practice, however, the parameters that go into these relationships are not so simple to ascertain. What these relationships do provide, however, is an essential source of insight into how the different elements of a fighter's design can influence sustained turn capability, and into how the developers of the Lavi sought to take maximum advantage of the means available to them.

Most classical, textbook treatments of fighter agility will tend to focus on two principal elements found under equation 7.3, as being the leading contributors toward maximizing an airplane's sustained turn rate: the airplane's wing loading, (W/S), and the airplane's thrust loading, (T/W). In marked contrast, the zero-lift drag coefficient, C_{Do}, is a relatively minor contributor. For a typical fighter configuration, for example, a 10 percent increase in the thrust-to-weight ratio would theoretically lead to an increase of roughly 6 percent in the airplane's sustained turn rate. A 10 percent decrease in the parasitic drag coefficient, on the other hand, would improve that same fighter's sustained turn rate by less than 1 percent. Only when the airplane moves into the supersonic regime, where wave drag becomes predominant, does the zero-lift drag coefficient become a leading player in deciding a fighter's maneuver potential.

Assessing even the relative sustained turn capabilities of different fighter designs, featuring different thrust loadings and different wing loading combinations, however, is not as simple as it might first appear. For a typical fighter design, decreasing the wing loading by 10 percent would improve the turn rate by 4 percent, making wing loading nearly as potent a tool as thrust loading for improving sustained turn rate. Decreasing a fighter's wing loading, however, requires a larger wing area, which will also tend to produce a heavier airplane.

There was also one other element, however, that the Lavi development team could tap into to maximize the fighter's turn performance: one other, key contributor, visible within equation 7.3, whose presence began to be felt as sustained turn rates climbed higher. That element was the pervasive influence of aerodynamic efficiency. A 10 percent improvement in the Oswald's efficiency would yield a 5 percent improvement in the available turn rate for a typical fighter. As fighter turn rates have climbed higher, however, aerodynamic efficiency has proven to be far less of a constant and far more of a variable than what textbook theory might imply.

By the 1960s, it had become readily evident that the classical drag polar described by equation 7.2, which had served the aviation industry so well at subsonic flight conditions and at modest load factors, did not completely capture the behavior of an aircraft in transonic flight, or at elevated loads. In the transonic flight regime, drag polars could become asymmetric, or shifted from the drag-axis, taking on a form that was slightly different from that seen in the classical textbooks:[4]

$$C_D = C_{Dmin} + (C_L - C_{Lmin})^2 / \pi A e$$
(7.5)

To complicate matters further, at elevated load factors it also became evident that there were other, higher-order terms, not captured by either equation 7.2 or equation 7.5. Far from being a constant parameter, the aerodynamic efficiency proved to be a function of the airplane's load factor. As a jet fighter's wings twist and bend under increasing load, aerodynamic efficiency erodes away, making the prediction of sustained or even instantaneous turn rates problematic.

In the jet age, therefore, Oswald's efficiency became yet another variable to keep track of, one that would typically decrease as both the load factor and the Mach number climbed.[5] By the time that the Lavi development team began to assemble their first conceptual sketches, it had already become evident that for a modern fighter the aerodynamic efficiency of the design could easily be as powerful of a player in fighter agility as the thrust-to-weight ratio or wing loading had historically been.

While this effect had been recognized by past developers, prior generations of fighter aircraft had made only modest attempts at harnessing it. The tools needed to improve thrust-to-weight ratio or to adjust the wing loading had been obvious. Adjustments could be achieved either by incorporating a larger jet engine or by building an airplane with a larger wing area. The means to achieve a meaningful improvement in aerodynamic efficiency, however, were not always readily evident. Historically, airplane developers were limited by whatever Oswald's efficiency their narrow selection of airfoils and planform arrangements could muster.

There were two elements, however, that coalesced at around the time of the Lavi's development and would change the manner in which developers thought about this subject. The first was tied to aeroelastic tailoring. By the 1970s, composite materials technology, in combination with advances in computational tools, allowed for the development of a wing structure that could control and channel aerodynamic bending to provide a more optimum airfoil shape for both cruise and maneuver conditions. The pioneer for this technique had been America's HiMAT unmanned demonstrator, which had been the first aircraft to utilize aeroelastic tailoring as part of a concerted effort to maximize fighter turn rate.[6] The second element that would give the Lavi an edge in any air-to-air engagement was its canard-delta planform. A properly integrated, close-coupled canard arrangement held out the potential to significantly increase the effective aerodynamic efficiency of a design, beyond what had been feasible with a traditional wing-and-tail arrangement. Experimental studies, for example, had demonstrated improvements of over 20 percent in the Oswald's efficiency at transonic flight conditions.[7] Increases of this magnitude had, historically speaking, been unthinkable.

The Lavi was therefore a made-to-order test case for showcasing the impact that decades of improvements to aerodynamic performance could potentially make. The Lavi, it should be recalled, was optimized for the attack role, not air-to-air combat. Although its wing loading was light, its thrust-to-weight ratio was less than that of the F-16, MiG-29, or other contemporary fighters. Taking our cue purely from the classical interpretations of fighter performance, and ignoring the effects of aerodynamic efficiency, it might have been expected that the F-16 would possess the higher sustained turn rate. But this simplistic, classical interpretation could also be misleading. In a classical sense, it would similarly have been expected that the F-15 should have exceeded the sustained turn capability of the F-16, by virtue of its own higher thrust-to-weight ratio and low wing loading. But the F-15 had made many compromises to its transonic performance to meet time-to-altitude and maximum speed objectives. Numerous fighter pilots would thereafter attest to the impact that this compromise had on the F-15's maneuver capabilities. As one Israeli F-15 pilot would humbly acknowledge, "An F-16 with a mediocre pilot could beat a good pilot in an F-15—the F-16 was the dominating factor, not the pilot."[8] Published reports suggest that for an airplane in a clean, air-to-air configuration in level flight, the F-16 could expect to see an Oswald's efficiency of around 0.85 at Mach 0.8 conditions, as compared to 0.68 for the F-15.[9] These efficiencies would, of course, erode at the elevated g-loads experienced during maneuver, but the relative advantage of the F-16 would remain intact.

Similarly, despite its inferior thrust-to-weight ratio, the developers of the Lavi were depending on the aerodynamic advantages of its closely coupled canard-delta design, working in combination with aeroelastic tailoring, to provide the Lavi with an edge in sustained turn rate. At Mach 0.8 and 15,000 ft altitude, the Lavi's sustained turn rate was projected to be 13.2 deg/sec, with an instantaneous turn rate of 24.3 deg/sec—when equipped for an air defense role, carrying two air-to-air missiles and 50 percent of its internal fuel. This compared to sustained turn rate values of 12.8 deg/sec for the F-16A and 11.8 deg/sec for the F-15C under these same flight conditions.[10] Despite its more modest thrust-to-weight ratio, the Lavi could be expected to more than hold its own in a turning engagement.

More importantly however, the relative advantage that the Lavi held would only have been further magnified when comparing aircraft that were loaded with stores, in an attack role. The Lavi was expected to experience far less degradation to its aerodynamic performance than its counterparts developed only a decade before. As an attack platform, the ability of the Lavi to avoid or engage potential adversaries over the battlefield was expected to be second to none.

Sustained turn rate, however, was not the only measure of dogfight agility. There was also ample evidence to suggest that on the modern aerial battlefield it would be the airplane with the highest *instantaneous* turn rate that would be the most likely to predominate. As air combat had come to be increasingly dependent on heat-seeking air-to-air missiles, and in particular with the advent of all-aspect heat-seeking missiles, dogfight capability had come to be characterized by a fighter's ability to point and shoot: rapidly bringing its weapons to bear before an opponent could either escape or fire off a shot of his own. This new missile technology meant that future dogfights would no longer be limited by the ability of a fighter to maneuver into an ideal firing position in a protracted turning engagement. Instead, the new measure of fighter capability had become how quickly it could bring its opponent within the lethal envelope of its own air-to-air arsenal.[11] Once again, the Lavi's canard-delta configuration, with its enhanced high angle of attack capabilities, would have been a crucial element in its success.

Like its predecessor, the F-16, the Lavi had flight control software that incorporated a maximum angle-of-attack restriction that prevented the pilot from exceeding 25° angle of attack under ordinary flight conditions.[12] This was not, however, the true limit of the Lavi's performance capabilities, any more than it had been for the earlier F-16. The F-16 actually reached its maximum lift performance at around 32° angle of attack. However, the airplane also became unstable at around 35°, as the rudder lost control authority and the effectiveness of the elevator continued to decline.[13] Despite these hazards, the Heyl Ha'Avir had reportedly experimented with an angle-of-attack override switch for its F-16s, allowing the pilot to exceed the conventional angle-of-attack limitations of their aircraft.[14]

Within this short-duration near-stall, or even post-stall flight envelope, the Lavi's canard-delta combination would have provided a decisive edge. The Lavi's performance potential at these higher angles of attack was expected to be demonstrated under the number-four prototype, which was to be equipped with a spin recovery chute. The fourth aircraft was also expected to validate the airplane's automated spin recovery software, another element aimed at ensuring the pilot's safety in this hazardous region of the flight envelope.[15] That aircraft, of course, never flew.

An airplane's maximum instantaneous turn rate will be dictated be the maximum, transient load factor that it can attain, as described by the relationship

$$n = \frac{qC_{Lmax}}{(W/S)} + (T/W)\sin\alpha$$
(7.6)

Although thrust-to-weight ratio does appear in this relation, it makes only a cameo appearance. The sine term ensures that its impact will be small. Far and away the more powerful contributors are the maximum lift coefficient, C_{Lmax}, and the airplane's wing loading, (W/S). The Lavi's combination of aeroelastic tailoring, canard-delta planform, and low wing loading would have ensured it an advantage in instantaneous turn rate.

Acceleration and Specific Excess Power

An entirely different set of metrics are used to evaluate fighter acceleration, with specific excess power being among the most commonly used yardsticks:

$$P_s = v[(T/W)\cos\alpha - n/(L/D)]$$
(7.7)

Note that specific excess power, like other measures of fighter acceleration, depends heavily on the airplane's thrust-to-weight ratio. The influence of wing loading on this relationship is less obvious, although it is still present: buried in the lift-to-drag ratio.

When calculated at 1 g loading conditions, specific excess power becomes a direct measure of the airplane's potential climb rate, measured in terms of ft/s (or m/s). The picture becomes more complicated, however, once maneuver loads come into play. As g-loading increases, the effect of the airplane's lift-to-drag ratio, (L/D), would likewise be magnified. An airplane with a decisive edge in acceleration in a straight line, at 1 g conditions, might not see that same advantage under even a modest, 3 g turn. This was where pilot tactics, and the principles of dissimilar air combat, would come into play.

For purposes of pilot training and tactics, a more complete picture is therefore needed: one that bridges the gap between measurements of specific excess power and measurements of turn rate. The solution, of course, is to draw a direct relationship between specific excess power and the available turn rate potential. If the lift-to-drag ratio term under equation 7.7 is expanded and the equation rearranged in terms of the airplane's load factor, a relationship can be arrived at that relates the load factor available to the airplane's specific excess power:

$$n=\left\{\left[\frac{(T/W)}{(W/S)}\cos\alpha-\frac{(P_s/v)}{(W/S)}-\frac{qC_{D_0}}{(W/S)^2}\right]\pi Aeq\right\}^{1/2}+(T/W)\sin\alpha$$

(7.8)

Using this formulation, and accounting for the effects of Mach number and g-loading on the aerodynamic performance of the airplane, it becomes possible to develop a more complete picture of the maneuvering envelope. This is typically portrayed in a graphical fashion as an E-M or "energy-maneuverability" diagram.

The E-M Diagram

The E-M diagram was first introduced during the mid-1960s, the brainchild of American fighter pilot Maj. John Boyd and mathematician Thomas Christie. Boyd was a Korean War veteran who later became an instructor at the U.S. Air Force Fighter Weapons School at Nellis Air Force Base. It was at Nellis that Boyd would publish his *Aerial Attack Study* in 1960, the U.S. Air Force's first fighter tactics manual for the jet age.[16] As a lieutenant colonel, Boyd would later go on to become a vocal proponent behind the development of the F-16. Boyd's greatest contribution to the world of air combat tactics, however, was made while he was still a major, in 1964, with the introduction of energy-maneuverability theory and the E-M diagram.[17]

An E-M diagram contains a great deal of embedded information that quantifies the ability of any particular fighter to either out-turn or out-accelerate its opponent, across a broad range of possible Mach numbers. The official E-M diagrams for today's operational fighters are closely guarded, for obvious reasons. Diagrams are occasionally released, however, for older generations of aircraft.

The vertical axis on the E-M diagram represents the turn rate of the respective aircraft, while the horizontal axis represents airspeed, measured in either knots or Mach number. Superimposed onto this plot are isocontours describing lines of constant specific excess power. These contours effectively map out the acceleration margin that the airplane has under each flight condition. A few key elements should stand out from this representation:

The isocontour where specific excess power, P_s, is equal to zero represents the maximum sustained turn rate that the fighter can achieve.

The outer boundaries of the contour map will be dictated by a combination of structural, thrust, and lift-limiting criteria. The contours of this boundary are often referred to as a "dog house" plot. This outermost limit also defines the maximum instantaneous turn rate.

The peak of this "dog house" boundary, where the airplane achieves its maximum turn rate, will define the maximum instantaneous turn rate at the specified altitude, as well as the "corner speed" of the fighter.

The E-M diagram provides insight into how a pilot can obtain the maximum advantage from his mount. A pilot flying an airplane that had an exceptional instantaneous turn rate, for example, might seek to lure his opponent into a turning engagement where each airplane would decelerate to this "corner speed." This tactic would maximize his own advantage. An opposing pilot flying an airplane with better acceleration but poor instantaneous turn performance, on the other hand, would likely seek to avoid such a contest, preferring instead to maintain his speed and momentum advantage.

The boundaries of the "dog house" plot will be defined by a variety of aerodynamic, engine, and airframe limitations. The upper left-hand boundary represents the maximum lift available to the airplane. This limit is typically defined by the airplane's C_{Lmax} limit, although fly-by-wire control systems can further restrict an airplane's maximum angle of attack. The upper right-hand boundary of the E-M plot, meanwhile, will be defined by the maximum allowable load factor of the airplane. Note that the definition of this limit may also depend on the selection of external stores that the airplane is carrying at the time. Finally, the right-hand limit of the dog house plot will represent either a dynamic pressure, structural limitation, or an engine thrust limitation.

Taken together, the E-M diagram illustrates both the limitations of the flight envelope for any particular fighter and the energy state of the airplane across a variety of flight conditions. Each E-M diagram, of course, represents the performance of a fighter at only one altitude and under only one particular payload and fuel combination. A series of such diagrams would be needed to map out all relevant altitude and payload conditions. By plotting the isocontours for specific excess power for any two competing or opposing aircraft onto the same E-M chart, it should become readily evident as to which airplane has an advantage at any particular airspeed, altitude, or payload combination. The developers of the early E-M diagrams also went one step further and simplified many of their charts by color-coding different regions of the flight envelope. Friendly aircraft were colored in blue, while opposing fighters were coded in red. A chart with more blue regions than red zones was therefore favorable for the friendly fighter.

As should be evident, however, obtaining even an approximate E-M diagram—without access to flight-test data—is a daunting task. Accurate representations encompassing the airplane's engine performance, as well as its lift and drag characteristics, would need to be known across a wide array of potential flight conditions. Most of the published lift and drag information available in the open literature, for example, was collected in wind tunnel studies performed under clean, 1 g load conditions.[18] Without a correction for g-load, most approximations will tend to overestimate the specific excess power and sustained turn rate of each airplane.

Other Measures of Air Combat Capability

Despite their utility, neither acceleration nor turn rate can completely describe on their own the full air combat potential behind a particular jet fighter design. Air combat capability is formed from a collection of attributes, which the pilot must learn to master and bring to bear. None of the foregoing analyses, for instance, take into account the responsiveness or control authority of an airplane's flight control system. During the Korean War, for example, the American F-86 Sabre was in many respects outmatched by the Soviet-built MiG-15 fighter. The MiG-15 combined lower wing loading with better high-altitude performance. Beginning with the F-86E model, however, the Sabre had the advantage of both a hydraulic control system and an all-moving horizontal tail, delivering substantially more control authority than that afforded by the mechanical control linkage of the MiG. Although the MiG might have appeared on paper to have both a turn rate and an acceleration advantage, the MiG pilot could not capitalize on this theoretical advantage, due to the Soviet fighter's antiquated control system. Added to this was the excessive flexibility of the MiG's wings, which at high-g loads could lead to "aileron reversal." These shortcomings would manifest themselves in a number of ways, some of them fatal. American pilots, for example, would report seeing MiGs losing control during evasive maneuvers. Years later, a number of American pilots had the opportunity to discuss their observations with their communist counterparts. As Lt. Raymond Nyls would recall one such interview, "He confirmed what we all suspected— that the MiG had a very nasty stall characteristic. They would go into a high-speed turn and pull it too tight, causing a stick reversal. They didn't have hydraulic controls, and it would do a sharp turn that would sometimes 'class-26' [write off] the aircraft from the excessive strain."[19] More recent innovations in control system technology, including fly-by-wire, computer-driven controls, and airplanes featuring relaxed static stability, can likewise provide an edge in control system response.

Similarly, while roll rate is also not usually regarded as a leading determinant of air combat success, in the right circumstances it too could play a role. A case in point is provided by Capt. Robert S. Johnson, an American World War II fighter ace who flew the P-47 Thunderbolt in twenty-eight victories against the Luftwaffe. The following account describes a training sortie in which Captain Johnson's P-47 was engaged in a mock duel with a far more agile RAF Spitfire. By all counts, the Spitfire pilot should have easily won this match. But as this story suggests, no amount of theoretical edge could supplant the role of a skilled pilot:

> We were at 5,000 feet, the Spitfire skidding around hard and coming in on my tail. No use turning; he'd whip right inside me as if I were a truck loaded with cement, and snap out in firing position. Well, I had a few tricks, too. . . . I kicked the Jug into a wicked left roll, horizon spinning crazily, once, twice, into a third. As he turned to the left to follow, I tramped down on the right rudder, banged the stick over to the right. Around and around we went, left, right, left, right. I could whip through better than two rolls before the Spitfire even completed his first. And this killed his ability to turn inside me. I just refused to turn. Every time he tried to follow me in a roll, I flashed away to the opposite side, opening the gap between our two planes. . . . Before the Spit pilot knew what had happened, I was high above him, the Thunderbolt hammering around. And that was it—for in the next few moments the Spitfire flier was amazed to see a less maneuverable, slower-climbing Thunderbolt rushing straight at him, eight guns pointed ominously at his cockpit.[20]

The lesson behind Captain Johnson's story should be no less clear in the jet age than it was in the era of piston-engined fighters. In the right hands, even a "truck loaded with cement" could be lethal. By extension, in the right hands, a superior fighter could be devastating.

Placing the Pieces into Perspective

In an air combat role, the Lavi would have boasted a sustained turn rate that was superior to that of most of its counterparts throughout the Middle East. On an instantaneous turn rate basis, the Lavi's advantage would have been even greater. These were a direct product of the Lavi's low wing loading and superior aerodynamic performance. On the other hand, the Lavi would also have suffered from a lower thrust-to-weight ratio than many of its contemporaries, resulting in slower acceleration, and lower climb rates. In short, in an air-to-air role the Lavi would have possessed counterbalancing advantages and disadvantages.

The Lavi, however, was intended to be not so much an air-to-air interceptor as it was an attack jet. As such, the developers of the Lavi had selected compromises that would permit a small warplane to hold its own in air-to-air combat, while still retaining their focus on its air-to-ground performance. Winning on the battlefield still depends on the ability to defeat troops, tanks, and artillery. Shooting down enemy fighters has been an unfortunate, if necessary, sideshow, and an attack jet that has to jettison its payload to engage opposing fighters has failed in its mission. Far more valuable would be an airplane with superior electronic countermeasures and faster penetration speed over the battlefield—one that would allow that aircraft to complete its primary mission before opposing air defenses had an opportunity to react. The objective behind the Lavi had therefore been not to provide an unbeatable air-to-air champion but rather to provide an attack jet that could take advantage of offsetting strengths and weaknesses in any air-to-air engagement.

It was no accident that the Lavi won the support of so many veteran Israeli generals, men such as Defense Minister Ariel Sharon and the chief of staff, Lt. Gen. Raful Eitan. For them, the Lavi was the airplane that would deliver the bomb loads needed to support the war on the ground—Israel's "flying artillery." It was also no accident that the Lavi had likewise won the support of so many leading Israeli air force pilots, including senior officers such as the

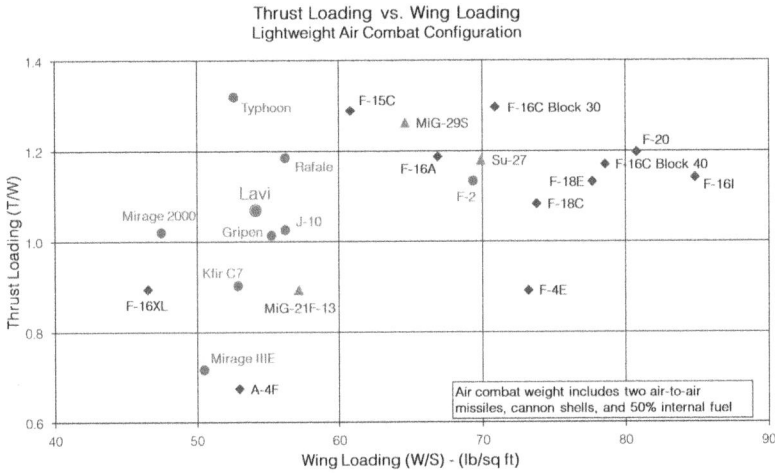

Thrust Loading vs. Wing Loading
Lightweight Air Combat Configuration

Fig. 38. The Lavi was intended to counterbalance its moderate thrust-to-weight ratio with low wing loading.

air force commander, Maj. Gen. Amos Lapidot, as well as combat veterans such as Brig. Gen. (Res.) Menachem Eini.

The Lavi was the product of the haunted, tortured memories that came out of the Yom Kippur War, born out of a nightmare battle in which Israel's survival had been very much in doubt. The design of this warplane had been a collaborative effort, spanning not only the many engineers who had developed the airframe, or the hundreds more responsible for its weapons and avionics, but also the many pilots and commanding officers who had shaped and refined its requirements, molding this airplane out of those tormented days when so many Israeli pilots had lost their lives. The Lavi had been built out of a uniquely Israeli perspective, aimed at the future wars that, sadly, Israel may yet again one day face.

. . .

A Classical Interpretation: Thrust Loading and Wing Loading

Diagrams charting the relationship between thrust loading and wing loading have been a staple of aircraft design and performance evaluations since the dawn of the jet age. These comparisons have proven to be an invaluable tool in airplane development efforts, helping to determine the available solution space that will allow a new airplane to meet its intended performance goals.

When comparing dissimilar aircraft, however, these charts can also become misleading. There is an aerodynamic component that remains absent in such a diagram. Moreover, charts plotted at takeoff conditions, for a fully loaded airplane, will not necessarily reflect which airplane will have the advantage in a lighter-weight, air-to-air configuration. Actual air combat will also take place at some altitude and airspeed, not at sea level static conditions, and will likely take place with much of the airplane's fuel capacity depleted. To be relevant to an assessment of dissimilar airplane configurations, the classical constraint diagram needs to be modified, to provide a comparison that is tailored to assess air-to-air potential.

A more equitable comparison of air combat capability requires that each aircraft be outfitted for the same mission, with similar, partial fuel loads. Ideally, the airplane's thrust loading would also be adjusted to account for the effects of thrust lapse, reflecting the appropriate altitude and Mach-number conditions for the scenario under review. This last step, however, can constitute a rather complex undertaking, requiring that the behavior of each aircraft engine be known or estimated. For the sake of simplicity, therefore, this final step can often be omitted—taking advantage of the fact that most jet engines will experience similar degrees of thrust lapse.

Comparing the Lavi to some of its contemporaries, it should be evident that the Lavi aimed for a thrust loading that was measurably lower than that of the F-16 or MiG-29, but with a counterbalancing decrease in wing loading. This trade-off was the result of a series of design compromises, which were necessary to maximize the Lavi's air-to-ground potential. For the Lavi, the weight of a larger, higher-thrust engine did not buy its way into a design focused on range and payload. The Eurofighter Typhoon, in contrast, was aimed at producing a fighter with a clear advantage in both thrust loading and wing loading, underlining its emphasis on the air-to-air mission. As an air-to-air platform, the Typhoon would have had a clear advantage over most of its contemporaries. To achieve this combined thrust loading and wing loading advantage, however, the Typhoon had to surrender fuel and payload capacity. Although both the Eurofighter and the Lavi were often described as "multirole" platforms, they were aimed at opposite ends of the air-to-air and air-to-ground spectrum.

As should be evident, a fair degree of insight can be obtained from a properly assembled thrust loading / wing loading diagram, although this chart alone does not always provide the entire story.

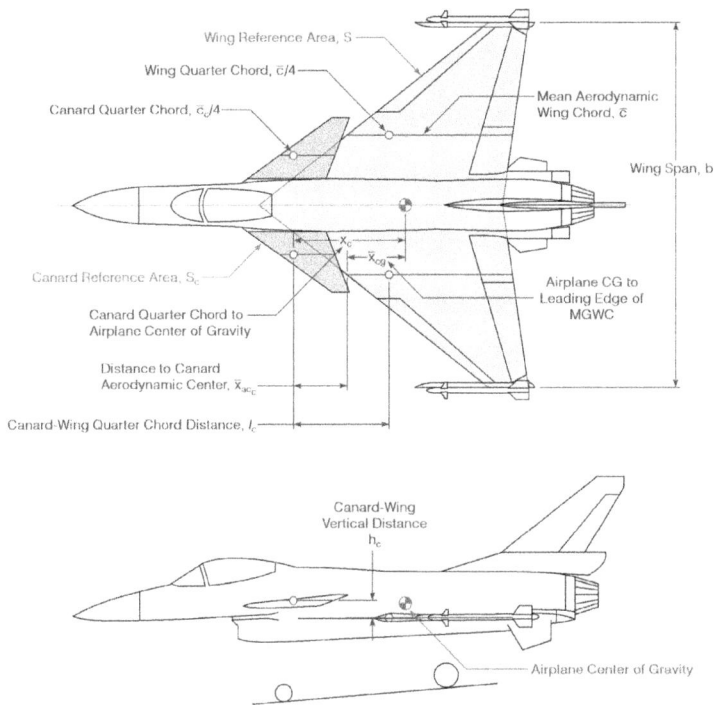

Fig. 39. Dimensional notations.

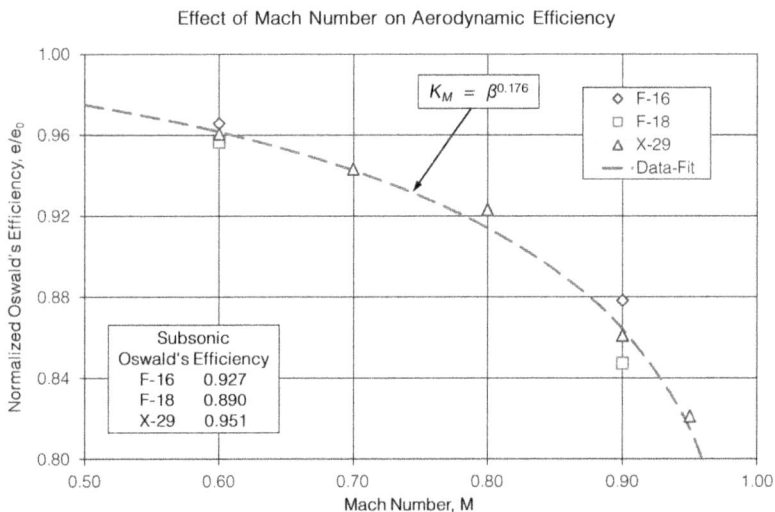

Fig. 40. Aerodynamic performance deteriorates as the Mach number increases.

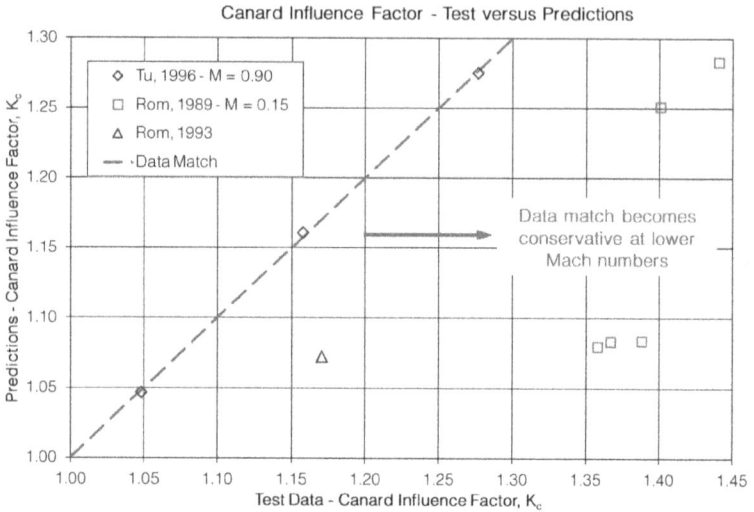

Fig. 41. Canard correction factor was calibrated for transonic (Mach 0.90) conditions.

Drag Polar Approximations

To complete even the most rudimentary of performance estimates, a reasonable approximation needs to be available for the drag polar. For the purposes of the estimates made here, the classical drag polar relation of equation 7.2 was deemed to be adequate, with the caveat that the Oswald's efficiency should be treated as a variable.

Numerous methods for estimating the zero-lift drag coefficient, C_{Do}, can be readily obtained from the open literature. The more sophisticated techniques will relate the airplane's wetted area and skin friction coefficient to an equivalent parasitic drag area, as well as providing guidance for the incremental drag impact from the addition of external stores and the effects of transonic drag rise.[1]

Estimating an airplane's Oswald's efficiency, however, can be more complicated. Empirical methodologies are readily available for estimating the subsonic Oswald's efficiency, based upon the wing aspect ratio and leading edge sweep angle, as well as for providing corrections to account for fuselage effects. None of these sources, however, provide a means for estimating the impact of a canard on the overall aerodynamic efficiency, nor do they provide correction factors for extending these subsonic efficiency estimates into transonic or high-g flight.

For the purposes of the mission analysis and combat radius studies conducted here, Oswald's efficiency was projected from the relationship

$$e = e_0 K_M K_c$$

where e_0 is the subsonic Oswald's efficiency, K_M is a correction factor to account for transonic Mach number effects, and K_c is a correction factor for the influence of the canard. It should be noted that if high-g maneuvers were also being considered, an additional correction factor, K_g, would need to be added.

The effect of transonic flight on the Oswald's efficiency was estimated using published flight-test data from a variety of fighter and strike aircraft,[2] from which an empirical relationship was thereafter derived:

$$K_M = \beta^{0.176}$$

where

$$\beta = (1 - M^2)^{1/2}$$

This relationship should prove to be fairly accurate, out to at least Mach 0.95.

Similarly, the experimental data was used to develop a relationship for the effects of the canard on aerodynamic efficiency,[3] resulting in the relationship

$$K_c = 1 + \frac{l_c}{\bar{c}}\left(\frac{S_c}{S}\right)\left[1 + \left(\frac{d\varepsilon_c}{d\alpha}\right)\right]\left(\bar{h}_c a_1 + a_0\right)$$

where the wing upwash on the canard, $(d\varepsilon_c/d\alpha)$, can be provided using published methods,[4] and where the empirical constants a_0 and a_1 were calibrated as follows:

$$a_0 = 0.3065$$

$$a_1 = 1.177$$

Comparing the influence of the Lavi canard to similar canard-delta configurations, it becomes readily apparent that the Lavi geometry was optimized to achieve the maximum benefit possible in terms of its aerodynamic efficiency. Relative to its wing size, the Lavi canard was the largest out of any of the production fighter configurations to be developed during the 1980s and 1990s, and it was also located in closer proximity to its wing. The Lavi canard-wing combination was optimized with the aim of maximizing the airplane's range, allowing a relatively small airframe to perform on a level far beyond what its size might suggest.

Table 14. Canard designs compared

Airplane	Canard area ratio (S_c/S)	Canard-wing axial spacing (l_c/c)	Canard-wing vertical spacing (h_c/c)	Wing upwash at the canard ($d\epsilon/d\alpha)_c$	Aerodynamic efficiency improvement (K_c-1)
IAI Lavi	0.12	0.56	0.13	9.71	34%
JA 37 Viggen	0.12	0.63	0.11	6.00	22%
Rockwell HiMAT	0.23	1.15	0.20	0.27	18%
Chengdu J-10	0.10	0.72	0.20	2.25	13%
IAI Kfir	0.04	0.55	0.10	12.39	13%
JAS 39 Gripen	0.10	0.64	0.07	3.39	11%
Dassault Rafale	0.05	0.71	0.09	4.92	9%
McDonnell Douglas x-36	0.19	1.16	0.00	0.27	9%
Chengdu J-20	0.10	0.76	0.04	1.45	7%
Eurofighter Typhoon	0.05	1.00	0.07	0.87	3%
Rockwell x-31	0.03	1.06	0.13	0.54	2%

Note: Projected influence of canard on aerodynamic efficiency: M = 0.90.

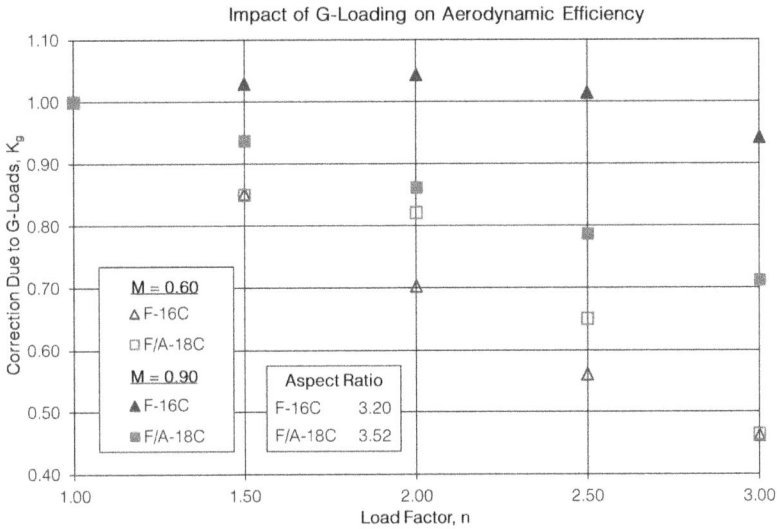

Fig. 42. The influence of maneuver loads on aerodynamic performance climbs rapidly as g-load increases but is less pronounced at transonic Mach numbers—where performance has already been eroded by compressibility effects.

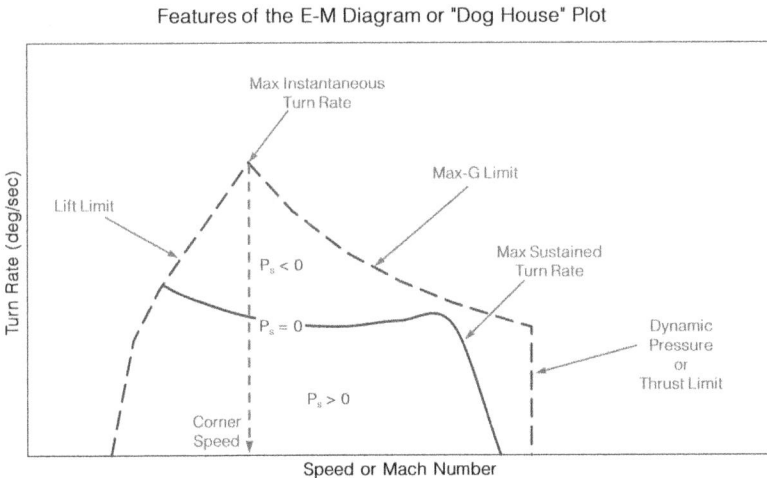

Fig. 43. The E-M diagram provides a roadmap to jet fighter maneuvering performance.

1. Roskam, *Airplane Design*, pt. 2, *Preliminary Configuration Design*; Raymer, *Aircraft Design*; Samoylovitch and Strelets, "Determination of the Oswald's Efficiency Factor."

2. Saltzman and Hicks, *In-Flight Lift-Drag Characteristics*.

3. Rom, Er-El, and Gordon, *Measurements of the Aerodynamic Characteristics*; Rom, Melamed, and Almosnino, "Experimental and Nonlinear Vortex Lattice Method Results"; Tu, *Numerical Study*.

4. Levy, *Prediction of Average Downwash Gradient*.

. . .

Estimating the Effects of Maneuver Loads on the Drag Polar

Relatively few sources in the open literature document the effects of g-loads on an airplane's Oswald's efficiency factor in a manner that is conducive to the prediction of jet fighter performance. Although this effect has been long recognized, the availability of quantitative studies is decidedly limited.

The reasons behind this apparent gap in the published literature are tied closely to the singular nature of the customers that are truly interested in predicting this phenomenon. There is relatively little interest in quantifying this effect within the civilian aircraft industry. High-g performance has generally been the reserve of military aircraft. Moreover, the test data necessary to quantify this effect is not easily obtained from any means short of flight test. Wind tunnel models may at best simulate aircraft performance at 1 g conditions.

Building on the relationship provided previously for describing Oswald's efficiency, the effects of g-loads can be expressed by the relation

$$e = e_0 K_M K_c K_g$$

where K_g is the incremental effect of g-loading on the aerodynamic efficiency.

A limited selection of flight-test data describing this effect is provided in the published literature and is portrayed graphically here, for both the F-16 and the F-18.[1] Two trends should be evident from this illustration. First, it should be apparent that the effects of g-loads are far more pronounced at lower Mach numbers, rather than under transonic conditions—where aircraft performance has already been eroded by compressibility effects. Second, it should be evident that wings having higher aspect ratios will, in general, be more susceptible to the effects of g-loads than their stiffer, lower aspect ratio counterparts.

Wing bend and twist effects are highly complex and are difficult to predict in advance using anything short of a combined structural and aeroelastic computer model. Even armed with these resources, the results would still need to be confirmed in flight test. The associated trends, however, relating performance loss to wing stiffness and Mach number effects, should nonetheless prove consistent across a wide variety of aircraft.

     1. Saltzman and Hicks, *In-Flight Lift-Drag Characteristics*.

. . .

Supersonic Performance

Supersonic flight offers its own nuances to jet fighter performance, only a fraction of which will be discussed here. The published literature provides a good introduction to this material, as well as empirical methods for estimating many of the parameters necessary for preliminary design.[1]

Some additional discussion, however, will be devoted to the subject of wave drag. The wave drag of an airplane can be related to its Mach number, its wing leading edge sweep angle, and most importantly, the Sears-Haack wave drag for an equivalent body of revolution. The Sears-Haack wave drag represents the minimum drag that would be produced from an idealized body of revolution, having an equivalent fineness ratio, (A_{max}/l), as the airplane under review:

$$\left(\frac{D}{q}\right)_{wave} = \frac{9\pi}{2}\left(\frac{A_{max}}{l}\right)^2$$

where A_{max} is the airplane's maximum cross-sectional area (minus the inlet capture area), and where l is the length of the airplane.

What makes the fineness ratio so important is the fact that it is squared. A short, stout fighter with a fineness ratio that is 10 percent greater than its longer, more slender counterpart can expect to see a 21 percent increase in its supersonic wave drag, just due to the effects of fineness ratio alone. This reality was part of the reason why area ruling was so important for the Lavi development team. Relative to many contemporary fighter designs, the Lavi was underpowered in the air-to-air mission. In subsonic flight, the Lavi could counteract this shortcoming with lower wing loading and better lift-to-drag performance. To maintain its supersonic performance, however, the Lavi relied heavily on area ruling to minimize its maximum cross-sectional area, and to come as closely as possible to an ideal Sears-Haack volume distribution. For an airplane that had been developed for the air-to-ground

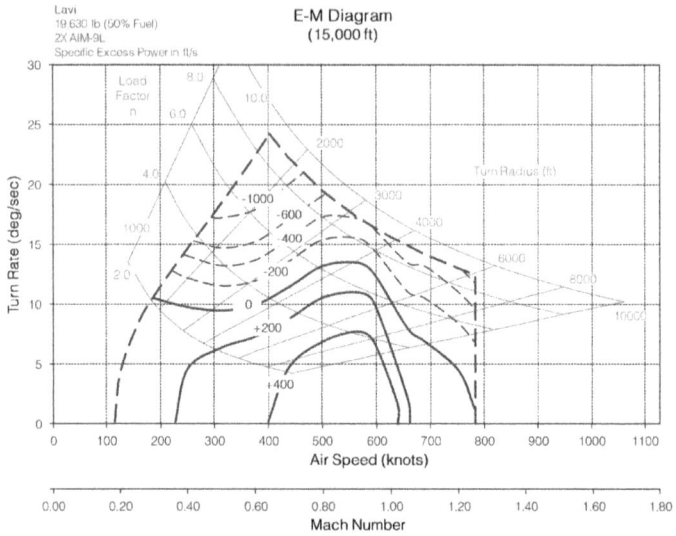

Fig. 44. Approximate E-M diagrams were calibrated to published sustained and instantaneous turn rates for the Lavi and F-16. Depicted here is the projected E-M diagram for the Lavi in a lightweight air-to-air configuration at 15,000 ft altitude, at maximum power.

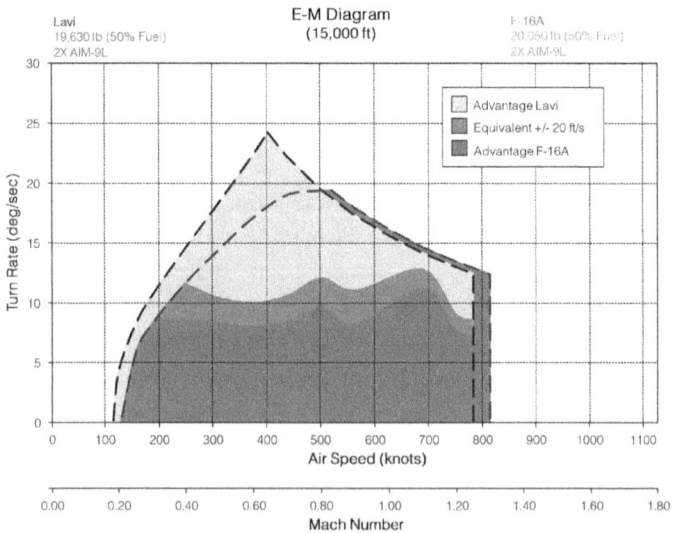

Fig. 45. Specific excess power for the Lavi is compared to an F-16A in an air-to-air configuration, at maximum power.

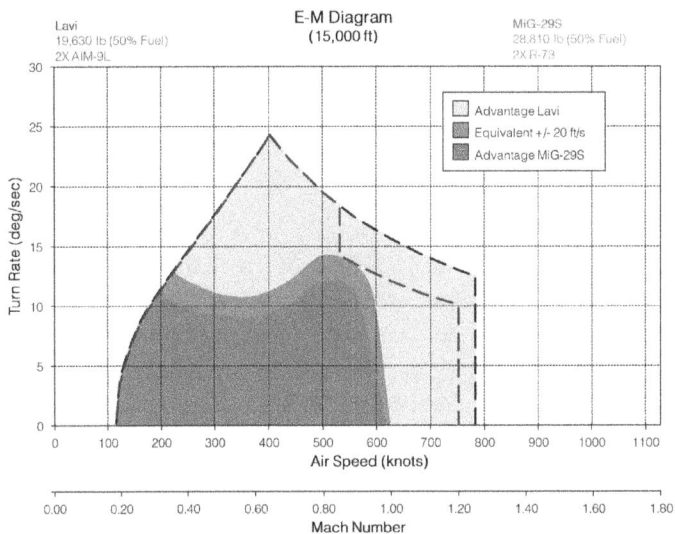

Fig. 46. Specific excess power for the Lavi is compared to the MiG-29s in an air-to-air configuration, at maximum power. The boundaries for the MiG's envelope became better established following the fall of the Soviet Union— and subsequent Russian attempts to market the MiG for export.

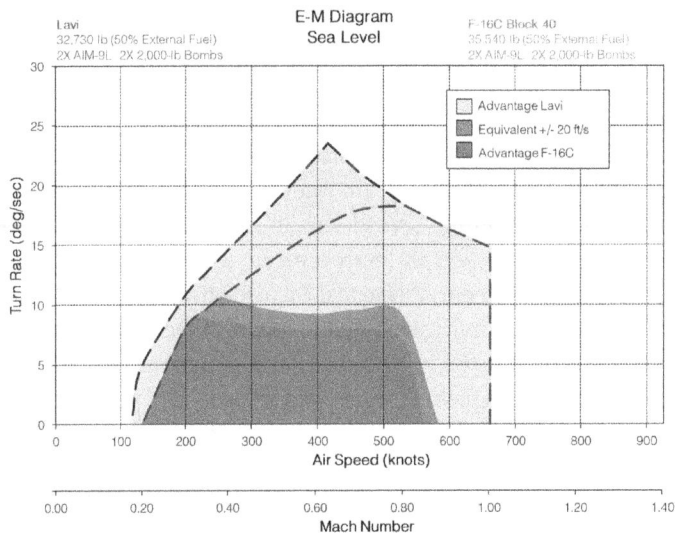

Fig. 47. Unlike the comparisons in prior figures, this back-to-back study was performed with an external bomb load, comparing the self-defense capability of the Block 30 F-16c to the Lavi. Thrust is set at maximum power.

mission first, this attention to detail was essential for maintaining its performance in the air-to-air mission.

1. Raymer, *Aircraft Design*; Roskam, *Airplane Design*, pt. 6, *Preliminary Calculation*.

. . .

Comparing E-M Diagrams

The E-M diagram provides a visual road map for many of the principles behind dissimilar air combat. It is a tool that illustrates, in ways that no other method can, how differences in airplane design can substantively alter how a fighter will be flown in combat.

To help shed some light on this subject, some *approximate* E-M diagrams have been assembled. These diagrams constitute a best, unofficial estimate of how the Lavi fighter would have performed in a maneuvering engagement, using the same methods cited previously for approximating the airplane's drag polar, and applying equation 7.8 to project specific excess power at each flight condition. Jet engine performance was approximated using the AEDsys software.[1] Relationships between Mach number, aspect ratio, and the effects of g-loading were projected from the limited pool of available flight-test data already published for jet fighter–type aircraft.[2] The airplane's lift curve slope was estimated using published, empirical methods for preliminary aircraft design.[3] The resulting performance charts should therefore be regarded as projections only—not official documents—but projections that have been calibrated against the published turn rates for the Lavi and F-16A. On a relative basis, these diagrams provide a means for exploring how an E-M diagram would be interpreted and what that diagram would imply for air combat tactics.

The first E-M diagram provides a picture for projected Lavi performance, in a lightweight, air-to-air configuration featuring two AIM-9L missiles and 50 percent of internal fuel. Reading from this diagram, the airplane's maximum sustained turn rate at Mach 0.8 and 15,000 ft altitude comes out to be 13.2 deg/sec, with a maximum instantaneous turn rate of 24.3 deg/sec. The Lavi's corner speed is projected to occur at around 400 knots—corresponding to Mach 0.64 at this altitude.

The second E-M diagram provides a direct comparison between the Lavi and an F-16A in an air defense role, employing color-coding to illustrate regions of the flight envelope where each airplane would be at a relative advantage in terms of specific excess power. In this instance, the blue regions of the flight envelope denote conditions where the Lavi would be at an advantage, while the red regions portray conditions where the F-16A would have superior excess power. The violet region highlights conditions where neither airplane has a specific excess power advantage of more than 20 ft/s. Note that both aircraft are assumed to be armed with two AIM-9L missiles and to carry 50 percent of their respective internal fuel.

From this second example, it should be evident that the Lavi would have an advantage during a tight, turning engagement at elevated g-loads. At lower g-loads, however, the F-16A would have the advantage and would be able to convert its excess power into either greater speed or greater altitude. It should be readily evident from this diagram as to just where and under what conditions each pilot would therefore prefer to engage his opponent. This is where the real value of the E-M diagram lies: in its ability to size up competing or opposing designs and to provide critical guidance as to appropriate tactics.

Also apparent from these comparisons are some of the flight control features unique to the F-16A. The fly-by-wire software in the F-16 has an angle-of-attack limiter that restricts the airplane to a maximum angle of attack of 25° under 1 g conditions, but to no more than 15° at maximum loading conditions. The F-16A's analog flight control system is also unique in that it allows the airplane to reach a maximum load factor of up to 9.3 g's. Later versions of the F-16 would restrict the airplane to 9.0 g's—widely considered to be the practical limit for pilot endurance.[4]

The third E-M diagram compares the performance of the Lavi in the point air defense role to the MiG-29s. The MiG-29 was developed with the objective of outperforming the F-16A in a visual range, maneuvering engagement. To achieve this, the MiG-29 sacrificed range and payload capacity to achieve a lower wing loading and a higher thrust-to-weight ratio. Later versions of the MiG-29 would add fuel and payload capacity to the airplane, eroding this advantage but making the airplane more attractive to foreign customers interested in multirole applications. The original MiG, however, was a truly formidable opponent in close-range, knife-fight scenarios.

The advantage of the Lavi over the MiG-29 would have been less pronounced than it was in relation to the F-16A at subsonic conditions. The Lavi would still have been able to outperform the MiG, however, during high-g encounters. Also evident from this comparison is the relatively poor performance of the MiG-29 at transonic conditions. Above Mach 0.85, the MiG-29 is limited to a maximum load factor of 7 g's.[5] It also experiences greater drag rise than either the F-16 or the Lavi, giving the Lavi a decisive advantage at transonic and supersonic conditions.

Finally, the fourth E-M diagram compares the performance of the Lavi in relation to a Block 40 F-16C in a long-range, low-altitude, air-to-ground role. Both airplanes are assumed to be equipped with two AIM-9L missiles, two 2,000 lb bombs, drop tanks, full internal fuel, and 50 percent of their maximum external fuel capacity. Under this comparison, the advantage of the Lavi is greater than it was in relation to the F-16A, where it was compared as a point air defense fighter. This is particularly true at transonic conditions, where the F-16 will experience greater drag rise due to its conformal weapons carriage.

In short, the Lavi was intended to combine superior air-to-ground performance with counterbalancing strengths and weaknesses in the air-to-air role.

1. Mattingly, Heiser and Daley, *Aircraft Engine Design*.
2. Saltzman and Hicks, *In-Flight Lift-Drag Characteristics*.
3. Roskam, *Airplane Design*, pt. 6, *Preliminary Calculation*.
4. Nguyen et al., *Simulator Study of Stall/Post-Stall Characteristics*, 34.
5. Gordon, *Famous Russian Aircraft*, 423.

NOTES

1. The First Lion

1. Laqueur and Rubin, *Israel-Arab Reader*, 173.

2. Sachar, *History of Israel*, 616.

3. Totals for Israeli and Arab air force inventories during the 1970s to mid-1980s were compiled from Chant, *Air Forces of the World*; Gunston, *Encyclopedia of World Air Power*; Gander, Ireland, and Jackson, *Modern Military Powers*; Pimlott, *Middle East Conflicts*, 51, 82.

4. Oren, *Six Days of War*, 136.

5. Arian, Talmud, and Herman, *National Security and Public Opinion*, 21. It should be pointed out that while anxiety over the impending Arab invasion permeated Israeli society in the weeks leading up to the Six-Day War, that anxiety did not extend to Israel's air force, where morale and confidence remained exceptionally high. As one of the pilots in Israel's 101st Squadron would later recall, "When [Chief of Staff] Rabin came to visit the squadron before the war, he was nervous and under pressure, and he was smoking heavily. He was unusually stressed. We sat in the briefing room and we told him, 'Yitzhak, do not worry. We will do the job for you.'" Shlomo Aloni, "101 Squadron, IDF/AF in the Six Day War," *Wings of Fame* 16 (1999): 140.

6. Gunston, *Encyclopedia of World Air Power*, 148–49; Bonds, *Illustrated Directory of Modern Weapons*, 37; Huertas, *Mirage*, 27.

7. Katz, *Night Raiders*.

8. Ronen, *Eagle in the Sky*, 45–60.

9. Tamir Eshel, "Tank Upgrading in the IDF," *Defence Update International*, no. 74 (August 1986): 17. From 1978 to 1989, *Defence Update International* was a monthly, English-language publication produced in Israel. The close ties that the editor and staff enjoyed with the Israeli defense establishment often ensured that they were the first to report on Israeli defense developments during this

period. Rights to publish the magazine were sold to a British house in September 1989. Shortly thereafter, the magazine went out of publication.

10. Steven, *Spymasters of Israel*, 252–82; R. Weiss and S. Aloni, *IAI Kfir in IAF Service*, 4–5.

11. The U.S. Navy and Marine Corps briefly leased twenty-five of the early model Kfir cis during the mid-1980s to serve in their Adversary squadrons, simulating Soviet MiG-21 and MiG-23 aircraft. The United States designated the airplane as the F-21A Kfir. "Navy Upgrades Flight Training Capability with Israeli F-21A Kfir," *Aviation Week & Space Technology*, October 21, 1985, 45, 52. For those not already familiar with it, *Aviation Week & Space Technology* (AW&ST) is the most widely circulated publication of record for news within the U.S. aerospace industry.

12. "'It's Like Lightening': Conversation with a Kfir Pilot," *Defence Update International*, no. 55 (1984): 54.

13. R. Weiss and S. Aloni, *IAI Kfir in IAF Service*, 10–11.

2. Superpower Relations

1. Nordeen, *Fighters Over Israel*, 90; Weizman, *On Eagles' Wings*, 183–85. Although it was President John F. Kennedy who ultimately agreed to the first officially sanctioned arms deliveries from the United States to Israel, the Israeli request for those arms had actually been delivered months earlier, by Prime Minister David Ben Gurion during a meeting with President Dwight D. Eisenhower, in 1959. It should also be pointed out that Brig. Gen. Yitzhak Rabin, who was then the head of the Operations Branch in the Israeli army, played a central role in drawing up the list of weapons requested. Rabin, of course, would also play a pivotal role years later in the decision to scrap the Lavi in favor of additional U.S.-supplied aircraft. Rabin, *Rabin Memoirs*, 54–55.

2. The early A-4 models that were supplied to Israel were primarily of the A-4H variety, with the exception of a few ex-navy A-4Es. Later models sold to Israel included the A-4N, which featured an increased maximum bomb load of up to 10,000 lb (4,540 kg). Gunston, *Illustrated Guide to the Israeli Air Force*, 100–105.

3. In November 1965 Israel dispatched a delegation to the United States to continue working out the details connected with the Skyhawk sale. The delegation was led by the Israeli air force commander at that time, Maj. Gen. Ezer Weizman—a man who would later play a central role in launching the Lavi program. Nordeen, *Fighters Over Israel*, 90–91; Weizman, *On Eagles' Wings*, 262–65; Rabin, *Rabin Memoirs*, 64–66.

4. Rabin, *Rabin Memoirs*, 130–31.

5. Rabin, *Rabin Memoirs*, 178.

6. Yonay, *No Margin for Error*, 299–302; Mersky, *Israeli Fighter Aces*, 81–84.

7. Gold, *Arms Control in the Middle East*, 127.

8. Pimlott, *Middle East Conflicts*, 82; Herzog, *Arab-Israeli Wars*, 239, 243, 285–87.

9. Kissinger, *Years of Upheaval*, 493.

10. Zumwalt, *On Watch*, 433.

11. Puschel, *U.S.-Israeli Strategic Cooperation*, 22.

12. Rabin, *Rabin Memoirs*, 261.

13. "The Kfir Comes of Age," *Defence Update International*, no. 55 (1985): 20.

3. The Lion's Den

1. Eliezer Cohen, *Israel's Best Defense*, 416.

2. Yonay, *No Margin for Error*, 308.

3. Eliezer Cohen, *Israel's Best Defense*, 66; Yonay, *No Margin for Error*, 137.

4. Huertas, *Israeli Air Force*, 88; Yonay, *No Margin for Error*, 138.

5. Eliezer Cohen, *Israel's Best Defense*, 93, 320; Yonay, *No Margin for Error*, 147, 307–9; Huertas, *Israeli Air Force*, 96, 104.

6. Yonay, *No Margin for Error*, 308.

7. Although the Swedish J-29 was judged to be an excellent fighter and an offer was initially made to sell the aircraft to Israel, the Swedes proved reluctant to close the deal. The offer to sell the jets to Israel eventually fell apart, ostensibly over financing issues—although the available evidence suggests that Swedish business interests in Egypt played a role in this debacle. Yonay, *No Margin for Error*, 139, 381.

8. Eliezer Cohen, *Israel's Best Defense*, 90; Yonay, *No Margin for Error*, 139–41.

9. Huertas, *Israeli Air Force*, 97.

10. Eliezer Cohen, *Israel's Best Defense*, 416.

11. Rubenstein and Goldman, *Shield of David*, 137.

12. Rubenstein and Goldman, *Shield of David*, 418–19.

13. Nordeen, *Fighters over Israel*, 142, 146.

14. Pimlott, *Middle East Conflicts*, 99–100.

15. Winchester, *Douglas A-4 Skyhawk*, 153; Aloni, *Israeli A-4 Skyhawk Units*, 34, 92.

16. Tsach and Peled, "Evolution of the Lavi Fighter Aircraft."

17. Eliezer Cohen, *Israel's Best Defense*, 420–21.

18. Eliezer Cohen, *Israel's Best Defense*, 421.

19. The proposed, twin-engined Aryeh fighter configuration continued to enjoy political support in Israel throughout the early to mid-1970s, due in part to the fact that an export customer had already been identified, in the form of the shah of Iran. The shah had expressed interest in acquiring the larger of the two proposed Israeli-developed fighter configurations, pushing this concept to

the forefront of Israeli planning. After Iran took delivery of its first F-14s in 1976, however, the likelihood of an Iranian purchase faded. Moreover, the subsequent fall of the shah's government in 1979 dashed any remaining hope of finding a major export customer for such a large and costly aircraft. Eliezer Cohen, *Israel's Best Defense*, 420–21; Peri and Neubach, *Military-Industrial Complex*, 56–57.

20. *Great Book of Modern Warplanes*, 145–46, 208–10.

4. The Next Lion

1. Gander, Ireland, and Jackson, *Modern Military Powers*, 124; Rearden, *History of the Joint Chiefs of Staff*, 90, 92.

2. Cooling, *Case Studies in the Achievement of Air Superiority*, 563.

3. Alternatively, the F-16XL could also carry a bomb load equivalent to the F-16's for up to twice the distance, while fully loaded with external fuel tanks. Robert Ropelewski, "F-16XL Shows Advances in Range, Ride Qualities," *AW&ST*, September 26, 1983, 62.

4. The Carter administration, unlike the preceding administrations of Nixon and Ford, failed to recognize that Israel's defense needs were more immediate than those of other U.S. allies. Under both Nixon and Ford, arms shipments to Israel were routinely given a priority status and expedited ahead of arms shipments to America's NATO allies. Under President Carter, no such priority was given. Rabin, *Rabin Memoirs*, 300.

5. I. Spector, *Loud and Clear*, 29, 370.

6. David Brown, "Gone with the Wind!" *Wings*, December 1989, 36.

7. Eliezer Cohen, *Israel's Best Defense*, 421.

8. "Israel: Seeking New Markets for Military Aircraft," *Business Week*, August 28, 1978, 48.

9. J. Weiss and C. Weiss, *I Am My Brother's Keeper*; Senior, *New Heavens*; H. Livingstone, *No Trophy, No Sword*.

10. Bernard Weinraub, "Plain-Spoken Hard-Liner for Israel," *New York Times*, February 15, 1983, pt. 1, 8.

11. "Israel: Seeking New Markets for Military Aircraft," 46, 48.

12. "Tide Turns against Israeli F-16s," *Flight International*, July 23, 1977, 264.

13. David A. Brown, "Israeli Air Force Facing Increased Material Threat, Reduced Budget," *AW&ST*, April 8, 1985, 39.

14. Gander, Ireland, and Jackson, *Modern Military Powers*, 146.

15. The U.S. Defense Department estimated at the time that clandestine Soviet acquisition of design documents from the F/A-18's APG-65 radar had saved the Soviets at least five years in development time and hundreds of millions of dollars in expenditures. Using this experience, the next generation in Soviet fighter radar became the first to incorporate a true look-down, shoot-down capability.

"Soviet Acquisition of Western Avionics Technology Concerns Defense Dept.," *AW&ST*, July 21, 1986, 79.

16. "Israel Demands U.S. Funds Prior to Talks on Lavi Alternatives," *AW&ST*, July 28, 1986, 20.

5. The Power of Decision

1. David A. Brown, "Israelis Review Decisions That Led to Lavi Cancellation," *AW&ST*, September 14, 1987, 23.

2. "Lavi Engine to Be Selected in Mid-May," *AW&ST*, March 30, 1981, 20.

3. The uprated versions of the F404, such as the F404-100 used by the F-20 Tigershark, could produce up to 18,000 lb (80.1 kN) of thrust in afterburner, or 11,000 lb (48.9 kN) at military power.

4. "U.S. Nears Lavi Transfer Approval," *AW&ST*, January 10, 1983, 21. One crucial statistic left out of these early range estimates was the anticipated loiter time, or time on target, for this close air support mission.

5. Tsach and Peled, "Evolution of the Lavi Fighter Aircraft," 831.

6. The key word here was "survivable." As the Lavi development program continued, it was to become a recurrent theme and one of the central reasons as to why the airplane was built. Brown, "Israelis Review Decisions," 22.

7. Peter Hellman, "The Fighter of the Future," *Discover*, July 1986, 45.

8. "Lavi or the Alternatives," *Defence Update International*, no. 79 (1987): 42.

9. Pratt & Whitney's initial dollar investment into Bet Shemesh was expected to be small: a meager $12 million. However, under the agreement, Pratt & Whitney was also expected to provide additional contract work for Bet Shemesh to supply spare parts for existing commercial aircraft engines. For a government-owned company whose financial viability had rarely, if ever, been assured, the infusion of additional work from the U.S. manufacturer was seen as a significant and attractive concession. Reiser, *Israeli Arms Industry*, 176–77.

10. "Lavi Engine to Be Selected in Mid-May," 21.

11. Eliezer Cohen, *Israel's Best Defense*, 421.

12. Klieman and Pedatzur, *Rearming Israel*, 109.

13. Nordeen and Isby, *M60 vs. T-62*, 22, 34; Rabinovich, *Yom Kippur War*, 281–83, 423–24, 457.

14. Sharon and Chanoff, *Warrior*, 451.

15. Nordeen, *Fighters over Israel*, 147.

16. Halperin and Lapidot, *G-Suit*, 76–77.

17. Halperin and Lapidot, *G-Suit*, 73–74, 77.

18. Hellman, "Fighter of the Future," 25, 27; Eliezer Cohen, *Israel's Best Defense*, 301–2. The Phantom flown by Shmuel Hetz and Menachem Eini was shot down by an SA-3 surface-to-air missile, which at the time was one of the newest Soviet

missiles. The Russians had yet to export this weapon to Vietnam or anywhere else outside of the Soviet Union, which was why the American ECM pods—designed to provide protection against the earlier SA-2 missile—proved to be so ineffective against this new threat. Yonay, *No Margin for Error*, 292–98.

19. Tamir Eshel, "Enter the Lavi," *Defence Update International*, no. 76 (October 1986): 6.

20. Armand J. Chapman, "History Benefits Next Generation Fighter Design," *Aerospace America*, May 1984, 50.

21. "Honing the Defenses with Updates," *AW&ST*, December 2, 1985, 88.

22. Eshel, "Enter the Lavi," 6.

23. "U.S. Defense Giants Eye Israel's New Jet," *Business Week*, February 22, 1982, 51.

6. Encountering Turbulence

1. Skinner, Anderson, and Anderson, *Reagan*, 443–44.

2. Skinner, Anderson, and Anderson, *Reagan in His Own Hand*, 213.

3. Silver, *Begin*, 1.

4. Shipler, *Arab and Jew*, 345–46.

5. Nakdimon, *First Strike*, 239–40. During that same press conference, Menachem Begin also expressed his personal gratitude to the pilots who had carried out the raid: "The target was surrounded by anti-aircraft guns, by land-to-air missiles, and by fighter planes, and yet they went in, into the lion's den, in order to defend their people. God bless them all." David K. Shipler, "Begin Defends Raid, Pledges to Thwart a New 'Holocaust,'" *New York Times*, June 10, 1981, A12.

6. The evidence for Iraq's nuclear weapons ambitions is overwhelming: L. Spector, *Nuclear Proliferation Today*, 165–91; Nakdimon, *First Strike*, 40–91. For an account of the Osirak raid from an operational point of view, see McKinnon, *Bullseye*.

7. Haig, *Caveat*, 87–88.

8. Arens, *Broken Covenant*, 28. Ironically enough, it would be President George Bush and Secretary of State James Baker who would one day again have to deal with their old "ally" Saddam Hussein and his regional and nuclear ambitions, following the Iraqi invasion of Kuwait in July 1990.

9. Nakdimon, *First Strike*, 244–46.

10. Haig, *Caveat*, 184.

11. Speakes and Pack, *Speaking Out*, 100.

12. Peter Hellman, "The Fighter of the Future," *Discover*, July 1986, 45. In Moshe Arens's own words, "You have got some people in the administration who would like to pick-up the dividends and kick us in the teeth at the same time." Bernard Weinraub, "Arens Says Strains in U.S.-Israeli Ties Are at a High Point," *New York Times*, February 20, 1983, pt. 1, 1, 9.

13. Herzog, *Arab-Israeli Wars*, 365–66.

14. I. Spector, *Loud and Clear*, 121.

15. Eliezer Cohen, *Israel's Best Defense*, 401, 488.

16. Arens, *Broken Covenant*, 26.

17. "Arens, Attacking U.S., Cites Need for Israeli Weapons Independence," *New York Times*, April 14, 1983, pt. 1, 4. Arens had been the first foreign ambassador that the newly appointed secretary of state had invited to meet with him when he took office in July 1982.

18. Shultz, *Turmoil and Triumph*, 443. George Shultz was later to lament that his support for the Lavi had been in vain. Had he known that the project would ultimately be canceled, he might have reconsidered his support for releasing the export licenses.

19. Bernard Gwertzman, "U.S. Allows Israel to Purchase Parts for New Fighter," *New York Times*, April 18, 1983, pt. 1, 1, 5.

7. Mysterious as a Ghost Ship

1. The UN Partition Plan of 1947 called for subdividing the British Mandate of Palestine to form separate Jewish and Arab states, based around the distribution of the Jewish and Arab populations. The British, however, continued to campaign against any plan for Israeli independence and, failing that, to campaign in favor of reducing the amount of territory that would be awarded to the Jewish state. It was only the personal intervention of Chaim Weizmann, who appealed directly to President Truman, that reversed the U.S. State Department's plans to acquiesce to British proposals. Had it not been for President Truman's decision to rein in his own State Department, there would undoubtedly have been a follow-on, British-sponsored resolution at the UN, calling for the territory allotted to the Jewish state to be cut in half. Eban, *Abba Eban*, 94.

2. Eban, *Personal Witness*, 149.

3. Brands, *Inside the Cold War*, x.

4. Brands, *Inside the Cold War*, 80.

5. Brands, *Inside the Cold War*, 102.

6. The quota system in force at the time allowed for a limited number of immigrants from each European country. Each consul could enforce its own interpretations and added requirements, however, ensuring that the quotas would remain unfilled. Antisemitism played no small part in this process. Wyman, *Paper Walls*; Wyman, *Abandonment of the Jews*.

7. Brands, *Inside the Cold War*, 124.

8. Loy Henderson was only one in a long line of diplomats who harbored a distinct anti-Israel bias and who came to dominate U.S. foreign policy and decision making at the State Department's Near East Bureau. Kaplan, *Arabists*.

9. Truman, *Years of Trial and Hope*, 162–64.

10. Truman, *Years of Trial and Hope*, 165.

11. A number of Americans did help Israel to acquire arms, including aircraft, during Israel's War of Independence. They did so despite threats of prosecution. Only one of them, however, was ultimately sentenced to jail time for violating U.S. neutrality acts and helping to smuggle weapons to Israel. Charlie Winters, a non-Jew, would spend eighteen months in prison for his role in helping to smuggle three surplus B-17 bombers to Israel in 1948. Decades later the Israeli government would grant Winters's dying request, allowing him to be buried in the land of Israel. H. Livingstone, *No Trophy, No Sword*, 136–37.

12. Eager to close the deal, North American Aviation assured the Israelis that a "green light," approving the sale of the requested fighters, would be provided in short order by the U.S. State Department. Israel had requested delivery of twenty-four F-86 Sabres, and in May 1954 North American Aviation authorized Canadair, which was building the airplane under license, to begin processing the order. The State Department, however, was contemplating no more than a token delivery of ten fighters to Israel, and even that paltry gesture was ultimately rejected. Gold, *Arms Control in the Middle East*, 83; Yonay, *No Margin for Error*, 139–40.

13. Rabin, *Rabin Memoirs*, 171.

14. Kissinger, *White House Years*, 864.

15. North, *Under Fire*, 154–55.

16. The initial memorandum of understanding governing strategic cooperation between the United States and Israel was suspended shortly after it was signed in December 1981, after Israel's Knesset formally annexed the Golan Heights. It was eventually superseded, however, by a formalized system of joint U.S.-Israeli military-to-military contacts, beginning with the first meeting of the Joint Political-Military Group in January 1984. Puschel, *U.S.-Israeli Strategic Cooperation*, 39, 49–50, 66–69, 81.

17. Haig, *Caveat*, 167.

18. Cannon, *President Reagan*, 324.

19. Haig, *Caveat*, 338–41, 86.

20. Shultz, *Turmoil and Triumph*, 12.

21. Shortly after he was named as the incoming secretary of state by President-Elect George Bush, James Baker described his own views on U.S.-Israeli relations in terms of a turkey shoot: "The trick is getting them where you want them, on your terms. Then you control the situation, not them. You have the options. Pull the trigger or don't." Arens, *Broken Covenant*, 27–28.

22. Tanter, *Who's At the Helm?*, 212.

23. Reagan, *Ronald Reagan*, 161.

24. Cannon, *President Reagan*.

25. Cannon, *President Reagan*.

26. Haig, *Caveat*, 85.

8. Funding Measures

1. "IAI Bases Lavi Fighter Project on 300 Aircraft Procurement," *AW&ST*, July 18, 1983, 23; "Lavi Engine to Be Selected in Mid-May," *AW&ST*, March 30, 1981, 20.

2. "IAI Bases Lavi Fighter Project on 300 Aircraft Procurement"; "U.S. Nears Lavi Transfer Approval," *AW&ST*, January 10, 1983, 20. Based on these figures and other sources, the target Lavi empty weight set at this time comes out to be some 14,800 lb (6,710 kg). This value would continue to grow at a modest pace to a value of around 15,310 lb (6,940 kg) at the time of the program's cancellation.

3. "U.S. Nears Lavi Transfer Approval," 20–22.

4. "IAI Bases Lavi Fighter Project on 300 Aircraft Procurement"; "U.S. Nears Lavi Transfer Approval," 20.

5. As a fraction of Israel's overall military spending, U.S. security assistance would reach its zenith in 1986, accounting for 27 percent of Israel's total defense expenditures. This fraction would gradually decline over the ensuing two decades, falling below 15 percent by 2008. Jeremy M. Sharp, *U.S. Foreign Aid to Israel*, 21–23.

6. Bernard Gwertzman, "House Votes Aid for Israeli Plane," *New York Times*, November 11, 1983, pt. 1, 14.

7. "U.S. Will Finance New Israeli Fighter Plane," *Congressional Quarterly Weekly Report*, November 19, 1983, 2438.

8. "Remarks of the President and Prime Minister Yitzhak Shamir of Israel Following Their Meetings," November 29, 1983, *Public Papers of President Ronald W. Reagan*, Ronald Reagan Presidential Library, http://www.reagan.utexas.edu/archives/speeches/1983/112983b.htm.

9. Organski, *$36 Billion Bargain*, 75–80.

10. Feuerwerger, *Congress and Israel*, 77. Feuerwerger's study of the sources of congressional support for Israel included a series of seventy-five interviews conducted with a range of representatives, including seventeen members of the House Foreign Affairs Committee. The interviews were conducted on a one-on-one basis during the term of the Ninety-Fourth Congress, from 1976 through early 1977. In order to obtain candid assessments from the various representatives, all of these interviews were conducted off the record, on an anonymous basis.

11. Organski, *$36 Billion Bargain*, 38–45. For a study into some of the likely cultural and historic origins behind the broad-based public support that Israel has enjoyed in the United States, see Stockton, "Christian Zionism."

12. *Congressional Quarterly Almanac*, 134.

13. Peter Hellman, "The Fighter of the Future," *Discover*, July 1986, 45.

14. "U.S. Will Finance New Israeli Fighter Plane"; "Reagan Wins Victory on Central America Plan," *Congressional Quarterly Weekly Report*, May 12, 1984, 1093.

15. The original batch of twelve Kfirs to Colombia was made up of Kfir c2s. The second batch was to consist of Kfir c7s. "And Another 12 to Cameroon," *Defence Update International*, no. 76 (October 1986): 14; Chant, *Air Forces of the World*, 13, 15; "Israel Seeks Kfirs, Upgrading Export," *Defence Update International*, no. 89 (1988): 42.

16. A handful of TC-2 and TC-7 Kfir trainers were also delivered to Colombia and Ecuador. There are also unconfirmed reports suggesting that up to seventy-seven retired Kfir airframes were eventually sold to South Africa, where they were fitted with French Atar engines and became the basis for South Africa's "Cheetah" fighters. The last such deliveries are reported to have taken place in the mid-1990s. Norton, *Air War on the Edge*, 302

17. Richardson, *Modern Fighting Aircraft*, 17.

18. Northrop's investment in the F-20 constituted the single-largest private R&D program ever undertaken by a U.S. defense contractor. Martin and Schmidt, *Case Study of the F-20 Tigershark*, 12.

19. Martin and Schmidt, *Case Study of the F-20 Tigershark*, 18; U.S. General Accounting Office, *Aircraft Procurement*, 5.

20. Gwertzman, "House Votes Aid for Israeli Plane."

21. "Funding for Israeli Fighter Triggers Debate in House," *AW&ST*, May 21, 1984, 24.

9. The Lion Unveiled

1. Rabin had failed to close a bank account in the United States when he left his ambassadorship—a minor infraction, but one that the public was not in the mood to overlook. Rabin, *Rabin Memoirs*, 309–13.

2. Klieman and Pedatzur, *Rearming Israel*, 73.

3. Reiser, *Israeli Arms Industry*, 103.

4. Reiser, *Israeli Arms Industry*, 74.

5. Central Bureau of Statistics, *Defence Expenditure in Israel*, 30.

6. U.S. Office of Management and Budget, *Fiscal Year 2013 Historical Tables*, 47–55, 211–12.

7. "Hyperinflation: Taming the Beast," *Economist*, November 15, 1986, 64.

8. Levran and Eytan, *Middle East Military Balance, 1986*, 135, 138.

9. "Honing the Defenses with Updates," *AW&ST*, December 2, 1985, 84.

10. Gander, Ireland, and Jackson, *Modern Military Powers*, 126.

11. David A. Brown, "Israeli Air Force to Decide on F-4 Conversion by Next Year," *AW&ST*, June 22, 1987, 65; Tamir Eshel, "New Life for an Old Workhorse," *Defence Update International*, no. 81 (June/July 1987): 56.

12. "IAI Super Phantom Conversion Would Boost F-4E Performance," *AW&ST*, June 22, 1987, 66.

13. Donald E. Fink, "Le Bourget Retrospective," *AW&ST*, June 29, 1987, 11.

14. "IAI Updating F-4 Fighter with PW1120 Engine for Israeli Air Force," *AW&ST*, April 1, 1985, 52; "Israelis Modify U.S.-Built Aircraft to Improve Combat Capabilities," *AW&ST*, July 21, 1986, 52.

15. Levran and Eytan, *Middle East Military Balance, 1986*, 140.

16. "Israel Aircraft Industries Modernizing Production," *AW&ST*, March 25, 1985, 20.

17. "Pratt & Whitney Wins Battle for Lavi Engine," *Flight International*, June 20, 1981, 1951.

18. Compare photos released to *Aviation Week* and published in the December 3, 1984, issue (page 24) with those published in the issue from January 14, 1985 (page 17).

19. "Israel's Flight Test Program Will Define Weapons Complement for Multirole Combat Aircraft," *AW&ST*, March 25, 1985, 20.

20. "Israel's Flight Test Program Will Define Weapons Complement." It was later revealed that the first four prototypes were all expected to be two-seat aircraft. The fifth prototype would have been the first single-seat fighter. Shmul, Erenthal, and Attar, "Lavi Flight Control System," *International Journal of Control*, 163–64.

21. "IAI Plans Initial Two-Seat Trainer Configuration," *AW&ST*, March 25, 1985, 19.

22. "Lavi Weight Change," *AW&ST*, June 17, 1985, 75. The most visible change to the Lavi wing was the addition of an auxiliary elevon at the wing trailing edge, to provide the added control authority necessary for the elevated payloads being envisioned.

23. The maximum weight values quoted for the F-16 are for the F-16C Block 25 aircraft, which was the model in production at that time. Later Block 40 and Block 50 F-16Cs increased the maximum takeoff weight for the airplane to 42,300 lb (19,190 kg) but also required an increase in the airplane's empty weight from 15,175 lb (6,880 kg) to 19,100 lb (8,660 kg). Bonds, *Illustrated Directory of Modern Weapons*, 43; Donald and Lake, *Encyclopedia of World Military Aircraft*, 242–43.

24. The Israeli Defense Ministry didn't even bother to hold a dedicated press conference to make this startling announcement. The first time that I came across it was in an advertisement titled "Featuring the Future," sponsored by Israel Aircraft Industries and published in the June 3, 1985, edition of *Aviation Week* (pp. 112–13).

10. Inside the Department of Defense

1. Cannon, *President Reagan*, 324–25.

2. McFarlane, *Special Trust*, 248–49.

3. North, *Under Fire*, 155–56. Whatever the source of Weinberger's anti-Israel bent, it was not lost on Israel's leading officials. In one interview, senior Israeli officials reportedly described Weinberger as "a prime candidate for psychoanalysis." Lucinda Franks, "Israel after Lebanon," *New York Times Magazine*, March 25, 1984, 30–38, 66, 69.

4. The member of the National Security Council responsible for bypassing Weinberger's restrictions and seeking Israeli assistance was none other than Marine lieutenant colonel Oliver North. N. Livingstone and D. Halevy, *Inside the PLO*, 252–56.

5. Zakheim, *Flight of the Lavi*, 3.

6. Zakheim, *Flight of the Lavi*, 4.

7. Zakheim, *Flight of the Lavi*, 22, 26.

8. Zakheim, *Flight of the Lavi*, 37–47.

9. Zakheim, *Flight of the Lavi*, 58.

10. Zakheim, *Flight of the Lavi*, 79.

11. Zakheim, *Flight of the Lavi*, 62, 69.

12. Zakheim, *Flight of the Lavi*, 78.

13. Zakheim, *Flight of the Lavi*, 157.

14. Speakes and Pack, *Speaking Out*, 325.

15. Reagan, *Ronald Reagan*, 511.

16. James K. Gordon, "U.S. Defense Dept. Claims Israelis Underestimated Lavi Fighter Costs," *AW&ST*, February 10, 1986, 32–33.

17. Zakheim, *Flight of the Lavi*, 83.

18. John D. Morrocco, "GAO Report on Lavi Indicates Spending will Exceed Cap," *AW&ST*, March 2, 1987, 20–21.

19. Gordon, "U.S. Defense Dept. Claims Israelis Underestimated Lavi Fighter Costs"; "Decision to Cancel Lavi Divides Israel," *AW&ST*, September 7, 1987, 24; "Israel Claims U.S. Defense Estimate of Lavi Cost Too High," *AW&ST*, February 24, 1986, 19.

20. U.S. General Accounting Office, *Foreign Assistance: Analysis of Cost Estimates*, 25.

21. Morrocco, "GAO Report on Lavi."

11. With the Sky at Stake

1. Peter Hellman, "The Fighter of the Future," *Discover*, July 1986, 37.

2. Zakheim, *Flight of the Lavi*, 78.

3. "Israel Considers Slowdown in Lavi Program," *AW&ST*, February 10, 1986, 32.

4. Aloni and Avidror, *Hammers*, 123.

5. I. Spector, *Loud and Clear*, 287.

6. Rabinovich, *Yom Kippur War*, 33.

7. Yonay, *No Margin for Error*, 325–31.

8. "IAF Chief Defends Lavi," *Flight International*, June 7, 1986, 15.

9. Eliezer Cohen, *Israel's Best Defense*, 422.

10. Zakheim, *Flight of the Lavi*, 100.

11. Zakheim, *Flight of the Lavi*, 100.

12. Zakheim, *Flight of the Lavi*, 135.

13. Zakheim, *Flight of the Lavi*, 151.

14. David A. Brown, "U.S.-Built Flight Control System Delays First Flight of the Lavi," *AW&ST*, July 28, 1986, 19–20.

15. "Israel Demands U.S. Funds Prior to Talks on Lavi Alternatives," and "Congressmen Urge Reagan to Release Lavi Funding," *AW&ST*, July 28, 1986, 19–20.

16. Representative Mel Levine to John Poindexter, July 17, 1986, Box 91093, James R. Stark Files, Ronald Reagan Presidential Library, Simi Valley CA. The cosigners of Mel Levine's letter represented a broad, bipartisan cross-section of Congress, including Representatives Jack Kemp (R-NY), Larry Smith (D-FL), Jim Courter (R-NJ), Les Aspin (D-WI), Dante Fascell (D-FL), Ben Gilman (R-NY), and Robert Torricell (D-NJ).

17. Zakheim, *Flight of the Lavi*, 171.

18. Zakheim, *Flight of the Lavi*, 174.

19. "Israelis Split Over Lavi Costs," *Flight International*, January 12, 1985, 8.

20. Haig, *Caveat*, 341–43.

21. McFarlane, *Special Trust*, 270–71.

22. Zakheim, *Flight of the Lavi*, 175.

23. "Senate Aid Bill Would Raise Military Grants," *AW&ST*, September 22, 1986, 25.

24. "Some Comments About the Lavi," *AW&ST*, June 1, 1987, 71.

25. "McDonnell Douglas May Produce the Lavi," *Defence Update International*, no. 73 (July 1986): 59; "IAI Discusses Future Partnerships," *AW&ST*, July 28, 1986, 19; "Israel Strong on Support for IAI Lavi Program," *AW&ST*, September 22, 1986, 28.

26. David A. Brown, "Israelis Review Decisions That Led to Lavi Cancellation," *AW&ST*, September 14, 1987, 23.

27. Zakheim, *Flight of the Lavi*, 75. Reports in the October 1985 issues of both *Inside the Pentagon* and *Defense News* reported that a USAF buy of the Lavi was being evaluated as a serious possibility.

28. David A. Brown, "Israel Air Force to Decide on F-4 Conversion by Next Year," *AW&ST*, June 22, 1987, 65.

29. Tamir Eshel, "Enter the Lavi," *Defence Update International*, no. 76 (October 1986): 5.

30. Eliezer Cohen, *Israel's Best Defense*, 243. Menachem Shmul would rack up a total of five kills as a Mirage pilot, three during the Six-Day War and one each during the War of Attrition and the Yom Kippur War. Aloni, *Israeli Mirage and Nesher Ace*, 81; Aloni, *Mirage III vs. MiG-21*, 66–67.

31. "The Lavi Takes Off," *Defence Update International*, no. 79 (1987): 3; Hirsh Goodman, "The Lavi Fighter," AW&ST, June 1, 1987, 58; "Lavi First Flight," IAI video, 10:43, January 1987, https://www.youtube.com/watch?v=cT44364ODNM. A single *New York Times* article would dispute the above three sources and claim that the Lavi first flew at 10:00 a.m. on January 1, 1987. No other news source, however, could corroborate this claim. "Israeli Army Reported to Want to Scrap Lavi," *New York Times*, March 4, 1987, pt. 1, 11.

12. In the Ministry of Defense

1. "Lavi Multirole Aircraft Begins Flight Testing in Israel," AW&ST, January 12, 1987, 19.

2. "Lavi Decision Imminent," *Flight International*, June 27, 1987, 30.

3. Tabulated statistics comparing the Lavi and Zakheim's proposed alternatives were assembled from a variety of sources. Basic performance data was drawn from "Lavi or the Alternatives," *Defence Update International*, no. 79 (1987): 31, 42–44; "Lavi Weight Change," AW&ST, June 17, 1985, 75. Payload values for the U.S.-built aircraft were compiled from "Specifications: U.S. Military Aircraft," and "Specifications: U.S. Gas Turbine Engines," AW&ST, March 9, 1987, 140, 163; Bonds, *Illustrated Directory of Modern Weapons*, 43, 53–54. Note that the F-16C data listed here is for a Block 40 aircraft, the version that would have been available to Israel in the early 1990s. Israel's prior F-16C deliveries had been from Block 30 stock, which featured an empty weight of 16,972 lb (7,700 kg), and a maximum takeoff weight of 37,500 lb (17,010 kg). *Jane's All the World's Aircraft 1991–92*, 401–5.

4. Zakheim, *Flight of the Lavi*, 94.

5. Levran and Eytan, *Middle East Military Balance, 1986*, 150.

6. "Lavi, F-16 Costs Compared," AW&ST, September 7, 1987, 25.

7. Claire, *Raid on the Sun*, 114, 143.

8. Unit costs for each airplane have been adjusted for lot size, using the methods described in Hess and Romanoff, *Aircraft Airframe Cost Estimating Relationships*, 5. The basic flyaway cost for each airplane, for a three-hundred-aircraft buy, was assumed to be $17.8 million for the Lavi (based on the results of the U.S. General Accounting Office investigation), $27.6 million for the F-15E, and $16.9 million for the F-16C (based on USAF estimates for an F-16

equipped with Lavi avionics). The Lavi, of course, proved to be far more sensitive to reductions in lot size, due to the smaller number of airplanes being produced worldwide.

9. Payload values at maximum load factor are not available for the F-15E. The estimates made here assume that the airplane is limited, at maximum payload, to 7.33 g's—analogous to the performance of the F-15C. Estimates for total airframe production worldwide were placed at 1,241 for the F-15 and 2,357 for the F-16, for all aircraft due to be delivered by 1991. Obaid Younossi, Kennedy, and Graser, *Military Airframe Costs*, 87.

10. Zakheim, *Flight of the Lavi*, 227.

11. Zakheim, *Flight of the Lavi*, 207.

12. Zakheim, *Flight of the Lavi*, 213.

13. Zakheim, *Flight of the Lavi*, 226.

14. "Lavi Fighter 'Vital' to Israel," *Flight International*, March 5, 1983, 576.

15. "Lavi or Not Lavi?" *Economist*, January 10, 1987, 29.

16. Zakheim, *Flight of the Lavi*, 233.

17. "Second Lavi Prototype Enters Flight Test Program," AW&ST, April 20, 1987, 58.

18. "Second Lavi Prototype Enters Flight Test Program."

19. Attar, *Some Interesting Phenomena from Lavi Test Flights*. This document is also available through the National Technical Information Service (U.S. Department of Commerce) as NTIS #N9220849.

20. Levran and Eytan, *Middle East Military Balance, 1986*, 135–36.

21. "Israeli Army Reported to Want to Scrap Lavi," *New York Times*, March 4, 1987, pt. I, 11.

22. "Lavi or the Alternatives," 42.

23. "Israel's Angry Young Men of War," *Economist*, September 19, 1987, 54; "New Chief of Staff for the IDF," *Defence Update International*, no. 81 (June/July 1987): 3; "Senior Appointments," *Defence Update International*, no. 83 (September/October 1987): 3.

24. Congressionally authorized funding levels were tabulated from the 1982 through 1986 editions of the *Congressional Quarterly Almanac*.

25. Levran and Eytan, *Middle East Military Balance, 1986*, 135.

26. Klieman and Pedatzur, *Rearming Israel*, 67.

27. S. Naaman, "Saar-5: New Technology Missile Corvette for the Israeli Navy," *Defence Update International*, no. 82 (July/August 1987): 58.

28. Donald E. Fink, "Israel Renews Debate on Lavi Development," AW&ST, June 1, 1987, 18.

29. Fink, "Israel Renews Debate on Lavi Development," 19.

30. Fink, "Israel Renews Debate on Lavi Development," 18.

31. John H. Cushman Jr., "Israel Presses U.S. to Ease Cost of Lavi Cutoff," *New York Times*, September 29, 1987, pt. 1, 15.

32. Cushman, "Israel Presses U.S. to Ease Cost."

33. "Israel Wins U.S. Financial Concessions to Cover Possible Cancellation of Lavi," *AW&ST*, July 13, 1987, 25.

34. Zakheim, *Flight of the Lavi*, 240.

13. Broken Wings

1. Robert Rosenberg, "National Pride vs. Economics," *U.S. News & World Report*, August 31, 1987, 36.

2. Rabin, *Rabin Memoirs*, 59, 238–41, 307–9.

3. Thomas L. Friedman, "Israel Puts Off a Decision on a New Plane," *New York Times*, August 17, 1987, pt. 1, 3.

4. Michael R. Gordon, "U.S. Is Pressing Israelis to Drop Costly Jet Effort," *New York Times*, August 12, 1987, pt. 1, 1, 5.

5. Zakheim, *Flight of the Lavi*, 248.

6. Thomas L. Friedman, "Israelis Decide Not to Construct Lavi Jet Fighter," *New York Times*, August 31, 1987, pt. 1, 1, 8.

7. "Bet Shemesh Engines: A New Start," *Defence Update International*, no. 71 (May 1986): 30; "Israel Selling Bet Shemesh," *AW&ST*, December 15, 1986, 27; "News Digest," *AW&ST*, August 31, 1987, 27.

8. The explanation given by Ben Nun for the proposed truncated Lavi production run was that the Israeli air force expected to purchase the U.S.-developed Advanced Tactical Fighter (later the F-22 Raptor) in the near future and would need to make room in the budget. The F-22, however, was never offered for export—either to Israel or to any other U.S. ally. Moshe Arens to John Golan, September 29, 2013.

9. Friedman, "Israelis Decide Not to Construct Lavi Jet Fighter"; "Decision to Cancel Lavi Divides Israel," *AW&ST*, September 7, 1987, 22.

10. Friedman, "Israelis Decide Not to Construct Lavi Jet Fighter"; "Decision to Cancel Lavi Divides Israel."

11. "International Partners Sought to Complete Lavi," *AW&ST*, September 14, 1987, 24.

12. "Decision to Cancel Lavi Divides Israel."

13. Friedman, "Israelis Decide Not to Construct Lavi Jet Fighter."

14. "Major American Lavi Contractors," *AW&ST*, June 1, 1987, 60.

15. Thomas L. Friedman, "Arens Quits Israeli Cabinet Post Over Jet Decision," *New York Times*, September 3, 1987, pt. 1, 6. The *New York Times* article goes on to confidently declare that Moshe Arens's political career was effectively finished. In Israel, however, the political system is organized around the national

party, not the local politician, and Arens was still very much a member of the upper echelons of the Likud Party. Following the next round of Israeli elections in 1988, Arens would again find himself in an Israeli Cabinet position, going on to serve as minister of defense for the second time in his career.

16. "IAI Proposes Flight Test Program to Extract More Data from Lavi," and "Lavi Cancellation Sets Back Pratt's PW1120 Engine Program," AW&ST, September 7, 1987, 22–25; James J. Harford, "Israeli Aeronautics after Lavi," Aerospace America, November 1988, 8.

17. Friedman, "Israelis Decide Not to Construct Lavi Jet Fighter"; "International Partners Sought to Complete Lavi," 23; "Israeli Air Force to Replace Lavi with F-16C," AW&ST, September 14, 1987, 23.

18. "IAI Proposes Flight Test Program to Extract More Data from Lavi," 22–23.

19. "South Africa Woos Lavi Workers," and "Israelis Cancel Lavi," Flight International, September 12, 1987, 2, 8.

20. "Israel Plans to Complete Third Lavi Prototype," AW&ST, September 28, 1987, 27–28.

21. "Washington Roundup," AW&ST, March 21, 1988, 15.

22. "U.S. to Test Arrow Antitactical Missile," AW&ST, December 21, 1987, 26–27.

23. "Lavi Cancellation Sets Back Pratt's PW1120 Engine Program," 25.

24. John D. Morrocco, "U.S. to Fund Phase 2 of Israeli Theater Missile Defense Study," AW&ST, March 21, 1988, 18. Following Weinberger's resignation, the Defense Department finally did reach an agreement with its Israeli counterparts, dividing up the costs for the Arrow demonstration program on an 80/20 basis. The Arrow often served as a test bed for technology that would eventually see use elsewhere in U.S. ballistic missile defense programs. As Michael Holtcamp, the U.S. program manager for the joint effort, would later testify, for example, the Arrow missile provided the United States with the very first test data ever obtained for infrared seeker performance in an endoatmospheric interceptor. John D. Morocco, "Intercept Boosts Arrow's Prospects," AW&ST, June 20, 1994, 26.

25. Dov S. Zakheim, "Bailing Out Israel," New York Times, October 6, 1987, pt. 1, 35.

26. Zakheim's role in Weinberger's Lavi cancellation campaign would continue to sour his relations with America's Jewish community for decades to come. Never was this more evident than in March 2002, when Zakheim withdrew his name as a candidate for president of Yeshiva University. Although Yeshiva University is ostensibly an apolitical center for higher education, combining opportunities for secular scholarship with programs in Jewish religious study, there had been an overwhelming public outcry against appointing a candidate who was perceived by many to have an anti-Israel history. Ami Eden, "Defense Official Drops Out of Running to Lead Yeshiva U," Forward, March 15, 2002; Adina

Levine, "Search Committee Decisions Question Yeshiva's Devotion to Zionism," *Yeshiva University Observer*, 2002.

27. Harford, "Israeli Aeronautics after Lavi," 8.

28. "Arens Says War Proves Need for Targeting Mobile Missiles," *AW&ST*, June 24, 1991, 26.

29. Harford, "Israeli Aeronautics after Lavi," 8.

30. Norton, *Air War on the Edge*, 378.

31. U.S. General Accounting Office, *Foreign Assistance: U.S. Funds Used*, 1–3.

32. David M. North, "Lavi TD Cockpit Reflects Pilot's Combat Experience," *AW&ST*, March 25, 1991, 46–53. As part of the reduced thrust and burner temperatures employed to extend the engine's life, the PW1120 maximum turbine metal temperature was reduced under the Lavi TD aircraft from 1,780 °F to 1,760 °F (from 1,010 °C to 1,000 °C). These metal temperatures should not be confused with the gas-path temperatures in the turbine or burner, which will be much higher.

33. North, "Lavi TD Cockpit Reflects Pilot's Combat Experience."

14. Jerusalem Takes Stock

1. The original Layout 33 concept study had proposed an aircraft with a payload of no more than 12,070 lb (5,470 kg)—more than the 10,950 lb (4,970 kg) provided by the venerable A-4 Skyhawk but less than the 13,390 lb (6,070 kg) available from the Kfir, and far less than the capabilities provided by the F-16A/B models of the day. Tsach and Peled, "Evolution of the Lavi Fighter Aircraft," 831.

2. Bernard Gwertzman, "U.S. Allows Israel to Purchase Parts for New Fighter," *New York Times*, April 18, 1983, pt. 1, 1, 5.

3. Kurzman, *Soldier of Peace*, 349–50.

4. Israel eventually eliminated a total of twenty-eight missile batteries during the course of the Lebanon War. "IAF vs. SAM: 28:0," *Defence Update International*, no. 78 (December 1986): 53–55; Nordeen, *Air Warfare in the Missile Age*, 159, 161.

5. Levran and Eytan, *Middle East Military Balance, 1986*, 68.

6. Levite, *Offense and Defense in Israeli Military Doctrine*, 59.

7. Bernard Weinraub, "Plain-Spoken Hard-Liner for Israel," *New York Times*, February 15, 1983, pt. 1, 8.

8. Under the final settlement proposal agreed to by Prime Minister Ehud Barak, Israel would have ceded sovereignty over 94 percent of the territory of the West Bank and Gaza, while the map of Israel's capital, Jerusalem, would have been redrawn to permit both Israel and the Palestinian Authority to claim the same city as their respective capitals. As proposed, the borders adjoining Israel's most strategically sensitive regions, near Israeli population centers in Tel Aviv, Haifa, and Jerusalem, would have been widened to encompass existing Jewish

settlements in the West Bank. In return, Israel would have ceded sovereignty over a similar stretch of territory adjoining the densely populated Gaza Strip. Enderlin, *Shattered Dreams*, 341, 351–57.

9. Clinton, *My Life*, 944.

10. Ross, *Missing Peace*, 766.

11. In April 2002, following a particularly gruesome terrorist attack on an Israeli Passover celebration in Netanyah, Operation Defensive Shield was launched, with Israeli troops tasked to root out the terrorist training and command centers, beginning with the city of Jenin. Goldberg, *Psalm in Jenin*.

12. Yehuda Amichai, "And Who Will Remember the Rememberers?" in *Open Closed Open*, 171. A veteran of Israel's War of Independence, Amichai is widely recognized as the most important and influential Israeli poet of the past half century.

13. Shoebat, *Why We Want to Kill You*, 21.

14. Post, *Mind of the Terrorist*, 28.

15. James J. Harford, "Israeli Aeronautics after Lavi," *Aerospace America*, November 1988, 8–10.

16. Klieman and Pedatzur, *Rearming Israel*, 210.

17. John D. Morrocco, "IAI Restructures, Seeks Civil Work," *AW&ST*, June 6, 1994, 70–71.

18. Israel Aircraft Industries' turnaround was remarkable enough to earn its president and CEO, Moshe Keret, a Laureate Award from *Aviation Week*. "1999 Aviation Week & Space Technology Laureate Awards," *AW&ST*, April 10, 2000, 15.

19. Klieman and Pedatzur, *Rearming Israel*, 210.

20. "World News Roundup," *AW&ST*, July 12, 1999, 19; "World News Roundup," *AW&ST*, January 10, 2000, 20; "World News Roundup," *AW&ST*, July 11, 2005, 20.

21. "Israel to Buy Fewer, More Advanced F-16s," *AW&ST*, April 11, 1988, 18.

22. For a brief time there was even talk about upgrading the A-4's old J52 engines to the newer J52-409 model. The newer version could deliver up to 12,000 lb (53.4 kN) thrust, 800 lb (3.6 kN) more than the previously employed model. These plans were eventually shelved due to budget pressures. "Industry Observer," *AW&ST*, April 11, 1988, 9.

23. "90 Years of Perfection," *Defence Update International*, no. 88 (June 1988): 4–8.

24. Robert Ropelewski, "Israel Wary of High Technology Weapons Buildup in the Middle East," *AW&ST*, July 25, 1988, 44–45; David A. Brown, "Aircraft Modernization Efforts Given Top Priority at Israel Aircraft Industries," *AW&ST*, September 10, 1990, 75–76; Michael Mecham, "Initial Phantom 2000 Operations Validate Israel's F-4 Update Program," *AW&ST*, June 17, 1991, 81, 85.

25. Mecham, "Initial Phantom 2000 Operations."

26. "IAI's Elta Div. Seeks EW Export Markets," *AW&ST*, September 26, 1988, 99.

27. The relevant performance demonstrated under the first two prototypes, in comparison, had comprised a minimum flight speed of 110 knots, a 23° maximum angle of attack, and a maximum load factor of 7.5 g's. Shmul, Erenthal, and Attar, "Lavi Flight Control System," *International Journal of Control*, 164, 178, 180.

28. Shmul, Erenthal, and Attar, "Lavi Flight Control System," *Active Control Technology*, 5–3.

29. U.S. General Accounting Office, *Israel*, 6.

30. Klieman and Pedatzur, *Rearming Israel*, 95.

31. "Israel Takes Delivery of U.S. Block 10 F-16s," AW&ST, August 1, 1994, 65.

32. David A. Fulghum, "USAF to Sell Surplus F-16s," AW&ST, August 22, 1994, 58.

33. The SPS-2000 electronic warfare systems installed in Israel's Peace Marble 3 F-16D aircraft would later be upgraded to the same SPS-2100 standard as Israel's F-15I fighters. Norton, *Air War on the Edge*, 334.

34. "Israel Tests Night F/A-18," AW&ST, March 15, 1993, 31.

35. "Israel Sees F-16ES Plans," AW&ST, January 17, 1994, 69.

36. "News Breaks," AW&ST, May 16, 1994, 17.

37. "Filter Center," AW&ST, October 17, 1994, 53; Davies, *Boeing F-15E Strike Eagle*, 181–83.

38. John D. Morrocco, "F-16 Scores Israeli Win in Fighter Export Battle," AW&ST, July 26, 1999, 29–30; "World News Roundup," AW&ST, September 10, 2001, 25.

39. The F-16I was also distinct enough from its predecessors to earn it a new designation in Israeli air force service: Soufa (storm). Previous Israeli F-16C/D models had carried the designation of Barak (lightning). Israel's F-16A/B aircraft, meanwhile, were designated by the name Netz (hawk). "F16I: The 'Storm' Is Coming to Israel," AW&ST, December 22, 2003, GMS6–GMS10.

40. "F16I: The 'Storm' Is Coming to Israel," GMS6; Norton, *Air War on the Edge*, 336.

41. Projections of Israeli air force inventories at the turn of the century were tabulated primarily from annual reports published by Israel's Jaffee Center for Strategic Studies: Levran and Eytan, *Middle East Military Balance, 1988–1989*, 192–93; Heller and Shapir, *Middle East Military Balance 1996*, 198; Brom and Shapir, *Middle East Military Balance 1999–2000*, 227. Other published reports, however, have differed from those of the Jaffee Center regarding the number of A-4 Skyhawks that remained in active service, with some suggesting that these aircraft had been retired at a more rapid rate. See, for example, David A. Fulghum, "Fighter Makers Clash as Israel Nears Decision," AW&ST, January 17, 1994, 68. The estimates tabulated here represent an average between these two assessments.

42. The Block 40 F-16C/D aircraft delivered to Israel in the early 1990s, like the F-16I, had featured a number of structural modifications to allow them to

carry heavier payloads. These included enlarged wheels and tires, which in turn required that the landing-gear doors feature a slight bulge. For comparison purposes, the Block 40 aircraft delivered for U.S. Air Force duty featured a maximum takeoff weight of 42,300 lb (19,190 kg) and an empty weight of 19,100 lb (8,660 kg) when fitted with an FII0-100 engine. The further increase in maximum takeoff weight provided for under the F-161 was needed to accommodate the conformal fuel tanks (900 lb / 410 kg), and their fuel (3,050 lb / 1,380 kg). "FI61: The 'Storm' Is Coming to Israel," GMS4; Norton, *Air War on the Edge*, 334–35; Donald and Lake, *Encyclopedia of World Military Aircraft*, 242–43.

43. Beginning in fiscal year 2000, U.S. economic aid to Israel was slowly phased out, at a rate of $120 million per year. Under an agreement reached with the House Appropriations Committee in January 1998, $60 million in military aid to Israel would be added during each year of the phaseout. Mark, *Israel*, 3, 12–13; Central Bureau of Statistics, *Defence Expenditure in Israel*, 30.

44. GDP comparisons for the 1980s were drawn from *Military Balance 1986–1987*. Other GDP comparisons that might be listed would include the AMX light attack aircraft, which was developed during the late 1970s as part of a cooperative effort between Italy and Brazil. Collectively, the two partners boasted a GDP that was 26 times the size of Israel's economy during the mid-1980s. Taiwan, on the other hand, enjoyed a GDP that was only 2.8 times the size of Israel's but, as is alluded to elsewhere, was aiming for a more modest indigenous aircraft. Japan, which developed the F-2 as a derivative from the F-16 fighter, sported a GDP that by the mid-1980s, was 55 times the size of Israel's. India, meanwhile, with a GDP that was over 8 times the size of Israel's, would require more than twenty years to develop its Light Combat Aircraft (later renamed the Tejas) into a production-ready fighter.

45. Saab has been somewhat cagey about releasing figures for the combat radius for the JAS-39.It has, however, released values for the ferry range, which, when compared with the equivalent ferry range for the F-16A, suggest a maximum combat radius of roughly 680 nm (1260 km) in a hi-lo-hi attack mission. Empty weight for the JAS-39A Gripen is 14,600 lb (6,620 kg), with a maximum takeoff weight placed at 27,498 lb (12,470 kg). While the empty weight is only slightly lower than that of the Lavi, the maximum takeoff weight is significantly less, another indication that the Gripen was sized to fit an air-to-air role, with a secondary attack capability. Keijsper, *Saab Gripen*, 118.

46. Vital statistics for Taiwan's Ching-Kuo are even more difficult to come by than those for the JAS-39 Gripen. Empty weight for the airplane is quoted as 14,300 lb (6,490 kg), with a maximum takeoff weight placed at 27,000 lb (12,250 kg). *Jane's All the World's Aircraft 1997–98*, 504.

47. Arens, *Broken Covenant*, 12.

15. America in the Mirror

1. Haig, *Caveat*, 146.
2. Weinberger, *Fighting for Peace*, 376.
3. Tanter, *Who's At the Helm?*, 3.
4. Ronald Reagan, "Recognizing the Israeli Asset," *Washington Post*, August 15, 1979, pt. 1, 25.
5. Puschel, *U.S.-Israeli Strategic Cooperation*, 39–50; Haig, *Caveat*, 328–29.
6. Puschel, *U.S.-Israeli Strategic Cooperation*, 81.
7. Puschel, *U.S.-Israeli Strategic Cooperation*, 94–95.
8. Puschel, *U.S.-Israeli Strategic Cooperation*, 96, 106.
9. Defense Department purchases from Israeli suppliers during the late 1980s have been tabulated from Puschel, *U.S.-Israeli Strategic Cooperation*, 96; Gold, *Israel as an American Non-NATO Ally*, 24, 27.
10. Gold, *Israel as an American Non-NATO Ally*, 6.
11. Gold, *Israel as an American Non-NATO Ally*, 27.
12. *Israel Line* (newsletter, Consulate General of Israel, New York), December 1992.
13. GDP comparisons were drawn for the year 1985 from *Military Balance 1986–1987*.
14. Dershowitz, *Reagan Administration and Israel*, 10.
15. Klieman and Pedatzur, *Rearming Israel*, 181–82, 193.
16. U.S. General Accounting Office, *Foreign Assistance: Analysis of Cost Estimates*, 25.
17. In a report to Congress from the comptroller general, the F/A-18 development effort had been placed at some $2.048 billion, in 1978 dollars. U.S. General Accounting Office, *Need to Demonstrate F-18 Naval Strike Fighter Weapon System Effectiveness*, 18.
18. The FS-X development effort was estimated to cost some $3.27 billion in 1995 dollars, with a unit flyaway cost of $56 million. Michael Mecham, "Japan's FS-X Fights Costs," *AW&ST*, January 23, 1995, 32–33.
19. McFarlane, *Special Trust*, 317.
20. Shultz, *Turmoil and Triumph*, 598.
21. McFarlane, *Special Trust*, 324.
22. Reagan, *Ronald Reagan*, 410.
23. Cannon, *President Reagan*, 325.

Appendix 1

1. McGeer and Kroo, "Fundamental Comparison."
2. R. Weiss and S. Aloni, *IAI Kfir in IAF Service*, 10–11.

3. Michael A. Dornheim, "X-31, F-16 MATV, F/A-18 HARV Explore Diverse Missions," AW&ST, April 18, 1994, 46–47.

4. Shanker and Malmuth, "Computational Treatment"; Batina, "Unsteady Transonic Flow Calculations."

5. Er-El and Seginer, "Vortex Trajectories and Breakdown"; Er-El, "Effect of Wing/Canard Interference."

6. This was an aspect that the Israelis were already familiar with from their flight experience with the Kfir. "'It's Like Lightning,' Conversation with a Kfir Pilot," *Defence Update International*, no. 55 (1984): 46–47.

7. Tsach and Peled, "Evolution of the Lavi Fighter Aircraft," 833.

8. The two scale models used for IAI's wind tunnel tests were built in the United States by Dynamic Engineering Corporation of Newport News, Virginia. "Israel Uses Lavi Model for Wind Tunnel Tests," AW&ST, December 2, 1985, 175.

9. Shmul, Erenthal, and Attar, "Lavi Flight Control System," *International Journal of Control*, 177.

10. "Attack Deterrent," AW&ST, April 8, 1985, 41.

11. Estimates for the effect of canard-wing interaction on aerodynamic performance were derived from Tu, *Numerical Study*; Rom, Er-El, and Gordon, *Measurements of the Aerodynamic Characteristics*; Rom, Melamed, and Almosnino, "Experimental and Nonlinear Vortex Lattice Method Results."

Appendix 2

1. Raymer, *Aircraft Design*, 413.

2. The Lavi development team used the moving-base flight simulator at the Netherlands National Aerospace Laboratory (NLR) as their primary site for evaluating the Lavi flight control software during this preflight development phase. Comparisons with equivalent results from a fixed-base simulator demonstrated that significantly better results could be obtained by fine-tuning their flight control software using the moving-base facility. Shmul, Erenthal, and Attar, "Lavi Flight Control System," *International Journal of Control*, 170–73.

3. Medina and Shahaf, "Post-Stall Characteristics."

4. Shmul, Erenthal, and Attar, "Lavi Flight Control System," *International Journal of Control*, 159.

5. Shmul, Erenthal, and Attar, "Lavi Flight Control System," *International Journal of Control*, 164.

6. Shmul, Erenthal, and Attar, "Lavi Flight Control System," *International Journal of Control*, 164.

7. Note that per these hand calculations, the "nominal" or average static margin for the F-16 would come out to be -4.5 percent—equivalent to the value of -4 percent quoted for the F-16 in the open literature. Nguyen et al., *Simulator Study*, 11.

8. Tamir Eshel, "Enter the Lavi," *Defence Update International*, no. 76 (October 1986): 7.

9. John Farley, "Vision of the Future," *Flight International*, January 23–29, 1991, 25.

10. David A. Brown, "U.S.-Built Flight Control System Delays First Flight of Lavi," *AW&ST*, July 28, 1986, 18–19.

11. William B. Scott, "Fighter, Helicopter Test Pilots Challenge Cockpit Design Concepts," *AW&ST*, November 16, 1987, 65; Peter Hellman, "The Fighter of the Future," *Discover*, July 1986, 37. In comparison, both the F-16A and Sweden's JAS-39 Gripen relied on a system of three flight control computers, rather than four, and those on the F-16A were analog rather than digital.

12. Shmul, Erenthal, and Attar, "Lavi Flight Control System," *International Journal of Control*, 164–65.

13. "IAI Bases Lavi Fighter Production on 300 Aircraft Procurement," *AW&ST*, July 18, 1983, 23.

14. Landfield and Rajkovic, "Canard/Tail Comparison."

15. "Lavi or the Alternatives," *Defence Update International*, no. 79 (1987): 43.

Appendix 3

1. "Lavi Contracts with U.S. Companies Detailed," *AW&ST*, January 21, 1985, 112; Hirsch Goodman, "The Lavi Fighter," *AW&ST*, January 1, 1987, 70.

2. "Honing the Defenses with Updates," *AW&ST*, December 2, 1985, 80.

3. David A. Brown, "Israelis Stress Need for U.S. Aid to Complete Lavi Development," *AW&ST*, March 25, 1985, 19–20.

4. Brown, "Israelis Stress Need for U.S. Aid."

5. "Honing the Defenses with Updates," 88.

6. Younossi, Kennedy, and Graser, *Military Airframe Costs*, 14, 87.

7. Hoskin and Baker, *Composite Materials for Aircraft Structures.*

8. Segal, "Supportability of Composite Airframes."

9. Shirk, Hertz, and Weisshaar, "Aeroelastic Tailoring."

10. "IAI Lavi: Custom-Built for Israel," *Flight International*, July 30, 1983, 236–37.

11. Lorell, *Use of Prototypes*, 34.

12. Pifko and Eidinoff, "Computational Structures Technology at Grumman," 405, 407.

13. Don Linn, "Douglas A-4 Skyhawk," *Airpower*, July 1991, 10–55.

14. *Jane's All the World's Aircraft 1991–92*, 401–5.

15. Lorell, *Use of Prototypes*, 53.

16. David M. North, "Lavi TD Cockpit Reflects Pilot's Combat Experience," *AW&ST*, March 25, 1991, 46.

Appendix 4

1. Care should be taken to recall that at the time that the Lavi engine selection was made, many of the engine variants that we today see in widespread service were either still under development or were no more than a distant dream. The F414, for example, would not enter into development for another decade, when the U.S. Navy launched its F/A-18E/F Super Hornet program. Similarly, the F110 engine, which would later go on to power Israeli F-16cs during the latter 1980s, was not even in the planning stages in 1982. Finally, the more advanced, higher-thrust versions of the F100, including the F100-PW-229 that would power Israeli F-15I's and F-16I's during the 1990s, were still in the earliest phases of conceptual design when the Lavi engine choice was announced. The most advanced version of the F100 that was available at the time that the Lavi engine was selected was the F100-PW-220.

2. Pushpindar Singh and Paul Mann, "LCA's First Flight Slips to Mid-1997," AW&ST, December 2, 1996, 52–53; Pushpindar Singh, "U.S. Nuclear Sanctions Could Kill India's LCA," AW&ST, July 20, 1998, 51; Michael Mecham, "HAL Wants Global Reach, but Not as Private Entity," AW&ST, March 11, 2002, 68; Neelam Matthews, "Second LCA Prototype Begins Flight Tests," AW&ST, August 5, 2002, 32–33.

3. St. Peter, History of Aircraft Turbine Engine Development, 89–103.

4. Kay, Turbojet History and Development, 2:105–14.

5. St. Peter, History of Aircraft Turbine Engine Development, 180.

6. Kay, Turbojet History and Development, 1:112–15; St. Peter, History of Aircraft Turbine Engine Development, 184.

7. St. Peter, History of Aircraft Turbine Engine Development, 280.

8. Gething, Modern Fighting Aircraft, 22.

9. Jane's All the World's Aircraft 1988–89, 733.

10. Pratt & Whitney's PWA 1480 alloy was the first single crystal alloy to see operational service, entering production on the JT9D-7R4 commercial aircraft engine in 1979. The alloy featured a melting point that was 50 °F higher than its directionally solidified predecessor, PWA 1422. This same technology was subsequently applied to Pratt & Whitney's military product line, including the Improved Life Core developed for the F100-220, as well as the PW1120 that powered the Lavi. Jerry Mayfield, "Single Crystal Technology Use Starting," AW&ST, October 1, 1979, 69–71, 73.

11. St. Peter, History of Aircraft Turbine Engine Development, 314–17.

12. Gunston, Development of Jet and Turbine Aero Engines, 176.

13. Performance parameters for the various engines have been tabulated at static sea level conditions. It should also be pointed out that the J79 variant listed, the J79-J1E, was the version used in Israel's Kfir C2 fighters. This version

was derived from the J79-GE-17 previously used in the F-4E Phantom and did not include the "combat plus" modifications for added engine thrust that were incorporated into later versions, as used under the Kfir C7. "Specifications: U.S. Gas Turbine Engines," *AW&ST*, March 9, 1987, 164–66; "Powerplants," *Defence Update International*, no. 55 (1984): 22–23.

14. "Specifications: U.S. Gas Turbine Engines"; "Powerplants."

15. Richardson, *Modern Fighting Aircraft*, 28; Mattingly, Heiser and Daley, *Aircraft Engine Design*, 303.

16. The range estimates provided here were based on a simplified mission profile evaluation for an aircraft sized around each engine alternative, carrying two 2,000 lb (910 kg) bombs, two AIM-9L Sidewinder missiles, and a fully loaded cannon.

17. "Lavi or the Alternatives," *Defence Update International*, no. 79 (1987): 34.

18. Eliot Cohen, *Gulf War Air Power Survey*, vol. 5, pt. 1, 651.

19. Klieman and Pedatzur, *Rearming Israel*, 98.

20. St. Peter, *History of Aircraft Turbine Engine Development*, 315.

21. Drewes, *Air Force and the Great Engine War*, 60.

22. Drewes, *Air Force and the Great Engine War*, xii.

23. "PW1120 Tests Planned in F-4 Phantom," *AW&ST*, December 16, 1985, 58.

24. Gunston, *World Encyclopaedia of Aero Engines*, 140.

25. *Great Book of Modern Warplanes*, 547.

26. Zipkin, *PW1120*, 2.

27. "Asia Specialist Cites Chinese Military Buildup," *AW&ST*, July 15, 1985, 24; "Decisions Near on Engine Selection for Range of International Fighters," *AW&ST*, August 4, 1986, 107–9; "News Digest," *AW&ST*, January 12, 1987, 33; "Industry Observer," *AW&ST*, March 2, 1987, 13.

28. It has been reported that after the United States had made it clear that no export licenses would be forthcoming for an American engine, three prototypes of China's proposed next-generation fighter were nonetheless constructed in the late 1980s, powered by Russian engines. This program would eventually be abandoned, however, in favor of renewed development of the J-10 fighter. David A. Fulghum, "China Pursuing Two-Fighter Plan," *AW&ST*, March 27, 1995, 44.

29. "Israeli Industry Reworks Goals in Wake of Lavi," *AW&ST*, March 14, 1988, 59; "Snecma to Deliver Atar 9K50 Powerplants for Use in Prototypes of Upgraded Kfir," *AW&ST*, October 30, 1989, 19; *Jane's All the World's Aircraft 1991–92*, 147.

Appendix 5

1. "Israel Explores Participation in U.S. Strategic Defense Initiative," *AW&ST*, June 17, 1985, 97; "Cost Trends for Fighter Avionics," *AW&ST*, December 2, 1985,

132; Michael A. Dornheim, "Lockheed Team Will Test ATF Cockpit in Boeing 757 Flying Laboratory," AW&ST, November 10, 1986, 23.

2. Tamir Eshel, "New Life for an Old Workhorse," *Defence Update International*, no. 81 (June/July 1987): 56; Hirsch Goodman, "The Lavi Fighter," AW&ST, June 1, 1987, 68.

3. *Jane's Avionics 1992–93*, 230.

4. Peter Hellman, "The Fighter of the Future," *Discover*, July 1986, 42; "Filter Center," AW&ST, May 27, 1985, 125.

5. Goodman, "Lavi Fighter," 69.

6. David A. Brown, "Combined Radar, ECM Functions Will Enhance Lavi Survivability," AW&ST, August 25, 1986, 111.

7. David A. Brown, "U.S. Flight Control System Delays First Flight of Lavi," AW&ST, July 28, 1986, 19.

8. Hellman, "Fighter of the Future," 68.

9. Goodman, "Lavi Fighter," 56, 68–69; David Hughes, "Company Bases Embedded System Specification Tools on Lavi Work," AW&ST, February 15, 1988, 92.

10. Brown, "U.S. Flight Control System"; Brown, "Combined Radar, ECM Functions," 113. Jovial was named after its developer, Jules Schwartz, who first developed Jovial as a derivative of Algol (the "international algorithmic language") in the 1970s. The new programming language saw use in U.S. avionics applications during the late 1970s and early 1980s, until it was displaced by Ada per government decree in the 1980s.

11. Hughes, "Company Bases Embedded System Specification Tools."

12. Beiser, "Lavi Avionics Development Methodology," 118.

13. Beiser, "Lavi Avionics Development Methodology," 118; "Electronic Intelligence," AW&ST, August 15, 1988, 99. Among the projects that IAI has reportedly applied the statecharts method to has been the development of avionics suites for their next generation of UAVs (unmanned air vehicles).

14. Brown, "Combined Radar, ECM Functions," 111.

15. Brown, "Combined Radar, ECM Functions," 113. Some sources mistakenly refer to the EL/M-2032 as being the "Lavi radar." The radar actually intended for the Lavi, however, was the EL/M-2035, from which the 2032 model was developed as a more compact derivative. The two radar sets share many common elements, including the same radar antenna. Where they differ is in their respective size, power, and range of operation, with the EL/M-2032 estimated to have a target tracking range of just over 16 nm (30 km), while the EL/M-2035 has a reported tracking range in excess of 25 nm (46 km). *Jane's Avionics 1992–93*, 38.

16. *Jane's Avionics 1992–93*, 38; Goodman, "Lavi Fighter," 57.

17. Hellman, "Fighter of the Future," 37, 39.

18. Goodman, "Lavi Fighter"; Brown, "Combined Radar, ECM Functions," 113.

19. David M. North, "Lavi TD Cockpit Reflects Pilots' Combat Experience," AW&ST, March 25, 1991, 47.

20. David A. Brown, "Aircraft Modernization Efforts Given Top Priority at Israel Aircraft Industries," AW&ST, September 10, 1990, 75–76.

21. Michael A. Dornheim, "Global Defense Cutbacks Stiffen Competition for Upgrading F-5s," AW&ST, July 22, 1991, 56–57.

22. Michael A. Dornheim, "Romania Gets Upgraded MiG," AW&ST, September 16, 1996, 72.

23. Gander, Ireland, and Jackson, *Modern Military Powers*, 138.

24. Hellman, "Fighter of the Future," 42.

25. Ball, *Fundamentals of Aircraft Combat Survivability Analysis*, 271–76.

26. Ball, *Fundamentals of Aircraft Combat Survivability Analysis*, 279.

27. Ball, *Fundamentals of Aircraft Combat Survivability Analysis*, 282.

28. Ball, *Fundamentals of Aircraft Combat Survivability Analysis*, 282–83.

29. Brown, "Combined Radar, ECM Functions," 111–13.

30. Brown, "Combined Radar, ECM Functions," 111–13. Conventional computer chip architecture employs a single layer of semiconductor, usually silicon, imprinted on the surface of the chip. Dense CMOS architecture, such as that found on the Lavi, alternates layers of semiconductor with layers of metal oxide, which acts as an insulator, to produce a computer chip that is two or three layers deep. This technique produces not only a smaller computer chip but, since the electrical impulses have a shorter distance to travel, a faster chip as well.

31. Philip J. Klass, "Israel's EW Firms Go Head-to-Head," AW&ST, September 11, 1995, 71.

32. "Israel's Flight Test Program Will Define Weapons Complement for Multirole Combat Aircraft," AW&ST, March 25, 1985, 60; Goodman, "Lavi Fighter," 56; Scott, "Fighter, Helicopter Test Pilots Challenge Cockpit Design Concepts."

33. Gunston, *Encyclopedia of World Air Power*, 178.

34. North, "Lavi TD Cockpit Reflects Pilots' Combat Experience," 46.

35. North, "Lavi TD Cockpit Reflects Pilots' Combat Experience," 47–52; John Farley, "Vision of the Future," *Flight International*, January 23–29, 1991, 23–24. The Lavi nose wheel could pivot up to 35° when taxiing the airplane.

36. Goodman, "Lavi Fighter," 69; Hellman, "Fighter of the Future," 44.

37. Hellman, "Fighter of the Future," 44; Farley, "Vision of the Future," 24; North, "Lavi TD Cockpit Reflects Pilots' Combat Experience," 52.

38. North, "Lavi TD Cockpit Reflects Pilots' Combat Experience," 52; "Lavi: The Next Lion," *Defence Update International*, no. 55 (1984): 35; "Israel's Flight Test Program Will Define Weapons Complement."

39. The Europeans also attempted to duplicate Israel's success with combining a helmet-mounted sight and display, with mixed results. Swedish developers ran into difficulty achieving the degree of miniaturization necessary to make a helmet display system practical and ultimately shelved plans for developing their own, opting instead to adapt the Striker helmet-mounted sight and display, developed for the Eurofighter Typhoon. The first Gripen fighters to be equipped with the system were delivered to South Africa in 2008. The French Rafale and the Eurofighter Typhoon, meanwhile, did not incorporate a helmet-mounted sight in production fighters until 2009. Keijsper, *Saab Gripen*, 88–89, 137; Williams, *Superfighters*, 58, 103, 142–43.

40. "VTAS Sight Fielded, Shelved in 1970s," AW&ST, October 23, 1995, 52.

41. Eric J. Lerner, "Toward the Omnipotent Pilot," *Aerospace America*, October 1986, 18–22.

42. "Filter Center," AW&ST, April 27, 1987, 165.

43. "Elbit's Helmet Mounted Sight," *Defence Update International*, no. 71 (May 1986): 31; "Avionics Companies Seek Greater Collaboration," AW&ST, June 22, 1987, 30.

44. Michael A. Dornheim, "U.S. Fighters to Get Helmet Displays after 2000," AW&ST, October 23, 1995, 48.

45. Goodman, "Lavi Fighter," 69–70.

46. Stanley W. Kandebo, "Navy to Evaluate Agile Eye Helmet-Mounted Display System," AW&ST, August 15, 1988, 94–99; "Filter Center," AW&ST, May 15, 1989, 69; Breck W. Henderson, "F-22 First U.S. Tactical Aircraft to Use True, All-Glass Cockpit," AW&ST, May 20, 1991, 52–53.

47. Kandebo, "Navy to Evaluate," 94–99; "Filter Center," AW&ST, May 15, 1989, 69; Henderson, "F-22 First U.S. Tactical Aircraft," 52–53.

48. Kandebo, "Navy to Evaluate"; Breck W. Henderson, "Kaiser Improves Helmet-Mounted Display to Boost Pilot's Kill Capability," AW&ST, June 19, 1989, 119–21.

49. Stanley W. Kandebo, "Advanced Helmet in U.S. Tests," AW&ST, March 27, 2000, 56–57.

50. Davies, *Boeing F-15E Strike Eagle*, 183.

51. Davies, *Boeing F-15E Strike Eagle*, 183. Technology, of course, stands still for no one. In 1989, for example, researchers at Israel's Weizmann Institute of Science announced that they had developed a new holographic display technology for use in helmet-mounted systems that promised to increase the available field of view by a factor of three over existing lenses. This technology, or its close cousins, will no doubt go on to equip the next generation of Israeli warplanes. "Filter Center," AW&ST, April 17, 1989, 59.

52. An even more sophisticated version of the joint helmet-mounted cueing system is slated for introduction on the F-35 Joint Strike Fighter, which is expected to field the first such helmet to have a binocular display, providing a full, panoramic 100 x 40 degree field of view. A capability of this magnitude is expected to ultimately supersede the need for the traditional head-up display, which is expected to be eliminated under this aircraft. David Hughes, "Aiming for More," *AW&ST*, August 16, 2004, 28–29.

53. For additional examples of U.S. weapons technology that benefited from Israeli experience throughout the 1980s and 1990s, see Eshel, "New Life for an Old Workhorse"; James K. Gordon, "U.S., Israel Attempt to Expand Research Cooperation," *AW&ST*, June 16, 1986, 31; Michael Melham, "Navy Evaluates Israeli R & D Programs for Use on U.S. Weapon Systems," *AW&ST*, June 1, 1987, 21.

54. Weizman, *On Eagles' Wings*, 124.

Appendix 6

1. *Jane's All the World's Aircraft 1991–92*, 405; John D. Morrocco, "Funding Cuts May Limit Carrier Air Wings to 16 A-12s," *AW&ST*, October 1, 1990, 18–19.

2. "Tactical Bombing of Iraqi Forces Outstripped Value of Strategic Hits, Analyst Contends," *AW&ST*, January 27, 1992, 62–63.

3. Eliot Cohen, *Gulf War Air Power Survey*, vol. 2, pt. 2, 148.

4. McKinnon, *Bullseye*, 80, 173.

5. JDAM kits employ global positioning signals, emitted by satellites, to provide them with guidance to a predetermined set of coordinates, rather than employing their own internal imaging systems or inertial navigation, as previous generations of precision-guided munitions had done. First introduced into U.S. service in 1999, the JDAM kits made it possible to retrofit existing iron bombs with a precision strike capability at a far more affordable cost.

6. "Lavi or the Alternatives," *Defence Update International*, no. 79 (1987): 42. Under the original, F404-powered design, the Lavi had been slated for only four hardpoints under its wings. "Lavi: The Next Lion," *Defence Update International*, no. 55 (1984): 38; Hirsch Goodman, "The Lavi Fighter," *AW&ST*, June 1, 1987, 58.

7. Nixon, *Transonic Aerodynamics*, 179.

8. Goodman, "Lavi Fighter," 54.

9. "U.S. Nears Lavi Transfer Approval," *AW&ST*, January 10, 1983, 21.

10. McKinnon, *Bullseye*, 170.

11. Gander, Ireland, and Jackson, *Modern Military Powers*, 121.

12. Gander, Ireland, and Jackson, *Modern Military Powers*, 115.

13. "Marietta to Produce Israeli Standoff Weapon," *AW&ST*, February 29, 1988, 33; "Have Nap Extends USAF's Reach," *Security Affairs*, February 1992, 4–5.

14. John D. Morrocco, "Israeli Have Nap Eyed as TSSAM Alternative," AW&ST, June 6, 1994, 79–80.

15. David A. Fulghum, "TSSAM Follow-On to Take Shape This Year," AW&ST, February 27, 1995, 51; John D. Morrocco, "Rafael Offers New Missile Upgrades," AW&ST, June 26, 1995, 25.

16. Bonds, Illustrated Directory of Modern Weapons, 121.

17. "News Digest," AW&ST, April 22, 1985, 30.

18. Tamir Eshel, "Enter the Lavi," Defence Update International, no. 76 (October 1986): 5.

19. Peter Hellman, "The Fighter of the Future," Discover, July 1986, 38.

20. Jeffrey L. Ethell, "Radar Combat and the Illusion of Invincibility," Aerospace America, January 1990, 16.

21. Nordeen, Fighters over Israel, 200.

22. Bonds, Illustrated Directory of Modern Weapons, 114–15, 231.

23. Michael Dornheim and David Hughes, "U.S. Intensifies Efforts to Meet Missile Threat," AW&ST, October 16, 1995, 37, 39.

24. "Python Capable, But Not for U.S.," AW&ST, October 16, 1995, 49.

25. David Hughes, "Luftwaffe MiG Pilots Effective with Archer," AW&ST, October 16, 1995, 39.

26. David A. Fulghum, "Finally, Pentagon Plans to Tap AIM-9X Builder," AW&ST, December 2, 1996, 21.

27. Dornheim and Hughes, "U.S. Intensifies Efforts," 36.

28. "Python Capable, But Not for U.S."

29. Fulghum, "Finally, Pentagon Plans to Tap," 23.

30. Anderegg, Sierra Hotel, 32.

31. Anderegg, Sierra Hotel, 10–11.

32. "Lavi Engine to Be Selected in Mid-May," AW&ST, March 30, 1981, 21.

33. The Barak (lightning) missile was developed for the Israeli navy to defend against low-flying antiship missiles, such as the French Exocet. As such it featured an extremely sensitive radar and a high rate of turn, all of which were packaged into a small 215 lb (98 kg) missile. The experience gained in developing this weapon could potentially have been invaluable in fielding an Israeli-developed, radar-guided air-to-air weapon. "IAI Develops Advanced Radar for Barak Vertical Launch System," AW&ST, April 15, 1985, 74.

34. John D. Morrocco, "Rafael Unveils Versatile 'Derby' Beyond-Visual Range Missile," AW&ST, May 7, 2001, 33.

35. David A. Fulghum and John D. Morrocco, "Israel Air Force to Grow in Size, Power and Range," AW&ST, April 10, 2000, 64. The Python 5 missile was officially unveiled at the 2003 Paris Airshow, where it was confirmed for the first time that the new missile would incorporate an Israeli-developed infrared

imaging seeker, similar to the one planned for the AIM-9X. This improved seeker technology had been the only remaining element for which the AIM-9X had been expected to have an advantage over the previous Python 4. At the time that it was unveiled, the Python 5 was already in low rate production, with operational service in the Heyl Ha'Avir slated for 2005. Combining its advanced seeker technology with the longer range and higher speed afforded by the Python rocket motor, the Python 5 has all but guaranteed that the Heyl Ha'Avir will continue to field the world's most lethal air-to-air missile for many years to come. Douglas Barrie and David A. Fulghum, "Double Vision: Israel Unveils Dual-Waveband I2R Dogfight Missile," AW&ST, June 23, 2003, 41.

36. Ethell, "Radar Combat," 16.

37. Ethell, "Radar Combat," 16. Burton, *Letting Combat Results Shape*. No stranger to controversy, Colonel Burton was widely known for his criticism of the U.S. Defense Department acquisition process. His findings on air-to-air missile reliability and kill rates were declassified in January 1987 and presented in hearings before the U.S. Congress in June of that year. Burton, *Pentagon Wars*, 21, 275.

38. "Commercial Operators Seek to Counter Growing Heat-Seeking Missile Threat," AW&ST, September 19, 1988, 43.

39. All of the BVR air-to-air kills were made by AIM-7 Sparrow missiles. The AIM-120 was not yet widely available at the time of the Gulf War. This kill total includes five helicopters shot down by fixed-wing, coalition aircraft, although it does not include another three Iraqi aircraft that flew into the ground while attempting to evade coalition fighters. In contrast, only one Iraqi fighter could be credited with a kill: a MiG-25 that shot down a U.S. Navy F/A-18 that was performing an attack mission during the first day of the air campaign. Eliot Cohen, *Gulf War Air Power Survey*, vol. 2, pt. 2, 113; Eliot Cohen, *Gulf War Air Power Survey*, vol. 5, pt. 1, 653–54.

40. U.S. Navy F-14s had similar long-range radar capabilities but had been intended to play a fleet air defense role rather than to secure air superiority across a crowded battlefield. The navy aircraft therefore lacked the electronic interrogation tools that the F-15 could employ to identify targets that failed to respond to a friendly IFF query.

41. O'Rourke, *Iraq War*, 55–57.

42. Cooling, *Case Studies in the Achievement of Air Superiority*, 565.

Appendix 7

1. These and other range-related evaluations were carried out for aircraft equipped with two 2,000 lb (910 kg) bombs, two AIM-9L Sidewinder air-to-air missiles, and a full complement of cannon rounds and loaded with maximum external fuel.

2. Heinemann, Rausa, and Van Every, *Aircraft Design*, ix. Ed Heinemann was the lead designer behind virtually every attack aircraft to come out of Douglas Aircraft during the 1940s and 1950s. Decades later, the famed airplane designer Burt Rutan would list Ed Heinemann as among the leading pioneers in aviation who had inspired him to become an aerospace engineer. Burt Rutan, "Confidence in Nonsense," *AW&ST*, March 24, 2003, 50–52.

3. For most applications, it is possible to simplify equation 7.3 by incorporating a small angle of attack approximation. Roskam, *Airplane Design*, pt. 1, *Preliminary Sizing*, 160.

4. Saltzman and Hicks, *In-Flight Lift-Drag Characteristics*, 12–13.

5. Saltzman and Hicks, *In-Flight Lift-Drag Characteristics*, 12–13.

6. Among the objectives of the HIMAT demonstrator was the ability to demonstrate a *sustained* turn capability of 8 g's when at Mach 0.90 and 25,000 ft altitude—a truly extraordinary achievement by any measure. Deets, DeAngelis, and Lux, *HIMAT Flight Program*, 5.

7. Tu, *Numerical Study*, 34, 47. The wind tunnel data used to substantiate the computational models presented under this study was collected at a Mach number of 0.90. Other researchers have documented even greater benefits for canard configurations at lower Mach numbers, in a subsonic environment. Rom, Er-El, and Gordon, *Measurements of the Aerodynamic Characteristics*.

8. Davies, *Boeing F-15E Strike Eagle*, 183.

9. Experimental values for Oswald's efficiency are available in the open literature for the F-16 and the F-18 at Mach 0.6, 0.9, and 1.3 conditions and for the F-15 at Mach 0.9 and 1.3 conditions. Values at Mach 0.8 have been interpolated from this data. Saltzman and Hicks, *In-Flight Lift-Drag Characteristics*, 50.

10. "U.S. Nears Lavi Transfer Approval," *AW&ST*, January 10, 1983, 20. Later literature sources, published after the Lavi had been officially canceled, would suggest a slightly lower turn rate for the airplane, quoting a sustained turn rate of 12.5 deg/sec and an instantaneous turn rate of 23.0 deg/sec. A relatively quick hand calculation, however, will confirm that these later figures corresponded to the performance of the Lavi Technology Demonstrator, which had seen its thrust-to-weight ratio artificially reduced to extend engine life and its approved, maximum angle-of-attack limit similarly trimmed. Shmul, Erenthal, and Attar, "Lavi Flight Control System," *International Journal of Control*, 163.

11. W. B. Herbst, "Dynamics of Air Combat," *Journal of Aircraft* 20 (July 1983): 594–98. Studies like this have suggested that future air combat will likely be dominated by two classes of jet fighters: the high angle of attack, point-and-shoot style of dogfighter, and a very high speed, slashing mode of attack made possible with a supercruise capability. The former approach to jet fighter design is probably best embodied by the U.S.-German X-31A Enhanced Fighter Maneu-

verability demonstrator, which was the first aircraft to demonstrate the "Herbst maneuver." The second class of air superiority fighters is best portrayed by the F-22 Raptor, which stands alone as the only dedicated supercruise fighter platform yet developed.

12. The maximum angle-of-attack limit for the F-16 is actually prescribed as a function of the airplane's g-load. At 1 g conditions, the airplane is limited to 25° AoA. At around 7 g loading conditions, however, the airplane's software limits the pilot to just over 20° AoA, and at 9 g's the airplane is limited to 15° AoA. These features were intended to keep the pilot from approaching too near to the stall limits of the airplane, where control effectiveness begins to suffer. Nguyen et al., *Simulator Study*, 34.

13. Beyond 50° angle of attack the F-16 enters "deep stall," where its elevator becomes completely ineffective and airplane recovery becomes a life-and-death matter. The advantages of a canard configuration in these near-stall and post-stall scenarios were convincingly demonstrated by the X-31. Not only did the canards on this airplane continue to provide pitch authority well into the post-stall regime, but they could also provide yaw authority through differential canard deflection. Michael A. Dornheim, "X-31, F-16 MATV, F/A-18 HARV Explore Diverse Missions," *AW&ST*, April 18, 1994, 46–47.

14. Norton, *Air War on the Edge*, 338.

15. Shmul, Erenthal, and Attar, "Lavi Flight Control System," *International Journal of Control*, 175–76.

16. Boyd, *Aerial Attack Study*.

17. Hammond, *The Mind of War*; Coram, *Boyd*.

18. A variety of both government-funded and private simulations, for example, have been built around the data collected by NASA Langley wind tunnel models for the F-16. This performance data, however, was collected entirely under 1 g conditions and omits the effects of maneuver loads on the airframe. A good example of this is provided by Nguyen et al., *Simulator Study*. Even at 1 g conditions, there will be measurable differences between wind tunnel and flight-test performance. These differences become magnified at higher loading conditions. A brief comparison of some of the differences between flight-test and wind tunnel predictions for the F-16A at 1 g conditions is provided by Webb, Kent, and Webb, "Correlation of F-16 Aerodynamics and Performance Predictions," 19-1–19-17.

19. Thompson, *F-86 Sabres*, 97–98.

20. Johnson, *Thunderbolt!*, 200–201. For a more complete review of the tactics of air-to-air combat, see Shaw, *Fighter Combat Tactics and Maneuvering*. The latter document includes descriptions not only for one-on-one fighter tactics but, more importantly, for aircraft operating in pairs or larger formations.

BIBLIOGRAPHY

Aloni, Shlomo. *Israeli A-4 Skyhawk Units in Combat*. Oxford: Osprey, 2009.

———. *Israeli Mirage and Nesher Aces*. Nothants, UK: Osprey, 2004.

———. *The June 1967 Six-Day War*. Vol. A, *Operation Focus*. Bat-Hefer, Israel: IsraDecal, 2008.

———. *Mirage III vs. MiG-21: Six Day War 1967*. Oxford: Osprey, 2010.

———. *101: Israeli Air Force First Fighter Squadron*. Bat-Hefer, Israel: IsraDecal, 2007.

Aloni, Shlomo, and Zvi Avidror. *Hammers: Israel's Long-Range Heavy Bomber Arm; The Story of 69 Squadron*. Atglen PA: Schiffer Military History, 2010.

Amichai, Yehuda. *Open Closed Open*. Translated by Chana Bloch and Chana Kronfeld. New York: Harcourt, 2000.

Anderegg, C. R. *Sierra Hotel: Flying Air Force Fighters in the Decade after Vietnam*. Washington DC: U.S. Air Force History and Museums Program, 2001.

Arens, Moshe. *Broken Covenant*. New York: Simon and Shuster, 1995.

Arian, Asher, Ilan Talmud, and Tamar Herman. *National Security and Public Opinion in Israel*. Tel Aviv: Jaffee Center for Strategic Studies, 1988.

Attar, Moshe. *Some Interesting Phenomena from Lavi Test Flights Related to Aircraft Stability and Control*. IAI TIC-91-1017. Tel Aviv: Israel Aircraft Industries, March 1991.

Ball, Robert E. *The Fundamentals of Aircraft Combat Survivability Analysis and Design*. New York: American Institute of Aeronautics and Astronautics, 1985.

Batina, John T. "Unsteady Transonic Flow Calculations for Interfering Lifting Surface Configurations." *Journal of Aircraft* 23 (May 1986): 422–30.

Beiser, Dan. "The Lavi Avionics Development Methodology." In *Proceedings of the 4th Israel Conference on Computer Systems and Software Engineering*, 112–19. Washington DC: IEEE Computer Society Press, 1989.

Bonds, Ray, ed. *The Illustrated Directory of Modern Weapons*. London: Salamander Books, 1985.

Boyd, John R. *Aerial Attack Study*. Washington DC: U.S. Air Force, August 11, 1964.

Brands, H. W. *Inside the Cold War: Loy Henderson and the Rise of the American Empire*. Oxford: Oxford University Press, 1991.

Brom, Shlomo, and Yiftah Shapir. *The Middle East Military Balance 1999–2000*. Tel Aviv: Jaffee Center for Strategic Studies, 2000.

Brown, Craig. *Debrief: A Complete History of U.S. Aerial Engagements, 1981 to the Present*. Atglen PA: Schiffer Military History, 2007.

Burton, James. *Letting Combat Results Shape the Next Air-to-Air Missile*. Washington DC: U.S. Department of Defense, 1986.

———. *The Pentagon Wars: Reformers Challenge the Old Guard*. Annapolis, MD: Naval Institute Press, 1993.

Cannon, Lou. *President Reagan: The Role of a Lifetime*. New York: Public Affairs, 2000.

Central Bureau of Statistics. *Defence Expenditure in Israel: 1950–2009*. Publication No. 1449. Jerusalem: State of Israel, June 2011.

Chant, Christopher. *Air Forces of the World*. London: Winchmore, 1983.

Claire, Rodger W. *Raid on the Sun*. New York: Broadway Books, 2004.

Clinton, Bill. *My Life*. New York: Alfred A. Knopf, 2004.

Cohen, Eliezer. *Israel's Best Defense*. New York: Orion Books, 1993.

Cohen, Eliot A., ed. *Gulf War Air Power Survey*. Vol. 2, pt. 2, *Effects and Effectiveness*. Washington DC: U.S. Department of Defense, 1993.

———. *Gulf War Air Power Survey*. Vol. 5, pt. 1, *A Statistical Compendium*. Washington DC: U.S. Department of Defense, 1993.

Congressional Quarterly Almanac: 98th Congress, 1983. Washington DC: Congressional Quarterly, 1984.

Cooling, Benjamin Franklin, ed. *Case Studies in the Achievement of Air Superiority*. Washington DC: U.S. Air Force History and Museums Program, 1994.

Coopersmith, Nechemia, and Shraga Simmons, eds. *Israel: Life in the Shadow of Terror*. Southfield MI: Targum Press, 2003.

Coram, Robert. *Boyd: The Fighter Pilot Who Changed the Art of War*. New York: Little, Brown, 2002.

Davies, Steve. *Boeing F-15E Strike Eagle*. Shrewsbury, UK: Airlife, 2003.

Deets, Dwain A., V. Michael DeAngelis, and David P. Lux. *HiMAT Flight Program: Test Results and Program Assessment Overview*. NASA TM-86725. Washington DC: National Aeronautics and Space Administration, June 1986.

Dershowitz, Toby, ed. *The Reagan Administration and Israel: Key Statements*. Washington DC: American Israel Public Affairs Committee, 1987.

Donald, David, and Jon Lake. *The Encyclopedia of World Military Aircraft*. New York: Barnes and Noble Books, 2000.

Drewes, Robert W. *The Air Force and the Great Engine War.* Washington DC: National Defense University Press, 1987.

Eban, Abba. *Abba Eban: An Autobiography.* New York: Random House, 1977.

———. *Personal Witness: Israel through My Eyes.* New York: G. P. Putnam's Sons, 1992.

Enderlin, Charles. *Shattered Dreams: The Failure of the Peace Process in the Middle East.* New York: Other Press, 2002.

Er-El, J. "Effect of Wing/Canard Interference on the Loading of a Delta Wing." *Journal of Aircraft* 25 (January 1988): 18–24.

Er-El, J., and A. Seginer. "Vortex Trajectories and Breakdown on Wing-Canard Configurations." *Journal of Aircraft* 22 (August 1985): 641–48.

Feldman, Shai. *Technology and Strategy: Future Trends.* Tel Aviv: Jaffee Center for Strategic Studies, 1989.

Feuerwerger, Marvin C. *Congress and Israel: Foreign Aid and Decision-Making in the House of Representatives.* Westport CT: Greenwood Press, 1979.

Gallagher, Gerald L., Larry B. Higgins, Leroy A. Khinoo, and Peter W. Pierce. *Fixed Wing Performance.* USNTPS-FTM-No. 108. Patuxent River MD: U.S. Naval Test Pilot School, 1992.

Gander, Terry, Bernard Ireland, and Paul A. Jackson. *Modern Military Powers: Israel.* London: Aerospace, 1984.

Gething, Michael J. *Modern Fighting Aircraft: F-15.* New York: Arco, 1983.

Gold, Dore, ed. *Arms Control in the Middle East.* Tel Aviv: Jaffee Center for Strategic Studies, 1990.

———. *Hatred's Kingdom.* Washington DC: Regnery, 2003.

———. *Israel as an American Non-NATO Ally: Parameters of Defense-Industrial Cooperation.* Tel Aviv: Jaffee Center for Strategic Studies, 1992.

Goldberg, Brett. *A Psalm in Jenin.* Tel Aviv: Modan, 2003.

Goldstein, Jonathan, ed. *China and Israel, 1948–1998.* Westport CT: Praeger, 1999.

Gordon, Yefim. *Famous Russian Aircraft: Mikoyan MiG-29.* Hinckley, UK: Midland Counties, 2006.

The Great Book of Modern Warplanes. New York: Salamander Books, 1987.

Gunston, Bill. *The Development of Jet and Turbine Aero Engines.* 2nd ed. Somerset, UK: Patrick Stephens, 1997.

———, ed. *The Encyclopedia of World Air Power.* London: Aerospace, 1980.

———. *An Illustrated Guide to the Israeli Air Force.* New York: Arco, 1982.

———. *World Encyclopaedia of Aero Engines.* 4th ed. Somerset, UK: Patrick Stephens, 1998.

Haig, Alexander. *Caveat: Realism, Reagan, and Foreign Policy.* New York: MacMillan, 1984.

Halperin, Merav, and Aharon Lapidot. *G-Suit: Combat Reports from Israel's Air War*. London: Sphere Books, 1990.

Hammond, Grant T. *The Mind of War: John Boyd and American Society*. Washington DC: Smithsonian Institution Press, 2001.

Heinemann, Edward H., Rosario Rausa, and K. E. Van Every. *Aircraft Design*. Baltimore MD: Nautical and Aviation Publishing Company of America, 1985.

Heller, Mark, and Yiftah Shapir. *The Middle East Military Balance 1996*. Tel Aviv: Jaffee Center for Strategic Studies, 1998.

Herbst, W. B. "Dynamics of Air Combat." *Journal of Aircraft* 20 (July 1983): 594–98.

Herzog, Chaim. *The Arab-Israeli Wars*. New York: Random House, 1982.

Hess, R. W., and H. P. Romanoff. *Aircraft Airframe Cost Estimating Relationships: Fighters*. N-2283/2-AF. Santa Monica CA: Rand, December 1987.

Hoak, D. E., and R. D. Fink. USAF *Stability and Control* DATCOM. Clayton MO: U.S. Air Force, Wright Aeronautical Laboratories, 1978.

Hoskin, Brian C., and Alan A. Baker. *Composite Materials for Aircraft Structures*. New York: American Institute of Aeronautics and Astronautics, 1986.

Huertas, Salvador Mafe. *The Israeli Air Force, 1947–1960*. Atglen PA: Schiffer, 1998.

———. *Mirage: The Combat Log*. Atglen PA: Schiffer, 1996.

Jane's Aero-Engines. Issue 11. Edited by Bill Gunston. Coulsdon, UK: Jane's Information Group, 2001.

Jane's All the World's Aircraft 1988–89. Edited by John W. R. Taylor. Coulsdon, UK: Jane's Information Group, 1988.

Jane's All the World's Aircraft 1991–92. Edited by Mark Lambert. Coulsdon, UK: Jane's Information Group, 1991.

Jane's All the World's Aircraft 1997–98. Edited by Paul Jackson. Coulsdon, UK: Jane's Information Group, 1997.

Jane's Avionics 1992–93. Edited by David Brinkman. Coulsdon, UK: Jane's Information Group, 1992.

Johnson, Robert S. *Thunderbolt!* Spartanburg SC: Honoribus Press, 1958.

Kaplan, Robert D. *The Arabists: The Romance of an American Elite*. New York: Simon and Schuster, 1995.

Katz, Samuel M. *The Night Raiders*. New York: Pocket Books, 1997.

Kay, Anthony L. *Turbojet History and Development, 1930–1960*. 2 vols. Ramsbury, UK: Crowood Press, 2007.

Keijsper, Gerard. *Saab Gripen: Sweden's 21st Century Multi-role Aircraft*. Hinckley, UK: Midland, 2003.

Kissinger, Henry. *White House Years*. Boston: Little, Brown, 1979.

———. *Years of Upheaval*. Boston: Little, Brown, 1982.

Klieman, Aharon, and Reuven Pedatzur. *Rearming Israel: Defence Procurement through the 1990s*. Tel Aviv: Jaffee Center for Strategic Studies, 1991.

Kozodoy, Neal. *The Middle East Peace Process: An Autopsy*. San Francisco: Encounter Books, 2002.

Kurzman, Dan. *Soldier of Peace: The Life of Yitzhak Rabin*. New York: Harper Collins, 1998.

Landfield, Joseph P., and Dario Rajkovic. "Canard/Tail Comparison for an Advanced Variable-Sweep-Wing Fighter." *Journal of Aircraft* 23 (June 1986): 449–54.

Laqueur, Walter, and Barry Rubin, eds. *The Israel-Arab Reader*. New York: Penguin Books, 1995.

Levite, Ariel. *Offense and Defense in Israeli Military Doctrine*. Tel Aviv: Jaffee Center for Strategic Studies, 1989.

Levran, Aharon, and Zeev Eytan. *The Middle East Military Balance, 1986*. Tel Aviv: Jaffee Center for Strategic Studies, 1987.

———. *The Middle East Military Balance, 1988–1989*. Tel Aviv: Jaffee Center for Strategic Studies, 1989.

Levy, David W. *Prediction of Average Downwash Gradient for Canard Configurations*. AIAA Paper 92-0284. New York: American Institute of Aeronautics and Astronautics, January 1992.

Livingstone, Harold. *No Trophy, No Sword*. Chicago: Edition Q, 1994.

Livingstone, Neil C., and David Halevy. *Inside the PLO*. Washington DC: Ethics and Public Policy Center, 1990.

Lorell, Mark A. *The Use of Prototypes in Selected Foreign Fighter Aircraft Development Programs*. R-3687-P&L. Santa Monica CA: Rand, September 1989.

Mark, Clyde R. *Israel: U.S. Foreign Assistance*. CRC Report IB85066. Washington DC: Congressional Research Service, May 21, 2002.

Martin, Tom, and Rachel Schmidt. *A Case Study of the F-20 Tigershark*. P-7495-RGS. Santa Monica CA: Rand, June 1987.

Mattingly, Jack D., William H. Heiser, and Daniel H. Daley. *Aircraft Engine Design*. Washington DC: American Institute of Aeronautics and Astronautics, 1987.

McFarlane, Robert C., with Zofia Smardz. *Special Trust*. New York: Cadell and Davies, 1994.

McGeer, Tad, and Ilan Kroo. "A Fundamental Comparison of Canard and Conventional Configurations." *Journal of Aircraft* 20 (November 1983): 983–92.

McKinnon, Dan. *Bullseye: One Reactor*. San Diego: House of Hits, 1987.

Medina, Moshe, and Manuel Shahaf. "Post-Stall Characteristics of Highly Augmented Fighter Aircraft." In *17th Congress of the International Council of the Aeronautical Sciences (ICAS)*, 2:1976–83. Washington DC: American Institute of Aeronautics and Astronautics, 1990.

Mersky, Peter. *Israeli Fighter Aces*. North Branch MN: Specialty Press, 1997.

The Military Balance 1986–1987. London: International Institute for Strategic Studies, 1986.

Mulvenon, James C., and Andrew N. D. Yang, eds. *The People's Liberation Army as Organization*. Santa Monica CA: Rand, 2002.

Nakdimon, Shlomo. *First Strike*. New York: Summit Books, 1987.

Nguyen, Luat T., M. E. Ogburn, W. P. Gilbert, K. S. Kibler, P. W. Brown, and P. O. Deal. *Simulator Study of Stall/Post-Stall Characteristics of a Fighter Airplane with Relaxed Longitudinal Static Stability*. NASA TP-1538. Washington DC: National Aeronautics and Space Administration, December 1979.

Nixon, David, ed. *Transonic Aerodynamics*. New York: American Institute of Aeronautics and Astronautics, 1982.

Nordeen, Lon. *Air Warfare in the Missile Age*. Washington DC: Smithsonian Institution Press, 2002.

———. *Fighters over Israel*. New York: Orion Books, 1990.

Nordeen, Lon, and David Isby. *M60 vs. T-62: Cold War Combatants 1956–92*. Oxford: Osprey, 2010.

Nordeen, Lon, and David Nicolle. *Phoenix Over the Nile: A History of Egyptian Air Power, 1932–1994*. Washington DC: Smithsonian Institution Press, 1996.

North, Oliver L., with William Novak. *Under Fire: An American Story*. New York: Harper Collins, 1991.

Norton, Bill. *Air War on the Edge: A History of the Israel Air Force and Its Aircraft since 1947*. Hinckley, UK: Midland, 2004.

Oren, Michael B. *Power, Faith and Fantasy: America in the Middle East, 1776 to the Present*. New York: W. W. Norton, 2007.

———. *Six Days of War*. Oxford: Oxford University Press, 2002.

Organski, A. F. K. *The $36 Billion Bargain: Strategy and Politics in U.S. Assistance to Israel*. New York: Columbia University Press, 1990.

O'Rourke, Ronald, ed. *Iraq War: Defense Program Implications for Congress*. Washington DC: Congressional Research Service, June 4, 2003.

Peri, Yoram, and Amnon Neubach. *The Military-Industrial Complex in Israel*. Tel Aviv: International Center for Peace in the Middle East, January 1985.

Pifko, Allan B., and Harvey Eidinoff. "Computational Structures Technology at Grumman: Current Practice / Future Needs." In *Computational Structures Technology for Airframes and Propulsion Systems*, 395–429.Washington DC: National Aeronautics and Space Administration, Office of Management, Scientific, and Technical Information Program, 1992.

Pimlott, John, ed. *The Middle East Conflicts*. New York: Crescent Books, 1983.

Post, Jerrold M. *The Mind of the Terrorist*. New York: Palgrave Macmillan, 2007.

Puschel, Karen L. *U.S.-Israeli Strategic Cooperation in the Post–Cold War Era*. Tel Aviv: Jaffee Center for Strategic Studies, 1992.

Rabin, Yitzhak. *The Rabin Memoirs*. Berkeley: University of California Press, 1979.

Rabinovich, Abraham. *The Yom Kippur War*. New York: Schocken Books, 2004.

Raymer, Daniel P. *Aircraft Design: A Conceptual Approach*. Washington DC: American Institute of Aeronautics and Astronautics, 1989.

Reagan, Ronald. *Ronald Reagan: An American Life*. New York: Simon and Schuster, 1990.

Rearden, Steven L. *The History of the Joint Chiefs of Staff*. Vol. 12, *1977–1980*. Washington DC: Office of the Chairman of the Joint Chiefs of Staff, December 2002.

Reiser, Stewart. *The Israeli Arms Industry*. New York: Holmes and Meier, 1989.

Richardson, Douglas. *Modern Fighting Aircraft: F-16*. New York: Arco, 1983.

Rom, J., B. Melamed, and D. Almosnino. "Experimental and Nonlinear Vortex Lattice Method Results for Various Wing-Canard Configurations." *Journal of Aircraft* 30 (March–April 1993): 208–9.

Rom, J., J. Er-El, and R. Gordon. *Measurements of the Aerodynamic Characteristics of Various Wing-Canard Configurations and Comparison with* NLVLM *Results*. AIAA-89-2217. New York: American Institute of Aeronautics and Astronautics, 1989.

Ronen, Ran. *Eagle in the Sky*. Tel Aviv: Contento De Semrik, 2013.

Roskam, Jan. *Airplane Design*. Pt. 1, *Preliminary Sizing of Airplanes*. Ottawa KS: Roskam Aviation and Engineering, 1989.

———. *Airplane Design*. Pt. 2, *Preliminary Configuration Design and Integration of the Propulsion System*. Ottawa KS: Roskam Aviation and Engineering, 1989.

———. *Airplane Design*. Pt. 5, *Component Weight Estimation*. Ottawa KS: Roskam Aviation and Engineering, 1989.

———. *Airplane Design*. Pt. 6, *Preliminary Calculation of Aerodynamic, Thrust and Power Characteristics*. Ottawa KS: Roskam Aviation and Engineering, 1989.

———. *Airplane Design*. Pt. 7, *Determination of Stability, Control and Performance Characteristics:* FAR *and Military Requirements*. Ottawa KS: Roskam Aviation and Engineering, 1989.

———. *Airplane Flight Dynamics and Automatic Flight Controls*. Ottawa KS: Roskam Aviation and Engineering, 1979.

Ross, Dennis. *The Missing Peace*. New York: Farrar, Straus and Giroux, 2004.

Rubenstein, Murray, and Richard Goldman. *Shield of David: An Illustrated History of the Israeli Air Force*. Englewood Cliffs NJ: Prentice-Hall, 1978.

Sachar, Howard. *A History of Israel: From the Rise of Zionism to Our Time*. New York: Alfred A. Knopf, 1979.

Saltzman, Edward J., and John W. Hicks. *In-Flight Lift-Drag Characteristics for a Forward-Swept Wing Aircraft*. NASA TP-3414. Washington DC: National Aeronautics and Space Administration, December 1994.

Samoylovitch, O., and D. Strelets. "Determination of the Oswald's Efficiency Factor at the Aeroplane Design Preliminary Stage." *Aircraft Design*, no. 3 (2000): 167–74.

Segal, A. "Supportability of Composite Airframes: The Lavi Fighter Aircraft." *Composite Structures* 10, no. 1 (1988): 105–8.

Senior, Boris. *New Heavens*. Washington DC: Potomac Books, 2005.

Shambaugh, David, *Modernizing China's Military*. Berkeley: University of California Press, 2002.

Shanker, Vijaya, and Norman Malmuth. "Computational Treatment of Three-Dimensional Transonic Canard-Wing Interactions." *Journal of Aircraft* 20 (May 1983): 456–61.

Sharon, Ariel, and David Chanoff. *Warrior: The Autobiography of Ariel Sharon*. New York: Simon and Schuster, 2001.

Sharp, Jeremy M. *U.S. Foreign Aid to Israel*. CRS Report R133222. Washington DC: Congressional Research Service, December 4, 2009.

Shaw, Robert L. *Fighter Combat Tactics and Maneuvering*. Annapolis MD: Naval Institute Press, 1985.

Shipler, David K. *Arab and Jew: Wounded Spirits in a Promised Land*. New York: Penguin Books, 1986.

Shirk, Michael H., Terrence J. Hertz, and Terrence A. Weisshaar. "Aeroelastic Tailoring—Theory, Practice, and Promise." *Journal of Aircraft* 23 (January 1986): 6–18.

Shmul, Menachem, Eli Erenthal, and Moshe Attar. "Lavi Flight Control System." *International Journal of Control* 59, no. 1 (1994): 159–82.

———. "Lavi Flight Control System: Design Requirements, Development and Flight Test Results." In *Active Control Technology: Applications and Lessons Learned*, 5-1–5-13. AGARD-CP-560. Neuilly sur Seine, France: Advisory Group for Aerospace Research and Development, May 1994.

Shoebat, Walid. *Why We Want to Kill You*. Newtown PA: Top Executive Media, 2007.

Shultz, George P. *Turmoil and Triumph*. New York: Charles Scribner's Sons, 1993.

Silver, Eric. *Begin: The Haunted Prophet*. New York: Random House, 1984.

Simon, Merrill. *Moshe Arens, Statesman and Scientist, Speaks Out*. New York: Dean Books, 1988.

Skinner, Kiran K., Annelise Anderson, and Martin Anderson. *Reagan: A Life in Letters*. New York: Free Press, 2003.

———. *Reagan in His Own Hand*. New York: Touchstone, 2001.

Speakes, Larry, and Robert Pack. *Speaking Out: The Reagan Presidency from Inside the White House*. New York: Avon Books, 1988.

Spector, Iftach. *Loud and Clear*. Minneapolis MN: Zenith Press, 2009.

Spector, Leonard S. *Nuclear Proliferation Today*. New York: Carnegie Endowment for International Peace, 1984.

Steven, Stewart. *The Spymasters of Israel*. New York: Random House, 1980.

Stockton, Ronald R. "Christian Zionism: Prophecy and Public Opinion." *Middle East Journal* 41 (Spring 1987): 234–53.

St. Peter, James. *The History of Aircraft Turbine Engine Development in the United States*. Atlanta GA: American Society of Mechanical Engineers, 1999.

Tanter, Raymond. *Who's At the Helm? Lessons of Lebanon*. Boulder CO: Westview Press, 1990.

Thompson, Warren. *F-86 Sabres of the 4th Fighter Interceptor Wing*. Nothants, UK: Osprey, 2002.

Truman, Harry. *Years of Trial and Hope*. Garden City NY: Doubleday, 1956.

Tsach, S., and A. Peled, "Evolution of the Lavi Fighter Aircraft." In *Proceedings of the 16th International Council of the Aeronautical Sciences (ICAS)*, 827–31.Washington DC: American Institute of Aeronautics and Astronautics, 1988.

Tu, Eugene L. *Numerical Study of Steady and Unsteady Canard-Wing-Body Aerodynamics*. NASA-TM-110394. Washington DC: National Aeronautics and Space Administration, August 1996.

U.S. General Accounting Office. *Aircraft Procurement: Air Force Air Defense Fighter Competition*. GAO/NSIAD-86-170BR. Washington DC, July 1986.

———. *Foreign Assistance: Analysis of Cost Estimates for Israel's Lavi Aircraft*. GAO/NSIAD-87-76. Washington DC, January 1987.

———. *Foreign Assistance: U.S. Funds Used for Terminating Israel's Lavi Aircraft Program*. GAO/NSIAD-90-3. Washington DC, October 1989.

———. *Israel: U.S. Military Aid Spent In-Country*. GAO/NSIAD-91-169. Washington DC, May 1991.

———. *Need to Demonstrate F-18 Naval Strike Fighter Weapon System Effectiveness Before Large-Scale Production*. PSAD-79-25. Washington DC, 1979.

U.S. Office of Management and Budget. *Fiscal Year 2013 Historical Tables: Budget of the US Government*. Washington DC, 2013.

U.S. Office of the Secretary of Defense. *The Military Power of the People's Republic of China 2006*. Washington DC, July 2006.

Webb, T. S., D. R. Kent, and J. B. Webb. "Correlation of F-16 Aerodynamics and Performance Predictions with Early Flight Test Results." In *Performance Prediction Methods*, 19-1–19-17. AGARD-CP-242. Neuilly sur Seine, France: Advisory Group for Aerospace Research and Development, May 1978.

Weinberger, Caspar. *Fighting for Peace*. New York: Warner Books, 1990.

Weiss, Jeffrey, and Craig Weiss. *I Am My Brother's Keeper*. Atglen PA: Schiffer Military History, 1998.

Weiss, Raanan, and Shlomo Aloni. *IAI Kfir in IAF Service*. Bat-Hefer, Israel: IsraDecal, 2007.

Weizman, Ezer. *On Eagles' Wings*. New York: MacMillan, 1976.

Williams, Mel, ed. *Superfighters: The Next Generation of Combat Aircraft*. Norwalk CT: Airtime, 2002.

Winchester, Jim. *Douglas A-4 Skyhawk*. Barnsley, UK: Pen and Sword Books, 2005.

Wyman, David S. *The Abandonment of the Jews*. New York: Pantheon Books, 1984.

———. *Paper Walls*. New York: Pantheon Books, 1985.

Yonay, Ehud. *No Margin for Error*. New York: Pantheon Books, 1993.

Younossi, Obaid, Michael Kennedy, and John C. Graser. *Military Airframe Costs: The Effects of Advanced Materials and Manufacturing Processes*. MR-1370-AF. Santa Monica CA: Rand, 2001.

Zakheim, Dov S. *Flight of the Lavi*. Washington DC: Brassey's, 1996.

Zipkin, M. A. *The PW1120: A High Performance, Low Risk F100 Derivative*. ASME 84-GT-230. New York: American Society of Mechanical Engineers, June 4, 1984.

Zumwalt, Elmo R., Jr. *On Watch*. New York: New York Times Book Co., 1976.

INDEX

Page numbers in italics refer to illustrations.

General Dynamics, 35–36, 135

Grumman: contract of, for wings and tail, 58–59, 69, 85, 90, 127, 243, 250–51; and Lavi coproduction, 133–34, 168. *See also* A-6 Intruder (Grumman); F-14 Tomcat (Grumman); X-29 (Grumman)

Hadish team, 24, 25–27, 28, 30–32, 46, 70

Haig, Alexander, 65–66, 68, 72, 80, 81–83, 85, 185

Harrari, Ovadia, 161

Heinemann, Edward H., 251–52, 254, 337, 397n2

helmet-mounted sight and display, 135–36, 301, 393n39, 393n51, 394n52; and Agile Eye, 304–5, 306; and DASH, 178, 292, 303, 305, 306; and HADAS, 303–4; and JHMCS, 306–7; and Soviet systems, 302, 322–23, 324; and VTAS, 301

Henderson, Loy, 76–77, 371n8

Hetz, Shmuel, 55, 369n18

high off-boresight missiles, 302, 322–26

Hod, Mordechai, 33, 124

Hughes, 107, 299, 300, 324

Hussein, Saddam, 62–64, 65, 113, 189, 370n8

Ikle, Fred, 114–15

Iran, 78, 99, 177, 317, 333, 335; Beirut bombing and, 132–33; as customer for Aryeh, 367n19; and fall of the Shah, 185–86; and Iran-Contra controversy, 85, 157, 183, 185, 194

Iraq, 2, 41, 53, 76, 78, 87, 306, 317; and Gulf War, 313–14, 331, 332–33, 396n39; Osirak raid and, 62–64, 65–66, 67, 111, 142–43, 184, 189, 370nn5–6, 370n8; as Soviet client, 14, 42

Israel: defense spending of, 101, 181, 203; GDP comparisons of, 181–82, 385n44, 386n13; Memorial Day in, 57; and sensitivity to casualties, 14–15, 56–57; Sinai withdrawal of, 2, 20–21, 47, 69; and state secrecy standards, 6, 20, 21, 106, 109, 319, 323

Israel Aircraft Industries (IAI): Arrow missile of, 152, 156, 162, 381n24; F-16 coproduction and, 31; Gabriel missile of, 10, 320, 328; layoffs from, 151, 157, 159–60, 161, 163, 173–74; and Lod airport, 7, 132, 136–37, 158. *See also* Elta; Kfir (IAI); Lavi (IAI); Nammer (IAI); Nesher (IAI); Shahal (IAI)

Israel Military Industries, 151

Ivry, David, 26, 28, 36, 46, 49, 51–52, 69–70, 116, 124, 188

J-10 (Chengdu), 214, 215, 216, 219–20, 356, 390n28

J-29 (Saab), 25, 367n7

J52 (Pratt & Whitney), 262, 265, 383n22

J57 (Pratt & Whitney), 263

J79 (General Electric), 262, 263, *278*; comparison of, to F100, 266, 267–68; and F-4, 103, 135, 265, 276–77; and Kfir, 8, 9, 389n13

JA-37 Viggen (Saab), 207, 208, 356

JAS-39 Gripen (Saab), 181–82, 261, 276, 385nn45–46, 388n11, 393n39; and canard design, 208, 214, 215, 356; and F404 engine, 44, 261, 262; and flight-test accident, 147, 226

jet engine evolution, 262–65, 389n10

Johnson, Lyndon B., 11–12, 14, 65, 78

Jordan, Hashemite Kingdom of, 41, 67, 88, 317; arms sales to, 6, 12, 42; and Six-Day War, 2–3, 53; as U.S. surrogate, 94, 111

Kaiser, 103, 175, 304–5, 306

Kasten, Robert W. (Bob), 132

Kemp, Jack F., 94, 97, 133, 377n16

Kennedy, John F., 11, 78, 92, 366n1

Keret, Moshe, 159, 383n18

Kfir (IAI), 30, 31, 35, 38, 39, 40, 45, 87, 100, *199*, 219, 232, *278*, 382n1; addition of canard to, 9–10, 104, 207, 208, 230, 356, 387n6; armament of, 320, 321; avionics suite of, 8, 27, 285, 290; evolution and variants of, 8, 27, 366n11; export of, 36, 95–96, 374nn15–16; and Israeli modernization planning, 34, 105, 179; and J79 engine, 8, 262, 265, 277, 389n13; Lavi as replacement for, 38, 72, 86, 109;

unveiling of, 20–21, 106
Kirkpatrick, Jeane, 81, 85, 194
Kissinger, Henry, 18, 75, 79–80
Knesset, 30–31, 39, 41, 69, 100, 145, 156

Labor Alignment, 37–38, 41, 46, 99–
100, 101, 151, 152, 154–56, 158
Lapidot, Amos: and Hadish team, 26,
28, 32, 46; as Israeli air force chief, 70,
104–5, 115, 124, 351; and Lavi development, 126–27, 130–31, 145, 215
Lavi (IAI): cockpit arrangement of, 55–
56, 90, 107–8, 135–36, 165, 299–301,
303–4, 310; combat radius of, 45, 87,
108–9, 141, 178, 181, 250, 270, 271–72,
335–37, 354–55; and conformal weapons carriage, 86, 316–17, 336, 364;
engine selection for, 44–45, 48–50,
259, 266, 268, 270, 271–73, 280–81,
394n6; flight test of, 107, 108, 136–37,
138, 147–48, 150, 160, 161, 164, 175–
76, 214, 226, 233, 289, 358, 384n27;
fly-by-wire technology of, 9, 107, 129,
136, 160, 210, 225–27, 230–31, 233,
236, 247, 249, 363, 387n2; in-flight
refueling system of, 147, 244, 257; and
Israeli public support, 155; and Layout
33 design, 45, 48, 163, 382n1; and
opposition in Israel's military, 30–31,
124–26, 148–49, 158, 380n8; program
costs of, 45, 49–50, 52, 87–88, 90,
93, 97, 102, 115, 116, 120–22, 123, 128,
139, 140, 142–45, 149, 151–53, 157–58,
161, 164, 167–68, 181, 190, 192, 273,
276, 285, 378n8, 379n9; and protests
over cancellation, 158–59; scrapped
prototypes of, 176; and support in
Israel's military, 30–31, 49, 50–52, 70,
104–5, 126–27, 130–31, 145, 350–51;
and Technology Demonstrator, 164–
65, 175–76; thrust-to-weight ratio of,
48, 86, 258, 337–39, 341, 342, 344, 350,
351, 362–63, 397n10; turn rate of, 86,
338–40, 343–44, 346, 350, 360–61, 362;
weights of, 45, 49–50, 86, 108, 140,
252–55, 257, 258, 270, 271–72, 280–81,
286, 287, 300, 316, 317, 373n2, 382n1.

See also Aryeh (IAI); Elbit; electronic
warfare; El-Op; Elta; helmet-mounted
sight and display
Lear Siegler, 129, 136, 160, 231
Lebanon War, 93, 172; air-to-air en-
gagements in, 56, 321; and impact
on Israeli elections, 69, 99, 101–2;
Reagan administration and, 67–69,
70–71, 72, 81–82, 90–91, 131, 186; and
surface-to-air missiles, 126, 168–69,
293, 317, 382n4
Levi, Moshe, 126–27
Levine, Mel, 130, 377n16
Libya, 5, 42, 317, 332, 335
Light Combat Aircraft. *See* Tejas (HAL)
Likud, 37–38, 40–41, 46, 72, 99, 101,
123, 145, 154, 158, 381n15
Long, Clarence D., 94, 97

Magister (Fouga), 7
Marshall, George C., Jr., 76, 93
Meir, Golda, 50, 169
Meir, Rafi, 159–60
Merkava, 10, 56, 89, 149
Meteor (Gloster), 24
MiG-15 Fagot, 348–49
MiG-21 Fishbed, 4, 15–16, 292, 366n11
MiG-23 Flogger, 366n11
MiG-25 Foxbat, 43, 396n39
MiG-29 Fulcrum, 323–24, 325, 342, 352,
361, 363
Mirage III (Dassault), 49, 161, 206, 207,
277, 332; evolution of, toward air-to-
ground role, 4, 6–7, 9, 12, 27, 33–34,
72; wartime experience of, 4, 16, 53–
54, 70, 136, 378n30
Mirage 5 (Dassault), 4–5, 8, 9, 12, 34
Mirage Milan (Dassault), 9
Modai, Yitzhak, 116, 123–24, 154
Mystère II (Dassault), 25–26
Mystère IV (Dassault), 25, 26, 27, 124

Nammer (IAI), 277
Nasser, Gamal Abdel, 1–2, 14–15, 16
National Security Council, 65, 74–75,
80, 84, 111, 113, 185, 376n4
Nesher (IAI), 8–9, 27, 262, 332
Nissim, Moshe, 145, 154, 158

Nixon, Richard, 64, 65, 71, 83, 100, 110–11, 368n4; and Cold War standoff, 15–16; and differences with State Department, 80; and F-4 deliveries, 14; national security advisor of, 75, 79; and Yom Kippur War, 17–19, 78–79, 92

North, Oliver, 80, 111–12, 376n4

Northrop, 59, 94–97, 135, 319. See also F-5E Tiger II (Northrop); F-20 Tigershark (Northrop); T-38 Talon (Northrop); YF-17 Cobra (Northrop)

Novi Avion (SOKO), 276

Ouragan (Dassault), 24, 124

PI80 Avanti (Piaggio), 208

Peled, Benjamin, 36, 49, 124; and F-16 licensed production, 28, 32, 33; and Hadish team, 24–27, 30–31; and Lavi, 30–31, 127; and Yom Kippur War, 29, 50, 51–52, 125–126

Peres, Shimon, 99, 101, 119, 126, 144, 154–55, 157–58, 159, 171

Pickering, Thomas, 118, 144, 156–57

Poindexter, John, 130, 377n16

Pratt & Whitney, 48–49, 95, 134, 157, 261, 369n9. See also F100 (Pratt & Whitney); J52 (Pratt & Whitney); J57 (Pratt & Whitney); PW1120

PW1120 (Pratt & Whitney), 141, 160, 219, 279; comparison of, to J79 engine, 266, 267–68; and F-4 upgrade, 103–4, 135, 174; and hot-section technology, 264, 389n10; Lavi as sized by, 270, 271–72; as Lavi candidate engine, 48–49, 106, 259; and Lavi Technology Demonstrator, 165–65, 382n32; and learning from F100 experience, 273–77; and production at Bet Shemesh, 157, 260, 263, 265

Rabin, Yitzhak, 99–101, 161, 171, 174, 176, 365n5, 366n1, 374n1; approval of, of Lavi production plan, 120; and Dov Zakheim, 115, 116, 144, 146; indigenous weapons and, 100; opposition of, to Lavi, 100, 145, 150–53, 157–58,

159, 184; and Pentagon delays, 128, 129, 168; rivalry of, with Shimon Peres, 154–55

Rada Electronic Industries, 287

Rafael: Derby missile of, 328–29; Lavi avionics and, 180, 297; Popeye missile of, 318–19; Python 3 missile of, 10, 322, 327; Python 4 missile of, 323–25, 328–29, 395n35; Python 5 missile of, 328–29, 395n35; Shafrir 2 missile of, 10; SPICE bomb kit of, 319–20

Rafale (Dassault), 181, 208, 214, 215, 298, 356, 393n39

Rahall, Nick J., 97

Raytheon, 324, 325

Reagan, Ronald, 64–65, 67, 68–69, 70, 72, 80, 95, 111, 131, 166; Cold War and, 62, 84, 192–93; endorsement of Lavi by, 90–91, 97, 98, 113–14, 184; and expanded U.S.-Israeli ties, xii, 81, 186–90; and internal feuds, 81, 85, 110, 119–20, 131–32, 185, 194; and letter urging cancelation of Lavi, 157; management style of, 84; misleading of, by staff members, 82–83, 183; and sympathy toward Israel, 61–62, 194

Ross, Dennis, 171

Rutan, Burt, 208, 397n2

Saar 4 missile boat, 10

Saar 5 missile boat, 149

Saudi Arabia, 42, 83, 94, 131, 144, 186, 332

Schapira, Avraham, 145

Schwimmer, Al, 159

Shahal (IAI), 163–64

Shamir, Yitzhak, 47, 90, 99, 126, 144–45

Sharon, Ariel (Arik): and Caspar Weinberger, 71; and Lebanon War, 69; and support for Lavi, 47, 51, 52, 158, 350; and Yom Kippur War, 50–51

Shmul, Menachem, 136–37, 138, 144, 164, 378n30

Shomron, Dan, 124, 148

Shultz, George P., 69, 71–72, 80–81, 83, 144, 157, 186–87; and Lavi, 72, 371n18; and Moshe Arens, 71, 72, 91; rivalry of, with Caspar Weinberger, 71, 110–11, 118–20, 128–29, 130, 193

Six-Day War, 47, 171; arms embargos and, 4–5, 10, 13; Israeli experience of, 1–3, 25, 33, 50, 70, 100, 124, 136, 321, 329, 365n5, 378n30; preemptive air strike in, 3–4, 317; U.S. reaction to, 11, 14, 21, 23

Speakes, Larry, 67, 119

Spector, Yiftach, 125

stability and control: and ground effect, 147, 226; and static margin, 223–29, 233–35, 236, 237–39, 242, 249; and supersonic flight, 234–36, 240–241; and transonic flight, 147, 231–33

surface-to-air missiles: and Hawk sales to Israel, 11, 92; in Lebanon War, 126, 169, 293, 382n4; in War of Attrition, 54–55, 369n18; in Yom Kippur War, 16–17, 28–30, 32, 49–51, 56–57, 125–26

survivability, 27–28, 56, 272–73. *See also* electronic warfare

Syria, 87, 88; and Lebanon War, 99, 126, 168–69, 293, 317, 321, 382n4; and Six-Day War, 2, 3, 53, 317; as Soviet client, 14, 42–43; and Yom Kippur War, 17, 29, 41, 50–52, 56, 125

T-38 Talon (Northrop), 134

Tadiran, 162, 174

Tanter, Raymond, 84, 185

Tejas (HAL), 44, 261, 385n44

Truman, Harry S., 75–76, 77, 371n1

Typhoon (Eurofighter), 181, 208–9, 214, 235, 261, 352, 356, 393n39

United Kingdom, 2, 7, 40, 68, 78, 106, 366n9, 371n1; and arms embargo, 5–6, 100; GDP of, compared to Israel, 189; and Spitfire, 24, 211. *See also* AV-8A Harrier (British Aerospace); Meteor (Gloster); Typhoon (Eurofighter)

United Nations, 1, 81, 194

United States: arms from, tied to Israeli concessions, 20–21, 70–71; arms from, tied to sales to Arab states, 12–13, 21, 42; and arms purchases by Israel, 188–89, 190, 306–7, 318–19; components

from, in Lavi, 58–59, 69, 85, 90, 107, 127, 129, 133–34, 136, 160, 231, 243, 250–51; and public sympathy for Israel, 93–94; and security assistance to Israel, xii, 17–19, 21, 78–79, 88–89, 91, 92–93, 97–98, 132, 149, 176–77, 181, 192, 373n5; and U.S.-Israeli memorandum of agreement, 186–88, 372n16; and U.S.-Israeli memorandum of understanding, xii, 81, 186, 372n16

U.S. Congress: foreign policy role of, 91–93, 373n10; and General Accounting Office, 121–22, 386n17; and Iran-Contra hearings, 157; and Middle East arms sales, 12, 83, 111; protests from, of contract delays, 129–30, 132, 168, 184, 377n16; and support for Lavi, 94, 97–98, 132–33

U.S. foreign policy, 79–80, 81–83, 84–85, 118, 122, 156, 157, 183–85, 193, 194. *See also* National Security Council; U.S. State Department

U.S. State Department: antisemitism and, 76–77, 80, 371n6; Baghdad Pact and, 78; and Bureau of Near East and South Asian Affairs, 74, 76–77, 80, 83, 118–19, 128, 156, 157, 184, 187, 371n8; and Bureau of Politico-Military Affairs, 74, 187

War of Attrition, 14–16, 54, 79, 321, 378n30

War of Independence, 24, 28, 39, 41, 47, 117, 372n11, 383n12

Weinberger, Caspar, 71, 81; and *Achille Lauro* hijacking, 112–13, 376n4; Arab monarchs and, 94, 111, 131, 144; and hostility toward Israel, 65–66, 68, 111–12, 184, 186, 376n3; and independent policy agenda, 64–65, 66–67, 131–32, 183, 185, 192–93; opposition of, to Lavi, 89–90, 110, 113–15, 122, 127, 138, 144, 150–51, 153, 155, 158, 163, 167, 189, 190, 194, 381n26; opposition of, to U.S.-Israeli joint programs, 156, 162, 381n24; rivalry of, with George Shultz, 71, 110–11, 118–20, 128–29, 130, 193;

and suspension of Lavi contract approval, 69, 105, 128–30, 132, 136, 168; and suspension of weapons deliveries, 66, 68–69

Weizman, Ezer, 59, 145, 307, 366n3; as air force commander, 37, 49; and launch of Lavi, 37–39, 41, 44–46, 49, 50, 58, 108; opposition of, to Lavi, 123–24, 154; political ambitions of, 37–38, 46

Wilson, Charles N. (Charlie), 94

wind tunnel tests, 30, 32, 213–14, 348, 358, 387n8, 397n7, 398n18

x-29 (Grumman), 250

x-31 (Rockwell), 208, 209, 214, 356, 397n11, 398n13

yf-17 Cobra (Northrop), 28, 32

Yom Kippur War, 8, 68, 70, 154, 172, 181, 203, 351; air-to-air engagements in, 56, 321, 329; Israeli casualties from, 28–30, 33, 38, 56–57; opening hours of, 17, 126, 169–70, 315; and preemptive strike option, 50–52, 125–26, 168–70; and surface-to-air missiles, 16–17, 28–30, 32, 49, 56–57, 125–26, 293; and U.S. airlift delay, 17–19, 21, 78; and U.S. military aid, 19, 78–79, 88

Zakheim, Dov: and Bureau of Near East and South Asian Affairs, 118–19; clashes of, with Menachem Eini, 117–18, 145; and delay of Lavi contracts, 127–28; and Lavi alternatives study, 127, 129, 138–39, 140–41, 142, 143–44, 148, 152–53, 378n3; and Lavi cost estimates, 115–16, 120–22, 123; lobbying of, for Lavi cancellation, 144–45; requests of, for Lavi program details, 116–17, 130–31; and suspension of Lavi contract approval, 128–29, 130; and termination of Lavi, 114–15, 122; and U.S. Jewish community, 163, 381n26

Zumwalt, Elmo R., Jr., 18

www.ingramcontent.com/pod-product-compliance
Lightning Source LLC
Chambersburg PA
CBHW030943150426
42812CB00065B/3150/J